God Befriended Me

Roy J. Myers, M.A.

I wish to dedicate this book, **God Befriended Me**, to my lover, friend and wife, Judy Myers, who has loved me, encouraged me, and helped me through all the stages of this book. Judy was so patient with me throughout this process and loved me unconditionally. I believe I would have given up on this project, if she had not been there for me. I can only say thanks and I love you; but that falls far short for what she has done for me. I love her dearly.

I wish to further dedicate this book to my Pastor and friend, Pastor Tim Stone, who originally gave me the idea for the book when he had us Elders do communion every month. Pastor Tim has constantly encouraged me to write and has even let me use his office to do that. Pastor Tim also helped in the publishing of the book and formulating the book's cover.

I wish to further dedicate this book to my good friend and cousin, Bruce Ebelt. He actually did most all of the editing of this book by taking time out of his busy schedule to do so. We have been friends since early childhood and he has always been there for me.

I wish to also dedicate this book to the Intercessory Prayer Group at Westlake Fellowship who constantly prayed for me during the writing of this book. Prayer more than anything else has guided me in the formation of this book. A tremendous thank you, for everyone who prayed for me at Westlake.

Table of Contents

Forward

Friendship with God....that's an intriguing concept. One that can be hard to wrap your brain around. Think about it for a moment. The Creator of the Universe, God Almighty, desires a relationship with you and I. After walking out my Christian journey for nearly half a century, this idea of God wanting to be my friend is still completely mind boggling to me. Yet, this is a truth found throughout Scripture.

What is so tragic, is this idea of a friendship with God is often lost and completely non-existent in most religious pursuits. So many see God as this unapproachable Deity that is anything but relational. As a result, they spend their life void of the very thing God so desperately desires for them. Referring to God, Jesus declared, "apart from Him, I can do nothing." The reality is that apart from this "friendship with God," our lives will amount to a whole lot of nothing. God longs for a real relationship with you and the only thing necessary for you to experience it is to receive it.

In this book, my good friend Roy Myers takes a detailed look at the concept of God befriending us. With a thorough study into the covenants of God, Roy meticulously weaves a narrative that helps to shed light on God's sincere desire for a relationship with all of mankind. I'm convinced that having read this book, you'll see clearly the reality that not only does God long for a relationship with you, that it is He who has initiated that relationship by pursuing you and removing all the obstacles that stand in the way.

I know of very few people who study God's Word with the passion and fervor that Roy does. His commitment to prayer and personal devotion speaks volumes about his own personal relationship with God. Day after day, week after week, year after year, I've watched my friend, Roy, walk out a real and tangible friendship with the Lord. This isn't simply something he's read about or a theological concept he's simply studied. This friendship with God is something he lives out daily. The pages of this book are not filled with theoretical religious ideas, but are based on the truth of Scripture and Roy's real life testimony of having experienced the reality of God befriending him.

Tim Stone, Senior Pastor – Westlake Fellowship / Montgomery, TX

Preface

"In the beginning God…" not only when the world was created, the universe and everything else that was made. God was in the beginning with me about writing this book on God Befriended Me. I had just finished my first book, The Five-Fold Ministry, and was able to publish it, when I was wondering what I was going to do next. My mind kept going back to the Covenants of God throughout the Bible. Someone else had just written a book on the same subject and I did not want to duplicate material. I talked to some friends of mine who had helped me with my first book, Reverend Clarence Dalrymple and his wife Pat. They encouraged me to write about what God was impressing and leading me to do. Therefore, I prayed about it and felt God leading me in the direction of this book, God Befriended Me. This is a discussion and possibly to some revelation of the Divine Covenants of God.

As I began writing different people in the church, I am apart of began to tell me they did not understand the Old Testament. I believe people do not understand the Old Testament because they do not understand that God is a covenant-keeping God. People are prone to want an experience with God rather than understand that Covenant relationship He wishes to establish with them. God is to be experienced, but it is much more than that. We must understand the importance of Covenant relationship and what it means to sit down with God in His Presence. Jesus shares that in the New Testament; that we have a Covenant Relationship with God. In the Old Testament God picks out particular individuals to befriend and makes a Covenant with them, but then He wants to befriend an entire nation, the nation of Israel. In the New Testament God reaches out to befriend the whole world through His Son, Jesus Christ. "For God so loved the world that He gave His only begotten Son, that whoever believes in Him should not perish but have everlasting life." (John 3:16)

The second most important fact to understand, is how Jewish people think and believe. This involves their culture, their way of life and how they view the Scriptures, especially concerning Covenants. From different sources, I have tried to recapture that within the context of the Scriptures.

Western thinking is completely different from Eastern and Jewish thinking. Not everyone wants to look at that. If I have erred in coming across with their way of thinking, I take full responsibility.

Probably the most important fact to understand about Covenants is what it means back in Bible times. Our Bible today is divided into the Old Testament and the New Testament. One must understand what that word "Testament" means back then and today. From BibleStudyTools.com sheds some light on what that word means. "The word Testament occurs twelve times in the New Testament as the rendering of the Greek word diatheke, which is twenty times rendered "covenant" in the Authorized Version and always so in the Revised Version…" Thus, throughout this book we will use that meaning. When we write Old Testament and New Testament, we will put in parenthesis beside it (Covenant), because I believe that is what God wanted us to see. Two different Covenants, but one Bible is being presented. The Old Testament (Covenant) is centered around the Law of God while the New Testament (Covenant) is centered around the person, the Lord Jesus Christ. You will see throughout this book that there are times when I repeat important facts, revelations and ideas. I believe a good teacher repeats important facts, revelations and ideas over and over again. Most people must hear something seven times before they will remember it.

Other people that have helped me in developing this book have been my Pastor, Tim Stone. He has done some of the final editing before and after putting it in book form. My cousin, Bruce Ebelt, has helped with the editing of God Befriended Me. I certainly wish to thank them both. Pastor Tim Stone is also helping me with the design of the book cover.

My wife, Judy Myers, has been patient with me during this endeavor and I love and appreciate that about her. She has always been there for me from beginning to the end.

My desire is to share what God has put in my heart to share and I pray that this subject brings revelation and understanding of the Covenants of God from the Old Testament as well as the New Testament, to born-again believers whether in denominational churches or non-denominational churches. May God bless our understanding of His Covenants.

Chapter 1
In The Beginning...

In the Beginning God created everything including man and woman. His great desire was to have a relationship with man, a Covenant relationship with man. God has always been a Covenant keeping God. To understand Covenant, you must understand how God thinks about Covenant. There are basically three steps in introducing man to that Covenant relationship. Man can't just enter that Covenant relationship. God initiates the process. First God reveals Himself to man and man if he is hungry for God will begin to follow God. "Blessed are those who hunger and thirst for righteousness, for they will be filled." (Matthew 5:6) There is only One Who has righteousness and that is God, Himself. As God reveals Himself to man, then man begins to follow God and seek Him with all their hearts. Perhaps the Psalmist David said it best. "When You said, Seek my face, My heart said to You, Your face, Lord, I will seek." (Psalms 27:8) Finally, God wants to enter into a Covenant with man. At this point man can choose to enter into a Covenant with God or follow from a distance. This is what we will be endeavoring to study as we look at the covenants of the Old Testament and then at the New Covenant that Jesus Christ, the Son of God, has brought us into with His death and resurrection.

The Hebrew word for Covenant is berith meaning to fetter or eat with. One must understand what a Covenant meant in Old Testament times because that is how people communicated and had relationships. The reason why it was hard to understand the Covenant relationship is because in the Old Testament there were three diverse types of Covenants. They are not alike and yet all three are reflected in the Old Testament. Most people define a Covenant as an agreement between two people. This is true in some cases, but not in all as we shall see. The first example of a Covenant in the Old Testament is the two-sided agreement between two people, most of the time of equal rank. Both parties accept the terms of the agreement. An example of this in the Bible is the friendship between David and Jonathan in 1 Samuel 18:3-4. "Then Jonathan and David made a covenant, because he (Jonathan) loved him as his own soul. And Jonathan took off the robe that was on him and gave it to David, with his armor, even to his sword and his bow and his belt." This Covenant was made the day that David killed Goliath. From that day forward David and Jonathan were in a Covenant relationship.

Another Covenant relationship between two people is the Covenant of marriage. In the beginning when Israel formed as a nation and Moses in the Books of the Law spelled out that relationship, it was not a problem. But as the nation drifted further and further away from God, couples began to have problems with the marriage Covenant. Toward the end of the Old Testament era, there was much divorce. Therefore, Malachi wrote: "Yet you say, "For what reason?" Because the Lord has been witness between you and the wife of your youth, with whom you have dealt treacherously; yet she is your companion and your wife by covenant." (Malachi 2:14)

The final example of a Covenant between two parties is called a political alliance. Israel was forced to make a political alliance or Covenant with the people of Gibeon. The Gibeonites dealt treacherously with Israel in chapter 9 of Joshua. They told Joshua and the leaders of Israel that they had come from a far place to make a Covenant with Israel. Joshua and the leaders did not consult God, but entered an alliance with them. Only after they entered a Covenant with the Gibeonites did they find out they were nearby neighbors. Once a Covenant like this is made, you cannot get out of it. You have sworn before God Almighty.

The second type of a Covenant in the Old Testament is a one-sided Covenant that is imposed by a Superior Being on an inferior being. Probably the best example of this is when God, as the Superior Being, commands a berith (Covenant) which man, the servant, is to obey. Joshua shared this type of Covenant with the nation of Israel just before he died. Observe this in Joshua 23:16. "When you have transgressed the covenant of the Lord your God, which He commanded you, and have gone and served other gods, and bowed down to them, then the anger of the Lord will burn against you, and you shall perish quickly from the good land which He has given you." This did happen to Israel after Solomon's reign as King of Israel, the nation of Israel and later Judah did forsake God and God allowed Assyria to take Israel and Babylon to take Judah. In both instances, only a remnant of the Jewish people remained in the land.

The third type of Covenant of the Old Testament is one that God has self-imposed obligation on Himself, for the reconciliation of sinners to Himself. In Psalms 89:3-4, God declares: "I have made a covenant with My chosen. I have sworn to My servant David. Your seed I will establish forever and build up your throne to all generations. Selah." He also stated this to Abraham: "And I will establish My covenant between Me and you and your descendants after you in their generations, for an everlasting covenant, to be God to you and your descendants after you." (Genesis 17:7)

God is interested in a Covenant relationship with man that is eternal. Most of the Old Testament Covenants was based on the Mosaic Law. This Mosaic Covenant was established when the children of Israel reached Mount Sinai. God spoke to Moses and explained the Covenant of Law to him. This is recorded in Exodus 19:5:" to Me above all people; for all the earth is mine." At that point in their history the Jewish people, after Moses explained the Covenant to them, agreed to the Covenant. It was a relationship based on "if you are willing and obedient, you shall eat the good of the land "(Isaiah 1:19). From these passages, the Old Testament Covenants were conditional on man and his ability or inability to obey the Law of God. The only problem with that is man's nature from the fall is sinful and rebellious of what God wants and desires. Several men (Noah, Abraham) in the Old Testament succeeded with the Covenant that God laid out for them. Usually the Covenant relationships that succeeded, as we said earlier, were with men who were hungry for God. There was a hunger for the things of God. This caused men and women to seek God. This hunger brought them into a love for God and a desire for God more than anything else. As a result, God changed their hearts and brought them into a tender Covenant relationship with Himself.

John Hagee, Pastor of Cornerstone Church in San Antonio, Texas, describes in his Prophecy Study Bible the Old Testament Covenant relationship with God. In his article in the Bible, The Idea of "Covenant" in the Bible, he describes that Covenant with God under the Law of God. "He (God) utilized a covenant style understood at the time: 1) a preamble identifying the absolute sovereign, 2) a brief history of relationship between the absolute sovereign and the subject people, 3) the benefits for and obligations of the subject people, 4) an oath of allegiance and its accompanying blessings for obedience and curses for disobedience, and 5) a list of witnesses and directions for keeping the covenant. Sometimes there followed instructions for periodic renewal of the covenant." This quote is from page 26 of that Bible. This Covenant with God under the Law of God is found in Exodus chapters 20 to 23, the whole book of Deuteronomy, and Joshua 24.

John Hagee goes on to describe the difference between the Old Testament (Covenant) and New Testament (Covenant) which comprises the whole of the Bible. "The Bible is divided into an Old Testament and a New Testament. "Testament" was a synonym for "covenant" in the English of the era of King James I. All of God's Word concerns an old and a new form of the way in which He provides for a personal, mutually committed relationship between Himself and those whom He calls and who respond in faith to Him. Various other Biblical covenants predate the "old covenant" (Old Testament) or elaborate aspects of it. People of God's covenant have a basis for saying, "My beloved is mine, and I am his." (Song of Solomon 2:16) This is also on page 26 of that Bible.

As John Hagee states in this article of his Prophecy Study Bible many Biblical scholars are returning to studying the Covenants of the Bible because that is how God has dealt with man from the beginning. God has not changed His ways. To understand how God deals with and wants to have fellowship with man and even resulting in a Divine relationship with God and man, we must study and understand the Covenant relationship. That will be the purpose of this study with the hope and desire that we come into that Divine Covenant relationship. But Covenant relationship in the Old Testament as well as the New Testament doesn't come immediately when an individual comes into relationship with God. In the Old Testament, God reveals Himself to the individual like Adam, Noah, and Abraham. Then usually there is a trial or test, before God reveals the

Covenant relationship to them. Finally, God reveals the Covenant relationship to them and what is stipulated in that relationship.

In the New Testament (Covenant), God reveals Himself in the person of Jesus Christ. "Therefore, having been justified by faith, we have peace with God through our Lord Jesus Christ, through whom, we have access by faith into this grace in which we stand, and rejoice in hope of the glory of God.... Much more then, having now been justified by His (Jesus) blood, we shall be saved from wrath (God's wrath) through Him (Jesus)." (Romans 5: 1, 2, 9) Adam's fallen race (you and I) accept Jesus' sacrifice for us and are saved from God's wrath. But many go no further into the New Covenant than that. Some don't even enter into the Covenant's two ordinances—water baptism and Communion or commonly referred to as the Lord's Supper. They understand very little of what the New Testament (Covenant) teaches. When ministers talk about a living relationship with the Lord, it is like a foreign language to them. Only churches and Messianic Jewish centers offering teaching along these lines that can bring someone into that Covenant relationship that God desires.

As stated before, our desire will be to bring people into that Covenant relationship with God, using both the Old Testament (Covenants) and the New Testament (Covenant) teaching found in the Word of God. There are principles found in the Old Testament Covenants that one will find in the New Testament Covenant. Since the Bible is a Jewish book one needs to study the Old Testament Covenants as well as the New Testament Covenant. God, the Holy Spirit, desires to bring us into that Divine relationship. May we prayerfully consider this as we study God's Divine Covenants. May we desire to be befriended by God with all of our heart.

Chapter 2
The Edenic Covenant

In every relationship with God, God is always pursuing us. We never pursue Him unless it is out of a selfish motivation. In other words, we want something from God. An excellent example of this is found in the New Testament. When Jesus Christ, the Son of God, began healing people around the Sea of Galilee and the Jordan River, word of mouth advertisement brought hundreds even thousands of people to Him, who needed healing and a miracle in their lives. But we are getting ahead of ourselves. Let us go back to the beginning and see the progression of man's relationship with God.

"In the beginning God created the heavens and the earth." (Genesis 1:1) In five days, God created everything from light and darkness, water, land, grass, fruit trees and plain trees, the sun, moon, and stars, and fish in the seas. This is all covered in twenty-four-hour days for five days. On the sixth day God created animals that roamed the land and finally He created man in His own image. "Then God said, "Let Us make man in Our image, according to Our likeness, let them have dominion over the fish of the sea, over the birds of the air, and over the cattle, over all the earth and over every creeping thing that creeps on the earth." (Genesis 1:26) Then God saw that man needed a helper. "And the Lord God said, "It is not good that man should be alone; I will make him a helper comparable to him." (Genesis 2:18) In a deep sleep that fell on Adam by God, God was able to perform the operation of creating woman and bringing her to Adam. This is described in Genesis 2:21-25. "And the Lord God caused a deep sleep to fall on Adam, and he slept, and He took one of his ribs and closed up the flesh in the place. Then the rib which the Lord God had taken from man, He made into a woman, and He brought her to the man. And Adam said: This is now bone of my bones and flesh of my flesh. She shall be called Woman, because she was taken out of Man. Therefore, a man shall leave his father and mother and be joined to his wife and they shall become one flesh. And they were both naked and not ashamed."

Thus far, we have given a background for the first Covenant that God made with man. Although, the word Covenant is not found in the first three chapters of Genesis, yet all the elements are there for a Covenant to be made. Since we are talking about a Covenant relationship, we must look at and define the elements involved in that relationship. Although, we will be discussing Divine Covenants that God has made with man, we will also be discussing from time to time Covenant relationships that men make with men and the Marriage Covenant that men make with women. Although, there is no statement in the Bible in Genesis that says this is a Covenant, the Covenant between Adam and God is laid out in Genesis the second chapter.

Before we move into this Edenic Covenant, we need to look at one other thing in the first chapter of Genesis. As stated at the beginning of chapter 1, God created the heavens and the earth. (Genesis 1:1) Everything that God creates is good and perfect. There are no flaws or imperfections. Therefore, when the Bible says, God created the heavens and the earth, both the heavens and the earth were perfect. We don't know how much time elapsed between Genesis 1:1 and Genesis 1:2. We do know that when Genesis 1:2 is written that chaotic changes had taken place. This Scripture refers to that in Jeremiah 4:23-26. "I beheld the earth, and indeed it was without form and void; and the heavens they had no light.... I beheld and the fruitful land was a wilderness, and all its cities were broken down at the presence of the Lord, by His fierce anger." From this Scripture in Jeremiah and Genesis 1:2 one can see that something had happened in the heavens. Satan had rebelled against God and had taken a third of the angels with him. Dr. Scofield in The Scofield Bible says, "Jeremiah 4:23-26...clearly indicates that the earth had undergone a cataclysmic change as a result of Divine judgment. The face of the earth bears everywhere the marks of such a catastrophe. There are not wanting intimations which connect it with a previous testing and fall of angels." J. Fennis Dake in his Dakes Annotated Reference Bible states clearly between Genesis 1:1 and 1:2 this statement. "Earth made chaos; end of earth's perfect state and first sinful career because of Lucifer's rebellion. Overthrow of the world that then was." J. Fennis Dake gives 2 Peter 3:5-7 as the proof text for this. "For this they willfully forget; that by the Word of God the heavens were of old, and the earth standing out of the water and in the water, by which the world that then existed perished, being flooded with water. But the heavens and the earth which now exist are kept in store by the same word, reserved for fire until the day of judgment and perdition of ungodly men." Some Bible scholars say this refers to Noah's flood, but notice there is no mention of darkness was upon the face of the deep. And the Spirit of God was hovering over the face of the waters." Now, the Hebrew word for "form" was tohow and it meant desolation, desert, a worthless thing, confusion, emptiness. Therefore, the word "void" means having no life. So, darkness covered the earth. As we said before, God does things that are perfect, therefore, He could not have done this. This was the devil's work. As it says in John 10:10, "The thief (the devil) does not come except to steal, to kill and to destroy..."

So why bring this up, if we are preparing to study Divine Covenants? I believe God knew the devil was on the earth. Only time would tell what form he would take. God wanted a person with which He could fellowship. But the person (Adam) must be tested to see if he would remain faithful to God. Therefore, God created a Garden (The Garden of Eden) full of fruit trees, where Man and Woman could live in harmony with God. God would allow one tree in the Garden to take the form of the devil's way.

But before we get into the temptation and the tempter's ploy, let's look at what a Covenant looks like. Arthur W. Pink in his book, The Divine Covenants, states what we have already stated that all the elements in the Edenic Covenant are already there. "It is true that the actual "covenant" does not occur in the Genesis record, in connection with the primordial transaction between God and man, but the facts of the case present all the constituent elements of a covenant...." (page 46). I share this to let you know that I am not alone in believing there was a Covenant between God and Adam.

Well, what is the definition and the essential elements of a Covenant? Arthur W. Pink states it clearly in The Divine Covenants. "...Briefly stated, any covenant is a mutual agreement entered into by two or more parties, whereby they stand solemnly bound to each other to perform the conditions contracted for. Amplifying that definition, it may be pointed out that the terms of a covenant are (1) there is a stipulation of something to be done or given by that party proposing the covenant; (2) there is a stipulation by the other party of something to be done or given in consideration; (3) those stipulations must be lawful and right, for it can never be right to engage to do wrong; (4) there is a penalty included in the terms of agreement, some evil consequence to result to the party who may or shall violate his agreement—that penalty being added as security." (page 41)

Mr. Pink goes on to describe how God and Adam entered into Covenant together. Because Eve is a part of Adam, she has entered into the same Covenant. Listen to Reverend Pink's description: "But of the tree of the knowledge of good and evil, you shall not eat, for in the day that you eat of it, you shall surely die." (Genesis 2:17) "Here are all the constituent elements of a covenant; (1) there are the contrasting parties; the Lord God and man (Adam); (2) there is a stipulation enjoined which man (as he was duty bound) engaged to perform; (3) there was a penalty prescribed which would be incurred in case of failure; (4) there was by clear and necessary implication a reward promised to which Adam would be entitled by his fulfillment of the condition; (5) the "tree of life" was the divine seal or ratification of the covenant…."

The only thing that Mr. Pink has left out of this description is the tempting agent, the devil and his part in the Covenant. Therefore, his definition is only partly correct. He also leaves out the fact that God wanted a relationship of love with Adam. A contract, as Reverend Pink describes Covenant, is more like a contractual type of relationship where there is a mutual benefit for both parties. God desires a love relationship and Covenant is a commitment of love. Ralph Smith in his paper-book, The Covenantal Structure of the Bible, is defining what Covenant means and says. He starts off by quoting Deuteronomy 6:4-5. "Hear O Israel! The Lord is our God, the Lord is one! You shall love the Lord your God with all your heart and with all your soul and with all your might."

From this Scripture, Mr. Smith shows the difference between a contract and a Biblical Covenant. "As these verses make clear, a covenant is a commitment of love. Since it creates a relationship fundamentally different from the mutual profit-seeking relationship of a contract, it must be established in a different manner. In the Bible, a covenant can only be established and sealed by an oath...." Ralph Smith actually gives us a better insight into Biblical Covenants than Reverend Pink. Mr. Pink's idea of a Covenant is more legalistic than Reverend Smith. Mr. Smith goes on to share what elements he considers to be important about Biblical Covenants. Some of Ralph Smith's elements are repetitious of Reverend Pink's elements while others shed a lot more light on the subject.

Next, we will look at Mr. Smith's elements of the Edenic Covenant and then look at what both left out. There are five points of the Eden Garden Covenant as presented by Mr. Smith. "(1) The entire passage (Genesis chapters 1 to 3) demonstrates the absolute Lordship of God who creates all things according to His will and plan. God's sovereignty in creation is especially seen in that all things are created by His Word... (Genesis 1:3,6,9,11,14,20,24,26,28,29) (This) corresponds to the tenfold Word of God in the Mosaic Covenant, the Ten Commandments. There is a hint of the Trinity in the Creation of Adam and Eve, both in the divine counsel— "Let Us make man in our image, after Our likeness." (Genesis 1:26) and in the very fact that human society is God's image, no less than the human individual. (2) Adam is the Lord of creation under God. He is the original King of the world and, with his Queen, has dominion over all creation. (Genesis 1:28) Adam is the original priest and prophet, since God speaks to Adam, who then teaches his wife the Word of God. (Genesis 2:16-18) His priestly responsibilities are seen in the command to guard the sanctuary (Genesis 2:15), for priests in later times were the guardians of the temple. His responsibility as the first husband and father included farming the garden (Genesis 2:15) and having children to fill the earth for the glory of God (Genesis 1:28). (3) These responsibilities constituted the commands of the Covenant. The ethical heart of the Covenant was the command not to eat of the tree of the knowledge of good and evil. (Genesis 2:17) God's gracious provision was to eat of all the trees except the one He named that was forbidden constituted a divine invitation to eat from the other, the tree of life. (4) The blessing and curse of the Covenant was set forth in the two trees."

"The tree of life would bring blessing, if Adam and Eve chose it rather than the tree of knowledge of good and evil. If they chose the forbidden tree, however, they faced the curse of death. It was as if the Lord was saying to Adam what Moses later said to Israel. "I call heaven and earth to record this day against you, that I have set before you life and death, blessing and cursing: therefore, choose life, that both you and your descendants may live." (Deuteronomy 30:19) (5) Had Adam chosen life, he and his posterity would have inherited the world and Satan would have been cast out. If Adam had refused Satan's temptation he would have understood the true meaning of good and evil, the very thing the tree and the test was supposed to teach him...If the lesson had been learned, Adam and Eve would have graduated into a higher status and all mankind after them would have enjoyed the Covenantal blessings they won."

The reason I chose to quote completely Ralph Smith's interpretation of the Edenic Covenant is because he gives a better understanding of the Covenant in my opinion than Mr. Pink's interpretation. It is important to know and understand this Covenant especially when the Holy Spirit can enlighten our minds about what Adam and Eve could have gained through obedience and what they lost through disobedience. From Reverend Smith, we can see the point of view of God's great love for man/Adam and how God would have preferred to walk in love and fellowship with Adam and Eve. In the later Covenants, we will see the great love that God has for mankind as a whole.

Let's summarize Ralph Smith's interpretation of the Edenic Covenant. In the first sentence of each of Mr. Smith's elements of that Covenant we see it summarized. "(1) The entire passage (Genesis chapters 1 to 3) demonstrates the absolute Lordship of God who creates all things (including the Garden of Eden, Adam, Eve, and Satan) according to His will and plan. (2) Adam is the Lord of creation under God. (3) Adam's responsibilities constituted the commands of the Covenant. (4) The blessing and curse of the Covenant were set forth in the two trees (Tree of life and the Tree of the knowledge of good and evil) (5) Had Adam chose life, he and his posterity would have inherited the world and Satan would have been cast out." Those are the main elements of Mr. Smith's Edenic Covenant. This is taken from his paper/book, The Covenantal Structure of the Bible on pages 19-20. This gives you a synopsis view of the Edenic Covenant. There are some things that are missing, which we will get into as we look at both views of this Covenant.

We might add that there are reasons why God gave a command about eating. The real issue behind this command was whether Adam and Eve would trust God and obey Him simply because He is God. "If Adam obeyed when tested, he would have manifested the faith and love that is the true heart of obedience." (page 19 Covenantal Structure of the Bible) Eating also refers to eating spiritually what God has set before you and giving thanks for His provision. When He tells you not to eat something, it is for your own good to abstain. Adam and Eve learned this the hard way and chose a life of independence rather than dependence on God. They already were children of God, because they were eating from His table and worshipping Him. Luke 3:38 calls Adam the son of God: "the son of Enos, the son of Seth, the son of Adam, the son of God." Adam and Eve were put in the Garden of Eden as a test of perseverance. If Adam passed the test, it would have been that he had persevered in faith and been blessed. God wanted to see if they would pass the test. Man was being tested and was given a free will to obey or not to obey. God was not forcing man to obey Him.

What you will not see in Arthur W. Pink's book, The Divine Covenants, or Ralph Smith's book, The Covenantal Structure of the Bible, is how Satan is not portrayed in their elements of the Edenic Covenant. He is mentioned, but to a great extent he is ignored. In the Biblical narrative, God says nothing to Adam and Eve about Satan or what he may attempt to do. In hindsight, we know the devil is on earth because of the Hebrew language in Genesis 1:1-2. From the description in those verses we know the devil is on earth, because he caused the devastation. From the first three chapters, except verses 1-2 of Genesis 1, it looks like God was ignoring Satan. Why did God not talk to Adam about Satan? I asked our

Apostolic Elder, Clarence Dalremple, and he gave me this explanation. He said that God had placed all the animals under the dominion of Adam, including the snake that spoke to Eve. When Adam and Eve started listening to the snake they violated their own chain of command. It is also true today. When we start listening to the devil through any person or thing, we are headed for trouble. Ephesians 4:27 says, "…nor give place to the devil." The word "place" is the Greek word topos meaning space, but limited by occupancy. This is taken from The Greek Dictionary of the New Testament in The Strong's Concordance on page 72. First Eve gave place to the devil in her life and then Adam followed suit. When we start listening to the devil, we stop listening to God, or we become double minded, having two minds. This is what the Apostle James refers to in James 1:5-9. "If any of you lack wisdom, let him ask of God, who gives to all liberally and without reproach, and it will be given him. But let him ask in faith, with no doubting, for he who doubts is like a wave of the sea driven and tossed by the wind. For let not that man suppose that he will receive anything from the Lord, he is a double-minded man, unstable in all his ways."

But we are getting ahead of ourselves. If one reads the first three chapters of Genesis, one realizes that Adam and Eve had a Covenant with God that was the best of all the Old Testament Covenants. There are several things about this Covenant that stand out. First, it was a pre-fall Covenant. Man had not sinned and he was walking in complete harmony with God. Adam and Eve were in a state of innocence and had no knowledge of sin or what sin meant. All the conditions of the Covenant had been explained to Adam by God. Adam in turned explained them to Eve. Part of the Covenant is in Genesis 1:28-30. "Then God blessed them (Adam and Eve), and God said to them, "Be fruitful and multiply; fill the earth and subdue it; have dominion over the fish of the sea, over the birds of the air, and over every living thing that moves on the earth. And God said, "See, I have given you every herb that yields seed, to you it shall be food. Also, to every beast of the earth, to every bird of the air, and everything that creeps on the earth, in which there is life, I have given every green herb for food; and it was so." Then in chapter 2 of Genesis, God puts one restriction or rule that man/Adam must follow. Genesis 2:15-18 shows that restriction or rule. "Then the Lord God took the man and put him in the garden of Eden to tend and keep it. And the Lord God commanded the man saying, "Of every tree of the garden you may freely eat, but of the tree of the knowledge of good and evil you shall not eat, for in the day that you eat of it you shall surely die."

Therefore, from this passage and Genesis 2:8-9 we know that there were two trees planted in the midst of the Garden of God. "The Lord God planted a garden eastward of Eden, and there he put the man whom he had formed. And out of the ground the Lord God made every tree grow that is pleasant to the sight and good for food. The tree of life was also in the midst of the garden, and the tree of the knowledge of good and evil." The final stage is set for the test, when Adam's wife, Eve, is formed from Adam's own rib. Adam is put to sleep by God after a long day of naming the animals. Eve is formed and brought to man. Evidently between chapter 2 and chapter 3 of Genesis, Adam explains God's instructions or the terms of the Covenant to Eve. Therefore, she is not without understanding of the Covenant with God nor of the consequences of that Covenant if it is broken. This can be understood by the answers she gives the devil, when he questions her.

Most probably, Adam and Eve for a while had sweet fellowship with God. I agree with most Bible scholars that this temptation or test came later. Many believe that the devil was in the snake for a while and talked to Adam and Eve daily, so that they became familiar with his voice and his questions. I personally, don't think the devil and the temptation took place immediately with Eve. There is a saying, "that misery loves company." The devil had already fallen and he wanted company. He was looking for an opportunity to deceive and tempt the one who had not heard directly from God—Eve. It's possible that God could have communicated the Covenant to Eve as well, but that isn't laid out in Scripture. Adam's responsibility was communicating to her the truth. At the heart of Satan's ploy is his attack of the weakest link. In fact, the Apostle Peter says this in 1 Peter 3:7: "Likewise you husbands, dwell with them with understanding, giving honor to the wife as to the weaker vessel, and as being heirs together of the grace of life, that your prayers be not hindered." Satan knows that she has gotten what she knows probably from Adam. That is why he attacked her rather than Adam. The devil does the same thing today. He will attack the weakest link in the family. Today it is not always the woman who is the weakest link, many times it is the man or the children.

At the heart of the temptation that broke the Covenant between Adam and God, was the fact that Eve listened to Satan. When Eve or we listen to the devil, we stop listening to God. Satan is always going to question what God has said to us. That is what he did with Eve. "Has God indeed said, "You shall not eat of every tree in the garden?" (Genesis 3:1b) Eve answers the question. From her answer, she tells the devil that they are not to eat of the tree of the knowledge of good and evil, because if they do so, they will die. But then the devil tells her God is wrong. "You will not surely die." He goes on to say that God is wrong about everything. "For God knows that in the day you eat of it your eyes will be opened, and you will be like God, knowing good and evil." (Genesis 3: 4b-5) The devil has contradicted everything that God told Adam and everything Adam told Eve about the Covenant restriction. Now Eve is forced to decide. Either God is wrong and the serpent is correct or God is right and the serpent/devil is wrong. That is when she started looking at the tree of knowledge of good and evil and began desiring it. "So, when the woman saw that the tree was good for food, that it was pleasant to the eyes, and a tree desirable to make one wise, she took of its fruit and ate. She also gave to her husband with her and he ate. Then the eyes of both of them were opened, and they knew they were naked; and they sewed fig leaves together and made them coverings." (Genesis 3:6-7) When this happened the Covenant with God was broken.

The devil was crafty in attacking what the woman knew and understood. Notice also that Adam was there when the serpent/devil talked to the woman and yet the devil didn't say anything to him. Adam also did not speak up or talk to the devil about what he was saying. We see this in the latter part of Genesis 3:6b. "She also gave to her husband with her, and he ate." The devil did not attack Adam. God had communicated with Adam everything about the Covenant relationship. From the first two chapters of Genesis, one can see that God communicated with Adam and God expected

Adam, as the head of the family, to communicate with Eve. Eve communicated what God had said, but she wasn't prepared for the devil questioning what God had said. It happens the same way today. God gives us a clear revelation of Who God is and of what He wants us to be, do and say. Then the devil comes along and starts questioning that clear revelation.

This brings us to the three things that happen to individuals that God wants to bring into a Covenant relationship with Him. First, God reveals Himself to them. God becomes so real to us and like Adam and Eve, we walk in the cool of the day with Him. We know this because the Word of God describes in Genesis 3:8 as this relationship. "And they heard the sound of the Lord God walking in the garden in the cool of the day...." From this verse we get the picture that this happened probably every day before the temptation by the devil. Adam and Eve walked and talked with God every day. That would have been like Heaven on earth. God had revealed Himself to them and they had such a beautiful relationship.

Second, the next step was to pass the test and forever be in Covenant relationship with God. The problem is they failed the test. Adam and Eve were so close, yet so far. They failed the test, but it is not over yet. God still wants them. God now must deal with the sin issue in their lives. At the root of the sin issue is disobedience. When God deals with the sin issue in their lives, He finds that Adam blames Eve and Eve blames the serpent/devil. In the beginning, they do not want to accept the responsibility of what they have done by saying, "I have sinned/disobeyed you."

One of the big questions that surfaces that has puzzled Bible scholars is where was Adam in proximity to Eve, when she yielded to the temptation that the devil sent her way. The serpent/devil knew exactly what God had told Adam. Therefore, he knew how to tempt Eve. Adam had communicated to Eve the Covenant that they were under. Some Bible scholars reject the idea that Adam was right there when Eve was tempted, but as we quoted earlier in Genesis 3:6b that Adam was right there next to Eve when she was tempted to eat the fruit. Therefore, Adam knew what was happening. 1st Timothy 2:14 says, "And Adam was not deceived, but the woman being deceived, fell into transgression."

Why didn't the devil tempt Adam instead of Eve? Perhaps he knew that if he could get Eve to capitulate Adam would too. Ralph Smith in his paper/book, The Covenantal Structure of the Bible, shares with us Adam's position on the Edenic Covenant. "When Satan approached Adam and Eve, Adam should have understood from Satan's challenge the real meaning of good and evil. Good and evil are not substances or things; rather the words good and evil describe our covenantal response to God. For man to submit to his Creator (God) is the essence of good and to rebel is the essence of evil, for man's whole life is defined in relation to God. Had Adam learned this truth by submission to God's will, he would have been confirmed in holiness by eating of the tree of life. We might say Adam had a choice of sacraments, the magical sacrament of Satan which promised power through disobedience to God, or the covenantal sacrament of God, which promised life and all good things by submission to Him." (page 20)

From the Covenant under which God placed Adam and Eve, man (Adam) has a choice. He is a free moral agent. He is not a robot. Adam could have interrupted the conversation that she was having with the devil and told the devil to leave. We have the same right, since the Cross of Jesus, to tell the devil to leave when we are being tempted. Just like Jesus did in the wilderness when He was tempted by the devil. Matthew 4:10-11 says, "Then Jesus said to him (the devil), "Away with you, Satan! For it is written, 'You shall worship the Lord your God, and Him only you shall serve." Then the devil left Him, and behold, angels came and ministered to Him." Adam chose not to do that. We will find out why he did that when God deals with Adam about his sin. That to disobey God was a choice Adam made.

Why did Adam choose not to intervene and stop the breaking of the Covenant with God? He knew what God promised if Eve and he broke the Covenant. Reverend Ralph Smith points out that Adam was looking to see what Eve would do. He believes that Adam's heart was evil. "What Adam actually did was more evil than most realize. When Satan addressed Eve, she yielded and ate the fruit. Then she gave some to Adam and he ate also. Nothing had happened to Eve, so Adam assumed it was safe to eat. But the fall had already occurred when Adam decided to let Eve eat." (page 20) Reverend Smith believes the fall happened in Adam and Eve's heart before the act was committed. "Then when desire has conceived, it gives birth to sin; and sin, when it is full-grown brings forth death." (James 1:15)

Notice that Adam and Eve did not physically die, when God pronounced judgment on them. This would come later—their physical death. But immediately, there was a death in their relationship with God. (James 1:15) Everything in chapter 3 of Genesis shows that Adam and Eve were troubled and terrified at the presence of God coming. The expelling of them from the Garden of Eden was another form of death. The Garden represented the presence of God and now they were cast out of His presence. Ralph Smith brings this observation. "In addition, the process of physical decay, the gradual "death" of their bodies began that day. Sickness and pain, fatigue and the sufferings of the body is the aging process were not part of the original creation. From the day they sinned, Adam and Eve "began to die" physically. Beyond the physical death they experienced, the whole creation began to experience a kind of death also…the entire animal and physical world was brought into the "bondage of corruption" (page 21)

As I said earlier, there is a difference of opinion about where Adam was when the snake/devil tempted Eve. Matthew Henry's Commentary, Genesis to Deuteronomy, Volume 1 says this: "The person tempted was the woman, now alone, and at a distance from her husband, but near the forbidden tree." (page 21) Although the Scripture seems to indicate that Adam was very close to her, he evidently heard everything that was said and did nothing. In fact, he participated in the temptation. Whether near or far the devil knows when to attack a child of God. He also knows who to attack. As the Apostle Paul said, "…lest Satan should take advantage of us; for we are not ignorant of his devices." (2nd Corinthians 2:11) As we said before, the woman in Scripture is the weaker vessel. 1st Peter 3:7 says, "Likewise you husbands, dwell with them (the wives) with understanding, giving honor to the wife, as to the weaker vessel, and as being heirs together of the grace of life, that your prayers may not be hindered."

Therefore, since Adam knew he would be living in disobedience to God's Covenant and to God, Himself, why did he partake of the forbidden fruit? There are several different views on this. First, he must have believed what Satan said, "You shall not surely die." He believed the lie of Satan and partook. A lot of individuals today believe the lie of Satan. They believe he will make them wise. They believe they will be able to discern between good and evil. But that is not always true. Everything is not always black and white. One must have the Holy Spirit to discern the difference. Learning to follow God and that still, small voice is most important. If only Adam and Eve had done what God commanded in the first place.

Secondly, Adam no doubt loved his wife and thought he would lose her or be separated from her. Human, fleshly love can only take us so far. This too has been played out in history repeatedly. What God said about them dying, does cause a separation unless they receive the sacrifice of God and become God's children through the redemptive work of the Holy Spirit. Therefore, Adam's fear of separation from Eve took place anyway when they both died.

Finally, God's truth of death and Adam's idea of death were different. Adam thought that death would be immediate, whereas God's truth of death was a gradual returning to the ground from whence Adam and Eve came. Adam finally understood it, when God explained death to him in Genesis 3:19. "In the sweat of your face you shall eat bread till you return to the ground, for out of it you were taken; For dust you are, and to dust you shall return." But then Adam realized the grave mistake he had made in yielding to temptation.

The Edenic Covenant not only had promises, but it also had judgments, if Adam failed to obey the Edenic Covenant. When Adam chose to listen to Eve, his wife and to the devil, he made a serious mistake. Adam knew the fruit came from the forbidden tree. Therefore, all three were punished—Adam, Eve, and the serpent. The serpent or snake, who allowed Satan to enter him, was cursed to be on his belly and crawl on his belly the rest of his life, plus the curse of death also was passed down to him. All snakes after him would have this punishment. "Because you have done this, you are cursed more than all cattle and more than every beast of the field; on your belly you shall go, and you shall eat dust all the days of your life. And I will put enmity between you and the woman, and between your seed and her Seed (Jesus); He (Jesus) shall bruise your head, and you shall bruise His (Jesus) heel. (Genesis 3:14-15) In verse 15 is the prophetic promise of Jesus coming to destroy the works of the devil. This setback did not take God by surprise. He knew before the foundation of the world was laid, that man/Adam was going to fall. In God's mind Jesus was already crucified before the foundation of the world was laid. Revelation 13:8 says, "And all who dwell on the earth will worship him (the dragon/the devil) whose names have not been written in the Book of Life of the Lamb (Jesus) slain from the foundation of the world." The devil's judgment and defeat has already been pronounced by our Father. God judged the serpent, but He also judged the devil that day.

The next Covenant judgment was against the woman/Eve. "To the woman He said, "I will greatly multiply your sorrow and your conception: In pain you shall bring forth children; your desire shall be for your husband and he shall rule over you." (Genesis 3:16) No doubt child bearing would have been easier for women of future generations, if she had not sinned in the Garden of Eden. Since that time child bearing has been painful for women. God had not really said anything about man being put over woman until the sin took place. Now God tells her prophetically that man shall rule over woman. God said, "…he shall rule over you." (Genesis 3:16b) Even in the New Testament, the Apostle Paul says the same thing in Ephesians 5:22-23. "Wives submit to your husbands as to the Lord. For the husband is head of the wife, as also Christ is the head of the church, and He is the Savior of the body." In the twenty-first century this is a real problem in the church. Only God can bring a balanced solution to this problem. Under the New Covenant that Jesus instituted, men and women are to submit to each other. I like the King James Version translation of this verse in Ephesians 5:21. "Submitting yourselves one to another in the fear of God." The word for submitting is hupodeiknumii meaning to exhibit under the eyes or to place oneself under. Therefore, we are to place others better than ourselves respecting God's wishes for each other. One can see how this takes place under the New Covenant after the Cross of Jesus Christ. As Jesus submitted Himself to the Father's will and plan, all in the Body of Christ should submit one to another.

The last Covenant judgment was against man/Adam, as he represented all of mankind that was to come after him. Some Bible scholars call Adam the Federal Head of the human race. The sin he committed in disobeying God, caused all of mankind after him to have participated in that sin. Adam because of his sin inherited a sinful nature (a disobedient nature) that he would pass down to all generations. Mankind could not avoid that sinful nature; the pain and suffering that would come because of that sinful nature. The only way to be delivered from that sinful nature and the results of sin and sins, was for God to send the Last Adam (Jesus Christ), God's only Son, to come and pay the penalty and price tag for sin for us. By the Last Adam (Jesus Christ) dying on the Cross, Jesus killed once and for all the Adamic nature thus setting us free from the sin nature that we inherited from Adam. When Jesus arose from the dead, we arose in Him as a heavenly man, a new creation in Christ Jesus. "And so, it is written, "The first man, Adam, became a living being, the last Adam (Jesus) became a life-giving spirit. However, the spiritual is not first, but the natural, and afterward the spiritual. The first man was of the earth, made of dust, the second Man is the Lord from heaven. As was the man of dust (Adam), so also are those who are made of dust; and as is the heavenly Man (Jesus), so also are those who are heavenly. And as we have borne the image of the man of dust (Adam), we shall also bear the image of the heavenly Man (Jesus)." (1sr Corinthians 15:45-49) The two Federal Heads, Adam and Christ are further explained in Romans 5:12-21, which we will discuss when we get to the New Covenant in the New Testament. Each of the Covenants in the Old Testament have aspects of the New Covenant in them, that prophetically show what is ahead in the New Covenant. For instance, in the Edenic Covenant is the aspect of living in obedience to God and walking in true fellowship with God, when you are walking in obedience with God.

God showed Adam in the Garden of Eden what his personal judgments were going to be. According to Genesis 1:17, Adam listened to the wrong person, his wife, Eve. "Then to Adam He (God) said, because you have heeded the voice of your wife, and have eaten from the tree of which I commanded you, saying, "You shall not eat of it." Evidently, Eve told him what tree it was and she was still alive. Therefore, he figured he wouldn't die. The reason today many individuals enter sin today as then, is because they listen to the wrong person and it is not always the woman in their lives. Many times, they listen to their co-workers at work or their children at home. Adam should have listened and obeyed God.

Listen to what God says Adam's Covenant judgment will be. "Cursed is the ground for your sake; In toil you shall eat of it all the days of your life. Both thorns and thistles it shall bring forth for you. And you shall eat of the herb of the field. In the sweat of your face you shall eat bread till you return to the ground, for out of it you were taken; for dust you are and to dust you will return." (Genesis 1:17b-19) God planted the Garden of Eden and Adam did not have to labor much for Eve and his food. But since he sinned (disobeyed God), now he would have to labor for the rest of his life. Sin or disobedience is always hard on the individual who does it. The Bible says in Proverbs 13:15b, "...but the way of the transgressors is hard." (NKJ Version) First, God says the ground is cursed because of you. The far-reaching results of Adam's sin was all the ground of the earth was cursed not only for Adam's generation, but for generations to follow. Paul mentions this in Romans 8:20-21. "For the creation was subjected to futility, (useless, ineffective), but because of Him who subjected it in hope; because the creation itself also will be delivered from the bondage of corruption into the glorious liberty of the children of God." There is coming a day of liberation for even the creation of the earth. Most Bible scholars believe that will take place during the millennial reign of Jesus Christ.

Secondly, God told Adam that he would eat bread by hard labor all the days of his life. This is what John Hagee, Pastor of Cornerstone Church in San Antonio, Texas, said about the Covenant judgment of man. "The disorder loosed in the soil and in all human enterprise reduces men to toilers who can never win for long in their efforts to make a living (Genesis 3:19). The struggle to get ahead of the chaos represented by thorns and thistles distracts men from God, their spouses, their children, and everything else that needs their attention." (John Hagee's Prophecy Study Bible, page 9) Therefore, Adam and Eve went from nearly a no labor situation to a labor of pain for the rest of their lives. This not only fell on Adam and Eve and their generation of people, but to all future generations to the present day. One can see this in Genesis 3:22-24. "Then the Lord God said, "Behold the man has become like one of Us, to know good and evil. And now, lest he put out his hand and take also of the tree of life, and eat and live forever"—therefore, the Lord God sent him out of the garden of Eden to till the ground from which he was taken. So, He drove out the man; and He placed cherubim at the east of the garden of Eden, and a flaming sword which turned every way, to guard the way to the tree of Life." This is the painful conclusion of the Edenic Covenant. Adam and Eve are driven from the Garden of Eden, which represents the very presence of God. Now both must find a way to draw near to God or hope that God will draw near to them.

There are some lessons that can be drawn from this broken Edenic Covenant. Probably, first and foremost the important lesson is that Adam did not really understand the choices he had made. He did not understand the Covenant that God was making with him. He could have chosen the tree of Life and lived forever. Instead he chose to listen to his wife, Eve, rather than listen to God. He chose the tree of knowledge of good and evil. He chose knowledge over Life (the Life of God) and it doomed him to death eventually.

The second most important lesson is always listen to God. It is better to listen to God rather than people. He listened to his wife not knowing she had been influenced by the devil. It is possible that he may have lost his wife, but he would have this consolation; he had listened to God. Maybe that is why he listened to her, he was afraid he would lose her. Let me interject this. It's not always the woman that is influenced by the devil, many times it is other people in our lives and at times our children. We must be constantly seeking God and wanting to do His will and pleasure. Our faith must be in God and following Him. Hebrews 11:6 says, "But without faith it is impossible to please Him. For he who comes to God must believe that He is and that He is a rewarder of those who diligently seek Him."

The third most important lesson to learn is obedience is better than disobedience. We have often heard the Scripture in 1st Samuel 15:22b. "...Behold, to obey is better than sacrifice, and to heed than the fat of rams." But in the beginning Adam didn't know about sacrifice. The problem is that God had given Adam a direct command not to eat of the tree of the knowledge of good and evil. He chose not to obey, not because he was deceived. 1st Timothy 2:14 says "And Adam was not deceived, but the woman being deceived fell into the transgression." Blessing comes out of obedience, while pain and suffering comes out of disobedience to God. In Deuteronomy 28:1-2 it says, "Now it shall come to pass, if you diligently obey the voice of the Lord your God, to observe carefully all the commandments which I command you today, that the Lord your God will set you on high above all nations of the earth. And all these blessings shall come upon you and overtake you, because you obey the voice of the Lord your God." In this instance the blessing according to Genesis 3:22 would have been life forever. However, the opposite is true if you choose not to obey God. Just like Adam and Eve you will be forced to leave the presence of God and according to Deuteronomy 28 says your life may become a curse. Deuteronomy 28:15 says, "But it shall come to pass, if you do not obey the voice of the Lord your God, to observe carefully all His commandments and His statutes which I command you today, that all these curses will come upon you and overtake you." And just like Moses wrote about all the blessings that the nation of Israel would experience if they listened to God and followed His commandments, he also listed the curses that would come upon Israel if they didn't listen to God and obey Him. And the curses were more enumerated than the blessings. Therefore, it behooves us to follow our God closely and listen to Him.

The fourth lesson to be learned by the Edenic Covenant is God did not leave Adam and Eve naked. Even though they failed the Covenant they had made with God and knew they had made a grave mistake, God still had mercy on them and sacrificed some animals, spilled some blood and clothed Adam and Eve. "And Adam called his wife's name Eve, because she was the mother of all living. Also, for Adam and his wife the Lord God made tunics of skin and clothed them." (Genesis 3:20-21) God had to sacrifice animals to clothe them. Blood had to be shed. This was a Divine picture of what was to take place some two thousand years later when Jesus Christ, the last Adam, was crucified for us. His blood paid for our sins past, present, and future. He killed the Adamic nature once and for all that day and clothed us with His righteousness. 2nd Corinthians 5:21 says, "For He (God) made Him (Jesus) who knew no sin to be sin for us, that we might become the righteousness of God in Him (Jesus)." "And so, it is written, "the first man Adam became a living being, the last Adam (Jesus) became a life-giving Spirit." (1st Corinthians 15:45) Adam and Eve died in the last Adam (Jesus) so they could live forever. You say how do you know that? The Apostle Peter gave us a startling revelation in 1st Peter 3:19-20 "...by whom also He (Jesus) went and preached to the spirits in prison, who formerly were disobedient, when once the longsuffering of God waited in the days of Noah, while the ark was being prepared, in which a few, that is eight souls were saved through water. "God always wants to give man a second chance. 1st Peter 3:9 says, "The Lord is not slack concerning His promise, as some count slackness, but is longsuffering toward us, not willing that any should perish bur that all should come to repentance."

The fifth lesson we should learn from the Edenic Covenant is the clothing of Adam and Eve by God shows the love and patience that God has for everyone. This is the prophetic view of God showing that God clothed them in the righteousness of Jesus Christ. "But of Him(God) you are in Christ Jesus, who became for us wisdom from God—and righteousness and sanctification and redemption—that as it is written, He who glories, let him glory in the Lord." (1st Corinthians 1:30-31) Therefore, even though Adam and Eve plunged the whole human race into sin and the sin nature, God our Father, is not finished with us. We are clothed today in the righteousness of Christ by God our Father through the work of the Holy Spirit.

With these lessons, we can learn a very valuable conclusion to the whole matter. All through the Bible, God never talks about Adam's success, but only his failure. When a person fails in their Covenant with God, there are usually tragic results in their testimony before God and man. As we shall see, God does not include Adam and Eve in the Faith Chapter of Hebrews 11. Adam is not acknowledged as a person of faith. Rather he is seen as a failure before God. Paul's letter to Timothy shows that Adam was not deceived when he ate of the forbidden fruit. This influenced his sons who were born to him after the fall. One of his sons, Cain, chose to live an earthily life rather than a spiritual life before God. Adam and Eve did teach Abel and Seth what God required to live before Him in righteousness. Cain took his living from the earth, while Abel was a keeper of sheep (a shepherd). Abel's sacrifice to God involved a spotless lamb that was slain and blood was shed. God accepted Abel's sacrifice. He did not accept Cain's sacrifice because it was of the earth-- earthy. I believe Adam taught his sons what sacrifice would please God. Only one obeyed and followed his directions. Cain thought any sacrifice would please God.

This is the final conclusion. Adam taught his sons well even though he had failed in God's Covenant with Him. It is sad that only one son obeyed and is in the Faith Chapter while Cain disobeyed God and after killing Abel was a wanderer and vagabond the rest of his life. We will look at the ones mentioned in the Faith Chapter and see what God saw in the ones mentioned from Adam to Noah. You cannot please God without faith.

Chapter 3
The Men of Covenant / Adam - Noah

Adam -

God is looking for Covenant men of faith throughout all generations. In fact, the Bible is so clear about that fact, it is stated in the faith chapter of Hebrews 11. "But without faith it is impossible to please Him, for he who comes to God must believe that He is, and that He is a rewarder of those who diligently seek Him." (Hebrews 11:6) Not only does God require faith, it is a must to walk with Him. God allowed the writer of Hebrews (Most believe it was Paul, the Apostle) to define faith. "Now faith is the substance (realization) of things hoped for, the evidence (confidence) of things not seen." (Hebrews 11:1) To be in Covenant relationship with God, faith is a requirement. Close to the end of the Bible, God let us know what men were walking by faith at the very beginning of time. Noticeably, Adam is missing from that list. Why would Adam be missing? Therefore, for a few minutes we will investigate why he is not included in the Faith chapter (Hebrews 11) and why when it counted, he faltered and failed.

First of all, the Bible says in Romans 12:3, "For I say, through the grace given to me, to everyone who is among you, not to think of himself more highly than he ought to think, but to think soberly, as God has dealt to each one a measure of faith." In the King James Version in my opinion this verse is a little clearer, especially the last of the verse. "...but to think soberly, according as God hath dealt to every man the measure of faith." (Romans 12:3b KJV) If God dealt to every man the measure of faith, then Adam had enough faith to do what was right. God had instructed him not to eat of the forbidden tree—the tree of the knowledge of good and evil. So, he had enough faith, enough understanding to obey God and do what was right. But he did not walk in faith toward God and thus Adam disobeyed God.

Secondly, Adam was not deceived by the serpent/the devil. The Scriptures are very clear about that. "And Adam was not deceived, but the woman being deceived, fell into transgression." (1st Timothy 2:14) Adam not being deceived means that Adam knew what he was doing when he disobeyed God and ate the forbidden fruit. By disobeying God, he was not acting in faith toward God. "But he who doubts is condemned if he eats, because he does not eat from faith; for whatever is not from faith is sin." (Romans 14:23) "Therefore to him who knows to do good and does not do it, to him it is sin." (James 4:17) From these two Scriptures we can see the magnitude of Adam's sin. Adam knew what God's Covenant required and willfully disobeyed that Covenant.

Finally, we have no record in the Bible during his earthily walk, that Adam ever repented of his disobedience. We believe he taught his sons, Cain and Abel, what a proper sacrifice God required. He knew what God required, because God had slain animals to clothe and cover Adam and Eve in their nakedness. That sacrifice of God required blood. Our sin and our nakedness before God requires a blood sacrifice. This is a prophetic view of what Jesus did for us at Calvary. Adam worked and labored in the fields to bring forth bread to eat for him and his family. This was the curse that God put on him. "Cursed is the ground for your sake; In toil you shall eat of it all the days of your life. Both thorns and thistles it shall bring forth for you, and you shall eat of the herb of the field. In the sweat of your face you shall eat bread till you return to the ground, for out of it you were taken; for dust you are, and to dust you shall return." (Genesis 3:17b-19) God also kicked him out of the Garden of Eden lest he eat of the Tree of Life and live forever in his sinful state. (Genesis 3:22-24) It is no wonder that Cain followed his father in tilling the ground. One can see that neither Adam nor Cain had a repentant attitude toward God. Since God had cursed the ground, we can see why Cain's sacrifice did not please God. Abel on the other hand became a shepherd of sheep. No doubt Abel saw that God used those animals possibly to clothe Adam and Eve in the beginning and that God revealed to Abel that perfect sheep according to human standards were acceptable to sacrifice to God.

Abel -

The only three men who are mentioned as men of faith in the beginning are Abel, Enoch, and Noah. Only Noah is recorded as having a Covenant relationship with God, we believe that Abel and Enoch must have a similar relationship, though it is not mentioned in Scripture. We know they had a relationship of faith with God. We believe that a faith relationship brought both Abel and Enoch into a Covenant relationship which requires something from the person. God required something of both Abel and Enoch as we shall see. Each man—Abel, Enoch, and Noah—had a particular emphasis of his life that honored God. Let us read what God says about them in the Faith Chapter—Hebrews 11:4-7.

"By faith Abel offered to God a more excellent sacrifice than Cain, through which he obtained witness that he was righteous, God testifying of his gifts, and through it he being dead still speaks."

"By faith Enoch was translated so that he did not see death, and was not found because God had translated him; for before his translation he had this testimony, that he pleased God."

"But without faith it is impossible to please Him, for he who comes to God must believe that He is, and that He is a rewarder of those who diligently seek Him."

"By faith Noah, being divinely warned of things not seen, moved with Godly fear, prepared an ark for the saving of his household, by which he condemned the world and became heir of the righteousness which is according to faith." These three men are considered among the heroes of faith. Only Noah has several chapters in Genesis about him. (Genesis 5:29-10) The other two men—Abel and Enoch—are just talked about briefly in a few verses.

Let us look at Abel first. In Genesis 4 we learn that Abel was the second son of Adam and Eve. Cain was the first-born son. The first-born son was important in Bible times and it is still important today. The reason the first-born son was important was "because it honored the rights and privileges of the families of the first-born son. After the father died…the first-born son assumed the father's authority and responsibility…" (Got

Questions.org. The Birthright) This was the beginning of human history so the right of the first-born had not yet been established. Later in Biblical times and the Far Eastern countries it would become very important. Later we shall see in Genesis how important being the first-born son was in Far Eastern Culture.

Since the fall in the Garden of Eden, Adam had to learn by trial and error what pleased God. The Covenant failure in the Garden had brought this about. There wasn't a Bible available to tell him how to approach God daily. He probably had to approach God every day to find out what pleased God concerning matters of the heart and sacrifice. It is possible he relayed all he had learned to his two sons—Cain and Abel.

However, there is another possibility that probably was more correct. Because Abel was a man of faith according to Hebrews 11:4, God revealed to Abel what sacrifice pleased Him. "By faith Abel offered to God a more excellent sacrifice..." (Hebrews 11:4a) In Genesis and Hebrews there is little said about Abel, except that he is a man of faith and his sacrifice pleased God. I believe Abel is the second man that God revealed Himself too. Adam is the first and he failed God. Out of the revelation of God to Abel, God shared with him what pleased Him. Abel understood that a sacrifice of blood and the sacrifice had to be without any blemishes to please God. I believe that came by revelation from God, Himself. Cain was not open to that revelation. Both Cain and Abel's occupation showed where they stood before God. Abel was a keeper of sheep and Cain was a tiller of the ground or farmer.

Listen to what Arthur W. Pink has to say about Cain and Abel in Gleanings in Genesis on page 58. "...Attention should be fixed not so much on two men themselves, as upon the differences between their offerings. So far as the record goes there is nothing to intimate that up to this time Cain was the worst man of the two, that is, considered from a natural and moral standard. Cain was no infidel or atheist. He was ready to acknowledge the existence of God, he was prepared to worship Him after his own fashion. He "brought the fruit of the ground an offering to the Lord." But mark three things. First his offering was a bloodless one and "without shedding of blood is no remission. (Remission means cancellation of the debt, forgiveness, pardoning.) Second, his offering consisted of the fruit of his own toil, it was the product of his own labors, in a word, it was the work of his own hands. Third, he brought of "the fruit of the ground" thus ignoring the Divine sentence recorded in Genesis 3:17, "Cursed is the ground." Abel "brought of the firstlings of his flock and the fat thereof," and to secure this, sacrifice had to be made, life had to be taken, blood had to be shed. The comment of the Holy Spirit upon this incident is, that "By faith Abel offered unto God a more excellent sacrifice than Cain." (Hebrews 11:4a) He does not state that Abel was more excellent, but that the offering which he presented was more pleasing and acceptable to his Maker."

I agree with most of what Mr. Pink said, except his idea that Abel was just an ordinary person. In Hebrews 11:4 and 6 it points out that Abel was righteous and pleasing to God because he had faith in God and he offered a sacrifice that pleased God. Cain thought within himself that he could offer to God a sacrifice, any sacrifice of the ground and it would please God. It might have cost Cain a lot of money and the sacrifice of the ground might have been beautiful, but he didn't check with God, what would be acceptable to Him.

Since Abel's life had to do with the sacrifice he presented to God, what does that say to us about the sacrifice that God will accept concerning us. There is only one sacrifice that God will accept and that is the sacrifice that Jesus Christ made on the Cross for us. God will not accept the sacrifice of anything else—time, money, property or talents or even ourselves. "Nothing in my hand I bring, simply to the Cross I cling." We must rest our lives, on the finished work of Jesus Christ at Calvary.

Enoch -

Enoch is the seventh man from Adam, that must have had a Covenant relationship with God. The Biblical narrative does not describe it, but in the simple phrase, "And Enoch walked with God…" one must believe that such a Covenant relationship existed. The name "Enoch" means dedicated.

Certainly, he was dedicated to God. Arthur Pink in his book, Gleanings in Genesis says this about Enoch. "He is one of but two men of whom it is said in Scripture that he walked with God. He is one of but two men who lived on this earth and went to heaven without passing through the portals of death. And he is the only one, except our blessed Lord, of whom it is written, "He pleased God." (page 74) This is a beautiful description of Enoch.

There are some details we can get from the Biblical narrative about Enoch. One of the first things we discover is that Enoch lived in an evil age. Listen to what Enoch says in the Book of Jude about the evil age in which he lived. "Now Enoch, the seventh from Adam, prophesied about these men saying, "Behold, the Lord cometh with ten thousands of His saints, to execute judgment on all, to convict all who are ungodly among them of all their ungodly deeds which they have committed in an ungodly way, and of all the harsh things which ungodly sinners have spoken against them." (Jude 14-15) Enoch was actually prophesying about the return of the Lord Jesus, His second coming. But these words were also true of Enoch's day. Enoch was living in a very wicked age. Mr. Pink describes that age and I totally agree with him. It was a terrible day in which to live. "...He (Enoch) seems to have stood alone in his fearless denunciations of the ungodly and his faithful testimony for God..." (page 74)

But there is another startling fact about Enoch before he was translated. Listen to what the Scriptures say about Enoch during his married life. "Enoch lived sixty-five years and begat Methuselah. After he begot Methuselah, Enoch walked with God three hundred years and begat sons and daughters. So, all the days of Enoch were three hundred and sixty-five years." (Genesis 5:21-23) So what is unusual about this? Enoch stood in contrast to the wicked generation about him. I am not talking about the people he did not know. I am talking about the people he knew. His sons, his daughters, and the people of his village or town were all a part of that wicked generation. All of them that remained alive died in the flood of Noah's day. There is no record that any followed the example of Enoch and walked with God, even among his children. No matter how bad the wicked got, Enoch persisted in walking with God.

Then we come to this Scripture in Genesis 5:24. "And Enoch walked with God; and he was not, for God took him." Matthew Henry's Commentary of Genesis to Deuteronomy, Volume 1 says this about Enoch's walk with God. "...He was entirely dead to the world, and did not only walk with God, as all good men do, but he walked with God as if he were in heaven already...Enoch it should seem, was a priest of the most High God...he was a preacher of righteousness and prophesied of Christ's second coming...The business of Enoch's life, his constant care and work; while other lived to themselves and the world, he lived to God. It was the joy and support of his life. Communion with God was to him, better than life itself..." (page49) "Can two walk together, unless they are agreed?" (Amos 3:3) Enoch agreed with God about his sinfulness and he wanted to change. Thus, God changed him. God made him a priest, thus he was able to offer to God pleasing sacrifices. They were in agreement every day as they walked together. Pride and unbelief left Enoch, as they walked together and he was conformed more into the image of God.

We do not know Enoch's wife's name. But one day she got up and made him breakfast. When she came back to find Enoch, he was not there. She sent the children out looking for him, but they could not find him. The neighbors and all of his acquaintances and everyone he knew looked for him but no one found him. God had taken him. God probably told him this was going to happen. He may have even shared this with all his family and because they lived in unbelief; they did not accept what God had shared with him. Think of this. Enoch did not have to go through the flood, for God had something better for him. God had taken him home to heaven.

The Amplified Bible translates Genesis 5:23-24 this way. "So, all the days of Enoch were 365 years. And Enoch walked (in habitual fellowship) with God, and he was not, for God took him." God took him alive to heaven. Some Bible scholars have trouble with this. They are trying to figure it out with their finite minds. When we look at this and then look at Hebrews 11:5 we will come to the same conclusion—God took him to heaven to be in everlasting communion with him. "Because of faith Enoch was caught up and transferred to heaven, so that he did not have a glimpse of death; and he was not found, because God had translated him. For even before he was taken to heaven he received testimony (still on record) that he had pleased and been satisfactory to God." (The Amplified Bible, Hebrews 11:5)

From www.bibleanswerstand.org? Q.A. Enoch we get this information about the Greek word "translated." The Greek word translated above in Hebrews 11:5a, but as "caught up and translated to "and concurrently "had translated" in The Amplified Bible is metal/qhmii this Greek word is transliterated as "metalithemi." Metalithemi is from meta (NT: 3326) denoting, "change of place or condition" and tithemii (5087), "to place." Thus, metalitheim means, "To transpose, put in another place and hence to transport, transfer, translate."

Why was Enoch translated or moved to heaven? In Hebrews 11:5b it tells us the reason for his translation to heaven. "...for before his (Enoch's) translation he had this testimony, that he pleased God." He so walked with God, that God saw fit to take him to heaven. As we said before, Enoch had a Covenant relationship with God. Enoch's wife and children must have had this conversation, "He was so heavenly minded, he was of no earthily good. Therefore, God took him to heaven." A preacher I once listened to said this: "He was so close to heaven, God just decided there was no reason to let him go back to earth." However, you look at it, Enoch had such a close Covenant relationship with God, that God Almighty took him. Enoch in this relationship with God, you might as well consider them to be friends. Friends tell everything about their lives to each other.

God wants to bring us into such a relationship with Him, that we are a Friend of God. I believe Enoch knew he was going to be taken home to heaven with God. This is that special relationship of friendship. When that happens, we begin to know what God is going to do next. This is made clear in the Scriptures. We are going to share something now, that we will develop later when we get to the Covenant of God with Abraham. James, the brother of Jesus, lets us know that Abraham was considered the Friend of God. "And the Scripture was fulfilled which says, "Abraham believed

God, and it was accounted (credited) to him for righteousness." And he was called the friend of God." (James 2:23) When God calls you his friend you have moved into Covenant relationship with Him. Jesus shared this relationship with His disciples and moved them into that Covenant relationship right before the Cross. "No longer do I call you servants, for a servant does not know what his master is doing; but I have called you friends, for all things that I have heard from my Father, I have made known to you." (John 15:15) This is the relationship that Enoch had with God. As I said before, I believe Enoch knew God was going to take him.

From Enoch's close walk with God and because he had become a friend of God, Enoch knew a flood was coming. I believe God shared with him the future of planet Earth. I am not alone in that belief. The noted Bible scholar, the late Arthur W. Pink, also shared this insight from one of the children of Enoch—Methuselah—in his book, Gleanings in Genesis. Names in the Old Testament and the New Testament mean something. Most often those names were prophetical of that period or the future. Thus, it is so with the name Methuselah. Mr. Pink gives us profound insight into the future with the Biblical definition of that name. Enoch gave Methuselah that name because he knew what the future of planet Earth held. God had revealed it to him. "The name of his son strongly implies that Enoch had a revelation from God. Methuselah signifies, "When he is dead it shall be sent," i.e. the Deluge (Newberry) In all probability then, a Divine revelation is memorialized in this name. It was as though God had said to Enoch, "Do you see this baby? The world will last as long as he lives and no longer. When the child dies, I shall deal with the world in judgment. The windows of heaven will be opened. The foundations of the great deep will be broken up, and all humanity will perish." ...Be this as it may—and it is difficult to escape such a conclusion—it is certainly implied that from the time of Methuselah was born, the world lost all of its attractiveness for Enoch and from that time on, if never before, he walked with God." (page 78)

Therefore, you see God had established a Covenant relationship with Enoch. As Enoch walked with God in Covenant relationship, God began to share with him what was going to happen on Earth. A flood was going to take place. God also shared with him why the flood was going to happen—the wickedness of man. This is recorded in Genesis 7:4. "So the Lord said, I will destroy man whom I created from the face of the earth, both man and beast, creeping things and birds of the air, for I am sorry that I have made them."

Probably, the last thing that God showed Enoch was His love and mercy for mankind. Notice that Methuselah lived nine hundred and sixty-nine years. "So, all the days of Methuselah were nine hundred and sixty-nine years and he died." (Genesis 5:27) No doubt, God was hoping that man would repent of his wickedness and turn to God. Methuselah is the longest reported living person in the Bible. According to the Bible, no one lived as long as he did. God gave man time to repent and live for Him. But only one man was counted just and righteous and that was Noah. For that reason, Noah found grace in the eyes of the Lord. "But Noah found grace in the eyes of the Lord." (Genesis 6:8) I believe God shared all this with Enoch before he took him. With this we conclude the Covenant relationship that God had with Enoch on earth.

Chapter 4
God's Covenant With Noah

To properly comprehend the Noahic Covenant, one must understand the period of time in which Noah was living when God approached him. The setting of this time is very important in understanding the Covenant. Noah was in total contrast to the people of his day. Most Biblical scholars believe there was a spiritual decline as a result of man's actions taken in Genesis 6:1-2. "Now it came to pass, when men began to multiply on the face of the earth, and daughters were born to them, that the sons of God saw the daughters of men, that they were beautiful, and they took wives for themselves of all whom they chose…"

The next three verses of Genesis 6 show that God did not approve of these marriages and the offspring they produced. Why was this? Most Biblical scholars believe that these sons of God referred to in these verses were fallen angels that the devil took with him when he fell. They also believe that the beautiful women came from the line of Cain. A reference is made about this in The Layman's Parallel Bible on page 15. It states what God felt about these bad marriages and what the results would be. "And the Lord said, "My Spirit shall not always strive with man forever, for he is indeed flesh, yet his days shall be one hundred and twenty years." (Genesis 6:3) God saw the results of these flesh marriages would be children from them" "Those were giants on the earth in those days, and also afterward, when the sons of God came to the daughters of men and they bore children to them. Those were the mighty men who were of old, men of renown." (Genesis 6:4) One would think the children would be great. "Renown" means honored, acclaimed and famous. (American Heritage Dictionary, page 1102) However, God did not look upon these individuals as great men, but self-made men. One can see the ungodly thought patterns these men were developing. God alone can look at people's hearts and the thoughts they generate.

"Then the Lord saw that the wickedness of man was great in the earth, and that every intent of the thoughts of his heart was evil continually."

(Genesis 6:5) God saw man's heart and it was constantly evil. It is no wonder He was grieved and sorrowful that He had made man. After seeing all of this, God makes this statement in Genesis 6:7. "So the Lord said, "I will destroy man whom I have created from the face of the earth, both man and beast, creeping things and the birds of the air, for I am sorry I made them." From Genesis 6:1 to verse 7, God sees no reason to continue putting up with His creation. He wants to destroy them all. One wonders what might have happened if God had not seen Noah. From what God says in verse 7 nothing would have remained on the earth. Everything about man had become evil and God would have destroyed the animal kingdom as well.

But then in Genesis 6:8 God observes Noah and He changes His mind about destroying everything. "But Noah found grace in the eyes of the Lord." The word for "grace" is the Hebrew word "cher" meaning kindness, favor, grace, pleasant, precious. God looked upon all mankind and all were wicked sinners except Noah. On one hand God was sorry that he had made man. On the other hand, God saw Noah and He was pleased and Noah found grace in God's sight. Grace that God bestows is the first step toward a Covenant relationship with Him. Most Christians really find grace in God's sight, but that is as far as they go with their relationship with God. Some even use grace as a license to sin. God loves them and saves them from their sins. But they don't want to walk further with God, therefore, they are in and out of sin. There is a deeper walk with God, that God would like for them to experience. Enoch and Noah, I believe experienced that deeper walk with God, therefore, they went a little further.

Let us look at the Scriptures, to see if this is true. "And Enoch walked with God; and he was not, for God took him." (Genesis 5:24) "This is the genealogy of Noah. Noah was a just man, perfect (blameless) in his generations. Noah walked with God." (Genesis 6:9) The Living Bible says of Noah, "He was the only truly, righteous man living on the earth at that time. He tried always to conduct his affairs according to God's will…" (Genesis 6:9) The Bible says this about Enoch and Noah that they both walked with God. What does that mean, "to walk with God?" The word "walk" in the Hebrew is "halak" means to walk continually with God. In my opinion it is a close Covenant relationship with God. Noah, Enoch and God were conversing every day. As a result of this walk with God, Noah was a just (righteous) man who was blameless. Noah and Enoch were basically taking that next step which would lead to God to make a Covenant with them. Words can't really tell which is first. Walking with God which leads to a Covenant relationship or a Covenant relationship which leads to walking closer and closer with God. But we will see that daily fellowship with God ultimately leads to the point when God chooses to cut Covenant with us.

Therefore, both Enoch and Noah had such a relationship with God, that they both entered into a friendship with God. As previously commented on, Jesus in the New Testament revealed what that friendship relationship with God looked like. "No longer do I call you servants, for a servant does not know what his master is doing; but I have called you friends, for all things that I have heard from My Father I have made known to you." (John 15:15) As we shall see God shared with Noah what was about to happen to earth, to the animals, and all of mankind. Not everyone has that Covenant relationship with God, so they do not know what is going to happen prophetically in the future.

We don't know how long it was when God revealed the future to Noah, but we know that He did. "And God said to Noah, "The end of all flesh has come before Me, for the earth is filled with violence through them; and behold I will destroy them with the earth. Make yourself an ark of gopherwood; make rooms in the ark, and cover it inside and outside with pitch." (Genesis 6:13-14) Not only is God unveiling the prophetic future to Noah, but He is also telling him how to save himself and his family. God tells Noah exactly the dimensions of the Ark; that it is at least three stories high to house all the animals, his sons, their wives and Noah and his wife. He further describes the door in the side of the Ark and the window close to the top, so that Noah and his extended family can see everything happening outside. This is all detailed in Genesis 6:14-16.

Then God begins again to tell Noah about the rain and flood He will bring upon the whole earth. "And behold, I Myself am bringing the flood of waters on the whole earth, to destroy from under Heaven all flesh in which is the breath of life and everything on the earth shall die." (Genesis 6:17) God is renewing the promise of judgment on the earth. But God goes a step further. He promises Noah that He will establish a Covenant with Noah after the flood. "But I will establish My covenant with you and you shall go into the ark—you, your sons, your wife, and your son's wives with you." (Genesis 6:18) From the wording of the Scripture this is like a Covenant that God is going to establish in the future with Noah and his sons. So, Noah must come through the building of the Ark and then the flood waters. This is a test of faith and then God will establish His Covenant with Noah. The Apostle Peter talks about the trial or test of your faith in 1st Peter 1:7KJV. "That the trial of your faith, being much more precious than of gold that perisheth, though it be tried with fire, might be found unto praise and honor and glory at the appearing of Jesus Christ."

Noah not only had to build the Ark God described, but he had to endure the scoffing and ridicule of the people as he built it. The people of that day had never seen rain or a flood. Noah was a preacher of righteousness and told the people they were going to be judged for their sins. He told them there would be rain and a flood that would cover the whole earth. He told them this judgment was because of their sins. The Apostle Peter describes that day in 2nd Peter 2:5. "...and (God) did not spare the ancient world, but saved Noah, one of eight people (Noah, his wife, three sons, and three daughters-in-laws), a preacher of righteousness describing the flood on the world of the ungodly." You can imagine that Noah and his family suffered a lot of abuse and scornful comments during that time.

After a revelation of God about the future, there is always a test or trial to make sure the revelation has become real to you and the ones following you. So, it was with Noah and his extended family. God then told Noah to come into the Ark—the clean animals, the unclean animals, the birds, the crawling animals, and the food he was to bring for his family and the animals. Notice after all these minute instructions Noah obeyed. "Thus, Noah did according to all that God commanded him, so he did." (Genesis 6:23) Noah was an obedient child of God and did everything God commanded him to do. As a result, when the Ark was finished, this was the command of the Lord to Noah. "Then the Lord said to Noah, "Come into the ark, you and all your household, because I have seen that you are righteous before Me in this generation." (Genesis 7:1) Noah also brought all the animals as well as his family into the Ark. "And Noah did according to all that the Lord commanded him. Noah was six hundred-year-old when the flood of waters covered the earth. So, Noah, with his sons, his wife, and his son's wives went into the ark because of the waters of the flood." (Genesis 7:5-7) After the animals were in the Ark with Noah and his family the Bible says, "...and the Lord shut him (Noah and his family and all the animals) in." (Genesis 7: 16b) No one else was allowed to enter the Ark. That was God's judgment on the earth and the inhabitants of the earth. The reason I shared all this about Noah, the Ark, his extended family, the animals is that it is all a part of God's Covenant with Noah, that Noah and his family would be spared. The only opinion that counts is God's opinion. He counted Noah and his family righteous, therefore, He spared them.

They had to go through the flood to show that they would persevere. When they came out of the flood, God extended His Covenant to Noah and his family. God waited until Noah built the Ark, Noah brought his family and the animals into the Ark, and then Noah endured the storm. This is what the Word of God says about total obedience to God. "By this we know that we love the children of God, when we love God and keep His commandments. For this is the love of God, that we keep His commandments. And His commandments are not burdensome." (1 John 5:2-3) We can't say we love God if we don't keep His commandments.

It is important that we note the day that Noah entered the Ark with his family and all the animals. "In the six hundredth year of Noah's life, in the second month, the seventeenth day of the month, on that day all the fountains of the great deep were broken up, and the windows of heaven were opened. And the rain was on the earth forty days and forty nights." (Genesis 7:11-12) Why is this important? In Scripture we don't hear God talking to Noah again for nearly a full year. Today, people would have given up on God if He didn't talk to them for a full year. But this isn't true of Noah. Finally, the Scriptures say that God remembered Noah. "...God remembered Noah, and every living thing, and all the animals that were with him in the ark…" (Genesis 8:1) This lets us know that God had not forgotten Noah, but it doesn't say that God said anything to Noah. However, Noah sees that God is beginning to move in his behalf. "The fountains of the deep and the windows of heaven were stopped, and the rain from heaven was restrained." (Genesis 8:2) Even though we have no evidence that God was talking to Noah, Noah opens the window in the Ark. Also, the Ark had come to rest on the mountains of Ararat. (Genesis 8:4) Another evidence that possibly God and Noah were in tune with one another even though we have no evidence of them talking is that Noah let two birds (a raven and a dove) out of the Ark to check on whether the waters were going down. When one is in Covenant relationship with God it is not always necessary to talk. During the last five years of my Dad's life, I lived with him. My mother was already in Heaven. Sometimes the television wouldn't be on, but we were just there in communion with each other. It's not necessary to talk all the time with the Lord. One can be in communion with Him without talking. In ministering to people at the end of a service, the Holy Spirit is in direct communion with you and yet He is not always talking. This is what I believe took place between God and Noah the year that Noah and his family were on the Ark. There was a deep communion and fellowship with the Lord and Noah. Noah just trusted his life and his family's life in the hands of God and God just silently directed Noah's steps.

How long approximately was the period of the flood? I tend to lean toward ideas about the length of the flood and how long Noah and his family stayed in the Ark from The Matthew Henry Commentary, Volume 1 Genesis to Deuteronomy, page 67 says this. "Noah's departure when he had his dismission. As he would not go without leave, so he would not out of fear or honor, stay in when he had to leave, but was in all points observant of the heavenly vision. Though he had been now a full year and ten days a prisoner in the ark, yet when he had found himself preserved there, not only for a new life, but for a new world, he saw no reason to complain of his long confinement…" Why is the length of time and the confinement important? As we said before, there is not a mention of God talking to Noah. As we discussed before there is the possibility of a communion and fellowship with God and Noah had that did not require talking. But there is the possibility that God wanted a silence there. "Be still and know that I am God, I will be exalted among the nations, I will be exalted in the earth." (Psalms 46:10) Perhaps God is wanting to know what Noah would do, what Noah's attitude would be, if God doesn't talk to him. The Scriptures doesn't say that God talked to him. How would we react to that? This maybe another test for Noah, before God extends His Covenant to him. Notice later it is God who extends the Covenant to Noah and not the other way around.

When Noah finally passes this last test, then God speaks to Noah and tells him and his family to come out of the Ark. Noah and his sons release all of the animals from the Ark. "Go out of the Ark, you and your wife, and your sons and your son's wives with you. Bring out with you every living thing of all flesh that is with you birds and cattle and every creeping thing that creeps on the earth, so that you may abound on the earth, and be fruitful and multiply on the earth." (Genesis 8:15-17) It is important to note that Noah waited for the commandment of the Lord. Noah and his family did not leave the Ark until God told him to leave the Ark.

Many Christians get upset and concerned when God doesn't immediately speak throughout a crisis or a tragic event. Yet God is still there and no doubt God's presence was there on the Ark. Even though there aren't any Scriptures to show that God spoke to Noah during that year and ten days, I believe God's presence was enough for Noah. Only in the fullness of time did God tell Noah to leave the Ark. God wanted Noah and his family to be safe when they left the Ark. The other side of the coin is often Christians move to quickly before God has told them to move. Noah did not leave the Ark until God told him to do so. Later when the Covenant is extended to Noah, these two lessons are very important. Listening to God and obeying God are very important lessons to learn in the Christian walk and especially when God extends His Covenant to you.

The command of God to Noah and his family as they are leaving the Ark with the animals is to be fruitful and multiply. "So, God blessed Noah and his sons and said to them, "Be fruitful and multiply and fill the earth." (Genesis 9:1) That is the command of God to us. Although the fruitfulness that God is talking about here to Noah and his family is to have more sons and daughters, but it also has to do with becoming more like God in His character traits, being obedient to Him, and putting your faith and confidence in God. God wants us to take on His likeness in our every day walk. God also asked Noah and his family to multiply. God put His blessing on Noah and his sons. Therefore, it was inevitable for them to multiply and to fill the earth. When we do what God asks us to do our children are going to become sons and daughters of God. The laws of sowing and reaping good automatically take place in our lives.

Before Noah entered into Covenant relationship with God, he had learned some valuable lessons that New Testament Christians should learn and know. Probably, the most important lesson was to seek God and live for Him. "But without faith it is impossible to please Him, for he who comes to God must believe that He is, and that He is a rewarder of those who diligently seek Him." (Hebrews 11:6) I believe God looked with grace at Noah, because Noah was seeking him. This is shown in the fact that Noah was 500 years old when he started building the Ark. No doubt his sons helped build the Ark, according to Bible scholars, they were approximately twenty to forty years old. Noah was 600 years old when the Ark was completed. It took 100 years to build the Ark. (Genesis 5:32; 7:6) During, this 100 years Noah was a preacher of righteousness to the wicked sinners of the day. The only ones who accepted this message of righteousness was his family and thus they were the only ones allowed on the Ark. The rest of that generation died in their wickedness.

The second lesson Noah learned was to obey God when He spoke to him. God warned Noah of things that were about to happen to the world in which he lived. "By faith Noah, being divinely warned of things not yet seen, moved with godly fear, prepared an ark for the saving of his household, by which he condemned the world and became heir of the righteousness which is according to faith." (Hebrews 11:7) This is a simple faith lesson that Noah learned. When God speaks and tells you to do something, you better do it, because God knows more than you. God told Noah that the world was going to be under water and all flesh would die. He told Noah to build an Ark to save his family and himself. Noah immediately got busy and built the Ark. As a result, he and his family were saved. That is a lesson in simple faith.

The last lesson Noah learned was he didn't become fearful, when he didn't hear from God. After Noah, his family and the animals entered the Ark at the command of God, they didn't hear from God for over a year. The next recorded time when God spoke was when He told Noah and his family to leave the Ark with the animals. I believe Noah and his family probably prayed every day, but according to Scripture, God didn't speak until over a year later. I believe they still believed in God during that period of time. Christians today have a hard time, if God doesn't answer when they call on His name. Christians in America are looking for instant communication with God. One needs to be prepared when God is silent and He is checking our motivation.

We do know that God didn't forget Noah, even though He may not have spoken to him. Genesis 8:1,4 says, "Then God remembered Noah, and every living thing, and all the animals that were with him in the ark. And God made a wind to pass over the earth, and the waters subsided.... Then the ark rested in the seventh month, the seventeenth day of the month, on the mountains of Ararat." From these Scriptures we see that God was still orchestrating the events of Noah's life, even though He might not have been talking to him. It is possible that God did talk to Noah on the Ark during the flood, but there is no record of it. There are periods of silence when God does not speak to His people. Another example of this is the four hundred years between the book of Malachi and the book of Matthew in the New Testament. It is during these times of silence that we have to trust God and what He has revealed to us in His Word just like Noah did. God saw through these lessons He taught Noah, that Noah could be trusted.

God's Covenant with Noah
Part II

After going through the flood and Noah showing that he was an obedient servant of God, it is no wonder that God showed him his grace and extended His Covenant to him. Even in the silence of God, Noah had remained faithful to God. No doubt Noah worshipped God on the Ark. In the report from the book of Genesis we have no evidence of his being disobedient. But as yet the Covenant of God had not been extended to Noah. It had only been promised. That is why we believe there is a difference in following God for a period of time and then God extending His Covenant to an individual.

In Genesis 6:18 God promises Noah a Covenant relationship. "But I will (in the future) establish my covenant with you and you shall go into the ark—you, your sons, your wife, and your son's wives with you…" I will speaks of a future event that has not yet happened. This event takes place when Noah and his family come out of the Ark and have a sacrificial meeting with God. Notice that in all of the previous Covenants we have talked about there is always a sacrifice of animals and that God is pleased with the sacrifice. God is a Covenant keeping God and the Covenants He extends always involve sacrifice of animals in the Old Testament (Covenant). However, in the New Testament or the New Covenant it is the sacrifice of God's Own Son on Calvary. Blood must be shed to cover sin in the Old Testament (Covenant) and the New Testament (Covenant) to remove sin. We will discuss this more in later Covenants.

"Then Noah built an altar to the Lord, and took of every clean animal and of every clean bird and offered burnt offerings on the altar. And the Lord smelled a soothing aroma. Then the Lord said in His heart, "I will never again curse the ground for man's sake, although the imagination of man's heart is evil from his youth; nor will I again destroy every living thing as I have done. While the earth remains, seedtime and harvest, and cold and heat, and winter and summer and day and night shall not cease." (Genesis 8:20-22)

God is pleased with the sacrificial offerings of Noah and notice these are all clean animal offerings. That is why God had Noah put five clean animals and clean birds. God constantly reveals the kind of sacrifices He is pleased with down to the last detail. Then God is talking with Himself about their being no more judgment like this again. He won't curse the ground anymore. This passage is the prelude to the Noahic Covenant. God is stating the first blessings of that Covenant. Since Noah has obeyed God by building the Ark, weathering the storm and the flood, coming out of the Ark at the command of the Lord, and shed a blood sacrifice of clean animals; God is going to bless Noah and his family. But this is only the beginning of that Covenant relationship with God.

The second principle of the Noahic Covenant is given in Genesis 9:1-4. "So, God blessed Noah and his sons and said to them, "Be fruitful and multiply and fill the earth. And the fear of you and the dread of you shall be on every beast of the earth, on every bird of the air, on all that move on the earth, and on all of the fish of the sea. They are given into your hand. Every moving thing that lives shall be food to you. I have given you all things, even as the green herb. But you shall not eat flesh with its life, that is, its blood."

This second principle of the Noahic Covenant has to do with all the animals and fish of the earth. Notice all are available for Noah and his family to eat. While It would seem, there is a contradiction with God's Covenant to Moses and the nation of Israel and the Covenant with Noah and his family, Dr. Spiros Zodhiates is his notes of The Hebrew-Greek Key Study Bible on page 14 talks about this seeming inconsistency. "There is no contradiction between this passage (Genesis 9:3) and Deuteronomy 14:7. ("Nevertheless of those that chew the cud or have cloven hooves, you shall not eat, such as these: the camel, the hare, and the rock hyrax; for they chew the cud but do not have cloven hooves; they are unclean for you. Also, the swine (pigs) is unclean for you; because it has cloven hooves, yet does not chew the cud; you shall not eat their flesh or touch their dead carcasses.") The former refers to man who did not live under the law of Moses. The latter command was addressed to Jews. Perhaps strict food laws were given the Jewish people to make them distinct from the other nations whose food was often closely associated with idolatry. (1 Corinthians 10:28) Therefore, Israel would be less susceptible to falling into temptation." As we look at the Covenants in the Old Testament (Covenant) and the New Testament (Covenant), we are going to find differences between how God handles and treats different individuals and nations at different times. Even today what God allows one person to do, He may not allow another person to do. As a person enters into Covenant with God it may be different with another person. Moral issues do remain the same. God does not allow people to lie, cheat, steal, murder or commit adultery.

I remember growing up in the Baptist Church we were taught this principle this way. "Others may, but you may not." They said some people have liberty in doing things, that God will not allow others to do. Some theologians call this dispensational truth. Every dispensation or time, God has set up certain rules for one generation that He does not set up for another. However, as you review it, you see that Noah and his family were allowed to eat clean and unclean animals, fish, and sea creatures.

This was a time when man was starting all over again with his relationship with God. One must remember that when God looked at Noah and his family before the flood, God was looking at Noah with the eyes of grace. "But Noah found grace in the eyes of the Lord." (Genesis 6:8) There were qualities about Noah that God liked. "...and Noah was a just (righteous) man, perfect (blameless) in his generation. Noah walked with God." (Genesis 6:9) Therefore, Noah was constantly seeking God to know His will and ways. Noah had passed the tests of building the Ark, bringing the animals with him, and remaining faithful to God during the storm. It is no wonder that God extended His Covenant to Noah and his sons. The only condition of this new Covenant was that Noah and his descendants were not to drink or eat of the animal's blood. God always considers the blood to be sacred, going back to the blood offered by Abel and then when his brother, Cain, slew him. God said his blood cried out from the ground. In Leviticus it talks about the life being in the blood. "for it (the blood) is the life of all flesh. Its blood sustains its life. Therefore, I said to the children of Israel. You shall not eat the blood of any flesh, for the life of all flesh is its blood. Whoever eats it shall be cut off." (Leviticus 17:14) The blood was to be poured out on the ground as God said. This was the acceptable condition by God.

Dr. Zoidhiates made one other explanation about the differences between the Noahic Covenant and the Mosaic Covenant. This explanation shows how God dealt with man at different times. This is on page 14 of The Hebrew-Greek Study Bible. "Throughout history God has dealt with man through covenants or agreements. Later the Jews regarded this (Noahic) covenant between God and Noah as the basis of relationship between God and all mankind, but the covenants with Abraham and Moses at Mount Sinai were seen as forming the basis of God's special relationship with Israel. Some believe that the stipulations laid on the Gentiles in Acts 15:20-29 find some of their source in the covenant between God and Noah. One feature of the covenant stands out. In spite of the fact that the distinction between clean and unclean animals existed (Genesis 7:2,8) God allowed the eating of any plant or animal. The only restriction was the eating of animal blood, for that is where the life of the animal resided. Later, Israel was forbidden to eat not only blood, but also the flesh of certain animals…"

God removed this distinction between clean and unclean animals in the vision that Peter had from the Lord in Acts 10:12-16a. "In it (the vision to Peter) were all kinds of four-footed animals of the earth, wild beasts, creeping things, and birds of the air. And a voice (the Lord's voice) came to him, "Rise Peter, kill and eat." But Peter said, "Not so Lord! For I have never eaten anything common and unclean." And a voice (the Lord's voice) spoke to him again the second time. "What God has cleansed you must not call common." This was done three times…" Peter identified the voice from heaven as the Lord's voice. God was trying to move Peter into God's New Covenant relationship with Him. It was time to move on past the Mosaic Covenant to a New Covenant relationship. Today, people have a hard time moving past the legalistic Covenant that they have been trapped in by the rules and regulations of their church or denomination. Not that they shouldn't obey the rules of life (The Ten Commandments). But there is more to a relationship with God than even those rules, which is what Jesus tried to teach in Matthew chapters 5 to 7. In those chapters, Jesus was dealing with the heart of man and not just the laws or rules.

The third principle of the Noahic Covenant was the foundation of human government. This principle states that man was not to take another person's life. God considered the blood of every person precious. Listen to what God spoke to Noah. "Surely for your livelihood I will demand a reckoning; from the hand of every beast I will require it, and from the hand of man. From the hand of man's brother, I will require the life of man. Whoever shed's man's blood, by man his blood shall be shed; for in the image of God, He made man." (Genesis 9:5-6) This is the instituting of capital punishment by God, Himself. Arthur W. Pink in his book, Gleanings in Genesis brings out some facts about this on page 115. "...Before the flood, there does not seem to have been any recognized form of human government designed for the suppression of crime and the punishment of evil doers. Cain murdered his own brother, but his own life was spared. Lamech also slew a man, but there is no hint that he had to defend himself before any tribunal that had been ordained by God. But now after the flood, capital punishment as the penalty of murder, is ordained by God, Himself, ordained centuries before the giving of the Mosaic law, and therefore, universally binding until the end of time. It is important to observe that the reason for this law is not based upon the well-being of man, but is grounded upon the basic fact that man is made "in the image of God""

Even though today, there is much debate about capital punishment whether it is cruel or not, God's Word stated here in Genesis states that God is for it. Actually, this is the formation of human government and God ordained it after the flood. It is interesting to note that this is apart of the Noahic Covenant. There is also New Testament precedent in Romans 13:1,2,4. "Let every soul be subject to the governing authorities. For there is no authority except from God, and the authorities that exist are appointed by God. Therefore, whoever resists the authority resists the ordinance of God, and those who resist will bring judgment on themselves...For he is God's minister to you for good. If you do evil be afraid; for he does not bear the sword in vain; for he is God's minister, an avenger to execute wrath on him who practices evil."

The fourth principle is what a lot of Bible teachers and preachers call "the law of sowing and reaping." This is a principle that God discussed with Himself—the members of the God-Head. Listen to what God said in Genesis 8:22. "While the earth remains, seedtime and harvest, and cold and heat, and winter and summer, and day and night shall not cease." This principle is seen when most people were farmers. They planted, they cultivated their crops—taking out the weeds and stones that were a detriment to the crops—and then in the spring of the year they brought forth a harvest. Ministers used this to teach about continually doing good and sowing money into the ministry. God does multiply your seed, if you sow it. But one thing was left out of the teaching which should have brought a significant understanding and that was as children of God we are in relationship with our Father. God rewards us as His children regardless of how much we sow. We need to just ask Him for what we need and He will give it to us, because He is a loving Father. This law of sowing and reaping tends to swing us back to a works mentality rather than a faith and trust mentality. This particular principle is for people in the world and not for people in a Covenant relationship with God. God had revealed Himself to Noah and Noah was walking in Covenant relationship with Him. When Noah prophesies over his sons, we will see that not all were walking in that revelation of God and not all are walking in Covenant relationship with God.

The last principle of the Noahic Covenant is the principle of fruitfulness and multiplying. Listen to what God tells Noah and his sons. "And as for you, be fruitful and multiply; bring forth abundantly in the earth and multiply in it." (Genesis 9:7) This is somewhat like the law of sowing and reaping, but there is a little difference. This is a command from your Father to do this. God is actually giving Noah and his sons things to do on the earth. Noah's role in this since is like the first man, Adam. God wants him and his sons to have dominion over everything on the earth just like Adam did in the Garden of Eden. Therefore, it must be noted that God gives Noah and his sons the principle of dominion over the animals and fish and then He follows up with the principle of being fruitful and multiplying. These two principles God had given to Adam and Eve, but they had failed in the Garden of Eden. This time Noah had succeeded in passing the test of obedience. Every time faith is involved there is also obedience. God tells His children what to do and by faith they obey Him. Noah built the Ark out of obedience and then he occupied the Ark during the flood out of obedience to God. Now God wanted Noah and his sons and their wives to be fruitful and multiply with many sons and daughters. As Mr. Pink says in Gleanings in Genesis the earth had been depopulated. "…There was a new beginning. Noah stood, like Adam stood, as the head of the human race. The need for this word was obvious. The earth had been depopulated. The human family had been reduced to eight souls…who formerly were disobedient, when once the longsuffering of God waited in the days of Noah, while the Ark was being prepared, in which a few that is, eight souls, were saved through water." (1 Peter 3:20) If then the purpose of man's creation was to be realized, if the earth was to be replenished and subdued, then man must be "fruitful and multiply." (page 116)

God's ultimate purpose in the creation of man is for our Father to have someone in which He could have fellowship and communion. His first creation—Adam—failed because of the temptation of satan. Now He still needs men and women to be born, so if they are willing they can be fashioned into sons of the living God. This is talked about in Hebrews 2:10-11. "For it was fitting for Him (Jesus), for Whom are all things and by Whom are all things, in bringing many sons to glory, to make the author of their salvation perfect through sufferings. For both He (Jesus) who sanctifies are all of one, for which reason He is not ashamed to call them brethren." God's eternal purpose is to have a family, with the elder brother being Jesus and we as God's sons are growing in grace and knowledge of Him. To cause that to happen at this point, Noah and his sons needed to be fruitful and multiply, another words having more children.

God's Covenant Extended to Noah
Part III

Then after God rehearses with Noah all the main points of His Covenant, during the time of worship, Noah offers a sacrifice to God and God extends His Covenant to Noah and his sons. It is important to note that God does not extend the Covenant to Noah until after a sacrifice of blood. God must have explained to Noah the importance of a clean animal sacrifice of blood and then for it to be completely burned with fire. This is stated in Genesis 9:8-17.

"Then God spoke to Noah and to his sons with him saying: And as for Me, behold I establish my covenant with you and with your descendants after you, and with every living creature that is with you: the birds, the cattle, and every beast of the earth with you, of all that go out of the ark, every beast of the earth. Thus, I establish my covenant with you: Never again shall all flesh be cut off by waters of the flood; never again shall there be a flood to destroy the earth. And God said. This is the sign of the covenant which I make between Me and you for perpetual generations: I will set my rainbow in the cloud, and it shall be for the sign of the covenant between Me and the earth. It shall be when I bring a cloud over the earth, that the rainbow shall be seen in the cloud: and I will remember my covenant which is between Me and you and every living creature of all flesh; the waters shall never again become a flood to destroy all flesh. The rainbow shall be in the cloud and I will look on it to remember the everlasting covenant between God and every living creature of all flesh that is on the earth. And God said to Noah, this is the sign of the covenant which I have established between Me and all flesh that is on the earth."

Notice this isn't a Covenant that Noah makes with God, but rather a Covenant that God makes with Noah and his descendants. This is what you would call a universal Covenant. God is saying in this Covenant, I am not going to destroy the earth with water again.

But there are some parts of the new Noahic Covenant that brings Noah and mankind as a whole into new revelation. Ralph Smith in The Covenantal Structure of the Bible on page 26 shares this. "Like later covenants, the Noahic covenant added new revelation that further amplified the new covenant. As in the pre-flood era each "new covenant" in the old covenant (testament) era ended with God's judgment on man's sin, because "in Adam" man cannot escape his sin. At the same time, however, the judgment of God in history were never merely negative. Each judgment furthered God's kingdom purpose by leading history unto Christ, the second (last) Adam who saved man." To understand what Mr. Smith is saying, one needs to study Romans 5:17-18. "(For if by one man's offense (Adam's sin) death reigned through the one, much more those who received the abundance of grace and of the gift of righteousness will reign in life through the One, Jesus Christ.) Therefore, as through one man's offense (Adam's sin in the Garden of Eden) judgment came to all men, resulting in condemnation, even so through one Man's righteous act (the Cross of Jesus Christ) the free gift (eternal life) came to all men, resulting in justification of life." Also, one needs to read and study 1st Corinthians 15:22. "For as in Adam all die, even so in Christ all shall be made alive." These two Scriptures point out the fact that if one remains in Adam, he or she will die in God's eternal judgment. However, if one receives and accepts the finished work of the Cross, God places that person in Christ through that work and they will live forever in Christ. "And so, it is written, the first man, Adam, became a living being. The last Adam (Jesus Christ) became a life-giving spirit." We will understand this better when we enter into the New Covenant in the New Testament.

Mr. Smith continues to discuss the radical changes to the earth after the flood. Noah and his family would have immediately recognized the changes to the earth and that they were in a new world. "The world changed radically after the flood. This probably included the geographical changes that caused the drift of the continents. If theories of a "water canopy"—the idea that the pre-flood world was "covered" by a cloud layer that produced a greenhouse effect, keeping the whole planet warm—are correct, radical changes in climate and in the surface of the earth would have been evident." (page 26) Therefore, the continents of Europe, Asia and Africa had separated completely from the continents of North and South America. There were also now weather conditions and weather systems over all the earth. Some areas were arid and desert while others had forests, grass and rock formations. Finally, there were four seasons over most of the earth: spring, summer, fall and winter. A lot of this is conjecture by Mr. Smith. We won't know for sure until we reach Heaven and God let's us know all things.

Another great change described by Mr. Smith is the loss of the Garden of Eden. "The greatest change, however, was the loss of the Garden of Eden. The sanctuary of God was no longer with men. No more was there a divinely ordained world-center to which men came to meet God, and no holy land close to the sanctuary. In these terms, the post-flood world is a world without God. This means that the re-creation of the world is incomplete, for it lacked two of the three parts of the Edenic world. In the original creation, God created the world (Genesis 1:1), then the land of Eden, and last of all the Garden (Genesis 2:8). After the flood there is a new world, but there is no new holy land. The new holy land is not re-created until Israel conquers Canaan. The sanctuary is not really created until Solomon's temple, the new Eden. This means that the re-creation of the world began after the flood continues for centuries until in the days of Solomon there is a Garden-Temple at the covenantal center of the world, surrounded by the holy land."

It is interesting to note that Mr. Smith talks a lot about the changes in the world, but also the changes to God's relationship with man. Noah chose to follow God and His directions all of his life. When we are reading about events after the flood there is no mention of Eden as a place in the world. Therefore, Mr. Smith is probably right that it was removed by God from the earth. This is a new world without a holy land. If man is to seek God, it will be his choice. Thus, we see God again wants man to choose worship and follow Him out of man's free will. With Noah as the head of the family, his family did choose to follow God for a while. God blesses Noah and his family with a new start. Only time will tell if the generations after Noah will follow God. God did give Noah the responsibility while he lived on earth of being prophet, priest and king. Mr. Smith outlines these responsibilities when he describes the Noahic Covenant on page 27 of his book, The Covenantal Structure of the Bible.

"Man (Noah) as prophet, priest and king is given new responsibilities. Noah was clearly the ultimate human authority in the new world and was the "King" of the race. He functions as priest in offering sacrifices (Genesis 8:20) and as a prophet in pronouncing blessings and curses on his sons (Genesis 9:25ff). But the primary difference in man's authority is judicial. Before the flood, man's judicial authority was confined to cases other than capital punishment. (Genesis 4:14-15) With the Noahic Covenant came authority and responsibility to execute murderers (Genesis 9:6). This was not permission to execute; God commanded it. Just as in the flood God, Himself, executed the whole race for its violence (Genesis 6:11-13). He commanded Noah to execute the wickedly, violent man. Ultimately this is merciful because the execution of individual murderers stops violence before it spreads to the point that it mandates the judgment of a whole society. This also represents historical growth—the Seed of the woman, as God's image, was given a share in God's judicial authority in order to protect the world from violence so that a man's historical mission could be accomplished."

In essence man has more authority to govern himself. With the command by God of capital punishment it lays the foundation for civil government. The judicial responsibility was laid on Noah and his succeeding generations to punish evil doers. But it was necessary for man to follow God to make sure that judicial responsibility was not perverted. As stated by Mr. Smith the prophetic future of man—the Seed (Jesus) of the woman—had to be protected so Jesus could come and save man from his sins and his sin nature.

Already Noah had fulfilled the responsibilities of prophet, priest and king. He was coming into that as he built the Ark and ordered his family and the animals into the Ark. His family (his wife, three sons and their three wives) would see him fulfill the responsibilities of prophet and priest while on the Ark and when the Ark landed. He definitely led out in all of these responsibilities.

The only limitation of the Noahic Covenant is the eating of blood in Genesis 9:4. "But you shall not eat flesh with it's life, that is, it's blood." You can eat the flesh of an animal as long as you drain the blood out of it before you cook it and eat it. Blood to God was considered to be the life of the animals and also with humans. Listen to what He told Israel in Leviticus 17:11-12. "For the life of the flesh is in the blood, and I have given it to you upon the altar to make atonement for your souls, for it is the blood that makes atonement for the soul. Therefore, I said to the children of Israel, 'No one among you shall eat blood, nor shall any stranger among you eat blood."

Noah offered "whole burnt offerings." Therefore, the animal was burned up completely. It could not be used for anything else after it was burned up. God had revealed to Noah the difference between clean and unclean animals. God would only accept clean animals as sacrifices to Himself. This is all important because man must learn to follow God's instructions explicitly and completely.

The final point of the Covenant is that God would never again destroy the earth with water. This was God's promise to Noah and his family. The sign that this was true was the rainbow in the sky. This was to remind God not to destroy the entire earth with water. "The rainbow shall be in the cloud, and I will look on it to remember the everlasting covenant between God and every living creature of all flesh that is on the earth. And God said to Noah, "This is the sign of the covenant which I have established between Me and all flesh that is on the earth." (Genesis 9:16-17)

The reason God would not destroy the earth with water, is because at that point He had not sent His Son, Jesus, to save mankind from their sins. The flood of water had cleansed the earth of the wickedness of man. Jesus Christ has come and His atoning sacrifice on Calvary has cleansed man of his sins and the sin nature. The next time God will judge the earth will be because men and women have rejected the sacrifice of God's Son. That judgment will be a judgment of fire that is prophesied in the Old and New Testament (Covenant). In the Old Testament (Covenant) in Psalms 105:25-26 it prophesies of the destruction of the earth. "Of old You laid the foundations of the earth, and the Heavens are the works of your hands. They will perish, but You will endure; Yes, all of them will grow old like a garment. Like a cloak you will change them, and they will be changed." In the New Testament (Covenant) in 2 Peter 3:10-13 the Earth's judgment is prophesied again. "But the day of the Lord will come as a thief in the night, in which the heavens will pass away, with a great noise, and the elements will melt with fervent heat; both the earth and the works will be burned up. Therefore, since all these things will be dissolved, what manner of persons ought you to be in holy conduct and godliness, looking for and hastening the coming day of God, because of which the heavens will be dissolved being on fire, and the elements will melt with fervent heat? Nevertheless we, according to His promise, look for new heavens and a new earth in which righteousness dwells."

Therefore, since there is another coming judgment by God of this Earth and the inhabitants of this Earth, our attention should be toward Heaven and what the Apostle Peter said in 1st Peter 3:14. "Therefore, beloved, looking forward to these things, be diligent to be found by Him in peace, without spot and blameless."

Noah's Response to God's Covenant

This brings us to the response that Noah and all of mankind made to the Noahic Covenant. There are differences of opinion about the response of man to this Covenant. Some believe that Noah, himself, had a bad response to the Covenant by planting a vineyard, harvesting the vineyard, making wine out of the vineyard, drinking the wine and getting drunk. We don't know if this is a one-time event or if Noah became a drunkard. This is what is recorded in Genesis 9:20-24. "And Noah began to be a farmer, and he planted a vineyard. Then he drank of the wine and was drunk, and became uncovered in his tent. And Ham, the father of Canaan, saw the nakedness of his father, and told his brothers outside. But Shem and Japheth took a garment, laid it on both their shoulders, and went backward and covered the nakedness of their father. Their faces were turned away, and they did not see their father's nakedness. So, Noah awoke from his wine, and knew what his younger son had done to him."

The fact that Noah decided to be a farmer and plant a vineyard is not sin in itself. The fact that he made wine and drank from it to the point of drunkenness, when one looks at other Scriptures, is sinful. The Apostle Paul call the continual practice of drunkenness a sin and that a person could not enter the Kingdom of God as a result of that sin. "Now the works of the flesh are evident, which are adultery, fornication, uncleanness, licentiousness, idolatry, sorcery, hatred, contentions, jealousies, outburst of wrath, selfish ambition, dissensions, heresies, envy, murders, drunkenness, reveries, and the like; of which I tell you beforehand, just as I told you in time past, that those who practice such things will not inherit the kingdom of God." (Galatians 5:19-21) We do not know if Noah continued to practice drunkenness after this one incident. The other word in this Scripture is the Hebrew word for "nakedness." That Hebrew word is 'errah and means disgrace, blemish, shame, and unclean. Up to this point nothing has been said bad or evil about Noah. God is constantly looking at Noah with grace in His eyes. Even in this one incident the Scripture does not record anything that God has to say about this good or bad. God does not say anything against Noah in Genesis chapter 9.

In the Old Testament (Covenant) wine was a drink of that day, because the water was not always good. This is what Zondervan Pictorial Bible Dictionary said about those times. "...In Old Testament times wine was not diluted... (page 895) It was often used as medicine or as a disinfectant." Talking to a Messianic group in the United States, First Fruits of Zion, I learned that in Old Testament times fermented wine was often used in celebration at the end of harvests, religious feasts, and weddings. Fermented wine among the Jewish people then and now means joy to the participants. However, it was not to be indulged in often, but to be drank temperately. Noah's over indulgence in fermented wine would have been looked down on in the average Jewish setting. But if he had not gotten drunk, they would not have considered it a sin. Messianic Jews and Conservative Jews today and during Bible times do not consider drinking fermented wine as a sin unless one over indulged in it.

We have no other record of Noah getting drunk. Only this one occasion is mentioned in Scripture. One indiscretion does not mean that Noah was a drunkard. Sometimes individuals take one indiscretion in Scripture as a license to sin. We should not use the Scriptures to justify our sins of indiscretion toward drinking or any other flesh trap. On the other hand, we tend to judge people who commit sin one time, not knowing that they may have repented of that sin. Probably, Noah knew from that day forward that his children, grandchildren, and great grandchildren were watching him, therefore, he did not over indulge again in wine drinking.

What transpired next between Noah and his youngest son, Ham, sheds a different light on the situation. Evidently, Ham wanted to show that Noah wasn't acting the part of being the leader. He definitely wasn't showing any respect for Noah, even if Noah appeared to be wrong in what he did. We are to honor our parents at all times, but he showed dishonor to his father, Noah. Listen to Arthur W. Pink's description of this sin in Gleanings in Genesis, page 124. "...Fearful had been the fall of Noah, but it was still a greater sin for Ham, on discovering the sad condition of his parent, to go out and report the malignant pleasure to his brethren.... For a child to go out and sneer at his parent's fall was wickedness of the worst kind, and evidenced a heart thoroughly depraved." Ham was advertising and proclaiming his father's sin rather than covering it as it talks about it in James 5:20. "Let him know that he who turns a sinner from the error of his way will save a soul from death and cover a multitude of sins." But that was not in Ham's thoughts when he proclaimed his father's sin to his brothers. This sin would be visited on Ham's children to the second and third generations.

Arthur W. Pink describes Ham's sin. "Ham's sin consisted of an utter failure to honor his father. He was lacking altogether in filial love. Had he really cared for his father at all he would have acted as his brothers did; but instead he manifested a total disrespect for and subjection unto his parent. And mark the fearful consequences: he reaped exactly as he had sown—Ham sinned as a son and was punished in his son (Canaan). The punishment meted out to Ham was that his son (Canaan) shall be brought into subjection to others, his descendants shall be compelled to honor, yea, "serve" others— "servant of servants" (verse 25) implies the lowest drudgery, slavery." (pages 124-125)

Although many Biblical scholars believe that Noah was wrong in getting drunk, there are a few who believe he was only acting as the custom of the day permitted. Ralph Smith shows in his book, The Covenantal Structure of the Bible, that he doesn't agree with Mr. Pink indicating that

Noah had not fallen into sin. On page 28 this is what he says about Noah becoming a farmer, planting a vineyard and making the fruit into wine. "Rejoicing in God, Noah planted a vineyard. He seems to be the first man to discover wine. At any rate, he drank the wine, a symbol of blessing and rest in the Bible. It was perfectly legitimate for Noah to drink wine and rest in his tent, because his work was done. It was the proper time to enjoy God's blessing. The Bible never condemned Noah for his drinking here. His son, (Ham) who attempted to steal authority and blessing symbolized in the robe of Noah, was condemned. His rebellion, however, was only a foretaste of what Noah's descendants would do later."

It is true God did not rebuke Noah for his drunken state. Most Israelites or Jews back then and Messianic Jews today believe wine is a symbol of joy and blessing. Noah did not uncover himself before his children and possibly his grandchildren. The real sin is how Ham, his youngest son reacted to all this. There is not another event written about Noah after this event, except for his prophetical utterances to his three sons. After that nothing else is written about Noah in the Book of Genesis.

The Last Role of Noah to his Family

In summary, this brings us to the last role of Noah toward his family. He is seen as King when he took charge of the building of the boat and ordering his family in the boat before the flood and out of the boat when God told him to leave the Ark. He has been seen in Scriptures as the Priest when he offered sacrifices of clean animals to God. Then God extended the Covenant to Noah and his family and this was a Covenant of Blessing, because to this point Noah and his family had obeyed the Lord. Now as Prophet, he prophesies over his three sons, blessing two of them and placing a curse on the youngest son, Ham. Evidently, Ham's disrespect of his father did have a bearing on what Noah prophesied over him. From this point on in the Book of Genesis the patriarchs would pronounce blessings and cursing over their children and God would honor the pronouncements by bringing it to past, Noah prophetically right after the show of disrespect of Ham, begins his pronouncements over his sons.

These pronouncements begin at Genesis 9:24-29. "Then he (Noah) said, "Cursed be Canaan; a servant of servants he shall be to his brethren. And he (Noah) said, "Blessed be the Lord, the God of Shem, and may Canaan be his servant. May God enlarge Japheth, and may he dwell in the tents of Shem, and may Canaan be his servant." And Noah lived after the flood three hundred and fifty years. So, all the days of Noah were nine hundred and fifty years; and he died."

After all of these events in Noah's life, God does not say anything to Noah good or bad since Noah and his family left the Ark. After his prophecies over his sons he lives three hundred and fifty years and God does not say anything good or bad about Noah. However, in the New Testament (Covenant) in the faith chapter of the Book of Hebrews this is recorded about Noah. "By faith Noah, being divinely warned of things not yet seen, moved with godly fear, prepared an ark for the saving of his household, by which he condemned the world and became heir of the righteousness which is according to faith." (Hebrew 11:7) God looked at the whole of Noah's life and saw faith and He was pleased. When God looks at the whole of our life, will He see faith or something else? Noah was not perfect, but he had a testimony that he pleased God. Nothing else good or bad is recorded about Noah, so we must conclude from the words in the Book of Hebrews that he pleased and honored God. He honored the covenant relationship with God.

A lot of Biblical scholars say Noah's drunkenness was his response to God's Covenant. Ralph Smith and his book on Divine Covenants shows something different. On page 28 of his book, he believes the tower of Babel was man's response and that response was one of rebellion. In Genesis 11:1-9 it shows man finding a place in the plain to build a tower to Heaven. Man wants to build his own religion apart from God. As we shall see, Ham's grandchild, Nimrod, had a role in starting this move away from God. Nimrod means rebellion and his kingdom started with the building of Babel. Mr. Smith has some interesting facts about the Tower of Babel. Listen to what he says about man's response to the Covenant with Noah.

"Sinful man was not content to inherit the blessings of the covenant and labor patiently for God's glory. Rather than seek from God a temple or a place of worship, man attempted to build his own new Eden, the tower of Babel (Genesis 11:4). The new race wanted a world center to preserve religion and political unity among themselves. The tower of Babel thus, was a declaration of independence from God. Man, himself would determine the way to heaven. In essence, the tower of Babel was the whole race of Noah's descendants imitating the sin of Canaan, which maybe described as plotting to steal his father's authority and set himself as a king. Canaan's true heir, Nimrod, the great hunter, led men in rebellion against the heavenly Father, seeking to "steal His robe, and set up a rival kingdom." (page 28)

From this excerpt from Mr. Smith's book, one can see the contrast of Noah's life and Covenant standing with God in contrast to his descendants' life and beliefs. They did not want to follow God the way Noah did. In fact, they wanted to be independent of God and chose rather to be in rebellion against God. They must have listened to Ham and Canaan and chose independence and rebellion, rather than live a life that pleases God. Notice they are not mentioned in the chapter of faith of Hebrews 11. This sounds a lot like the generation of today. When one reads Genesis 11:1-4, there is no mention of God or one's Covenant relationship with God at all.

"Now the whole earth had one language and one speech. And it came to pass, as they journeyed from the east, and they found a plain in the land of Shinar, and they dwelt there. Then they said to one another, "Come let us make bricks and bake them thoroughly." They had brick for stone, and they had asphalt for mortar. And they said, "Come let us build ourselves a city, and a tower whose top is in the heavens, let us make a name for ourselves, lest we be scattered abroad over the face of the whole earth." (Genesis 11:1-4) Had Noah's descendants consulted God about all this? Were they even in fellowship with God? There is no mention of the Noahic Covenant or of God at all. This was the generation that came along after Noah. Who is the ruler of this city, this country and the land of Shinar? All of this is explained in Genesis 10 and it is there we get all these questions answered.

"The sons of Ham were Cush, Mizraim, Put, and Canaan...Cush begat Nimrod; he begun to be a mighty one in the earth. He was a mighty one before the Lord; therefore, it is said, "Like Nimrod the mighty hunter before the Lord." And the beginning of his (Nimrod) kingdom was Babel, Erech, Accad, and Calneh, in the land of Shinar." (Genesis 10:6, 8-10) The name Nimrod means "the Rebel." As Mr. Pink says in Gleanings in Genesis on page 131; he talks about the form of that rebellion. "...the form which Nimrod's rebellion assumed was to head a great confederacy in open revolt against God. This confederacy is described in Genesis eleven and that it was an organized revolt against Jehovah is clear from the language of Genesis 10:9. "Nimrod, the mighty hunter before the Lord," which...means that he pushed his own designs in brazen defiance of his Maker.

It is interesting to note, that Noah had prophesied that Ham's generation would be servants to the other two sons. But in the natural, Ham's generation in the beginning seemed to be getting the upper hand. Although Noah had cursed Canaan and said he would be servant to his brethren—his uncles. It looks like the opposite is happening. Many years later the prophetic word of the Lord through Noah would come to pass.

Listen to God blessing Shem and his generations after him. Through Shem would come the Jewish race, the Messiah, Jesus Christ, the Son of the living God. Japheth for all intents and purposes is also blessed and chooses to dwell in Shem's tents. Japheth generations are the Gentile nations that turn to God and dwell in the tents and blessings of the Jewish people. That blessings are the salvation that comes through receiving Jesus Christ as Lord and Savior. This came as a result of Shem and Japheth honoring and respecting their father, Noah.

Ham's son, Canaan, and the generations that follow choose only to rebel against God and Noah's Covenant. Led by Nimrod, that generation try to build a temple in Babel and make a name for themselves. Their response to God's Covenant of blessing by rebelling will cause God to change the languages of the people and scatter them over the face of the earth.

God always has a response to rebellion and walking independently of Him. Notice what God did to their response of rebellion in Genesis 11:5-9. "But the Lord came down to see the city and the tower which the sons of men had built. And the Lord said, "Indeed the people are one and they all have one language, and this is what they began to do; now nothing that they purpose to do will be withheld from them. Come let Us go down and there confuse their language, that they may not understand one another's speech. So, the Lord scattered them abroad from there over the face of all the earth, and they ceased building the city. Therefore, its name is called Babel, because there the Lord confused the language of all the earth; and from there the Lord scattered them abroad over the face of all the earth."

I am not the only one who believes that this city, Babel, and this tower was planned by Nimrod (the Rebel) and those who followed him had a plan of rebellion against God. Ralph Smith in The Covenantal Structure of the Bible on page 28 shows the basic religious philosophy of Babel and what it's intent would be. "God visited the tower of Babel. He saw that men were unified against the Kingdom of God. The Babel system allowed wicked men like Nimrod to establish a political tyranny upon the basis of a false religion from which it would be difficult for anyone to escape. The result would only have been a repetition of the days before the flood, an age of universal corruption. To preserve a remnant and confound the rebellious purpose of men, God confused man's language. This meant more than using different words for the same object. Different groups of men had different perspectives on the world and man's work in it (Genesis 11:7,9). This led to mutual mistrust and the breakdown of the Babel establishment."

As Mr. Smith goes onto say that men scattered all over the world. Everywhere they went to some degree they imitated Nimrod and formed little Babels all over the world. They would build buildings like Babel, but they were called different things like pyramids. Everywhere they would form a false religion to false gods. But there would be a remnant that believed in God and God would make a Covenant relationship with them. This Noahic Covenant was with the whole Gentile world as well as the

Jews. The promise of God in this Covenant is that God would never again judge the world with a flood of water. The sign of the promise of God about this is the rainbow in the sky. God isn't saying He won't ever judge the world, but He won't do it with a flood of water again. His next judgment according to prophetic prophecy will be by fire.

In Summary...

To summarize what we have said thus far, let us remember some of the key elements of a Covenant relationship with God. The first two elements of what we have learned about this Covenant relationship are faith and obedience. Abel, Enoch and Noah were men of faith. They heard from God and by faith acted upon what they heard. They obeyed God in what He told them to do. One cannot move in Covenant relationship with God unless they follow God by faith and do what He says.

The next element of a Covenant relationship with God involves the right sacrifice. These men knew the sacrifice that God would accept because God had revealed it to them. Abel offered to God a sacrifice that pleased God, therefore his sacrifice was accepted and Cain's was rejected. Noah offered clean animals to God as a sacrifice. How did these men know that? I believe God revealed it to them. Today, the only sacrifice that pleases God is the sacrifice that God's Son, Jesus, made for us on Calvary. "Nothing in my hands I bring. Simply to Thy Cross I cling." If we are going to walk in Covenant relationship with God, we must continually cling to the finished work of the Cross, His Son made for us there.

Another element of the Covenant relationship with God are what Biblical scholars call positions of authority. The men who are in Covenant relationship are placed in positions of authority. Generally, one of the first men who exercised these positions of authority was Noah. These positions of authority were Prophet, Priest, and King. One only has to look at Noah's life and one can see him moving in these positions of authority. Only if you were in Covenant relationship with God were you allowed to operate in those places of authority. Noah operated as King when his family obeyed him in helping build the Ark, gather then animals, and leave the

Ark when Noah told them to do that. Certainly, Ham was not an obedient son, but the other two sons obeyed him and because they honored their father, he honored them. Noah was the Priest of his home when he sacrificed to God acceptable sacrifices. Noah was the Prophet of his home when he prophesied over his sons both blessings and cursing and God honored his prophecies and allowed them to come to pass. One's Covenant relationship with God determines if you are positionally able to operate before God as Prophet, Priest and King.

There is another element of Covenant relationship with God which is being God's own friend. This is not necessarily you calling God your friend. It is God calling you His friend. Noah had this relationship with God. God chose Noah to be His friend. We know this because Noah knew what was going to happen to the world. God had told him about the flood destroying the world. In Genesis 6:17 it says, "And behold, I Myself am bringing flood of waters on the earth, to destroy from under heaven all flesh in which is the breath of life, and everything that is on the earth shall die." God went on to tell Noah to build an Ark for him and his family. This is a Covenant mark of friendship God had with Noah. We will see this Covenant mark again when we study Abraham. Listen to what Jesus told His disciples before He was crucified. "No longer do I call you servants, for a servant does not know what his master is doing; but I have called you friends, for all things that I have heard from My Father I have made known to you." (John 15:15) Jesus explained to His disciples several times that He was going to suffer and die and be raised the third day. You know you are walking in Covenant relationship with God, when He begins revealing the future to you and His secrets, and His mysteries to you. Oh God, cause us to draw close to you!

Finally, just like with Enoch, the Covenant relationship is a daily walk with God. Every day we must be continually seeking God. We will never have arrived in this earth walk. There was a day when God took Enoch and he was not. There will be a day when God will take us and we will no longer be here. "...But without faith it is impossible to please Him for he who comes to God must believe that He is, and that He is a rewarder of those who diligently seek Him." (Hebrews 11:6)

Chapter 5
The Abrahamic Covenant

Before there is a call by God, there is an appearing by God. There must be a revelation of God, before there is a calling to God. This was the principle in Abraham's life. One cannot get a picture of the calling of Abraham by God looking at the Old Testament (Covenant) first. One must listen to the testimony of Stephen in the book of Acts, chapter 7. "And he (Stephen) said, "Men and brethren and fathers, listen: The God of glory appeared to our father, Abraham, when he was in Mesopotamia, before he dwelt in Haran, and said to him, "Get out of your country and from your relatives and come to a land that I will show you." Then he (Abraham) came out of the Chaldeans and dwelt in Haran. And from there, when his father was dead, He moved him to this land in which you now dwell." (Acts 7:2-4) From this Scripture we get the setting of the first appearing of God to Abraham and then Abraham's calling. The Greek word for "appear" is sptavw which means to look at, behold, to allow one's self to be seen, to appear. In other words, Abraham had a revelation of God and then God instructed him to leave the city of Ur and the country of Mesopotamia.

This appearing of God to Abraham causes Abraham to listen to God. Arthur W. Pink describes this "appearing" in Gleanings in Genesis, page 138. "The God of Glory appeared unto Abraham, when he was in Mesopotamia." This is the first recorded "appearing" of God after the banishment of our parents (Adam and Eve) from Eden. It was probably the earliest of all theophanic manifestations that we read of in the Old Testament (Covenant), and which anticipated the Incarnation as well as marked the successive revelations of God. We do not hear of God appearing to Abel or Noah. Great then was the privilege thus conferred upon Abraham, the one who afterwards was termed the "friend of God."

Mr. Pink believes like I do that Abraham received a revelation of God, which would turn his world upside down. Revelation does that to you. It makes you follow God no matter what the cost. This revelation would prove to cost him the place of his birth (Ur) and eventually all his family except his wife (Sarah). Without a revelation of God and of His Son (Jesus), we will live mediocre Christian lives. This first step in the life of Abraham is important, because then He began to influence Abraham's earthily father's decisions.

The next information about Abraham is where he had this revelation and what was God's instructions to him? Mr. Pink, like me, believes Abraham got these instructions in the city of Ur in Mesopotamia. "And God said unto him (Abraham), "Get thee out of thy country and from thy kindred and come into the land which I will show thee." This command from God came to Abram in Mesopotamia, in the city of Ur of the Chaldees which was situated near to the Persian Gulf. The time of Abram's call is significant. It occurred shortly after the destruction of Babel and dispersion of the nations." (Gleanings in Genesis, page 138)

Most Bible scholars believe God wanted Abraham to leave Ur of the Chaldees, because it was steeped in idolatry and worshipped the moon god. According to Joshua 24:2 Abraham's family worshipped idols. "And Joshua said to all the people, "Thus says the Lord God of Israel, your fathers, including Terah the father of Abraham and the father of Nahor, dwelt on the other side of the River (the Euphrates) in old times; and they served other gods." God wanted Abraham to leave their influence that they had on his life. Sometimes people have to leave the influence of family in order to follow God. Today, this happens a lot in third world countries and in the Middle East. Jesus talking to multitudes who wanted to follow Him said this, "If anyone comes to Me and does not hate his father and mother, wife and children, brothers and sisters, yes, and his own life also, he cannot be My disciple." (Luke 14:26) Our supreme love for Jesus, must be above all other loves.

What does that mean? It means that sometimes family can pull you away from God and what God wants for your life. You must love the Lord above all things and people. In many foreign countries today, especially Muslim countries you have to count the cost of discipleship to our Lord Jesus Christ. This information is taken from a magazine published by

Barnabasaid. The article in the magazine is entitled, Praying for the Persecuted Church, page 37. The article talks about people who face torture and even death if they convert to Christianity from Islam. Countries that used to be strongly Christian in recent years have converted from Christianity to Islam and are now persecuting Christians. One such country mentioned in this magazine is Sudan. There is Christian persecution throughout the Middle East, African and Asian countries according to the magazine. Therefore, even today Christians are suffering persecution for the cause of Jesus Christ.

But there were some conflicting, cultural issues in the case of Abraham. He had a revelation of God in Ur. God appeared to him and from the beginning told him what he was to do. This is the first step in coming into a Covenant Relationship with God. The question then becomes why didn't Abraham leave his father, his mother and his brothers and go to the land of Canaan? Mr. Pink thinks he was walking in disobedience to God until after Terah, his father, died.

"In order to learn what response Abram made to God's call it is necessary to revert again to the previous chapter. "And Terah took Abram, his son, and Lot the son of Haran, his son's son and Sarai, his daughter-in-law, his son Abram's wife, and they went forth with them from Ur of the Chaldees, to go into the land of Canaan and they came to Haran and dwelt there." (Genesis 11:36) From these words we discover a two-fold failure on Abram's part. Three things were commanded him (Abram) by God; he was to leave his own country, he was to separate himself from his kindred, and he was to go forth unto a land which Jehovah had promised to show him. In respect to the first requirement Abram obeyed, but with the last two he failed. He left Chaldea, but instead of separating himself from his kindred, Terah his father, and Lot his nephew accompanied him. Terah means "delay" and thus it proved to be so. Terah accompanying Abram resulted in a delay of at least five years in Haran which means "parched." Abram's response to God's call then, was partial and slow, for observe that in Isaiah 51:2 we are expressly told that God called Abram "alone" yet in the end he "obeyed." (Gleanings in Genesis, page 141)

This is a long quotation, but I wanted you to see Mr. Pink's thoughts and ideas about Abraham and why he considered him slow in obeying God. Mr. Pink goes on to say that he believes those sins of reluctance to leave his kindred were blotted out. I believe Abraham's decision to wait until his father, Terah, died goes deeper than that. Mr. Pink, I believe is looking at it from a Western Hemisphere mind set. We tend to look at the Bible from a Western point of view, rather than an Easterner's point of view. The Bible is written from an Easterner's and Jewish mind set, which is different from the Western Hemisphere mind set.

The New Manners and Customs of Bible Times by Ralph Gower on page 54 gives us a clue as to the mind set of the Easterner during Abraham's time. Under the heading of The Father it says this, "The family was therefore a "little kingdom" that was ruled by the father. He ruled over wife, children, grandchildren and servants—everyone in the household. Children were brought up to accept the authority (Exodus 20:12) and if they refused to accept it, thereby threatening the security of the family unit, they could be punished by death. (Deuteronomy 21:18-21) "On the death of the father, succession normally passed to the eldest son. Isaac was a special case. According to the family law practiced in Abraham's time, it was possible for a man to have a child by a secondary wife. Ishmael was born to Abraham and Hagar in this way. (Genesis 16:1-2) But if any child was born subsequently to the first wife, then the child in the case of Isaac became head of the family. The same law was followed in Jacob's case. Rachel was always to be his first wife. Therefore, it was her elder son, Joseph, who became Jacob's heir and was given the distinctive coat to show it (Genesis 37:3-4) even though he was born long after his stepbrothers."

This also is a long quotation, but it gives the complete family law of Eastern culture in Old Testament (Covenant) times at the time of Abraham and his descendants. Seeing that Abraham had a revelation of God, does not mean under the culture of the day, he could leave his father, his father's wife and children or even Ur of the Chaldees unless Terah, his father was in agreement with him doing so. Terah was still his father and over him under Eastern family law.

Ralph Glover is not the only authority on Manners and Customs of Biblical times that believes this. Fred H. Wright wrote a book, Manners and Customs of Bible Lands, who echoed some of the same sentiments. He wrote a chapter on the Parental Position in the Home, pages 103-106. In this chapter he writes the Supremacy of the Father under the Patriarchal system on page 103. "Under the patriarchal administration, the father is supreme in command. The authority which the father has, extends to his wife, to his children, his children's children, his servants, and to all his household, and if he is the sheik, it extends to all the tribe...When Abraham, Isaac, and Jacob lived in tents in the Land of Promise, they were ruled by the same system..."

Since this is true and Abraham seemed to honor his earthily father, that is the reason he could not leave him in Ur and later in Haran. It seems Abraham's father, Terah, honored Abraham by leaving Ur of the Chaldeans and trying to go into Canaan. "And Terah took his son Abram and his grandson Lot, the son of Haran (Haran was deceased—Genesis 11:28) and his daughter-in-law Sarai, his son Abram's wife, and they went out with them from Ur of the Chaldeans, and they came to Haran and dwelt there. So, the days of Terah were two hundred and five years and Terah died in Haran." (Genesis 11:31-32)

Evidently, Abraham shared with his father, Terah, what God wanted him to do in leaving Ur of the Chaldeans. Abraham probably told Terah he was supposed to leave him and Lot. Terah, the patriarchal head of the family, probably said let me lead you to Canaan before I die. In other words, Terah honored the revelation that Abraham had. As the leader of the family, he went as far as he could and that was Haran. We don't know why they did not go all the way to Canaan. But Abraham honored his earthily father by staying with him until he died. I believe God honored that act. As soon as Terah died, Abraham started toward Canaan.

Look at this phrase in Genesis 12:1a. "Now the Lord had said to Abram..." Notice the Scripture says, "had said." That is a past tense verb.

God "had said" to Abram in Ur. Now God refreshes our memory of what He had said to Abram.

> "Get out of your country,
> From your kindred
> And from your father's house,
> To a land that I will show you."
> "I will make you a great nation;
> I will bless you
> And make your name great;
> And you shall be a blessing."
> "I will bless those who bless you,
> And I will curse him who curses you,
> And in you all the families of the earth
> Shall be blessed." (Genesis 12:1-3)

From what we read in The New Manners and Customs of the Bible, the oldest child, after the father passed away, would lead the family from that point on. In this case it was Abraham. This is still followed in the Middle East today. So, it is no wonder that Lot followed, Abraham to Canaan. "So, Abram departed as the Lord had spoken to him, and Lot went with him. And Abram was seventy-five years old when he departed from Haran." (Genesis 12:4)

I tend to agree with Ralph Smith and his preliminary statements about the Abrahamic Covenant in The Covenantal Structure of the Bible, page 30. "The Abrahamic covenant revealed the plan of salvation with greater clarity than even before. In both the post-fall promise and the covenant with Noah the saving grace of God is revealed, but the plan of salvation is rather obscure. With Abraham the promise of the new covenant is considerably expanded, providing a much clearer vision of the future salvation. Thus, the Abrahamic covenant becomes the "reference covenant" for the rest of the covenants in the old covenant era. The Mosaic, the Davidic, and the Restoration covenants are all explicitly grounded in the Abrahamic covenant…"

One can see that God got Abraham's attention in Ur. Though it took a little time to get out of Ur of the Chaldeans, it took a lot longer time for Abraham to get free of his family and their connection to idolatry. This is where the grace of God came in. The Abrahamic covenant points to faith as well as grace. That faith is declared in Hebrews 11:8. "By faith Abraham obeyed when he was called to go out to the place which he would afterward receive an inheritance. And he went out, not knowing where he was going." It took faith to leave people and places that you are familiar with and go to a place that you know nothing about. But in Genesis 12:1-3, God is promising him that He will make out of him a great nation and He promises to bless him abundantly. Because of Abraham's quick obedience God blesses him time and time again. When we obey God quickly, He tends to let blessings follow us and overtake us.

Since the fall of Adam and the flood, everything that was God-centered in the world had been swept away by the flood. The Garden of Eden did not exist anymore and that was where the presence of God was. There were several spiritual areas lacking in the world. Idolatry was beginning to run rampant in the world. But this did not catch God by surprise. Ralph Smith shares what the Abrahamic Covenant does to remedy this situation. First, God chooses and calls a man, Abraham, and then He chooses where that family is going to live, Canaan. On page 30 of his book, The Covenantal Structure of the Bible, he talks some about this action. "Before the call of Abraham, the world of that day, like the world of Noah, lacked a God-appointed world center. It also lacked a unified priestly system. Abraham's own family worshipped idols (Joshua 24:2) but there were some true priests...In these circumstances Abraham was chosen to be the progenitor of a race of priests that would culminate in the Savior of the world. From the time he was chosen, men were required to relate to God through Abraham."

There are four things that occur as a result of the Abrahamic Covenant. We learn through the writings of Paul that we are justified by faith in Romans the fourth chapter. Paul declares that as a result of us believing on Jesus we are justified by faith. "But to him who does not work but believes on Him (Jesus), his faith is counted for righteousness." This refers up to verse three. "For what does the Scripture say? "Abraham believed God, and it was accounted to him for righteousness." (Romans 4:6,3)

This faith is not based on the works of the law or works period. King David described that faith in Romans 4:5-8. "...just as David also describes the blessedness of the man to whom God imputes (charges) righteousness apart from works. Blessed are those whose lawless deeds are forgiven, and whose sins are covered. Blessed is the man to whom the Lord shall not impute (charge) sins." Although this is recorded in Romans 4, Paul is actually quoting Psalms 32:1-2. Paul is showing that even in the Old Testament (Covenant) Abraham followed God, believed in God, and that faith was counted as righteousness even before Abraham was circumcised. He only was circumcised and circumcised his sons as an act of obedience to God. But circumcision did not make him righteous, his faith in God did. That is why the Abrahamic Covenant is a Covenant of faith. When you do what God asks you to do, you are walking in the faith of our father, Abraham. "Because it is of faith that it might be according to grace, so that the promise (Jesus) might be sure to all the seed, not only to those who are of the law (Jews) but also to those who (Gentiles) are of the faith of Abraham who is the father of us all (Jews and Gentiles)." (Romans 4:16)

The second thing was the receiving of the Holy Spirit by faith. It is that same faith that Abraham had. This is brought out in Galatians 3:5-6. "Therefore He (Jesus) supplies the Spirit to you and works miracles among you, does He do it by the works of the law, or by the hearing of faith? — Just as Abraham believed God, and it was accounted to him for righteousness." Paul was writing to the Galatians because they had entered back under the law. He starts off chapter three of Galatians by analyzing their situation. He lets them know they received the Holy Spirit by faith. He is letting them know that if they continue in faith, they are sons of Abraham even though they are Gentiles. "Therefore, know that only those who are of faith are sons of Abraham. And the Scripture, foreseeing that God would justify the nations by faith, preached the Gospel to Abraham beforehand saying, in you all nations shall be blessed. So, then those who are of faith are blessed with believing Abraham." (Galatians 3:7-9) Paul then identifies the fact that Jesus Christ "redeemed us from the law" so we should receive the "blessing of Abraham"." Christ has redeemed us from the curse of the law having become a curse for us (for it is written Cursed is everyone who hangs on a tree), that the blessing of Abraham might come upon the Gentiles in Christ Jesus, that we might receive the promise of the (Holy) Spirit through faith." (Galatians 3:13-14) We can choose the fact that Jesus has redeemed us from the curse of the law and now we are under the blessings of Abraham.

The third thing of the Covenant involved Abraham inheriting the land of Canaan. Abraham gets a promise from God that the land in which he is living (Canaan) will someday belong to Abraham's descendants. This land would be "a God-appointed world center." (page 30) Abraham is walking through it as though it were his. This is a promise that God makes to Abraham. "Then the Lord appeared to Abram and said, "To your descendants I will give this land." And then he (Abram) built an altar to the Lord, who had appeared to him." (Genesis 12:7) This is the first time that God appears or reveals Himself to Abram in the promise land. God had not promised land to him until Abram began walking in the land. These are all Covenant promises that God made to Abram and his seed after him. We are of the seed of Abraham because we are walking and living by faith in Jesus Christ.

The Garden of Eden had been a place of worship and communion for Adam and Eve before they sinned. After the flood there was no place designated by God as a place of worship until Abram moved to Canaan. When he stepped on the land and God made this Covenant promise to him, it was time to worship God. Listen to what Arthur W. Pink in his book, Gleanings in Genesis, says about all this on page 144. "At the first appearing the God of Glory called upon Abram to separate himself from his place by nature; but at this second appearing He reveals Himself to Abram for communion, and the result is that Abram erects an altar. There was no "altar" for Abram in Ur or Haran. It is not until there is a real separation from the world that fellowship with God is possible. First the obedience of faith and then communion and worship." One will notice that periodically Abram erects altars to God through out the land of Canaan where he worships and sacrifices to the Lord, his God. Usually, at those times something spiritual has transpired between God and Abram and it is a renewing of the Covenant Relationship.

The fourth thing of the Covenant involves Abram becoming a priest to God. There is no mention of Abram becoming a priest until he builds this altar in Genesis 12. Noah and Abram (Abraham) are the first priests mentioned in the Bible. Ralph Smith said this about Abram on page 30, The Covenantal Structure of the Bible. "In these circumstances, Abraham was chosen to be the progenitor of a race of priests that would culminate in the Savior of the world. From the time he was chosen, men were required to relate to God through Abraham. Those who blessed Abraham would be blessed and those who cursed Abraham would be cursed (Genesis 12:1-3) ...Wherever Abraham settled, he dug wells and built altars (Genesis 12:7-8; 13:4,18; 21:34; 26:15) establishing that location as a "sanctuary" world center. Most importantly, the covenant promised the "Seed of Abraham" the center of God's plan, who (Jesus) would bring blessing to the whole world."

We have looked at some of the Covenant Promises to Abraham. There is one thing we should point out before we get into the Abrahamic Covenant. You may have noticed that in the beginning when Abraham is called to leave Ur and Haran, his name is called Abram. That is the name his earthily father, Terah, gave him. Later, right before Abram is circumcised, God changes his name to Abraham, which name (Abraham) means a father of many nations. God reserves the right as our Heavenly Father to change our name just as He chose to change Abram's name from Abram to Abraham. This takes place in the 17th chapter of Genesis. Abraham's character changed when his name was changed. He became the father of faith as well as the father of many nations. The name Abraham stuck and that is what most people call him today. Prophetically, he did become the father of many nations and his believing in God caused God to call him righteous. Has God given you a new name in Glory?

The Covenant Relationship

Dr. Ralph Gower gives us a good overview of the Covenant Relationship that Abraham had with God in his book, The New Manners and Customs of the Bible on page 287-288. "In Old Testament times God chose to enter in a close relationship first with an individual (Abraham), then with his immediate family and finally with his descendants so that they would gradually be prepared for his personal coming and for a deeper relationship than had hitherto been possible. Abraham was the individual (Genesis 12:1-2) and the covenant relationship entered into with Abraham and his family (Genesis 15:9-18) was renewed with his grandson Jacob (Genesis 28:13-15) and with Moses (Exodus 3:6; 24:3-8)"

Dr. Gower goes on to explain the Covenant Relationship in regard to Moses and the law. God isn't interested in us having a religion or religious experiences per se, but rather us coming into a Divine relationship with Him. As we get into the terms of the Abrahamic Covenant we will see also that God was interested in the things that Abraham was interested in, such as family, land, riches and cattle. All of these things are apart of the Covenant that God makes with Abraham. In the process, Abraham grows in his relationship with God to the point Abraham trusts God with himself and everything he has. Let us look at the Covenant with Abraham and God as it unfolds. Remember God extends the Covenant to Abraham and not the other way around.

The Abrahamic Covenant

In Genesis 12:1-3 God explains to Abram that He is going to show him land he hasn't seen before. He also promises Abram that He will make of his seed a great nation. Finally, God promises Abram that He will bless those who bless Abram and curse those who curse Abram. This is the Covenant Promises that God made to Abram in Ur of the Chaldeans. In all of this Abram still hasn't done what God has asked him to do from the beginning which is to separate himself from his family. This is only done after Abram, Sarai, and Lot return from Egypt. God causes circumstances to make Abram finally do what God had asked him to do in the beginning. Abram after leaving Egypt returns to the place where he worshipped God in the beginning—Bethel. We learn from the narrative that Abram again calls on the Lord.

From the Scriptures at this point, we learn that Lot has as much wealth as Abraham. "Lot also, who went with Abram, had flocks and herds and tents. Now the land was not able to support them, that they might dwell together, for their possessions were so great that they could not dwell together. And there was strife between the herdsmen of Abram's livestock and the herdsmen of Lot's livestock. The Canaanites and the Perizzites then dwelt in the land." (Genesis 13:5-7)

From this we can see that God engineered the events ahead for a separation of Abram and Lot. According to the cultural customs of the day, it was not right for Lot to leave Abram. Abram was still the Patriarch of the family since Terah had died. Abram being the spiritual head of the family saw what lies ahead if Lot was not given space for his family and his cattle. Therefore, he spoke to Lot about separating from him. "So, Abram said to Lot, "Please let there be no strife between you and me, and between my herdsmen and your herdsmen; for we are brethren. Is not the whole land before you? Please separate from me. If you take the left, then I will go to the right; or if you go to the right, then I will go to the left." (Genesis 13:8-9) It is the Patriarch's duty to make sure there is no strife between him and his nearest kin—Lot. According to Matthew Henry's Commentary, Genesis to Deuteronomy, Volume 1, page 90-91, Lot is rich in goods and cattle as a result of being with Abram. This is apart of the Covenant Blessing that was on Abram. We will see from this point on that Lot is selfish and has been following Abram for what he could get out of the relationship, namely the blessing of God. Lot is not in Covenant Relationship with God nor does he know God like Abram does. God revealed Himself to Abram not to Lot. This will become abundantly clear in the chapters that follow. A lot of people attach themselves to the blessed and Covenant keeping Christians. That will only last for awhile and then circumstances will cause them to leave thinking they are blessed themselves. Evidently Lot felt this way.

Arthur W. Pink in his book, Gleanings in Genesis, page 149 makes this observation. "Abram foresaw there was a danger of a falling out between himself and his nephew (Lot), that what had begun with the servants would probably end with the masters. Deprecating the thought of friction between brethren, he proposed they should separate. The wisdom which is from above is first pure and then peaceable…" Lot did not give Abram the right for the best land. He chose the best for himself which shows his selfish nature. "And Lot lifted his eyes and saw the plain of Jordan, that it was well-watered everywhere (before the Lord destroyed Sodom and Gomorrah) like the garden of the Lord, like the land of Egypt as you go toward Zoar. Then Lot chose for himself all the plain of Jordan and Lot journeyed East. And they separated from each other." (Genesis 13:10-11)

It would look like Lot took advantage of Abram and Abram let him. But looking behind the scenes and what God says to Abram after Lot leaves, one actually sees that Abram is rewarded because of his Covenant with God. In Genesis 13:14-17 shows that Abram got the better of Lot in his Covenant with God. While Lot chose the East and it looks good to the natural eyes and the natural man, there are going to be some draw backs that Lot had not counted on in the long run. Because Lot left Abram, the man under God's Covenant blessing, in the end Lot will lose everything and all that he will have left is his sinful daughters. God shares with Abram the blessings of the land his descendants are going to receive. Notice that God does not share this with Abram until after Lot leaves and goes East. By circumstances I believe God maneuvered Lot away from Abram so that He could bless him. In the beginning when God appeared to Abram, He told Abram to leave his kindred—all those who were related to him. When we are under the Covenant of God, sometimes God maneuvers us away from people who will harm our relationship with Him. This is something to Selah—meditate on. "And the Lord said to Abram after Lot had separated from him: "Lift your eyes now and look from the place where you are—northward, southward, eastward and westward; for all the land which you see I give to you and your descendants forever. And I will make your descendants as the dust of the earth; so that if a man could number the dust of the earth, then your descendants could also be numbered. Arise, walk in the land through it length and its width, for I give it to you." (Genesis 13:14-17)

Therefore, from what God told Abram, the land that Abram gave Lot; Abram didn't have the power to do that. All the land was going to Abram and his descendants according to God's will and pleasure. The land was the first provision of the Covenant that God made with Abram and it was an everlasting Covenant. There are men and countries today that are trying to take this land away from Abram's descendants and God will not allow that to happen. When God makes a Covenant, it is sealed in Heaven at the throne of God.

Abram Rescues Lot

Genesis chapter 14 shows how Abram rescues Lot, his nephew. Abram still loved Lot and his family, although they had separated from him and were now living in Sodom and Gomorrah. Lot is in the middle of a war called the Battle of the Kings. To give you an idea of the Kings involved in this battle, we will take it as it is written in Genesis 14:1-2. "And it came to pass in the days of Amraphel king of Shinar, Arioch king of Ellasar, Chedorlaomer king of Elam, Tidal king of nations (Goyim), that they made war with Bera king of Sodom, Birsha king of Gomorrah, Shinab king of Admah, Shemeber king of Zebolim, and the king of Bela (that is Zoar)." The kings in the first verse won the battle and probably Abram would not have got involved but in verses 11-12 of chapter 14 of Genesis they took all the goods of Sodom and Gomorrah and Lot and all his goods too. One of the residents of Sodom and Gomorrah escaped and came and told Abram all about it. Now notice this that Abram considered Lot to be his brother and when he was taken captive by these Kings, he went to rescue him. "Now when Abram heard that his brother was taken captive, he armed his three hundred and eighteen trained servants who were born in his house and went in pursuit as far as Dan" (Genesis 14:14) Needless to say, he rescued Lot and brought back all the goods as well as the men and women.

There are some important lessons to be learned about Covenant relationship with God from what took place in this chapter. First, although

Lot has chosen to live in Sodom and in this battle, he is captured and taken prisoner, he does not realize that he is no longer under the Covenant of Abram. He walked out from underneath that Covenant when he left Abram and moved to Sodom. When one is in Covenant relationship with God, one is under Divine protection. What happens to Lot in the chapters ahead and how he loses everything but his earthily life, is a picture of what happens to Christians who move away from the presence of God and His Covenant relationship with them. Twice Abram rescues him from messes that Lot has gotten himself into because of "the lust of the flesh, the lust of the eyes and the pride of life." (1 John 2:16)

As a result of this battle that Abram fights, when he rescues Lot, he is able to get a lot of goods from the Kings. However, he does not take anything from the Kings of Sodom and Gomorrah. When Abram returns with all the goods, he meets Melchizedek, King of Salem. There are a lot of different opinions about Melchizedek. Let's skip what everyone else says and look at the Scriptures. To get a good understanding of Melchizedek, one must look at Genesis 14:18-20 and then compare it to Hebrews the 7th chapter. But before you look at those verses, read John 8:56-58. Jesus said this about Abraham. "Your father Abraham rejoiced to see my day, and he saw it and was glad. Then the Jews said to Him, "You are not yet fifty years old, and have you seen Abraham?" Jesus said to them, "Most assuredly I say to you, before Abraham was, I Am."

How could Jesus have seen Abraham? Like Jesus said, before Abraham was, I Am. Now let us look at Genesis 14;18-20. "Then Melchizedek, King of Salem bought out bread and wine: he was priest of God Most High. And he (Melchizedek) blessed him (Abram) and said:"

"Blessed be Abram of God Most High
Possessor of heaven and earth
And blessed be God Most High,
Who has delivered your enemies into your hand."
"And he (Abram) gave him(Melchizedek) a tithe of all."

From this Scripture, we see that Melchizedek blessed Abram. In return Abram gave Melchizedek a tenth or tithe of all the goods he had taken from

King Chedorlaomer and the other Kings. Why would he tithe to this person if he was merely a man? One tithes to God and not to man. Therefore, he must be more than a man. With this in mind turn to the 7th chapter of Hebrews. Read the first four verses of Hebrews 7.

"For this Melchizedek, King of Salem, priest of the Most High God, who met Abraham returning from the slaughter of the kings and blessed him. To whom also Abraham gave a tenth part of all, first being translated "king of righteousness" and then also king of Salem, meaning "king of peace," without father, without mother, without genealogy, but made like the Son of God, remains a priest continually. Now consider how great this man was to whom even the patriarch Abraham gave a tenth of the spoils." (Hebrew 7:1-4) Then drop down to verses 9 and 10 of Hebrews 7. "Even Levi, who receive tithes, paid tithes through Abraham, so to speak, for he (Levi) was still in the loins his father (Abraham) when Melchizedek met him."

Now ask the Holy Spirit to enlighten your eyes of understanding. Only God can bless anyone. We can say, "God bless you", but only God can bless someone. The Scripture says Melchizedek blessed Abraham returning from the spoils. Abraham gave him tithes. We tithed to God; we don't tithe to man. The Scripture describes Melchizedek as the King of Righteousness and the King of Peace. The name Melchizedek means righteousness and His kingdom means peace. We are given righteousness and peace because we are in Jesus. This man was already righteous and peaceful. That was His nature. At that point in history, He didn't have a father or mother or genealogy. He is like the Son of God, Jesus Christ and is forever a priest.

I believed Jesus appeared in human form to Abraham as is recorded in John's Gospel. Abraham had a revelation of Jesus Christ. Whether that was Melchizedek or not, we will find out in eternity when we get to Heaven. All of our questions will be answered there. What does this have to do with a Covenant relationship with God? I believe under His Covenant with Abram, He instructed Abram to tithe and revealed Jesus to him during this time. This is what Matthew Henry says about this subject in Matthew Henry's Commentary, Volume 6, Acts to Revelation, page

917. "Many Christian writers have thought him (Melchizedek) to be Jesus Christ, Himself, appearing by a special dispensation and privilege to Abraham in the flesh, and who was known to Abraham by the name Melchizedek, which agrees well to Christ and what is said in John 8:56. "Abraham saw his day and rejoiced." Much may be said for this opinion, and what is said in verse 3 does not seem to agree with any mere man; but then it seems strange to make Christ a type of Himself. (3) The most general opinion is that he was a Canaanite King, who reigned in Salem, and kept up religion and the worship of the true God; that he was raised to be a type of Christ and was honored by Abraham as such."

Abraham in Genesis 14 also dealt with the King of Sodom. This King was a worldly person and very wicked. The King of Sodom offered Abram all the goods that Abram had brought back and restored to his city. Abram under the Divine Covenant of God refused everything and told the King of Sodom in essence that he served God. You can read Abram's testimony before the King of Sodom in Genesis 14:22-24. We are under the New Testament (Covenant) and have the right to testify about Jesus every day.

Starting Genesis 15, God promised Abram to protect him. "After these things the word of the Lord came to Abram in a vision saying, "Do not be afraid, Abram. I am your shield, and your exceeding great reward." (Genesis 15:1) God wanted Abram to know that he didn't have to be afraid of the Kings around about him, including the King of Sodom. This was a Covenant Promise Abram walked and lived in from the time he started walking by faith in God. Today, we have that same Covenant Promise under the New Covenant when we walk and live in Jesus.

Abram's great fear was the fact that Sarai was childless and if she didn't have a child, his heir would be Eliezer of Damacus. "Then Abram said, "Look, You have given me no offspring: indeed one (Eliezer) born in my house is my heir." (Genesis 15:3) But listen to what God promises Abram. This is the second promise of the Divine Covenant of God. "And behold, the word of the Lord came to him, saying, "This one shall not be your heir, but one who will come from your own body shall be your heir. Then He brought him outside and said, "Look now toward heaven, and count the stars if you are able to number them." And He said to him, "So shall your descendants be." (Genesis 15:4-5)

Now, Abram had a choice to make. It probably would have been easy for Abram to doubt God's promises to him, but according to Genesis 15:6 he believed and trusted what God told him. "And he believed in the Lord, and He accounted it to him for righteousness." This verse is quoted by the Apostle Paul in the New Testament (Covenant) in Romans 4:3. "For what does the Scripture say? Abraham believed God, and it was accounted to him for righteousness." Then in verse 5 of the same chapter, Paul explains what verse 4 meant. "But to him who does not work but believes on Him who justifies the ungodly, his faith is accounted for righteousness." The faith of God is we just trust Him to bring what He has promised to pass. Therefore, the promise of a child that would inherit all that Abram had promised by God to him. When we get to chapter 16 of Genesis, we learn that Sarai knows what God has promised and her lack of faith is evident when she gives Abram her maid servant, Hagar.

But before we look at the chapter under Covenant eyes, let's see that God again promises Abram all the land. "I am the Lord, who brought you out of Ur of the Chaldeans, to give you this land to inherit it." (Genesis 15:7) God goes over the history that Abram and He have had together. Notice up to this point, God is sharing with Abram the Covenant Promises. He has not yet extended His Covenant to Abram. Abram is a lot like us, when God promises us something. We say, "How is God going to bring this to pass?" So, Abram expresses his concern in Genesis 15:8. "And he said, "Lord God, how shall I know that I will inherit it?" At this point, God extends the Covenant to Abram. Genesis 15:9-12 shows the Covenant sacrifices that must be made and how the devil through the vultures tries to destroy that Covenant Relationship. Abram continually has to make the vultures leave. Those birds represent the negative thoughts, ideas and suggestions that bombard our minds as we seek to walk in Covenant relationship with God. Abram had the same battle. Abram then experiences the presence of God in a spectacular way. "So, He said, "Bring Me a three-year-old heifer, a three-year-old female goat, a three-year-old ram, a turtledove, and a young pigeon. Then he brought all three to Him and cut them in two, down the middle, and placed each piece, opposite the other; but he did not cut the birds in two. And when the vultures came down on the carcasses, Abram drove them away. Now when the sun was going down, a deep sleep fell upon Abram; and behold horror and great darkness fell upon him." (Genesis 15:9-12)

The animals that God had Abraham bring were clean animals. According to studylight.org every animal that God told Abraham to bring were in the list of sacrificial animals under the Mosaic law. What God was arranging here with Abram was the sacrifices needed to cut a Covenant with Abram. The Zondervan NIV Bible Commentary: Volume 1 Old Testament, says this about the animals, their cuttings and arrangement on pages 24-25. Dr. John H. Sailhamer says this, "17 The act of dividing the animals and walking through the parts was apparently an ancient form of contractual agreement (cf. Jeremiah 34:18). While the meaning of the details may remain a mystery, fortunately the writer of Genesis has explained the custom: On the day the Lord made a covenant with Abram."

Notice that before this chapter on the Divine Covenant, that God did not immediately enter into Covenant Relationship with Abram. First, God promised Abram certain provisions and then watched to see if Abram would obey Him when He commanded him to do something for example like leaving Ur of the Chaldeans. Most every time Abram quickly obeyed the Lord. Then God promised Abram the land that he was sojourning in and finally a child would be born to Sarai and Abram. Abram's servant, Eliezer, would not be Abram's heir. Even though Abram questioned God about his inheriting the land, God chose to extend His Covenant to Abram.

Again, Abram followed God's instructions carefully, choosing the animals and the birds, and cutting the animals down the middle and laying them out. Evidently, Abram knew what was happening and would not let the vultures land on the sacrifices. Abram's part in the Covenant making was the preparation of the sacrifices and making sure the vultures didn't take them away or land on them. Arthur W. Pink in Gleanings in Genesis, page 169 had this to say about the Covenantal Sacrifices. "It has been pointed out by another that each of the three animals named here were tame ones, not wild and needing to be captured by Abram; instead, they were the willing servants of man's needs. Each one foreshadowed a distinctive aspect of Christ's perfections and work. The heifer of three years seems to have pointed to the freshness of his vigor; the goat, gave the sin offering aspect; the ram is the animal that is in the Levitical offerings was connected especially with consecration. The birds told of One from Heaven. The "three years" thrice repeated, suggested perhaps the time of our Lord's sacrifice, offered after "three years" of service! Note that death passed upon them all, for without shedding of blood is no remission and where no remission is there can be no inheritance. The "dividing" of the animals indicated that this sacrifice was to form the basis for a covenant (cf. Jeremiah 34:18-19). The "driving way" of the fowls seems to have shown forth the energy of faith."

In practical application we have taken the sacrifice of Jesus Christ on the Cross and His blood, as our sacrifice and His precious blood to wash away all our sins. The vultures (the devil) is constantly trying to bring us under condemnation and the blood is sufficient enough for our sins. We constantly have to cast down the thoughts, the imaginations of the heart, and the fleshly ideas of the mind, just like Abram had to chase away the vultures. The Sacrifice of Jesus and the blood of Jesus is sufficient to take away our sins and our sin nature. "But if we walk in the light as He is in the light, we have fellowship with one another, and the blood of Jesus Christ, His Son, cleanses us from all sin." (1 John 1:7) We need to dismiss the devil's accusations against us, as already been washed away by the blood of Jesus. As a preacher once told me, "You can't stop the birds from flying overhead, but you can stop them from making a nest where you live."

God Almighty was inviting Abram to the Covenant Table. After Abram had split the three animals and sacrificed the birds and chased away the vultures, Abram fell asleep and the Bible says…"and behold, horror and great darkness fell upon him (Abram)." (Genesis 15:12b) Matthew Henry's Commentary, Volume 1 says this about that time. "1. A deep sleep fell upon Abram, not a common sleep through weariness and carelessness, but a divine ecstasy, like that which the Lord caused to fall upon Adam

(Genesis ch. 2:21) that being hereby wholly taken off from the view of things sensible, he might be wholly taken up with contemplation of things spiritual." (page 103) Suffice it to say that God and Abram met in Holy Covenant Relationship. That is when God in this spiritual state spoke to Abram and told him what the future would be. God, our Father, would like for us under the New Covenant to enter into a deeper spiritual relationship with Him. How often we are too busy or we have to much of the world in us to enter into that relationship with our Father that would cause us to cry out Abba Father. (Romans 8:15; Galatians 4:6)

"Then He said to Abram: "Know certainly that your descendants will be strangers in a land that is not theirs, and will serve them, and they will afflict them four hundred years. And also, the nation whom they serve I will judge: afterward they shall come out with great possessions. Now as for you, you shall go to your fathers in peace; you shall be buried at a good old age. But in the fourth generation they shall return here for the iniquity of the Amorites is not yet completed." (Genesis 15:13-16)

In that moment, when God extended the Covenant to Abram and cut Covenant with him, that God answered the question Abram had at the beginning. "And he (Abram) said, "Lord God, how shall I know that I will inherit it?" In those moments of Holy Communion with God as they broke Covenant with one another, notice Abram is not told to do anything but listen to God. Because Abram has forsaken all his kin and the world (King of Sodom) in obedience to God, God has extended His Covenant to Abram. Notice this Covenant Relationship was not extended in Ur of the Chaldeans or later in Haran. It was extended to Abram when he fully obeyed the Lord and did what God asked him to do. God will extend His Covenant to us when we fully follow the Lord and do what He has commanded us to do, no matter what that may be. What is often strange most of the time, God's pleasure is different with each individual.

The last thing that happens before Abram comes out of Holy Communion, is that Abram sees the smoking oven and the burning torch that passes through the pieces of the animals. This is the symbol of God that He is ratifying the Covenant between them. (Genesis 15:17) In Genesis

15:18-21 the Covenant is completely extended. "On the same day the Lord made a covenant with Abram saying: "To your descendants I have given this land, from the river of Egypt to the great river, the river Euphrates—the Kenites, the Kenezzites, the Kadmonites: the Hittites, the Perizzites, and the Rephaim; the Amorites, the Canaanites, the Gergasites, and the Jebusites."

Bible critics use the number of years God said the Israelites would be in bondage in an attempt to discredit the Bible. There is some conflict according to them concerning the figure in Genesis 15 which says 400 years and what it says in Exodus 12:40-41 which says 430 years. Dr. Spiro Zodhiates in his The Hebrew-Greek Key Study Bible on page 22 gives a clarification about the 400 years mentioned in Genesis 15:13-16 and the 430 years mentioned in Exodus 12:40-41. "God gave Abraham a preview of events in his family's history before they actually possessed the land which he had promised them. They would first be temporary residents in a strange land for 400 years and become slaves. Their bondage in Egypt was certainly a part of God's overall plan. Four hundred years is a round figure. There is no conflict with the 430 years mentioned in Exodus 12:40-41. The four generations of their sojourn should be understood as four life times. One hundred years would have been a conservative estimate for one life time in patriarchal times. The events surrounding Israel's departure from Egypt would be a judgment upon that nation. The interval of their sojourn in Egypt would be given to the Amorites, who possessed Canaan at that time. Israel's campaign against them was a matter of God's judgment."

Needless to say, when God gave Abram this Covenant, from that day forward it would be the foundation of how God dealt with Abram. From this point, Abram is now in Covenant relationship with God. He needs to listen to God and ask God about each new thing that is happening in his life. The question will be, how will Sarai react to what God has promised Abram especially under this new Covenant Relationship? Abram will find out when he returns to her after his meeting with God.

Sarai's Plan to Help God

Just like us today, after we have had an encounter with God, there is a temptation or test that follows. So, it was with Abram. As soon as he returns home and no doubt shared with Sarai his Covenant Relationship with God and what God had promised, especially about having an heir, she probably wanted to help Abram and God, if possible. Sarai knows that Abram needs an heir and yet she is barren at the moment. She might have heard Abram say that God had promised a son to them through them, Sarai and Abram. Maybe she is thinking how this can happen—I am barren. At this point she figures she needs to help God with this since Abram and she are advanced in years and beyond child bearing. Before we judge Sarai, let us take a step back and examine our own life and how many times we have tried to help God. Sarai would have her Egyptian maid servant, Hagar, bear an heir for Abram and her.

Sometimes this happened in Middle Eastern countries. The maid servant would be employed to produce a male heir, in the place of the wife, if she was barren. Sarai's Egyptian hand maiden, Hagar, was given to Abram to be his second wife. Anything of Egypt in the Bible is most always considered of the flesh. This is a carnal arrangement proposed by Sarai. This is nothing new. It happens all the time and God lets it happen to show us our lack of faith in Him. Even father Abram, the father of faith, sees this as an opportunity to get an heir. Isn't that what God promised—an heir? Notice Abram and Sarai have not talked or consulted God about this. God will let us go our merry way and then He will confront us with the truth. Let's listen in on what Sarai says to Abram. "So, Sarai said to Abram, "See now, the Lord has restrained me from bearing children. Please, go into my maid, perhaps I shall obtain children by her." And Abram heeded the voice of Sarai. Then Sarai, Abram's wife, took Hagar her maid, the Egyptian, and gave her to her husband Abram to be his wife, after Abram had dwelt ten years in the Land." (Genesis 16:2-3)

Notice that Sarai started all of this. Abram had just been in the presence of God and was promised in the Covenant with God the land they are dwelling in and a son. Abram doesn't go to God about Sarai's proposal.

He does not seek God's will in the matter. Maybe he is thinking this is God's way of providing me a son. It is only after having relations with Hagar and a son is conceived and born, that he will learn in the days to come that this isn't the will of God. This is going to cause problems in his household for years to come. Abram became married to the flesh (Egyptian) and that union will only produce flesh. Egyptian people and the things of Egypt in the Bible are considered flesh. "So, he went into Hagar, and she conceived. And when she saw that she had conceived, her mistress became despised in her eyes. Then Sarai said to Abram, my wrong be upon you! I gave my maid into your embrace, and when she saw that she had conceived, I became despised in her eyes. The Lord judge between me and you." (Genesis 16:4-5)

Now things are much more complicated than when it was just Abram and Sarai. If Abram had spent some time in prayer before this relationship with Hagar, the Egyptian, God would have told him what to do and that this would not be a blessed relationship. Even after Hagar saw she conceived and was going to have a child, as a servant to Sarai, she is duty bound to submit to Sarai and even give the child to Sarai as heir. But it is not turning out that way. Now Abram has a relationship with the flesh. "Then when desire has conceived, it gives birth to sin; when it is full-grown brings forth death." (James 1:15) This is a description of what Abram brought about with his flesh relationship with Hagar. The birth of Ishmael will produce sin and death in the years ahead. Today the descendants of Ishmael want to destroy and kill the descendants of Abram. When we don't pray about our decisions but launch ahead without God's directions, we are going to produce "Ishmaels" who will produce sin and death.

The complexity of the situation takes place in the next several verses, when Abram is told about what is transpiring between Sarai and Hagar. Again, Abram does not pray about the situation, but tells Sarai to handle it. We need to pray about all the situations and people in which we are involved with. "...praying always with all prayer and supplication in the Spirit, being watchful to this end with all perseverance and supplication for all the saints." (Ephesians 6:18) Instead, Abram turns everything over to Sarai. Hagar does not realize she is still under Abram and Sarai. Abram reminds Sarai of this fact. Sarai does not gently rebuke Hagar. "So, Abram said to Sarai, "Indeed your maid is in your hand; do to her as you please." And when Sarai dealt harshly with her (Hagar), she fled from her presence." (Genesis 16:6)

It is interesting to note that the Angel of the Lord finds Hagar in the wilderness running away from Sarai. Many Bible scholars believe the Angel of the Lord in the Old Testament (Covenant) is actually Jesus Christ in his pre-incarnate form. I guess we will know in Heaven. Anyway, the Angel of the Lord tells Hagar to go back and submit to Sarai. He also tells her she will have a male child and he is to be called Ishmael. The Angel of the Lord gives a prophetic word to Hagar and all of it happens as He says. "And the Angel of the Lord said to her. "Behold you are with child, and you shall bear a son. You shall call his name Ishmael, because the Lord has heard your affliction. He shall be a wild man; His hand shall be against every man, and every man's hand against him, and he shall dwell in the presence of his brethren." (Genesis 16:11-12)

When Ishmael is born, he is a son of Abram. Is this a fulfillment of the Covenant Promise of God? No, this son is born outside of the Covenant. This is not a fulfillment of God's promise to Abram. Ishmael is still a son of Abram, but he is a son outside of the Covenant of God. Therefore, Ishmael cannot inherit the promises that Abram's true Covenant son will inherit. Ishmael is born outside of the will of God and is therefore a fleshly son of Abram.

The Changing of Abram's Name

In chapter 17 of Genesis, God explains more about their Covenant Relationship and changes Abram's name to Abraham. Notice at the end of chapter 16 of Genesis in verse 16 it gives Abram's age when Ishmael is born. "Abram was eighty-six years old when Hagar bore Ishmael to Abram." Then Chapter 17 of Genesis verse 1 states Abram's age when God talks to Abram the next time. "When Abram was ninety-nine years old, the Lord appeared to Abram and said to him, "I am Almighty God, walk before Me and be blameless." It seems God may not have talked to Abram for over thirteen years. Some Bible scholars believe God was silent toward Abram, because he had listened to Sarai and followed her advice in taking Hagar to be his second wife and had Ishmael. A lot of times communication between us and God is lost when we follow the advice that is fleshly and leads us to fleshly ways.

Whenever God changes a person's name in the Old Testament (Covenant), He changes their character. When God changed his name from Abram to Abraham, it became a prophetic word over Abraham's life. The name "Abraham" means "father of a multitude." This was given in The Index of Proper Names by Rev. A.T. Chapman and can be found in The First Scofield Bible, page 1382. But also, Genesis 17:5, God says he will be a father of many nations. "No longer shall your name be called Abram, but your name shall be Abraham; for I have made you a father of many nations." At the end of Abraham's life, that is what he became. All of his offspring became heads of many nations. This would be the third promise of the Abrahamic Covenant.

Going on with chapter 17 of Genesis, God appears (reveals Himself) to Abraham again. "When Abraham was ninety-nine years old, the Lord appeared to Abram and said to him, "I am God Almighty, walk before me and be blameless. And I will make My covenant between Me and you and will multiply you exceedingly." (Genesis 17:1-2) Thirteen years have passed since Hagar gave birth to Ishmael. In this chapter God renews His covenant with Abraham and institutes the Covenant sign, which is circumcision. Listen to the Covenant Promises that God shares with Abraham from Genesis 17. God is explaining the Covenant in simple terms, so Abraham can understand it. God describes also the act of circumcision. (Genesis 17:6-14)

"I will make you exceedingly fruitful; and I will make nations of you and kings shall come from you. And I will establish my covenant between Me and you and your descendants after you in their generations, for an everlasting covenant to be God to you and your descendants after you. Also, I give to you and your descendants after you the land in which you are a stranger, all the land of Canaan, as an everlasting possession; and I will be their God. And God said to Abraham: As for you, you shall keep my covenant, you and your descendants after you throughout their generations. This is my covenant which you shall keep, between Me and you and your descendants after you: Every male child among you shall be circumcised, and you shall be circumcised in the flesh of the foreskin, and it shall be a sign of the covenant between me and you. He who is eight days old among you shall be circumcised, every male child in your generations, he who is born in your house or bought with money from any stranger who is not descendants. He who is born in your house and he who is bought with money must be circumcised, and my covenant shall be in your flesh for an everlasting covenant. And the circumcised male child who is not circumcised in the flesh of his foreskin, that person shall be cut off from his people; he has broken my covenant." (Genesis 17:6-14)

In this passage God states all of the provisions of the Abrahamic Covenant. God promises the land to Abraham and his descendants, but He also qualifies it with the act of Circumcision for all the males free or slave that are Abraham's descendants. From this we get the fact that God qualifies all His Covenants. Adam was not to eat of the tree of knowledge of good and evil. Noah was to build the Ark or ship to house his family which included his sons and their wives and Noah's wife as well. They were to enter the Ark at the command of God they and the animals during the flood. Obeying God was necessary for Noah and his family's salvation. God's Covenant with Abraham had promises about the land and the son he would have through Sarah, but there was the stipulation that all males had to be circumcised. We will see that the New Testament (Covenant) had qualifications as well. We will look at it when we get to it.

But this is not all that God promised Abraham. God then precedes to tell Abraham, he is going to have a son through Sarai and God also changes her name from Sarai to Sarah. Her earthily father called her Sarai meaning quarrelsome, but her Heavenly Father (God) calls her Sarah. As with Abraham God changed his name to be God like in character. Now Sarai name is changed to Sarah, so that it is more God like in character. The Hebrew name "Sarah" means Princess. God commanded her name change before the birth of the son, Isaac. This is all a part of the same Covenant with Abraham. "Then God said to Abraham, "As for Sarai, your wife, you shall not call her Sarai, but Sarah shall be her name. And I will bless her and give you a son by her; then I will bless her, and she shall be a mother of nations, kings of peoples shall be from her." (Genesis 17:15-16)

To Abraham this is a funny situation. This is the first detailed account of how God is going to supply an heir to Abraham. Abraham is now one hundred years old and Sarah is ninety. From this point on in history it is harder for older adults to have children. No doubt you have been in similar situations, where you have wondered how God is going to do what He has promised to do. Perhaps he is hoping he can hide this laughter from God. This is a faith situation, but listen to what Abraham says in his heart, but not out loud to God. It is very important that you see that Abraham says this in his heart, but he does not voice or confess it out loud. "Then Abraham fell on his face and laughed, and said in his heart, "Shall a child be born to a man who is one hundred years old? And shall Sarah, who is ninety years old bear a son? And Abraham said to God, "Oh that Ishmael might live before you." (Genesis 17:17-18)

What you see here is Abraham not voicing his doubts about the ability of God to do something that physically looks impossible. Instead Abraham is asking God to consider Ishmael. We tell God what is humanely possible rather than allow God to do the impossible. Then God answers all of Abraham's doubts and objections. "Then God said," No Sarah your wife shall bear a son, and you shall call his name Isaac (Laughter): I will establish My covenant with him for an everlasting covenant, and with his descendants after him. And as for Ishmael, I have heard you. Behold, I have blessed him, and will make him fruitful, and will multiply him exceedingly. He shall begat twelve princes and I will make him a great nation. But my covenant I will establish with Isaac, whom Sarah shall bear to you at the set time next year." (Genesis 17:19-21)

God answers all of Abraham's questions. Even the ones that Abraham did not voice but laughed about. Now Abraham must act in faith by circumcising everyone, including Ishmael and himself. This is the

Covenant Sign of the Abrahamic Covenant. This act of circumcision will also appear when we get to the Mosaic Covenant and still be the Covenant Sign of that Covenant as well. The Abrahamic Covenant is the foundational Covenant for Abraham and all his descendants—the Jewish people. The reason it is the foundational Covenant is because it is a Covenant of faith and all the Jewish people were in Abraham when he acted in faith toward what God told him to do, step by step. Each individual Jew or non-Jewish person must accept God by faith and live in that Covenant of faith. Romans chapter 4 explains why the Abrahamic Covenant is a Covenant of faith for everyone—Jew and Gentile. Here are some of the verses in Romans 4 in which that is explained but it would be good to study the entire chapter.

"Does this blessedness (the blessedness of faith in God) then come upon the circumcised only, or upon the uncircumcised also? For we say that faith was accounted to Abraham for righteousness. How then was it accounted? While he (Abraham) was circumcised or uncircumcised? Not while circumcised but while uncircumcised. And he received the sign of circumcision, a seal of the righteousness of the faith which he had while still uncircumcised, that he might be the father of all those who believe, though they are uncircumcised that righteousness might be imputed (given) to them also...Therefore it is of faith that it might be according to grace, so that the promise (Jesus) might be sure to all the seed, not only to those who are of the law (Jews), but to those (Gentiles) who are of the faith of Abraham, who is the father of us all." (Romans 4:9-11, 16)

"So, Abraham took Ishmael his son, all who were born in his house and all who were bought with his money, every male among the men of Abraham's house, and circumcised the flesh of their foreskin that very same day, as God had said to him. Abraham was ninety-nine years old when he was circumcised in the flesh of his foreskin. And Ishmael his son was thirteen years old when he was circumcised in the flesh of his foreskin." (Genesis 17:23-25) Although, Abraham did not understand how God was going to provide an heir as apart of the Covenant, he did immediately obey God and had all the males circumcised in his house including Ishmael and himself. To me that was an act of faith on the part of Abraham. No doubt, God knew Abraham's heart and honored that act of faith. Abraham would learn through this, that God is the God of the impossible.

Arthur W. Pink in his book, Gleanings in Genesis on page 182 brings out some remarkable facts about the 13-year period of silence that God demonstrated toward Abraham when he listened to his wife Sarah and took Hagar as his second wife in chapter 16 of Genesis. God doesn't appear to Abraham in chapter 17 until 13 years later. This is Mr. Pink's explanation for the silence of God those 13 years. Mr. Pink also discusses the importance of the number 13. Meaning that we learn there was an interval of just thirteen years between the incident mentioned in Genesis 16 and that recorded in Genesis 17, between Abram hearkening to the voice of Sarah and the Lord's appearing to him anew, and that this interval is one of spiritual bareness and is passed over in silence. "Ere we turn and consider the gracious revelation which the Lord made to Abram at the close of this interval let us first ask and ponder an important question…Why had Abram to wait all this while before the Lord appeared to him again? Is not the answer to be found in Romans 4:19? "And being not weak in faith; he considered not his own body now dead, when he was about a hundred years old, neither yet the deadness of Sarah's womb." God was about to act in grace, but ere grace can be displayed the creature has first to come to the end of himself: ere divine power is put forth man must learn his impotency…Not till Abram's body was "dead" would God fulfill His Word and give him a son…It might be tersely expressed thus: The Lord has a reason for His delays. God not only does that which is right and best but He always acts at the right and best time…"

I believe Mr. Pink has some valuable points for us to look at here, that we can see through Abraham's life. Thirteen years of silence from God says one thing to me. Abraham had leaned on the arm of flesh (Hagar's flesh) and he must learn that, that is not God's way. Before we point at Abraham, each of us may want to look at times when we have leaned on the flesh. Silence from God sometimes means, He is not pleased with our decision. This quotation from Mr. Pink's book helps to show why God delays in answering. Mr. Pink also pointed to some reasons why there is a delay and why God is not answering our prayers. "Are you anxiously exercised over God's delay? He has some wise purpose for it. He had with Abram and He has with you. From seventy-five—his age when he left Haran—to one hundred—when Isaac was born—was a long time to wait, but sequel evidenced the Lord's wisdom. God has more than one reason for His delays. Often it is to test the faith of His children, to develop their patience, to bring them to the end of themselves. His delays are in order that when He does act His delivering power may be more plainly evident, that what He does may be more deeply appreciated, and that in consequence He may be more illustriously glorified." (page 184)

Mr. Pink's description of God's delays and reasons for those delays, teaches us that God is always in His wisdom looking out for us. Sometimes as His children we are not prepared for immediate answers. We haven't grown enough spiritually for immediate answers. Those 13 years was like the year of silence with Noah; it was a period of growing spiritually learning to trust God no matter what—whether He appears and talks to you or not.

Notice through all this in chapter 17 of Genesis, God is causing Abraham to humble himself before God. Actually, in chapter 17 of Genesis, God is renewing the Covenant with Abraham. God had every right to walk away from Abraham, but He did not. As a result of God appearing to Abraham and telling him to be blameless or perfect, Abraham falls on his face before God. God from that point on is promising Abraham the Covenant; Abraham would be a father of many nations; he would be fruitful; many kings would come from his loins. Abraham fell on his face again when he heard Sarah was going to have a male son by him. God makes Abraham know that He is going to do all this.

Next God deals with Sarah in chapter 18 of Genesis. But before this happens in chapter 18, God is revealed to Abraham in the form of three men. Matthew Henry says, "These three men were three spiritual heavenly beings, now assuming human bodies, that they might be visible to Abraham and conversable with him. Some think that they were all created angels, others that one of them was the Son of God, the angel of the covenant, whom Abraham distinguished from the rest (v.3) and who is called Jehovah v.13." (Matthew Henry, A Commentary on the Whole Bible, Volume 1 Genesis to Deuteronomy, page 115) Another writer calls this a theophany. "A theophany is a manifestation of God in the Bible that is tangible to the human senses. In its most restrictive sense, it is a visible appearance of God in the Old Testament (Covenant) period, often, but not always in human form...Many commentators believe this could be a Christophany, a preincarnate appearance of Christ." (gotquestions.org. a theophany)

Personally, I believe this is a theophany in which the Trinity is revealed. There are three persons in the God-head; Father, Son and Holy Spirit. Genesis 18:2-4 says, "So he (Abraham) lifted his eyes and looked and behold, three men (Father, Son, and Holy Spirit) were standing by him; and when he (Abraham) saw them, he ran from the tent door to meet them, and bowed himself to the ground, and said, "My Lord, if I have found favor in your sight, do not pass on by your servant, Please let a little water be brought to wash your feet, and rest yourselves under the tree..." The fact that Abraham bowed down to them, says to me that these three men represent God in the Trinity at least in this initial meeting. Someone may ask, why be interested in this revelation of the three men in regard to the Covenant Relationship with God? It is because Abraham recognized that these three men represented God in flesh like people. Only a Covenant Relationship with God, would enable Abraham to know that this is God in the flesh.

The next thing that happens is God tests both Sarah and Abraham. It is evident that one of the men was God the Father and Abraham knew this by revelation. God uses the same words He used in chapter 17 of Genesis in verse 10 of Genesis chapter 18. "And He said, "I will certainly return to you according to the time of life, and behold Sarah your wife shall have a son..." And in actuality the Scripture calls Him "Lord" in verses 13 and 14. In the original Hebrew the word "Lord" is Jehovah in both verses. The Hebrew word is Yhovih meaning self-existent One or Eternal One, the Jewish national name of God-Jehovah (3068) (Strong's Concordance; Hebrew and Chaldean Dictionary, page 47)

Abraham laughed in his hearing this in Genesis 17:17, but now it is Sarah who seems to be caught off guard by what the Lord is saying. This is the third time Abraham has heard this, therefore, he is probably not laughing anymore. Because of their age, Sarah does laugh about it. "Now Abraham and Sarah were old, well advanced in age; and Sarah had passed the age of child-bearing, therefore Sarah laughed within herself, saying, "After I have grown old, shall I have pleasure, my lord being old also?" (Genesis 18:11-12) Notice this is a laugh within herself, but God knew she had laughed within herself. Listen to what God said to Abraham. "And the Lord said to Abraham, "Why did Sarah laugh saying, "Shall I surely bear a son since I am old?" "Is anything too hard for the Lord? At the appointed time, I will return to you, according to the time of life, and Sarah shall have a son." (Genesis 18:13-14) Sarah tries to deny it, but the Lord tells her, "No but you did laugh." (Genesis 18:15)

Again, God is dealing with them according to Covenant. God is letting both of them know what is going to happen to them in the future. Unless one is walking in Covenant Relationship with God, He will not tell them what is happening next. Some call this a prophetic vision, but this is really the results of walking in Covenant Relationship. If God says something one time to us about the future, most everyone of us believe it will come to pass just as God said it. But God told Abraham four times he was going to have a son and even told him what to call his son. His name would be Isaac (Laughter).

Abraham the Intercessor

Then the three men (God the Father, God the Son and God the Holy Spirit) got up to leave. But the Lord decides to tell Abraham what He is going to do with Sodom and Gomorrah. This is what the Lord told Abraham about Sodom and Gomorrah. "Because of the outcry against Sodom and Gomorrah is great, and because their sin is very grievous, I will go down now and see whether they have done altogether according to the outcry against it that has come down to Me and if not, I will know." (Genesis 18:20-21) Abraham knew they were very wicked and that Lot, his wife and daughters were living in Sodom and Gomorrah. Therefore, he began to intercede and plead with the Lord about the righteous that might be there in Sodom and Gomorrah. It is estimated by Biblical scholars there were between 600 to 1200 people in Sodom and Gomorrah at its destruction.

It is interesting to note how bold Abraham was in interceding for Sodom and Gomorrah in Genesis 18. I believe the reason Abraham interceded to the Lord so strongly for Sodom and Gomorrah was because of Lot, his nephew, Lot's wife, and his children that lived in Sodom. Looking back at the war the kings of Sodom and Gomorrah had with Chedorlaomer one can see that Abraham wasn't really interested in Sodom and Gomorrah. He was only concerned about his nephew, Lot. Listen to what Genesis 14:12, 14, and 16 says. "They also took Lot, Abram's brother's son who dwelt in Sodom and his goods and departed…Now when Abram heard that his brother was taken captive, he armed his three hundred and eighteen trained servants who were born in his house and went in pursuit as far as Dan…So he (Abraham) brought back all the goods, and also brought back his brother Lot and his goods, as well as the women and people."

Abraham cared for Lot and he must have prayed often for Lot. Lot had made some bad choices and now he was going to suffer for it. After that battle with the Kings, Lot went right back to Sodom to live and maintain his earthily riches. That battle in Genesis 14 did nothing to change Lot's mind and cause him to move away from Sodom. "Bad company corrupts good habits." (1st Corinthians 15:33) Lot would not willing leave Sodom and all it evil influences.

The difference between Abraham and Lot is Abraham had a Covenant Relationship with God. Lot's relationship with God was distant and far removed. It is for sure that Lot did not confer or commune with God about the decisions he made. After Lot left Abraham as is described in Genesis 13, he got further and further away from God, until one day he was living in Sodom and he and his family were under the evil influences of that city. In all of this, Abraham was praying and interceding for Lot. Intercession is apart of the Covenant Relationship, we have with God. "Let us therefore come boldly to the throne of grace, that we may obtain mercy and find grace to help in time of need." (Hebrews 4:16) And that is exactly what Abraham did, when he knew God was going to Sodom and Gomorrah to see if it needed to be destroyed. Abraham knew God would destroy it because those five cities in the plain were very wicked. Therefore, his overriding concern was for Lot and his family.

One can tell that Abraham was an intercessor. He stands before God and each time Abraham talks to God about a lesser number of righteous people. (Genesis 18:16-33) Because of Lot and his family, Abraham is asking God to spare Sodom. Each time he humbles himself before God saying, "I am but dust and ashes…" (Genesis 18:27) Finally, the Lord tells Abraham if he finds 10 righteous people in Sodom, He won't destroy it.

The Sin of Lot

In chapter 19 of Genesis, one can immediately see that Lot doesn't have a Covenant Relationship with God. To put it in New Testament (Covenant) terms Lot is a very carnal Christian, along with his wife and children. They have become worldly Christians. However, Peter in the New Testament (Covenant) called Lot a righteous man. Listen to what the Apostle Peter says in 2nd Peter 2:7. "…and delivered righteous Lot, who was oppressed with the filthy conduct of the wicked." Although Peter considered Lot to be a righteous man, we will still see that there is such a contrast between Abraham and Lot.

Reverend Wick Brooman, a contributor of The Zondervan Pictorial Bible Dictionary, page 493 says this about Lot, Abraham's nephew. "(2) Decision and destiny. Due to a conflict between their herdsmen, Abraham suggested that his nephew (Lot) choose another place. Lot prompted by selfishness, chose the environs of Sodom, a city that had already been notorious because of its wickedness. (Genesis 13:5-13) This fatal choice determined his subsequent destiny. It was Abraham now who maintained the greater spiritual status (Covenant Relationship with God). (Genesis 13:14-18) … (4) Depravity and degeneration. Angels then visited Lot in Sodom to hasten his departure from the imminent dooms decreed upon the wicked city. Though originally only a sojourner (Genesis 19:9) Lot acted like a citizen: he had imbibed their mores and standards. Look at his willingness to sacrifice his daughters' chastity (Genesis 19:8); his utter ineffectiveness in dealing with his sons-in-law (Genesis 19:14); his hesitation in leaving the doomed city (Genesis 19:15); his unwillingness to leave the comforts of the city."

From this quotation, one can see how far Lot had wandered away from God. In fact, he was beginning to believe like the men of Sodom. In Genesis 19, we know though he did recognize the angels God had sent to him and he did respect them. "Now the two angels came to Sodom in the evening, and Lot was sitting in the gate of Sodom. When Lot saw them, he arose to meet them and he bowed himself with his face toward the ground." (Genesis 19:1)

Notice that Lot Is sitting at the city gate entrance of Sodom. Fred H. Wight in his book, Manners and Customs of Bible Lands, page 240, believes that Lot was a judicial judge for Sodom. "City gates is a place for holding court. One of the most important uses of the gates of an ancient city was for holding court. Stone seats were provided for the judges. Thus, Lot sat in the gate as a judge (Genesis 19:1) …" From this we understand that Lot was in an official capacity in Sodom. In mark contrast, he had lost all touch of what God wanted in his life. In the pages of Genesis that talks about Lot, God never extends His Covenant to Lot. Lot is a very selfish, greedy person. In New Testament (Covenant) terms we would call him a carnal Christian.

However, he does know that these are angels from God visiting him. He does reverence their presence. He invites them to his house; they decline, but on his insistence, they come to his house. Lot knows how wicked Sodom is and that is why he insists on there coming to his house. He goes on to cook a good meal with unleavened bread. This shows he knows what to cook for his Divine guests. I believe the guests are Angels unlike the three men who visited Abraham. I believe the three men were God, the Trinity, visiting Abraham. Genesis 19 does not say men but says angels.

The Angels then told Lot what was going to happen to the city of Sodom. "Then the men (two Angels, Genesis 19:1) said to Lot. "Have you anyone else here? Son-in-law, sons, your daughters, and whomever you have in the city—take them out of this place! For we will destroy this place, because the outcry against them has grown great before the face of the Lord, and the Lord has sent us to destroy it." (Genesis 19:12-13) Notice, that the three angels did not know who was apart of Lot's family. They only knew Lot. Therefore, Lot's family may not have had any relationship with God.

Lot did try to get his sons-in-law to leave the city. But they only laughed at him. They thought Lot was joking. This shows how backslidden Lot was; his own sons-in-law didn't consider him a good witness. Another thing that happened when the angels tried to persuade Lot to leave Sodom with his family also shows his backslidden condition. Genesis 19:16a says, "And while he lingered..." shows Lot wasn't in any hurry to leave Sodom, even though he knew it would be destroyed. Notice people today are not willing to leave their sinfulness. Even though those sinful habits, those sinful flesh traps will destroy them.

The Angels finally had to act. "And while he lingered, the men (Angels) took hold of his hand, his wife's hand, and the hands of the two daughters, the Lord being merciful to him (Lot) and they brought him out and set him outside the city." (Genesis 19:16) Then Lot argued with the Angels over where to go. The Angels suggested the mountains while Lot wanted to go to Zoar which means a little one. I believe the name of this city is significant. Zoar means a little one—a little sin. This is only in the eyes of man; in God's sight sin is sin. God hates sin. One can see how Lot's attitude toward sin had changed since he had been living in Sodom. That happens to anyone who rubs shoulders with the world. The Angels finally agree, but later in chapter 19 of Genesis Lot leaves even Zoar and flees to the mountains when he see the destruction of Sodom and Gomorrah.

The Angels in the meantime rain down fire and brimstone on Sodom and Gomorrah. To show how depraved Lot's wife was, she is told not to look back at the city of Sodom. But in her rebellious state, she looks back and is turned into a pillar of salt. "But his wife looked back behind him, and she became a pillar of salt." (Genesis 19:26) Jesus in talking about people who are left behind when He comes for the Church, His Bride, are those who have attached themselves to this world in Luke's Gospel chapter 17:31-32 Jesus mentions Lot's wife. "In that day, he who is on the housetop, and his goods are in the house, let him not come down to take them away. And likewise, the one who is in the field, let him not turn back. Remember Lot's wife." Notice that Lot's wife's name is not given. She became as Sodom and Gomorrah. She received the same judgment. So, will all those who want to hold onto this world's goods when our Lord returns. Also, those servants working in the field of the Lord and turn back to the world. Now we understand what our Lord and Savior, Jesus Christ, was talking about in Luke 17:31-32.

Now why did the Angels and the Lord wait until Lot and his family were out of Sodom and Gomorrah and had entered Zoar? It is simple to understand. Lot did not have a Covenant Relationship with God. Lot had very little relationship with God if any. This represent Christians who follow the Lord from a distance and only seek God when they are in a crisis. Usually, they depend on others to pray and intercede for them. This is the explanation when we read Genesis 19:27-29. Abraham was interceding for Lot. "And Abraham went early in the morning to the place where he had stood before the Lord. Then he looked toward Sodom and Gomorrah, and toward all the land of the plain, and he saw, and behold, the smoke of the land which went up like the smoke of a furnace. And it came to pass, when God destroyed the cities of the plain, that God remembered Abraham, and sent Lot out of the midst of the overthrow, when He overthrew the cities in which Lot dwelt." It was Abraham's position of prayer that saved Lot and his daughters from certain destruction. No doubt Abraham had a life of prayer and intercession. God had extended His Covenant Relationship to Abraham and Abraham used that relationship to cause God to decide to remove Lot and his daughters from Sodom. Covenant Relationship with God has its rewards. People with that Covenant Relationship with God enables them to plead with God for their loved ones.

But because Lot was selfish and had all but lost his relationship with God; he lost all of his wealth, his home and his wife. He did not have a Covenant Relationship with God nor did God even approach him about it. He did not seek God first and his life shows it. "But seek first the kingdom of God and His righteousness, and all these things shall be added to you." (Matthew 6:33) God does not extend Covenant Relationship to everyone. God looks to see where our heart is. "Do not lay up for yourselves treasures on earth, where moth and rust destroys and where thieves break in and steal; but lay up for yourselves treasures in heaven, where neither moth nor rust destroys and where thieves do not break in and steal. For where your treasure is, there your heart will be also." (Matthew 6:19-21)

It is true we can be saved and make it to Heaven, but like Lot have little or no relationship with God. Many people just want to barely get into the Kingdom of God. Apostle Peter called Lot righteous (2nd Peter 2:7) and yet his life was anything but victorious over the world, the flesh and the devil. Lot's latter days does not show any victory in this life, but defeat. He had caused his daughters to live in wicked Sodom and they had taken on the sin and life style there. This is brought out in chapter 19 of Genesis verses 30 to 38. Unknown to Lot each daughter made Lot drunk with wine and they committed the sin of incest. They wanted children that would carry on the name of Lot, but that was not the way to do it. They should have sought God and He would have given them wise counsel on what to do. He probably would have provided godly men for them.

Sad to say, Lot had other options. He could have returned to Abraham and gotten suitable mates for his daughters. He could have started over under Abraham's leadership. But he went to the mountains instead and they lived in a cave. Because Lot was not praying nor did he have a Covenant Relationship with God, his daughters determined his destiny on earth. We do not hear about Lot anymore, but the sons that were born through his daughters, Moab and Ben-Ammi, produced nations that would later attack Israel, the descendants of Abraham, in the Wilderness.

Abraham, A Sojourner in the Land of the Philistines

In the meantime, Abraham decides to move and go into the country owned by the Philistines. Abraham forgets his Covenant Relationship with God. Abraham again acts in fear like he did in Egypt calling his wife his sister. This is true, but not the whole truth. She is his half-sister because she is the daughter of Abraham's father, but not by the same mother. "But indeed, she is truly my sister. She is the daughter of my father, but not the daughter of my mother; and she became my wife." (Genesis 20:12) The problem with Abraham is he doesn't believe God can protect him when he tells all the truth—that Sarah is his wife. He is afraid that Abimelech does not fear God and will kill him for his wife. This is the second time that Abraham has shown his lack of faith in God about protecting him from a worldly leader. Yet, God in His mercy tells Abimelech the truth about Sarah. There is no Scriptural evidence that God got after Abraham and chastised him. In a dream God reveals the truth to Abimelech and tells him to have Abraham, a Prophet, to pray for Abimelech, his family and kingdom. Abimelech restores Sarah to Abraham and has Abraham pray over him, his family, and his servants under the direction of God. He also gives Abraham sheep, oxen, male and female servants and a thousand pieces of silver. "So, Abraham prayed to God and God healed Abimelech, his wife and his maidservants. Then they bore children, for the Lord had closed up all the wombs of the house of Abimelech because of Sarah, Abraham's wife." (Genesis 20:17-18)

What does this have to do with a Covenant Relationship with God? There are a few things one can get from Abraham's experience with Abimelech. First, Abimelech recognizes and sees the relationship that Abraham has with God. God reveals that to him in a dream and even Abimelech's life is altered by Abraham's relationship. Secondly, God blesses Abimelech, his family and the Philistines when Sarah is restored. She is blessed and protected by that Covenant Relationship God has with Abraham. Abraham is her covering before God. Finally, Abraham is now seen as a Prophet, because God called him to be a Prophet and uses that title of Prophet when God spoke to Abimelech in the dream. By the way this is the first time that the title Prophet is used in Scripture.

Therefore, Abraham has become in actuality a Prophet, Priest and King over his household. God called Abraham a Prophet to Abimelech. As a Prophet, Abraham knew what God was planning to do. A Prophet and a Covenant Keeper know what is coming next. (Genesis 18:17-21) At different places, Abraham had erected altars and offered sacrifices to God, making him a Priest before God. (Genesis 12:8; 15:9-18; 18:1-15) A Priest of God also intercedes for others. (Genesis 18:16-33; 19:27-29) Abraham was also considered a King or lord over his family and servants. (Genesis 18:17-21) Even Sarah called Abraham, her husband, lord. "...as Sarah obeyed Abraham, calling him lord, whose daughters you are if you do good and are not afraid with any terror." (1st Peter 3:16) The word "lord" in this passage is kurios meaning supreme in authority, master, a respectful title, a lord wielding authority for good.

In the Far East, Oriental customs prevail and thus it was at Abraham's dwelling. In Manners and Customs of Bible Lands by Fred H. Wright on page 103 it describes Abraham's position as lord over his house. "Oriental meaning attached to the word "father." The Oriental idea of the family is a little kingdom within itself, over which the father is the supreme ruler. Every company of travelers, every tribe, every community, every family must have a "father," who is the head of a group...The Oriental mind cannot conceive of any band or group without somebody being "the father" of it...Supremacy of the father under the Patriarchal system...Under the Patriarchal administration the father (Abraham) is supreme in command. The authority which the father has, extends to his wife, to his children, his children's children, his servants and to all his household, and if he is the Sheik, it extends to all the tribe."

Thus, with Abraham, whatever Abraham said in his house was law. That is why Sarah obeyed Abraham when in Egypt he told her to call him (Abraham), her brother. That is why possibly Lot did not return to Abraham and come under his rule. Lot did not want to be under Abraham again. To apply this to us as Christians, we are under God our Father, and must do as He says, otherwise we are in rebellion. That is why, it is so important to have a Covenant Relationship with God. In this Covenant

Relationship, we come to know what God's heart is and what He desires for us and from us.

We maybe a lot like Abraham. God promised Abraham a son. Abraham then tried to bring that about by having Hagar, the Egyptian, to become his wife and by having a child by her in the flesh. Often, we try to help God out when He doesn't need our help. God knows what He wants to do and we should yield to Him in all things.

The Birth and Test of Isaac

Chapter 21 of Genesis, begins with God visiting Sarah and she giving birth to a son, Isaac. Sarah laughed about it, when she was told she was going to have a baby, but God always fulfills His promises. The birth of Isaac is the fulfillment of one of God's Covenant Promises. "And the Lord visited Sarah as He had said, and the Lord did for Sarah as He had spoken. For Sarah conceived and bore Abraham a son in his old age, at the set time of which God had spoken to him. And Abraham called the name of his son who was born to him—whom Sarah bore to him—Isaac (laughter). Then Abraham circumcised his son Isaac when he was eight days old, as God had commanded him. Now Abraham was one hundred years old when his son Isaac was born to him. And Sarah said, "God has made me laugh, so that all who hear will laugh with me. She also said, "Who would have said to Abraham that Sarah would nurse children? For I have born him a son in his old age." (Genesis 21:1-7)

I wanted to quote this whole passage to show that God did not need any help fulfilling His Covenant Promises. "God is not a man, that he should lie, nor a son of man, that He should repent? Has He said, and will He not do it? Or has He spoken, and will He not make it good?" (Numbers 23:19) Notice that both Abraham and Sarah did everything in regard to the Covenant of God. They called this new son, Isaac, according to the commandment of God. They circumcised him on the eighth day as God commanded, even as all the males in Abraham's house were circumcised. Therefore, they were walking in obedience to God. When one walks in faith toward God, they obey what God says.

God promised Abraham and Sarah, that Isaac would be born in a set time. In the 18th chapter of Genesis, God promises Abraham the birth of Isaac at a certain time. "Is anything to hard for the Lord? At the appointed time I will return to you, according to the time of life, and Sarah shall have a son." (Genesis 18:14) There was an appointed time of God for the birth of Isaac. "For Sarah conceived and bore Abraham a son in his old age, at the set time of which God had spoken to him." (Genesis 21:2) God promised it twice. The first time in Genesis 17:21 and then He repeats it again in Genesis 18:14. "But My Covenant I will establish with Isaac, whom Sarah shall bear to you at this set time next year." (Genesis 17:21) God works according to His calendar, not according to our calendar. There is a fulness of time with God. This is mentioned in the New Testament in the coming of Jesus Christ. "But when the fulness of time had come, God sent forth His Son (Jesus) born of a woman, born under the law to redeem those who were under the law, that we might receive the adoption of sons." (Galatians 4:4-5) We call this the time element or timing of God. Everything in Covenant Relationship has to do with the timing of God. It is when God wants to bring things about and in Abraham's case it was different than Abraham's timing. Both Abraham and Sarah laughed within themselves, but the good thing is they did not express doubt in words. That is why when Isaac was born, they could see that nothing was too hard for God. We get off the track of faith when we express our doubts and fears.

It is fitting that the name Isaac means to laugh. "From the Hebrew name Yitzchag meaning "he will laugh, he will rejoice derived from tzachag meaning to laugh. The Old Testament explains this meaning by recounting that Abraham laughed when God told him that his aged wife Sarah would become pregnant with Isaac. (See Genesis 17:17)" This is taken from www.netfind.com/search--Issac Bible Name Meaning/Search Here and Browse Results...

The next important thing about Isaac is he began to grow up. This brings us to the point in Isaac's life where he is weaned from his mother's milk. "So, the child grew and was weaned. And Abraham made a great feast on the same day that Isaac was weaned." (Genesis 21:8) This is a very significant happening in the life of Isaac. Biblical scholars say that in the

Old Testament children were weaned from 18 months to five years depending on the health of the child. There is some cultural background taken from Got Questions/What Was the Significance of Weaning a Child in the Bible (Genesis 21:8)? "According to Jewish custom, the time when a child was weaned is cause for celebration. A weaned child has survived the fragile stage of infancy and can now eat solid food rather than breastfed from his or her mother." There was "High infant mortality rates existed in ancient cultures…Because of the risks that infants faced, the celebration of a child's weaning was a natural and important part of the culture. If a child had developed past the need for the physical support of a mother, then he or she had reached a new stage of life that greatly increased the likelihood of good health." (Got Questions…) One of the realities that takes place with Isaac coming to the place of being weaned away from his mother's milk and able to eat solid food, is he is less under his mother's supervision and more or less under his father's supervision. We will see the expression of this when we reach Genesis 22.

Matthew Henry makes this observation in the Matthew Henry Commentary, Volume I Genesis to Deuteronomy, page 132. "And then it was that Abraham made a great feast for his friends and neighbors, in thankfulness to God for His mercy to him. He made this feast, not on the day that Isaac was born, that would have been too great a disturbance to Sarah; nor on the day he (Isaac) was circumcised, that would have been too great a diversion from the ordinance; but on the day he was weaned, because God's blessing upon the nursing of children, and the preservation of them through the perils of the infant age, are signal instances of the care and tenderness of the divine providence, which ought to be acknowledged to its praises."

Now Isaac has learned from Sarah, his mother, about God and how he was brought into this world. He learned what Sarah's appreciation and worship of God and all that God has taught her. Now the learning is switched for Isaac and now he will learn from his father, Abraham, about God and the worship of God. After the weaning, Isaac comes under his father's supervision. Abraham from that point on will be Isaac's instructor. There is a day when we are no longer under guardians and stewards, but are under our Heavenly Father's instruction. "Now I say that the heir, as long as he is a child, does not differ at all from a slave though he is master of all, but is under guardians and stewards until the time appointed by the father (our Heavenly Father)." (Galatians 4:1-2)

The sad commentary of the church today is that there are so many baby Christians that have not been weaned from the mother's milk (Church milk). Because of this, they cannot feed on solid food. A lot of Christians say, "I go to church to be fed." But when will those individuals start feeding themselves and others. Listen to what the writer of Hebrews says. "For though by this time you ought to be teachers, you need someone to teach you again the first principles of the oracles of God, and you have come to need milk and not solid food. For everyone who partakes only of milk is unskilled in the word of righteousness, for he is a babe. But solid food belongs to those who are of full age (mature), that is, those by reason of use (practice) have their senses exercised to discern both good and evil." (Hebrews 5:12-14)

Abraham Choosing Isaac Over Ishmael

It must have been during the Feast of Weaning that Sarah saw Ishmael laughing at Isaac. By this time Ishmael must have been 13 or 14 years of age. Evidently, Sarah realized that Ishmael would try to take advantage of Isaac. Normally, the first born of Abraham would be heir of all that Abraham had. Isaac would be God's choice of the firstborn of Abraham. God had already told Abraham that Isaac would be the child that would be blessed and would inherit God's Covenant Promises. In Genesis 17:19, 21, God tells Abraham that His Covenant would be through Isaac. "Then God said, "No Sarah your wife shall bear a son, and you shall call his name Isaac; I will establish My covenant with him for an everlasting Covenant, and with his descendants after him...But My covenant I will establish with Isaac whom Sarah shall bear to you at this set time next year."

So, when Sarah saw Ishmael scoffing (or laughing) at Isaac, she went to Abraham and told him to get rid of the bond woman and her son. "Therefore, she said to Abraham, "Cast out this bondwoman and her son;

for the son of the bondwoman shall not be heir with my son, namely with Isaac." (Genesis 21:10) This Scripture along with the following Scriptures are found in Galatians the fourth chapter. But before we get into those we have to see that to some extent Abraham's flesh was tied to Hagar and his son, Ishmael. They have been living in the same tent with Abraham and Sarah. But when Isaac is born the true nature of Ishmael is revealed. Listen to what Arthur W. Pink says about Ishmael and Isaac in Gleanings in Genesis, page 215. "Fourth…it is to be noted that it was the birth of Isaac which revealed the true character of Ishmael. We know practically nothing of Ishmael's life before the birth of Isaac, but as soon as the child of promise made his appearance the real nature of Hagar's son was made manifest. He may have been very quiet and orderly before, but as soon as the child of God's quickening power came on the scene, Ishmael showed what he was by persecuting and mocking him. Here again the type holds good. It is not until the believer receives the new nature that he discovers the real character of the old…It is not until we are born again we learn what a horrible and vile thing the flesh is…"

Now, Abraham has a choice to make. Does he keep Ishmael, a type of the flesh, and his mother, Hagar or does he listen to Sarah and what God said all along? The Scripture shows that Abraham is in turmoil. "And the matter was very displeasing in Abraham's sight because of his son (Ishmael)." (Genesis 21:11) When we see our flesh as Abraham saw his, we need a revelation from God. Abraham must have turned to God for an answer. God had an answer for him. "But God said to Abraham, "Do not let it be displeasing in your sight because of the lad (Ishmael) or because of your bond woman (Hagar). Whatever Sarah has said to you, listen to her voice; for in Isaac your seed shall be called. Yet I will also make a nation of the son of the bondwoman, because he is your seed." (Genesis 21:12-13) Getting rid of your fleshly inclinations is not a happy time. The flesh produces sorrow and pain as it did with Abraham. Now let us look at Galatians 4:21-31. Paul quotes this same passage in Galatians four. The Apostle Paul describes the relationship that Abraham had with Sarah, his wife, and Hagar, who Sarah had given to him to be his wife.

"For it is written that Abraham had two sons; the one by a bondwoman, the other by a free woman. But he who was of the bondwoman was born according to the flesh, and he of the free woman through promise, which things are symbolic. For these are the two covenants; the one from Mount Sinai (Law) which gives birth to bondage, which is Hagar—for this Hagar is Mount Sinai (Law) in Arabia, and corresponds to Jerusalem which now is, and is in bondage with her children (to the Law)—but the Jerusalem above (free in the Spirit) is free, which is the mother of us all." (Galatians 4:22-26)

Hagar is a second wife to Abraham that is a wife of the flesh. She gives birth to a son, Ishmael, who is a son after the flesh. Sarah on the other hand is the first wife to Abraham and is a wife after the Spirit and she gives birth to a son, Isaac, a son of promise after the Spirit. Paul is using this happening in the Old Testament (Covenant) as a symbol or allegory. A symbol or allegory represents a deeper meaning than is on the surface. This is what the Apostle Paul does with the life of Abraham and the birth of the two sons. Ishmael is representing the son of the flesh and is in bondage to the law (Covenant of Law) that was taught by the lower Jerusalem. Whereas, Isaac represents the son of the Spirit and freedom(The New Covenant). Paul sums up everything in Galatians 4:28-31. "Now we, brethren, as Isaac was, are children of promise. But, as he who was born according to the flesh then persecuted him who was born according to the Spirit, even so it is now. Nevertheless, what does the Scripture say? "Cast out the bondwoman (Hagar) and her son (Ishmael) for the son of the bondwoman shall not be heir with the son (Isaac) of the freewoman (Sarah). So, then brethren, we are not children of the bondwoman (Hagar, Law) but of the free (Sarah, Spirit)."

Abraham was at a moment of decision. He could rely on his physical love for Hagar and Ishmael or he could follow what God was directing him to do and obey the Covenant he had made with God. God told him he would take care of Hagar and Ishmael. Abraham knew if they stayed, there would be constant conflict between Ishmael (flesh) and Isaac (Spirit). Only one could be acknowledged as the first-born son of Abraham. Abraham waited until he heard from God and he obeyed what God told him to do.

"Do not let it be displeasing in your sight because of the lad or because of your bondwoman. Whatever Sarah has said to you, listen to her voice; for in Isaac your seed shall be called." (Genesis 21:12) He waited for God to speak and although it hurt his flesh, he obeyed God immediately. "So, Abraham rose early in the morning, and took bread and a skin of water; and putting it on her shoulder, he gave it and the boy (Ishmael) to Hagar, and sent her away…" (Genesis 21:14a)

One thing I see about Abraham in all of this, is he immediately obeys God. He does not argue or complain. He just obeys the Lord and does what God says. He hears from God one day and does what God says the next day. To walk in Covenant Relationship with God, one must obey God and do what God says. The Scripture shows that God did provide for Hagar and Ishmael. They did not die. Egypt in the Scriptures is a type of the flesh. Hagar found Ishmael an Egyptian wife. If the Holy Spirit is to have His way, the flesh must leave. We call this in New Testament (Covenant) terms, crucifying the flesh. "And those who are Christ's have crucified the flesh with its passions and desires." (Galatians 5:24)

Abraham and Abimelech

Earlier in Chapter One of this book, we discussed Covenants between men. The latter part of this chapter deals with the Covenant Relationship between Abraham and Abimelech. Abimelech acknowledges God blessings upon Abraham's life. That is one thing the world will acknowledge usually; the blessings of God upon Christians when they walk with God. The blessings of God upon Abraham comes from him walking in Covenant Relationship with God. Thus, Abraham experienced that blessing and Abimelech knew it. The Old Testament (Covenant) is full of Covenants between men, as is seen in this chapter. "So, Abraham took sheep and oxen and gave them to Abimelech and the two of them make a covenant." (Genesis 21:27)

Abimelech is the Philistine King of Gerar near Gaza. At this time in history, Abraham chose to make a Covenant or treaty with him, so he could talk to Abimelech about a well Abimelech's servants had taken from him.

It seems that Abimelech, to stay in the good graces of Abraham, is willing to restore the well to Abraham. Although it is not stated that way, Abraham plants a tamarisk tree in Beersheba. It was a small tree with blue-green leaves that identified the spot where Abraham and Abimelech made a Covenant together.

Evidently, Abimelech knew that God would do whatever Abraham asked God to do. In the twentieth chapter of Genesis Abimelech, his family and his Kingdom would have suffered had Abraham not prayed for Abimelech, his family and Kingdom. Abimelech had taken Sarah to possibly be his wife, but God in a dream warned Abimelech that he and all he had would die, if he did not restore Sarah to Abraham. Abraham prayed and Abimelech and his family and all that he had was restored, after Sarah was given back to Abraham. (Genesis 20:1-18) A man walking in Covenant Relationship with God exerts great influence and power on those around him. That is why Abimelech wanted to make a Covenant with Abraham.

The Test of the Abrahamic Covenant

Genesis 22 presents the Test of the Abrahamic Covenant. Every Covenant of God has a Test. Noah's Test was to build and enter the Ark at the command of God. He went on to live out his days loving and serving God. If Noah had not built the Ark and entered the Ark at the command of God, Noah and his family would have been destroyed with the rest of mankind. Noah's Covenant would have failed. But he was an obedient servant of God. For God to extend the Covenant to an individual, they "must believe that He is, and that He is a rewarder of those who diligently seek Him." (Hebrews 11:6b)

The Covenant has been extended to Abraham. But now God must test Abraham. What will He test Abraham about? He will test Abraham about his love for Isaac. God must be the supreme love of Abraham's life. Abraham has come to love Isaac; it seems more than God. "Now it came to pass after these things that God tested Abraham, and said to him, "Abraham!" And he said, "Here I am." And He (God) said, "Take now your son, your only son Isaac, whom you love, and go to the land of Moriah, and offer him there as a burnt offering on one of the mountains of which I shall tell you." (Genesis 22:1-2)

You have to see that God is testing or touching someone God has given him. Notice that God does not recognize Ishmael as Abraham's son. He says, "Take now your son, your only son Isaac, whom you love." (Genesis 22:2c) God only recognizes the promise son of the Covenant, therefore, He does not consider Ishmael at all. Ishmael is a son of the flesh. "Now this I (Apostle Paul) say, brethren, that flesh and blood cannot inherit the kingdom of God; nor does corruption inherit incorruption." (1st Corinthians 15:50) Only the son that God promised will inherit all that God promises.

The second phase to notice in this exchange between God and Abraham is "...whom you love..." (Genesis 12:26b). At the heart of God is sacrifice. You can see this with God's only Son, Jesus. In the mind of God, Jesus is slain from the foundation of the world. (Revelation 13:5) But this has to do with Abraham's love for his son. God will not allow anything to come before Him. Possibly, Abraham's love for his son, may have become greater than Abraham's love for God. Possibly, God wanted to make sure that did not happen. This test to Abraham will remove all idolatry from Abraham's heart, if it existed. God would be first above all things. Since Isaac is a part of the Covenant Promises of God, Abraham must see that even the Promises of God will not be first in Abraham's heart and life. It must be God alone.

Again, Abraham has to decide what is going to be first; the Covenant of God or God, Himself. In Genesis 22:3-4 we see the answer of Abraham. "So, Abraham arose early in the morning and saddled his donkey and took two of his young men with him and Isaac his son; and he split the wood for the burnt offering and arose and went to the place of which God had told him." Abraham immediately obeys God. He did not wait around a few days to think about it. He even cuts his own wood for the burnt offering. When it is time to sacrifice, Abraham quickly does what God has asked him to do.

On the way up Mount Moriah, Isaac asks Abraham who or what is going to be the sacrifice. "But Isaac spoke to Abraham his father and said, "My father!" And he said, "Here I am, my son." And he said, "Look the fire and the wood, but where is the lamb for a burnt offering?" (Genesis 22:7) The Word of God says it better than I can. Abraham as yet has not told his son what God has said. I imagine it was hard for Abraham to talk about this sacrifice. But the King James Version says it better than any version I have read. "Abraham said, "My son, God will provide Himself a lamb for the sacrifice. So, they both went together." (Genesis 22:7 KJV) What I see in this translation is that God would be the Lamb that would be sacrificed two thousand years later. It is a prophetic word hidden in the Scriptures that only the Holy Spirit can reveal.

Abraham and Isaac came to the place that God had showed him. Abraham does exactly what God told him to do. "Then they came to the place of which God had told him. And Abraham built an altar there and placed the wood in order, and he bound Isaac his son and laid him on the altar, upon the wood. And Abraham stretched out his hand and took the knife to slay his son." (Genesis 22:9-10) A lot of doubters and unbelievers would say, "Abraham what are you thinking and doing?" Abraham had a faith that far surpasses ours at times. He loved God and was willing to do whatever God said. The writer of Hebrews shares what Abraham was thinking at that time.

"By faith Abraham, when he was tested, offered up Isaac, and he who had received the promises offered up his only begotten son, of whom it was said, "In Isaac your seed shall be called, accounting that God was able to raise him up, even from the dead, from which he also received him in a figurative sense." (Hebrews 11:17-19) The writer of Hebrews was showing us that Abraham believed God could raise Isaac from the dead, since God had ordered Abraham to kill Isaac. Abraham had seen the deadness of Sarah's womb and how God had brought life to her womb. She was able to conceive and bear a son, Isaac. Since, God could do that, Abraham believed He was able to raise Isaac from the dead. Abraham was still moving in faith and believing God for a positive outcome in this situation.

Abraham's hand was stretched out to slay his son, when he heard the Angel of the Lord cry out to Abraham.

"But the Angel of the Lord called to him (Abraham) from heaven and said, "Abraham, Abraham." And he said, "Here I am." And He said, "Do not lay your hand on the lad, or do anything to him: for now, I know that you fear God, since you have not withheld your son, your only son from Me." (Genesis 22:11-12) What God was saying is you have passed the test. "Abraham you will not even withhold your only son, Isaac, from Me." Every Covenant, God extends has a test and wants to see His sons and daughters pass the test. This was the test of the Abrahamic Covenant and Abraham had passed with flying colors. It was a test of faith and Abraham had shown God that he trusted God with the outcome.

As a side note, before we get into the blessings that God was going to bestow on Abraham, we need to look at this name—"the Angel of the Lord." Many Biblical scholars believe "the Angel of the Lord" is Jesus, Himself—the preincarnate Logos. Hear what Dr. Steven Barabas says about "the Angel of the Lord" in the Zondervan Pictorial Bible Dictionary, page 40. "In the Old Testament (Covenant) we find the oft-recurring phrase, "the Angel of the Lord," in which, in almost every case, this messenger is regarded as Deity and yet is distinguished from Jehovah (Genesis 16:7-14; 22:11-18; 31:11-13, Not all the references in the Dictionary). There is good reason for thinking that He is the pre-incarnate Logos, His appearance in Angelic or human form foreshadowing His coming in the flesh." I agree with Dr. Barabas. I believe "the Angel of the Lord" is the pre-incarnate Son of God, Jesus Christ. This may or may not be a side issue. God the Father commanded Abraham to kill his son, Isaac. But then has His pre-incarnate Son, Jesus, tell him not to kill his son. Only Deity could stop him from killing his son. It is fitting that Jesus stops Abraham, because two thousand years later, He is the sinless Son that is offered for the sins of the world. A type of Jesus is Isaac, but could not fulfill all of that because Isaac is not sinless.

Then, God did an amazing thing. He provided Abraham with a substitute sacrifice. "Then, Abraham lifted up his eyes and looked, and there behind him was a ram caught in the thicket by its horns. So, Abraham went and took the ram, and offered it up for a burnt offering instead of his son. And Abraham called the name of the place, "The Lord Will Provide" as it is said to this day, "In the Mount of the Lord it shall be provided." (Genesis 22:13-14) Abraham in his heart sacrificed his son, just like God has in His heart sacrificed His Son from the foundation of the world. This is but a type and shadow of that which is to come. We could never bring a sacrifice worthy enough to wash away our sins. Therefore, God provided the sacrifice for us. We just need to accept His sacrifice (Jesus) as our sacrifice, Jesus. Even so, God showed Abraham another picture of His provision for him, with the ram that he (Abraham) sacrificed instead of his son, Isaac.

The Picture Within A Picture

After Abraham passed the Covenant Test, God tells him what this means for generations to come through the loins of Abraham. Abraham is now under Covenant Blessings. "Then the Angel of the Lord (Jesus) called to Abraham a second time out of heaven, and said, "By Myself I have sworn, says the Lord, because you have done this thing, and not withheld your son, your only son (Isaac), in blessing I will bless you, and in multiplying I will multiply your descendants as the stars of heaven and as the sand which is on the sea shore; and your descendants shall possess the gates of your enemies. In your seed all the nations of the earth shall be blessed, because you have obeyed my voice." (Genesis 22:15-18) In other words, Abraham all the blessings I promised to you in the beginning are going to come to pass. Certainly, all this was not fulfilled in Abraham's lifetime. But Abraham knew God would do it. When God said, "In your seed (Jesus) all the nations of the earth shall be blessed…" (Genesis 22:18) He was talking about His Son, Jesus, coming to this earth to bless them with salvation and a Covenant Relationship.

Not only later the multitude that would be his descendants—Israel—would possess the land of Canaan that God promised them, but they would gain control of their enemies. That is yet to happen but will happen during the Millennial reign of Christ. The salvation, healing, deliverance, and restoration comes to believers no matter what nation when they receive the Lord Jesus as their Lord and Savior. In that way all the nations of the earth will be blessed. They will receive the seed of Jesus and be blessed. At this point, in the life of Abraham we can see how as John Hagee calls The Picture Behind the Picture. We are taking a quotation from John Hagee's Prophesy Study Bible on page 33. This quotation is the paragraph at the bottom called, The Greater Only Son.

"That is the obvious story on the surface. What then is the hidden picture? Commentators have long noted how this incident illustrates the salvation that God would one day provide for the world through Jesus Christ. The similarities are obvious. Isaac was Abraham's only legitimate son, and Christ is the only Son of God. Abraham loved God so much that he was willing to sacrifice his son. God loved the world so much He was willing to sacrifice His Son (Jesus). Isaac did not resist the will of his father; Christ did not resist the will of His Father. Isaac carried the wood for the sacrifice on Mount Moriah; Christ, at least until He was weary, carried His own Cross up to Golgotha. Even the site of Abraham's sacrifice is near the site where Jesus was crucified. The author of Chronicles identifies Mount Moriah as the mount where the temple in Jerusalem was built. (2nd Chronicles 3:1)"

"However, there is one more amazing parallel, which has to do with the way God provided Abraham with a substitute sacrifice. Over in a nearby thicket was a wild ram. "So, Abraham went and took the ram and offered it up for a burnt offering instead of his son." (Genesis 22:13). God has done the same for us. He has provided, not a ram, but the Lamb. Christ through His death on the Cross, has become our substitute. He died so that we might live."

There you have it, The Picture Behind the Picture. It is actually a prophetic word for the future. In fact, Abraham had a Revelation of Jesus Christ in the time during which he offered up Isaac. Having, the Angel of the Lord tell him what to do at the end when Abraham spared Isaac's life may have led to the Revelation of Jesus, that Jesus mentioned in John 8:56. "Your father Abraham rejoiced to see my day, and he saw it and was glad."

Jesus in this Scripture is talking about unbelieving Jews. This is what they said when Jesus stated that Revelation that Abraham had. "Then the Jews said to Him, You are not yet fifty years old, and have you seen Abraham." (John 8:57) This is when Jesus gives them a most startling Revelation. "Jesus said to them, "Most assuredly I say to you, before Abraham was, I AM." (John 8:58) Jesus by saying this identified Himself as the God, I AM. The Jews only had two choices just like us when God reveals Himself to us. We can accept that Revelation into our hearts and lives and let it change us, or we can reject it. The Jews chose to reject Jesus and the Revelation He had given them. "Then they took up stones to throw at Him, but Jesus hid Himself and went out of the Temple, going through the midst of them and passed by." (John 8:59) It was not yet the time for Jesus to lay down His life. Needless to say, Abraham in the Old Testament (Covenant) had a Revelation of Jesus Christ and saw what Jesus was going to do for mankind. He saw the blessing that was going to come through Jesus Christ.

Abraham's Last Days

As God said, Abraham's last days on earth were filled with unparalleled blessing. Abraham's seed had been established through Isaac. Even with God giving him the seed, Isaac, Abraham's love was tested by God. Would Abraham love Isaac more than God or would he love God more than Isaac? Abraham passed the test and Abraham showed God, he loved Him supremely. As a result, God blessed Abraham even more. "Now Abraham was old, well advanced in age; and the Lord had blessed Abraham in all things." (Genesis 24:1)

In Genesis 23, Abraham had to part with Sarah. Sarah had lived one hundred and twenty-seven years. Her passing must have been a great blow to Abraham. Now he must find a burial place in Canaan for her. He was living among the Hittites, the sons of Heth. He finally negotiates and buys a burial cave in a field belonging to Ephron, the Hittite for four hundred shekels of silver. Ephron would have given him the field and the cave, but Abraham insists on buying it. In my opinion, this shows Abraham's intention of staying in the land that God had promised him and Abraham's descendants. Back then, they saw through this, that Abraham's integrity of being a wise business man. He was considered by the Hittites at this time to be a wise, spiritual man who had a strong Covenant Relationship with his God. This spoke volumes to them of Abraham's integrity and honesty.

In Genesis 24, Abraham sees the need of his son, Isaac, finding a wife. In those days, the fathers usually found the wives for their sons. This was apart of the culture of the countries of the East. Abraham doesn't want Isaac to have a wife from the Hittites. Although Abraham negotiated with the Hittites for a burial site for Sarah, he did not want Isaac to marry one of their young women. The Hittites were a people given to idolatry. Abraham is getting old; therefore, he calls his oldest servant, Eliezer, to him and gives him instructions about getting Isaac a wife. Listen to the instructions he gives his servant, Eliezer of Damascus. So, Abraham said to the oldest servant (Eliezer) of his household, who ruled over all he had, "Please put your hand under my thigh, and I will make you swear by the Lord, the God of heaven and the God of the earth, that you will not take a wife for my son, from the daughters of the Canaanites among whom I dwell, but you shall go to my country (Haran) and to my kindred and take a wife for my son Isaac." (Genesis 24:2-4)

Got Questions.org says the reason Abraham didn't want his servant to get a Hittite wife is because the Hittites were an idolatrous people. They worshipped the sun, moon, stars and various nature gods. As we know choosing a wife is very important in Covenant Relationship. Back then as we said the marriages were arranged by parents. Therefore, Abraham wanted a wife for Isaac who would be open and could be persuaded to worship God Almighty. Abraham also told his servant not to take Isaac back to where he, Abraham, lived with his father, Terah. The city was also called Haran after his brother, Haran, and showed the influence that Haran had on the place. This would be the city where Eliezer would end up when looking for a wife for Isaac. Abraham's final warning to his servant is in Genesis 24:6. "Beware that you do not take my son (Isaac) back there." Why would Abraham say that? Abraham knew his brother's family was there and it would be a temptation for Isaac to return there. He might want to stay there. The land of Canaan is where God's Covenant Promises are to be fulfilled. God had promised Abraham that His Covenant and the Covenant blessing would be extended to Isaac in the land of Canaan. This Covenant Promise is found in Genesis 17:7-8.

"And I will establish My covenant between Me and you and your descendants (Isaac, later Jacob and later still Israel) after you in their generations for an everlasting covenant to be God to you and your descendants. Also, I give to you and your descendants after you the land to which you are a stranger, all the land of Canaan, as an everlasting possession and I will be their God." The Abrahamic Covenant extends to all of Abraham's descendants through Isaac. Down in verses 19 and 20 of Genesis 17, God makes it clear that it is through Isaac that God will continue to extend His Covenant. Abraham told God to look at Ishmael as the promised son and the son in which God would extend His Covenant. God totally rejected that thought from Abraham. "And Abraham said to God, "Oh, that Ishmael might live before You." Then God said: "No, Sarah your wife shall bear you a son, and you shall call his name Isaac; I will establish My covenant with him for an everlasting covenant, and with his descendants after him." (Genesis 17:19-20)

Eliezer does swear by an oath, that he would do all in his power to bring back a bride for Isaac. The servant, Eliezer, does end up in Nahor, which city name is used interchangeably with the city name Haran. Abraham is hoping and believing his brother's family (Nahor) will have a suitable bride for Isaac. When Eliezer gets to the outskirts of Nahor, Rebekah, "who was born to Bethuel, son of Milcah, the wife of Nahar," (Genesis 29:15) comes out with a pitcher of water. The servant of Abraham in advance has set a fleece before the Lord. A fleece in the Bible is asking God for a sign in order to determine God's guidance. He asks God that when he asks for a drink of water from her pitcher, that she will not only give him a drink of water but will also give water to all of his camels. He must have had quite a few camels. A lot of mature and immature Christians use this way of praying to get God's guidance. Rebekah comes with her pitcher of water and Eliezer asks her for a drink. She gives him a drink of water and offers to give all of his camels a drink of water, fulfilling the fleece that Eliezer had just prayed. "And when she (Rebekah) had finished giving him

(Eliezer) a drink, she said, "I will draw water for your camels also, until they had finished drinking." (Genesis 24:19)

Eliezer's next step was to find out whose family this young girl belonged. He rewards her for her work by giving her jewelry. That was the custom of that day. "So, it was, when the camels had finished drinking, that the man took a golden nose ring weighing half a shekel, and two bracelets for her wrists weighing ten shekels of gold, and said, "Whose daughter are you? Tell me, please, is there room in your father's house for us to lodge?" (Genesis 24:22-23) When she tells him, her name is Rebekah and that she is the daughter of Bethuel and this is Milcal's son, whom she bore to Nahor. She also told him that they had room for him. At that point Eliezer worshipped God, because he knew that God was directing his steps. I believe all of this is the result of the Covenant Relationship that Abraham had with God. All in Abraham's household was guided and blessed by that Covenant Relationship.

Next, Eliezer meets the family and this family was from the line of Nahor, Abraham's brother. That is what Abraham had been praying and interceding for all this time. Rebekah tells Laban, her brother, and he goes and meets Eliezer and brings them to their house, beds Eliezer's camels and bring Eliezer into his house. The customs of that day took over then and he was considered a guest and provided for as far as food and lodging. Guests could stay for an extended amount of time, usually as long as they wished.

But before Eliezer would eat anything he explains his mission and talks about Abraham and his son, Isaac. "So, he said, "I am Abraham's servant. The Lord has blessed my master greatly, and he has become great; and He has given him flocks and herds, silver and gold, male and female servants, and camels and donkeys. And Sarah my master's wife bore a son to my master when she is old; and to him he has given all that he has. Now my master made me swear, saying 'You shall not take a wife for my son from the daughters of the Canaanites, in whose land I dwell; but you shall go to my father's house and to my kindred, and take a wife for my son.' And I said to my master, 'Perhaps the woman will not follow me.' But he said to me, 'The Lord, before whom I walk, will send His angel with you and prosper your way; and you shall take a wife for my son from my kindred and from my father's house. You will be clear from your oath when you arrive among my kindred; for if they will not give her to you, then you will be released from my oath." (Genesis 24:34-41) From this passage, you see both the providential dealings of God and how God has directed Eliezer's steps. One also can see the faith of Abraham in guiding the servant of Abraham, Eliezer. Abraham knew that God would bring him to the right family and to the right young daughter that Isaac would have as a bride from Abraham's kindred or father's house. He would release Eliezer from the oath if they would not let the young girl go.

At this point, Eliezer begins to share the fleece he had prayed to the Lord about the young girl who would give him water and his camels water. (Genesis 24:42-44) He goes on to explain that before he finished speaking, Rebekah appears and he approaches her to give him a drink of water. Not only does she give him a drink but pours water in the troughs for the camels as much as they needed. He then asks the family if they will let Rebekah go. "Now if you will deal kindly and truly with my master, tell me. And if not, tell me, that I may turn to the right hand or to the left." (Genesis 24:49) Then you hear both Laban and Bethuel say that this is from the Lord. They are willing to let Rebekah go with Eliezer and to become Isaac's bride. (Genesis 24:50-51) As customary, Eliezer gives them gifts both to Rebekah, but also to her family. That was the custom of the day and was called a dowry. This is what a young man or family is willing to pay for a bride.

Everything seems to be happening according to God's plan, until the next morning. Eliezer wants to take Rebekah and leave. But her family is not so sure about that. This is a big decision on the part of Rebekah. She probably will not see her family any more. Therefore, listen to what they say to Eliezer and then what they ask Rebekah. "And he said to them, 'Do not hinder me, since the Lord has prospered my way; send me away so that I may go to my master.' So, they said, 'We will call the young woman and ask her personally. Then they called Rebekah and said to her, 'Will you go with this man?' and she said, 'I will go.' So, they sent away Rebekah their sister and her nurse, and Abraham's servant and his men. And they blessed Rebekah…" (Genesis 24:56-60a)

This was a tremendous test for Rebekah. She is leaving all she knows even her understanding of God and gods. Although, Laban and Bethuel acknowledge that this errand of Eliezer that Abraham put upon him and describe it as from the Lord. They do want Eliezer to take Rebekah and go to Canaan, but their understanding of God is different from that of Abraham and his household. They acknowledge God but they also worship other gods. Laban has compromised his beliefs about God and gods. He may have worshipped Jehovah God, but he also worshipped idols. Abraham has the true Revelation of God and of Christ. His family in Haran do not. Rebekah is leaving all this behind and we will see that she comes into a relationship with God that explains the twins in her womb later. Rebekah does tell Laban and Bethuel that she wants to go with Eliezer. (Genesis 24:58)

Laban and Bethuel bless Rebekah with this saying before she leaves. "Our sister, may you become the mother of thousands of ten thousands, and may your descendants possess the gates of those who hate them." (Genesis 24:60) It is good to leave the idolatrous situation and to be blessed by even those who do not understand God spiritually. Then Eliezer returned with Rebekah and when she saw Isaac, I believe she knew she had made the right decision. Eliezer tells Isaac all the details of finding his bride, Rebekah. The very fact that Rebekah gave Eliezer a drink of water and also his camels, shows she had a servant's heart. To follow God, one must have a servant heart. "Then Isaac brought her into his mother Sarah's tent; and he took Rebekah and she became his wife, and he loved her. So, Isaac was comforted after his mother's death." (Genesis 24:67)

When you are walking in obedience to the Covenant of God as Abraham was, God will move in your behalf. He will take care of those around you including your servants like he did with Eliezer, Abraham's servant. I don't believe Eliezer would have been able to be successful in this errand to bring back a bride for Isaac, if he too had not been walking in covenant relationship with God. That is why Covenant Relationship is so important.

Your whole household learns to trust God and walk with Him when you are walking in Covenant Relationship. Plus, God is continually telling you what is ahead prophetically.

Genesis 25 is a fulfillment of God's prophetic word over Abraham. In Genesis 17:5-6, God tells Abraham he would be a father of many nations. "No longer shall your name be Abram, but your name shall be Abraham; for I have made you a father of many nations. I will make you exceedingly fruitful, and I will make nations of you and kings shall come from you." This comes to pass when Abraham marries Keturah in the last years of his life. Of course, God had promised Abraham that even Ishmael would found a nation. Prophetically, God told him this when He told him Isaac would be the seed of promise in Genesis 17:20. "And as for Ishmael, I have heard you. Behold, I have blessed him, and will make him fruitful, and will multiply him exceedingly. He shall begat twelve princes, and I will make him a great nation."

This came to pass after Abraham sent Hagar and Ishmael away. He raised up a nation in the wilderness of Paran. This was the beginning of nations that would come out of Abraham. Keturah bore him Zimram, Jokshan, Medan, Midan, Ishbak, and Shual. (Genesis 25:2) These sons later form all of the Arabic nations that we see today. Christianity.stackexchange.com shared this information that the Ishmalites later became what is called the Bedouins today and also shared the information about Keturah's sons. This was a fulfillment of the prophetic word that God gave Abraham in Genesis 17:5-6.

All of the account of Abraham's life is a result of Abraham following God by faith and trusting God's Covenant Promises. He was obedient to God. Every time God told him to do something, he did it and usually immediately. God extended His Covenant to him as a result of his obedience and faith. In one of the last chapters before Abraham's death it opens the chapter with this statement. "Now Abraham was old, and well advanced in age; and the Lord had blessed him in all things." (Genesis 24:1)

Summary of the Abrahamic Covenant

There are several Revelations a New Testament (Covenant) believer can receive from the Abrahamic Covenant. The first thing is that Abraham had to have a Revelation of God in order to follow God wherever He might lead. One must have a Revelation of God. It is hard to follow God without Divine Revelation. For Abraham this took place in Ur of the Chaldeans. "The God of glory appeared (revealed Himself) to our father Abraham when he was in Mesopotamia before he dwelt in Haran." (Acts 2:2b) God revealed Himself to Abraham and then gave him his marching orders.

The next revelation Abraham had to have in order to follow God, was the earthily bondages had to die. As we discussed earlier, Abraham's father, Terah, was still leading him around. It is true, Terah was trying to lead him where God told Abraham to go, but God wanted Abraham to just follow him. The earthily ties of his father had to die. "And Terah took his son, Abram, and his grandson Lot, the son of Haran, and his daughter-in-law, Sarai, his son Abram's wife, and they went out with them from Ur of the Chaldeans to go to the land of Canaan, and they came to Haran and dwelt there. So, the days of Terah were two hundred and five years and Terah died in Haran." (Genesis 11:31-32) Notice who is leading Abraham when they leave Ur. Terah is leading his whole family out of Ur. The earthily bondages and ties have to die before one can hear the voice of God clearly. These earthily bondages can become soul ties. Notice God waited until Terah died before He led Abraham into Canaan. God was full of mercy and grace toward Abraham. The culture of the day had to die in Abraham before he could move on with God.

The third revelation one gets in studying about Abraham is that he is considered to be the father of faith. Faith is usually a revelation of something God wants you to do and you must take each step that God is leading you to take. As soon as Terah died, Abraham left Haran with his wife, Sarah, and his nephew Lot. Faith and obedience to God are tied together. Abraham followed God and obeyed God taking each step that God showed him. This is what God said about the faith of Abraham. "By faith Abraham obeyed when he was called to go out to the place which he would afterward receive as an inheritance. And he went out, not knowing where he was going. By faith he sojourned in the land of promise as in a foreign country, dwelling in tents with Isaac and Jacob, the heirs with him of the same promise." (Hebrew 11:8-9) A former Bible College teacher of mine, J.W. Luman, said that faith is knowledge in action. The knowledge that Abraham was given by God was Spirit-revealed knowledge that enabled him to go to a country that he did not know. God promised him, he would inherit that land, the land of Canaan. Abraham believed God's Covenant Promises about the land. Then later God promised him a son through Sarah his wife.

Probably, one of the greatest revelations in Abraham's Covenant Relationship was staying faithful to God when Abraham was tested. God after giving Abraham a son, Isaac, God asked Abraham to sacrifice him as a burnt offering. God wanted Abraham to kill him. Many of us might not understand why God would ask such a thing of Abraham. Our western culture gets in the way of understanding why God requires sacrifice. If we will admit the truth, it is hard for us to understand the Cross of Jesus Christ. Why would God require His Son, Jesus, to die two thousand years later? Sin has to be atoned for and God requires a blood sacrifice. Many of us might not have stayed true to God like Abraham did, if we were under similar circumstances. This is what God says about it in Hebrews 11. "By faith when he (Abraham) was tested offered up Isaac, and he who had received the promises offered up his only begotten son, of whom it was said, 'In Isaac your seed shall be called,' accounting that God was able to raise him up, even from the dead, from which he also received him in a figurative sense." (Hebrews 11:17-19) In every situation, Abraham just trusted God with the outcome. His being faithful when tested, promoted him for the blessing of God the rest of his life. This is what God said in Genesis about Abraham at the end of his life. "Now Abraham was old and well advanced in age and the Lord blessed Abraham in all things." (Genesis 24:1)

Abraham had moved in his Covenant Relationship with God as being God's friend. This status of being God's friend enabled Abraham to know things in advance before they happened. James, Jesus' brother, said this about Abraham in James 2:23. "And the Scripture was fulfilled which says, 'Abraham believed God, and it was accounted to him for righteousness.' And he (Abraham) was called the friend of God." In Genesis 18, God considered Abraham his friend and shared with him what He was going to do to Sodom and Gomorrah. Even after Abraham talked to God about sparing Sodom and Gomorrah, if God could find ten righteous people there. God was not able to find ten righteous people. But Abraham still interceded for his nephew, Lot, and his family. As a friend of God and a prophet, Abraham knew that Sodom and Gomorrah were going to be destroyed. God had let him know that. We can know things that are going to happen if we have become a friend of God. Jesus actually defines what qualifies you to be a friend of God in John 15:14-15. "You are my friends if you do whatever I command you. No longer do I call you servants, for a servant does not know what his master is doing; but I have called you friends, for all things that I have heard from My Father I have made known to you." If you cross reference this to Genesis 18:17-19, God the Father says the same thing when He tells Abraham about Sodom and Gomorrah. "Shall I hide from Abraham what I am doing, since Abraham shall surely become a great and mighty nation, and all the nations of the earth shall be blessed in him? For I have known him, in order that he may command his children and his household after him, that they may keep the way of the Lord, to do righteousness and justice, that the Lord may bring to Abraham what He has spoken to him." Both God the Father and God the Son say the exact same thing about friendship with both of them. If you walk in Covenant Relationship with God and do what He says, you will become a friend of God and God will show and enlighten your minds to the future of your life and those around you.

There is a closer relationship with God discussed in the New Testament (Covenant) than being a friend of God. Jesus Christ, God's Son, wants not only to bring us into being a friend of God, but also to that of being sons and daughters of God walking in fellowship with our Father every day and sitting at His table enjoying that fellowship. John, the Beloved Apostle, talks about that relationship in 1st John 3:1-3. "Behold, what manner of love the Father hath bestowed upon us, that we should be called the sons of God: therefore, the world knoweth us not, because it knew Him not.

Beloved, now are we the sons of God, and it doth not yet appear what we shall be: but we know that, when He shall appear, we shall be like Him; for we shall see Him as He is. And every man that hath this hope in Him purifieth himself, even as He is pure." (KJV) We will discuss this more when we get to the New Testament (Covenant).

Chapter 6
The Covenant Relationships Of Isaac And Jacob

Isaac, The Meditator

God appeared to Isaac and Jacob and extended the same Covenant that Abraham had, to both of them. Therefore, they were living under the Abrahamic Covenant. We know they both had that Covenant Relationship, but there were differences. Abraham gave all his wealth as well as his spiritual mentoring to Isaac. Isaac knew his father Abraham in a different light, when Abraham offered up Isaac as a sacrifice to God; that God was first in Abraham's life. In Genesis 25:5-6, shows us the priorities as far as children were concerned in Abraham's life. "And Abraham gave all that he had unto Isaac. But unto the sons of the concubines, which Abraham had, Abraham gave gifts, and sent them away from Isaac, his son, while he yet lived, eastward unto the east country." (KJV) Abraham did not want them to become a hindrance or a distraction to Isaac in his life. When Abraham died, both Isaac and Ishmael buried him next to Sarah in the cave of Machpelah. (Genesis 25:9) But God only extended the Covenant to Isaac, but not to Ishmael. God had already told Isaac and Rebekah that Jacob would receive the Covenant, even though Isaac wanted to give it to Esau. We don't know how God would have brought that about, because Rebekah and Jacob tricked Isaac into giving it to Jacob. In Abraham's case, God chose Abraham to give it to him. We will investigate some of these differences as we study the lives of Isaac and Jacob.

We know that Isaac had a deep relationship with God, because before Rebekah arrived to be his wife, he went out into the fields to meditate and pray. "And Isaac went out to meditate in the field in the evening; and he lifted his eyes and looked and there the camels were coming." (Genesis 24:63) It is important to realize that a Covenant Relationship with God comes about by already being in an intimate relationship with God. No doubt the loss of his mother, Sarah, had a profound effect upon his life. It was only when Rebekah came and comforted him that he was able to rise above that setback. Davis Dictionary of the Bible on page 353 had this to say about Isaac's disposition. "In disposition he (Isaac) was retiring and contemplative; affectionate also and felt his mother's death deeply." It took a gentle woman like Rebekah to help him with his mother's death. She no doubt helped him when Abraham died as well.

The next event in Isaac's life was the birth of his two son, Esau and Jacob. But this was a trial also. One must understand in those days to be barren as Rebekah was, was not a good thing. The New Manners and Customs of Bible Times by Ralph Gower on page 58 says this about women who seemingly could not have children. "If a woman could not have children, it was therefore seen as a curse from God because it was as good as extinction." Different women in the Bible saw barrenness as evil. Ralph Gower goes on to say this, "Rachel told Jacob that if she had no children she would die." (Genesis 30:1) Just like Sarah, it looked like Rebekah was not going to have children. In Sarah's case, God promised her a son, Isaac. In Rebekah's case, Isaac interceded for his wife. "Isaac was forty years old when he took Rebekah as his wife, the daughter of Bethuel the Syrian of Padan Aram, the sister of Laban the Syrian. Now Isaac pleaded with the Lord for his wife, because she was barren; and the Lord granted his plea, and Rebekah his wife conceived." (Genesis 25:20-21)

This didn't happen immediately. He must have pleaded with God a long time. According to Dr. Steve Barabas in The Pictorial Bible Dictionary on page 283 he says this about Isaac's intercession to God. "At the age of 40 he married Rebekah a kinswoman from Mesopotamia (Genesis 24), but he and his wife were childless until, in answer to prayer twin sons, Esau and Jacob, were born to them when he (Isaac) was 60 (Genesis 25: 20, 26)" According to Genesis 25:26 this is correct. "Afterward his brother came out, and his hand took hold of Esau heel; so, his name was called Jacob. Isaac was sixty years old when she bore them." This means they waited on God and prayed for twenty years before they had children. Jesus said in The Amplified Bible on page 1178, Luke 11:9 "So I say to you, Ask and keep on asking, and it shall be given you; seek and keep on seeking and you shall find; knock and keep on knocking, and the door will be opened to you."

This was not the only problem with Rebekah's conception. It was apparent that she was going to have twins and they seemed to be fighting in her womb. Perhaps, she had learned from Isaac the best thing to do was to ask God about it. So, Rebekah did just that. In Genesis 25: 22-24 Rebekah gets an answer from the Lord. "But the children struggled together within her, and she said, "If all is well, why am I this way? So, she went to inquire of the Lord. And the Lord said to her. "Two nations are in your womb, two peoples shall be separated from your body; One people shall be stronger than the other, And the older shall serve the younger."

It is interesting to note that God had a prophetic word for Rebekah. Why did God not share that word first with Isaac? Perhaps, Isaac would not have been open to that word. It is probably for sure that Rebekah shared the word of the Lord with Isaac, but later we see he had no intention of following it. What God was telling Rebekah, was that He was not going to pay attention to the traditional view of the first born receiving the birth right and the blessing of the father, Isaac. Instead, "the older (Esau) would serve the younger (Jacob)" God is prophesying what is going to happen. Thus, we see that God is already applying the Covenant He promised to Abraham to Isaac and his family. This will be taken up in Genesis 26.

In Old Testament times, the father and mother usually sought God about what to name their children. So, it was with Isaac and Rebekah. In Genesis 25:25-26 listen to what they called their two boys. "And the first came out red. He was like a hairy garment all over; so, they called his name Esau (literally hairy). Afterward his brother came out, and his hand took hold of Esau's heel; so, his name was called Jacob (Supplanter, Deceitful). Isaac was sixty years old when she bore them." Names were usually prophetic utterances of their character and nature. Esau would become a man of the fields (world) where he hunted game. Isaac would eat of the venison he cooked and that caused him to love Esau. On the other hand, Jacob lived in tents. Tent dwellers usually shepherded sheep. He stayed close to home and maybe because of the prophetic word God gave Rebekah for Jacob or because he took care of the sheep of the family, she loved him. Therefore, already the family was divided over the two sons, Esau and Jacob.

Arthur W. Pink in his book, Gleanings in Genesis, on page 238 gives us some more characteristics of the character of the two sons. "Next we are told that Esau was "a man of the field." (v.27) In the light of Matthew 13;38— "the field is the world"—it is not difficult to discern the spiritual truth illustrated in the person of Esau. He was typically a man of the world. In sharp contrast from what we are told of Esau two things are said of Jacob: --he was "a plain man; dwelling in tents." (v.27) The Hebrew word for "plain" is "tan," which is translated in other passages "perfect," "upright," "undefiled." This reference is to Jacob's character. The dwelling in tents denotes that he was a stranger and pilgrim in this sense; having no abiding city but seeking one to come."

But we are getting a little ahead of ourselves. We need to look at Isaac and how God reaffirms the Covenant He gave Abraham to Isaac. This is covered in Genesis chapter 26. God had already told Abraham that Isaac was the promise seed of the Covenant, right before Abraham's death. Right after Abraham would have killed his only son, Isaac, he was stopped by the Angel of the Lord, Whom we believe to be Jesus. God reaffirms His promise to Abraham.

Genesis 22:15-18 says this. "Then the Angel of the Lord (Jesus) called to Abraham a second time out of heaven and said, "By Myself says the Lord, because you have done this thing, and have not withheld your son, your only son, in blessing I will bless you, and in multiplying I will multiply your descendants (Isaac, Jacob, etc.) as the stars of the heaven and the sand which is in the seashore; and your descendants shall possess the gate of their enemies. In your seed (Isaac) all the nations of the earth shall be blessed, because you have obeyed my voice." Because of Abraham's faith and obedience to God, future generations, Isaac included, would be blessed. When we obey God, our children are going to be blessed.

Isaac at Gerar

God does not change His mind, even when Isaac looks like he is going contrary to what God has told Rebekah and Isaac to do. But we will look at that when we examine Genesis chapter 27. In chapter 26 of Genesis a famine develops in the land of Canaan where Isaac, Rebekah, and their family are living. Isaac goes to Gerar where the Philistine King, Abimelech lives. Isaac is known for his digging wells and providing food, shelter and water for his sheep. This typifies our Lord Jesus Christ in being the Chief Shepherd of the sheep. Isaac leaves the well of Beer Lahai-roi (well of the living one) and goes to Gerar (lodging place), which is the last city before entering into Egypt. All the places mentioned in Genesis are very significant and speak of the spiritual life that Isaac is entering into. Isaac is going from a place where he has seen the Lord to just a lodging place. But the fact that he stayed at Gerar is significant also, because in this chapter God tells him not to leave Canaan.

This is what Arthur W. Pink says about the departure of Isaac from the well named Lahai-roi to go to Gerar. "We have just looked at Isaac by the Well of Lahai-roi; did he remain there? What do you suppose is the answer? Could you not supply it from your own experience? "And there was a famine in the land, beside the first famine that was in the days of Abraham. And Isaac went unto Abimelech, King of the Philistines unto Gerar." (Genesis 26:1) Isaac's departure from the Well of Lahai-roi to Gerar typifies the failure of the son (the believer) to maintain his standing in the presence of God and his enjoyment of Divine fellowship." (Gleanings in Genesis, page 230)

Then we see the grace of God manifested to Isaac and his family in Gerar. God for the first time reveals Himself to Isaac. God appears (reveals Himself) to Isaac and gives him instructions about what to do in this famine. "Then the Lord appeared to him (Isaac) and said: Do not go down to Egypt; dwell in the land of which I tell you. Sojourn in the land and I will bless you. For to you and your descendants I will give all this land, and I will bless you and keep you; for to you and your descendants I will give all these lands, and I will perform the oath (Covenant) which I swore to Abraham your father. And I will make your descendants multiply as the stars of heaven; I will give to your descendants all these lands; and in your seed (Jacob) all the nations of the earth shall be blessed; because Abraham obeyed My voice and kept My charge, My commandments, My statutes and My laws." So, Isaac dwelt in Gerar." (Genesis 26:2-6)

There are three things that appear in this passage. The first important thing is that God appears to Isaac for the first time. The word "appeared" comes from the Hebrew word Ra'ah and generally it means to see, to see intellectually, to make one feel or know, to perceive (in the sense of hearing). (The Hebrew-Greek Key Study Bible; Lexicon of the Old and New Testaments by Dr. Spiro Zodhiates, pages 1635-1636) Isaac had a Revelation of God, Himself and God gave Isaac specific instructions which he followed as recorded in Genesis 26:6.

The second major thing God did while He was revealing Himself to Isaac; He reaffirmed the Covenant God had made to Abraham and extended it to Isaac. When God said in Genesis 26:3b "...and I will perform the oath (Covenant) which I swore to Abraham, your father...", God was telling Isaac I will perform the Covenant promised to Abraham, to Isaac, and his descendants. The word for "oath" is Sh'buw'eh which means something sworn, swearing, an oath or a covenant confirmed by an oath. (The Hebrew-Greek Key Study Bible; Lexicon of the Old and New Testaments edited by Dr. Spiro Zodhiates, page 1641)

The most important thought after all this is the fact that Isaac obeyed God. He allowed God to direct his life. It is one thing for God to reveal Himself to you. It is another thing for you to get instructions from God, but the most important thing is for you to obey God and do what He says. By staying where he was in the land of Canaan, he was giving God an opportunity to bless and meet all of his needs both physically and spiritually.

One thing Isaac did not do, he did not go immediately back to Beersheba (Well of Seven or Well of the Oath) and the well at Laha-roi (Well of the Living God) which would have put him right in the middle of Canaan. All of these places and wells are spiritually important to Isaac and his walk with God. Instead Isaac stayed in the border city of Gerar. It is possible he was looking to Abimelech to supply all his physical needs like food and shelter. A lot of times we are looking to the arm of flesh to satisfy our needs. But God is going to engineer circumstances to cause him to move back to Beersheba. That is very important, that he waits on God to tell him what to do. He was under the Abrahamic Covenant of Promise. He is actually the only son of Abraham, that did not leave the Promise Land, Canaan. We will see that Abraham, Isaac, and Jacob are not actually perfect pictures of the eternal. Abraham is a type and shadow of God our Father, who to a great extent showed how he was the father of faith, just like our Heavenly Father is. Abraham was not perfect about faith, but he obeyed God and it was counted to him for righteousness.

Isaac is a type and shadow of the Son of God, laying down his life in obedience to his father, Abraham. He could have fought Abraham about laying on the altar and being sacrificed, but he did not. He was a willing sacrifice and willing to obey his father, Abraham and die. God's own Son, Jesus Christ, was not a type or shadow, but the reality and willingly laid down His life for us and paid for all our sins with His own blood.

Finally, Jacob is a type and shadow of the Son of God in the flesh who came to Haran (a type of the world) to get a bride. His father, Isaac, told him not to take a bride from the Hittites, but to go to Haran and secure a bride from there. He came to Haran and fell in love with Rachel and he finally marries her. Leah is a type of the fleshly bride that Laban made him marry and was always trying to get Jacob to love her through her fleshly efforts. We have people in the church today who are trying to enter Heaven through their fleshly efforts. Rachel on the other hand is a type and shadow of the Bride of Christ. She has compromised her faith with the idols she stole from her father, Laban. Jacob finally sets her free from idolatry, when he takes the idols and hides them under the terebinth tree which was by Shechem (Responsibility). Right after this Rachel who had already bore Joseph, gives birth to a second child, Benjamin and in doing so because of hard labor she passes away. Benjamin means son of my right hand. These two sons, Joseph and Benjamin, are Jacob's favorite sons throughout his life.

These three pictures in the Old Testament (Covenant) are but types and shadows of the real. Types and shadows break down, because they are not reality. When Bible teachers teach about types and shadows, they should make clear that they break down and that the reality of God, Himself, in the New Testament (Covenant) is better than the types and shadows. God uses types and shadows to enlighten us to some degree and help teach us the truth and the reality. Jesus in the New Testament (Covenant) used parables, earthily stories with a heavenly meaning, to teach His disciples. Parables are another example of types and shadows. The reality of our spiritual walk is in Jesus Christ alone. Only the Holy Spirit can make that a reality to us.

We kind of took a little detour and now let us go back to the life of Isaac and what he learned in his walk with God. Probably, Isaac had it in mind to leave the Promise Land, Canaan and go to Egypt, because of the famine in Canaan. When this trial happened, Isaac had gone to Abimelech in Gerar right on the border of Canaan and Egypt. This Abimelech is not the same Abimelech that Abraham had encountered a hundred years earlier. Most Bible scholars believe that this was the son of the Abimelech that Abraham had encountered. Bible scholars also believe he was given the same name on purpose, because of his royal heritage. (International Standard Bible Encyclopedia, Bible Study Tools. Com. Abimelech) At that point there was an intervention by God. "Then the Lord appeared to him and said. "Do not go down to Egypt; dwell in the land (Canaan land) of which I tell you. Sojourn in the land, and I will be with you and bless you; for to you and your descendants I will give all these lands and I will perform my oath (Covenant) which I swore to Abraham your father. And I will make your descendants multiply as the stars of heaven; and I will give your descendants all these lands; and in your seed all the nations of the earth will be blessed; because Abraham obeyed My voice and kept My charge, My commandments, My statutes, and My laws." (Genesis 26:2-5) In this intervention of God, God is confirming His Covenant that He made with Abraham and extending it to Isaac. God is letting him know that if he stays in Canaan, He is going to take care of Isaac and all of his family and servants. This lets Isaac know he is not alone and God's blessings are going to be upon him and his family and even his descendants. "And my God shall supply all your need according to His riches in glory by Christ Jesus." (Philippians 4:19) So, what does Isaac do? "So, Isaac dwelt in Gerar (Lodging Place)." (Genesis 26:6) We shared this before, but it bears repeating. Isaac obeyed God and stayed out of Egypt.

Then a second trial arises about Isaac's wife, Rebekah. Rebekah is a very attractive woman and the men of Gerar ask him about his wife, Rebekah. Rather than tell the truth, he lies and tell them that she is his sister, because Isaac is afraid they will kill him to get Rebekah. "And the men of the place (Gerar) asked him (Isaac) about his wife (Rebekah). And he said, "She is my sister"; for he was afraid to say, "She is my wife," because he thought, "lest the men of the place should kill me for Rebekah, because she is beautiful to behold." (Genesis 26:7) Isaac has the same fear problem that Abraham had. They are both men of faith, but they both lied about their wives, because they are afraid they will be killed for them. (Genesis 20:1-18) Many times people of faith in God, are tripped up because of their fears.

Listen to what Arthur W. Pink says in his book, Gleanings in Genesis, page 231, about Abraham and Isaac participating in the same sins. "...Isaac thus repeated the sin of Abraham (Genesis 20:1-2). What are we to learn from Isaac thus following the evil example of his father? First the readiness with which Isaac followed in the way of Abraham suggests that it is easier for children to imitate their vices and weaknesses of their parents than it is to emulate their virtues, and the sins of their parents are frequently perpetuated in their children. Solemn thought this! But second, Abraham and Isaac were men of vastly different temperament, yet each succumbed to the same temptation. When famine arose each fled to man for help. When in the land of Abimelech each was afraid to own his wife as such. Are we not to gather from this that no matter what our natural temperament may be, unless the grace of God supports and sustains us, we shall inevitably fall! What a warning!"

We were born with Adamic tendencies from our forefather, Adam. So, in many ways we may not have the temperament of our forefathers, but we have their sinful tendencies. Only the Cross of Jesus Christ can take care of those sinful tendencies. Abraham and Isaac were looking forward to the Cross of Jesus Christ, while we were looking back at that Cross and the death of our Old Man. "Knowing this, that our old man (old nature) was crucified with Him (Jesus Christ), that the body of sin might be done away with, that we should no longer be slaves of sin." (Romans 6:6)

"Now it came to pass, when he (Isaac) had been there a long time, that Abimelech, the King of the Philistines, looked through a window, and saw, and there was Isaac showing endearment (caressing) to Rebekah his wife. And Abimelech called Isaac and said, "Quite obviously she is your wife; so how could you say, "She is my sister?" And Isaac said to him, "Because I said, 'Lest I die on account of her' And Abimelech said, "What is this you have done to us? One of the people might soon have lain with your wife and you would have brought guilt on us." So, Abimelech charged all of the people, saying, "He who touches this man or his wife shall surely be put to death." (Genesis 26:8-10)

Knowing the fleshly nature of fallen man, during this long period of time that Isaac and Rebekah had been in Gerar, it was a miracle of God that none of the men touched Rebekah. Knowing they were under the Abrahamic Covenant and that Covenant had been extended to Isaac by God, one can see that God kept the men away from Rebekah. God caused Abimelech to see Isaac caressing Rebekah and from that he knew that they were married. You don't do that in Middle Eastern countries unless you are married. Even then most men and women are not that intimate in public in those countries. God had arranged all of this and showed the lies to Abimelech that Isaac had said. Actually, what Abimelech said kept the men from Rebekah and took care of Isaac's fear. If they touch Isaac or his wife, Rebekah, they would die. One can see the hand of God in protecting Isaac and Rebekah, but God is also making them look odious in the eyes of the Philistines. From this point on Isaac and his wife would be watched by the Philistines. One has to know that God's Covenant Relationship with Isaac was protecting them in the midst of an idolatrous people. Abimelech knew that Isaac and his wife, Rebekah, did not worship idols like his people did. The whole way of life was different from the Philistines and Abimelech's command only isolated Isaac and Rebekah even more.

Although, Isaac had not moved back to Beersheba (the Well of the Oath, or the Well of the Seventh), where I believe God wanted him, God was still blessing him. Arthur W. Pink in his book, Gleanings in Genesis, page 231, he states that Isaac "was out of communion with God." I have a hard time believing that. Isaac was still in the land of Canaan. He had not gone to Egypt but had lived a long time in the border town of Gerar. It is during his time there that God chooses to bless him. "Then Isaac sowed in that land and reaped in the same year a hundredfold; and the Lord blessed him. The man began to prosper and continued prospering until he became very prosperous; for he had possessions of flocks and possessions of herds and a great number of servants. So, the Philistines envied him." (Genesis 26:12-14) Maybe God did want Isaac in Beersheba. God has the ability to engineer circumstances to where He wants a person to be. That is what I believe was happening to Isaac.

Evidently, Mr. Pink believes if you are being blessed by God, you could still be out of communion with God. From the Biblical account of Isaac's life in Genesis chapters 24 to 28, there are no references that say where God wanted Isaac to live in the Promise Land. The only command God gave him was to stay in the land of Canaan and if he did that God would bless Isaac. Isaac did stay in the Promise land and God did really bless him a hundredfold and he prospered to the point that the Philistines were envious of him. He is the only Patriarch that did stay in Canaan, the Promise Land, all the days of his life.

In the beginning of our study of Isaac and his Covenant walk with God, we discovered that Isaac would go out into the fields, meditate and pray to God. "And Isaac went out to meditate in the field in the evening; and he lifted his eyes, and looked, and there the camels were coming." (Genesis 24:63) The word "meditate" is the Hebrew word siach meaning to talk, consider, to pray. I have not found anything in the Scriptures to show during Isaac's life time that Isaac was out of fellowship with God. I do believe God does at times direct His people through circumstances and even other people can get us to the place where God ultimately wants us, as we shall see with Isaac and Rebekah. From the Scriptures, I see that Isaac was a quiet, and reserved man who spent a lot of time meditating and communing with God. But to say someone is out of communion with God, because God isn't appearing to him every day or every month is to me a little extreme. I believe circumstances in Isaac's relationship to the Philistines will ultimately move Isaac and his family where God wants him.

It would seem that the Philistines were envious of Isaac and his success in everything he put his hand to do. It looks like they want Isaac to leave, because the next thing they do is stop up all his father Abraham's wells. Of course, Abraham had no doubt given these wells to Isaac. "Now the Philistines had stopped up all the wells which his father's servants (Abraham's servants) had dug in the days of Abraham his father, and they had filled them with earth." (Genesis 26:15) From this Scripture, it would seem the Philistines are trying to discourage Isaac and Rebekah from staying at Gerar. Then Abimelech, the King of the Philistines, asked them to leave because Isaac is much to prosperous for them. "And Abimelech said to Isaac, "Go away from us, for you are much mightier than we." (Genesis 26:16) This is the last straw. Because of Isaac's prosperity they have asked Isaac to leave. We know that it is that Covenant blessing that is following and overtaking Isaac, which the Philistines do not understand. "Yes, and all who desire to live Godly in Christ Jesus will suffer persecution." (2 Timothy 5:12) He does obey Abimelech and moves down in the valley of Gerar.

When Isaac is set up in the valley of Gerar, he attempts to open up again the wells his father Abraham had dug. He called each well after the names his father had called them. In that valley they found a well of running water. "Also, Isaac's servants dug in the valley and found a well of running water there." (Genesis 26:19) But this caused another controversy with the Philistine herdsmen in the valley of Gerar. They claim the water as their own. Isaac calls that well Esek or well of contention. As one might gather each well was a place in God spiritually that Isaac was encountering. God was using the trouble with the wells to move Isaac closer to where He wanted him to be. Sometimes God uses people and situations to draw us closer to Himself. (Genesis 26: 17-22)

As one can see, Isaac is not a person of confrontation. He moves to another location and has his herdsmen dig another well. But the Philistine herdsmen quarrel over that well too. Therefore, Isaac calls it Sitnah or well of enmity (Genesis 26:21). Isaac will not stand his ground and fight for these wells, even though he has plenty of herdsmen and servants. There is a difference between Abraham and Isaac. Remember Abraham used his own hired servants to get Lot and his family back. Abraham also confronted Abimelech about some wells that Abimelech's servants had seized. (Genesis 21:22-28) Isaac is more mellow and nonconfrontational than Abraham. He moves on to find another place where he and his family can live without quarreling and fighting. Isaac did not stay at Sitnah but moved on to another place.

Most every Bible scholar I have read said that Isaac needed to get back to Beersheba. Their reasons are that is where God visited him and revealed Himself to him in the beginning of his walk with God. Isaac finally, moves back to Beersheba and God appears (reveals) Himself to Isaac again. "Then he (Isaac) went up from there (Rehoboth) to Beersheba. And the Lord appeared (revealed Himself) to him the same night and said, "I am the God of your father Abraham: do not fear, for I am with you and I will bless you and multiply your descendants for My servant Abraham's sake." So, he built an altar there and called on the name of the Lord, and he pitched his tent there; and there Isaac's servants dug a well." (Genesis 26:23-25)

We do not see any corrective tones in what God said to Isaac. Rather it is God reaffirming Isaac and His Covenant relationship with him. God is telling him, He is the God of Abraham and that He is going to be with Isaac and bless him. Because Isaac has obeyed God and remained in the land of Canaan and did not go to Egypt, he will be blessed. The Bible even confirms that Isaac at Gerar was blessed a hundred-fold. His flocks have increased and now he has two wells that are supplying water for his flocks and herds. Isaac like Abraham has received the blessing of God, spiritually and materially. Some individuals would be changed and become proud by all of this, but from the Biblical record we see no change in Isaac. Riches have not changed his heart toward God or man. In fact, we see Isaac building an altar to God in Beersheba, meaning the Well of the Oath, and there he calls on God. "For whoever calls on the name of the Lord shall be saved." (Romans 10:13) He is at peace with God and his Covenant with God. I believe at this point in his life, Isaac is beginning to understand his Covenant Relationship with God. All of this is in the timing of God. We don't walk in Covenant Relationship with God, until He is ready for us to do that. This Covenant Relationship with God is going to affect his relationship with the Philistines and their leaders. Our Covenant Relationship with God will affect our relationship with our family, friends, and others we come in contact with.

This brings us to the next phase of Isaac's life, which is his relationship to the Philistines and their leaders. Worldly leaders like Abimelech have become jealous and even contentious over the favor of God in Isaac's life. They don't realize that it is because Isaac is walking in Covenant Relationship with God. This started when Isaac and his family were in Gerar and then later in the valley of Gear. Each step toward Beersheba, God continues to bless Isaac and cause everything to overtake him with the blessing of God. Finally, it dawns upon Abimelech and his leaders that Isaac has favor with God and the best thing they can do is to be at peace with Isaac through an earthily Covenant on an earthily scale. This is not like God's Covenant with Isaac. Because the Covenant that God has with Isaac is one that God started and not Isaac. God is superior to Isaac and that Covenant depends on God not Isaac. The Covenant that Abimelech and Isaac agree upon are two equal men having a Covenant relationship. But even with this Covenant with Abimelech, Isaac has the upper hand, because he has the favor of God upon his life and he is walking in Covenant Relationship with God. Probably, Abimelech is afraid that down the path of life, Isaac might seek revenge because of how he and the Philistines have treated Isaac in the past. With God on Isaac's side, Abimelech and his people would not have a chance. This leads us to the Scripture where Isaac and Abimelech make a Covenant.

"Then Abimelech came to him from Gerar with Ahuzzath, one of his friends, and Phichol the commander of the army. And Isaac said to them, "Why have you come to me, since you hate me and sent me away from you?" But they said, "We have certainly seen that the Lord is with you. So, we said, 'Let there now be an oath (covenant) between us, between you and us; and let us make a covenant with you, that you will do us no harm, since we have not touched you, and since we have done nothing to you but good and have sent you away in peace. You are now the blessed of the Lord." (Genesis 26:16-29)

Isaac shows some fear, because most every time Abimelech comes to him, he is telling Isaac to move or go somewhere else. However, this time is different, because Abimelech has come to the conclusion that the favor of God is upon Isaac's life. He recognizes that Isaac has a living relationship with his God. He does not know it is a Covenant Relationship. When Isaac and Rebekah were blessed in Gerar with their family, with all the servants and cattle, herds and riches, the Philistines were also blessed. When Abimelech and the Philistine leaders asked them to leave and they did, the blessing and favor of God also left the city. It goes back to what God had promised Abraham in Genesis 12:3. "I will bless those who bless you, And I will curse him who curses you; and in you all the families of the earth will be blessed." In my opinion, Abimelech and his friends were missing out on the blessing of God. Therefore, they came to Isaac to "mend fences," make things right, and to make a Covenant with him.

When we are walking in Covenant Relationship with God, the favor of God will be upon our lives and the world will take notice of what we have in God. Not all, but many will want to come and ask about our relationship with God. Evangelization will be a result of our walk with God. People look at individuals, when they see a life of peace and harmony that they do not see in the world. That is when they start asking questions and we are able to witness to them of the saving power of Jesus Christ. Abimelech and his friends saw the blessings and the peace of God on Isaac's life. Isaac did not get upset when they told him to leave Gerar. He just left. He did not strike back, when the herdsmen in the valley of Gerar started quarreling and claiming his wells as their wells. He just moved on until he found a place where he could live in peace with God and man. Now, Abimelech and his friends wanted to make peace and a Covenant with Isaac, and so they did.

A Covenant among men usually starts with a feast and ends with the two parties or men swearing an oath of peace between them. Covenants between men in Old Testament (Covenant) times involved feasting and drinking, which occurred between Isaac and Abimelech and Abimelech's friends. "So, he (Isaac) made them a feast, and they ate and drank. Then they arose early in the morning and swore an oath (Covenant) with one another; and Isaac sent them away, and they departed from him (Isaac) in peace." (Genesis 26:30-31)

From this point on, Isaac does not have anymore trouble with Abimelech and the Philistines. He lived with them in peace. Although, we are not told that the Philistines accepted God and started worshipping God, they did respect Isaac and his Covenant Relationship with God. A lot of individuals will not receive the Lord Jesus Christ, but overtime if we are faithful to Him, they will respect our relationship with Jesus. Some may overtime receive the Lord Jesus Christ as their Lord and Savior through our witness.

"It came to pass the same day that Isaac's servants came and told him about the well which they had dug, and said to him, "We have found water. So, he called it (the well) Shebah. Therefore, the name of the city is Beersheba to this day." (Genesis 26:32-33) I do not think it was a coincidence that his servants found water in the well at Beersheba the same day. I believe God was blessing his endeavors to be at peace with his neighbors. "If it is possible as much as depends on you, live peaceably with all men." (Romans 12:18) Trying to live peaceably with all people should be the goal of every Christian. (Genesis 26:32-33)

The Choosing of Brides in Eastern Countries

Fred H. Wright, an authority on manners and customs in Bible lands, wrote a book called Manners and Customs of Bible Lands. On page 126 of this book he addresses this situation. "It is well known in the East(ern)(countries) the parents of a young man select a bride for him. This custom goes back to early Old Testament (Covenant) times. When Esau married against the wishes of his parents, he carried ill will. (Genesis 26:34-35)" Mr. Wright goes on to present an argument why parents insisted on their rights in this sub topic, Reasons for Parental Privilege, on page 126 of the same book. "Why did parents usually insist on their right to select a bride for their son? The new bride was to become a member of the bridegroom's clan, and therefore, the whole family was interested in knowing if she would be suitable. There is evidence that at least sometimes the son or daughter was consulted. Rebekah was asked it she was willing to go and become the wife of Isaac. (Genesis 24:58) But the parents felt they had a right to make the choice."

In this situation, one has to remember that the sons brought their new brides home to his parents of the sons and they lived under the same tent or roof with the parents of the son and all of the other children the son's parents had. Going on in Manners and Customs of Bible Lands, pages 130-134, Esau brought his new brides home to his parent's home probably unannounced. From the Scriptures we can see Esau did not consult his parents about the marriages. Usually, it was only one wife at a time; but he brought home two. This probably strained the relationship between Esau and his parents, when Esau chose Hittite wives.

There is another reason why Esau marrying two Hittite women strained the relationship of Esau and his parents. This quotation is taken from Got Questions. Org./Hittites. "The religions of the Hittites were a pluralistic worship of nature. They believed in various gods over the elements of earth, sky, weather, etc., and these gods were often listed as witnesses on treaties and oaths. As in most pagan societies, this nature worship led to desperate practices which brought the wrath of the true God on them..." Therefore, these two women who had lived in idolatry now were living with Isaac and Rebekah. How do I know that? Because in the next chapter (Genesis 27) Rebekah gets the choice clothes of Esau that were in the house to clothed Jacob so he could deceive his father Isaac. (Genesis 27:15) Evidently, from this Scripture they had moved out of the tents and into a house. From this we know that Esau and his two wives were living with Isaac and Rebekah.

But what does all this say about Esau? First of all, he was in rebellion against his parents and what was traditionally done by parents; the choosing of the bride or brides for their son. One thing I did not bring up, is these two women came from an immoral background. "From some time after 2200 B.C., the Hattians (Hittites) were overrun by a vigorous Indo-European speaking people from the north, who became Heth's ruling class while adopting the older and often immoral Hittite culture." (The Zondervan Pictorial Bible Dictionary, page 366) Esau knew what Isaac and Rebekah stood for, but no doubt the immoral and idolatrous society he was in swayed him and he chose two brides of that society. He knew he was in rebellion but chose to go that way anyway.

Earlier in Genesis 25:27b Esau has already chosen a life of the field to hunt and bring slayed animals home from the field. From the Scriptures we learn that the field is considered to be the world. Matthew 13:38, the Scripture says, "The field is the world, the good seed are the sons of the Kingdom, but the tares are the sons of the wicked one (the devil)." Esau's life revolved around the world. Secondly, he had become a skilled hunter. He killed animals and prepared venison a lot of times for his father, Isaac. Arthur W. Pink in his book, Gleanings in Genesis, page 238 says this about Esau. "Esau was a cunning hunter." (v.27) The hunter tells of the roving, daring, restless nature that is a stranger to peace. A glance at the Concordance will show that the word "hunter" is invariably found in an evil connection (cf. 1 Sam.24:11; Job 10:16; Ps. 140:11; Prov. 6:26; Micah 7:2; Ezek. 13: 18). "Search" is the antithesis, the good word, the term used when God is seeking His own. Only two men in Scripture are specifically termed "hunters," namely Nimrod and Esau, and they have much in common. The fact that Esau is thus linked together with Nimrod, the rebel, reveals his (Esau) true character."

God had already prophesied to Rebekah that the elder (Esau) would serve the younger (Jacob). (Genesis 25:23) Does it surprise you that Esau started out wrong? Esau is linked to a rebel (Nimrod) already in Genesis.

Esau is not considering his parent's ideas and suggestions and not even asking their advice before he chooses two women to marry only highlights this fact.

Esau Sells His Birthright

Another step of rebellion, Esau shows is when he sells his birthright to Jacob. He was a mature young man when he did this. He has chosen an occupation of a hunter which depends on a person finding wild animals and killing them. This is all left to chance. One day he comes in from the field evidently without any game. He smells what Jacob is cooking for himself. Jacob is cooking pottage or lentils without any meat. Esau is extremely hungry. Jacob asks for the Birthright. The Birthright is very important and was usually given to the firstborn son, which is Esau. According to Jamison, Fauset and Brown Commentary of the Whole Bible, page 30, is what the Birthright was all about. (The Birthright includes "…the rights and privileges of the firstborn (son)—which was very important—the chief being that they were the family priests (Exodus 4:22) and they had a double portion of the family inheritance (Deuteronomy 21:17)."

Zondervan Pictorial Bible Dictionary, page 126 says this about the Birthright and what Esau did with his Birthright. "From time immemorial a man's firstborn son has been given privileges above those of his younger brother. This is illustrated today by the order of succession to the throne (in Britain for instance)…The birthright included a double portion of the inheritance (Deut. 21:15-17) and the privilege of priesthood; but in Israel God later set apart the tribe of Levi instead of the firstborn for that service…Esau lost his birthright by selling it to Jacob for a mess of pottage, and no regret could undo the loss he had brought upon himself. (Genesis 25:27-34; Hebrews 12:16)"

This is what Jacob is bargaining with Esau about—Esau's Birthright. Listen to what Esau says when Jacob begins bargaining with him about the Birthright in Genesis 25:31-34. "But Jacob said, "Sell me your birthright as of this day." And Esau said, "Look, I am about to die, so what profit shall this birthright be to me?" Then Jacob said, "Swear to me as of this day," So, he swore to him, and sold his birthright to Jacob. And Jacob gave Esau bread and stew of lentils (little beans), then he ate and drank, arose, and went on his way. Thus, Esau despised his birthright."

The selling of the Birthright by Esau actually happened before Esau married the two Hittite women. But it shows that Esau was more concerned about the appetites of his flesh than he was of spiritual matters including being the Priest of his house after Isaac's death. Because he was so hungry coming from the field he thought he was going to die. Evidently, he did not catch any game that day. He was living with Isaac and Rebekah and they would not have let him die. Temptations come in many forms and this one was the savory stew pottage of Jacob. Listen to what Jamisson, Fauset and Brown Commentary of the Whole Bible, page 30 says. "(Esau says) I am running a daily risk of my life, and of what value will the birthright be to me; so he despised or cared little about it, in comparison of gratifying his appetite—he threw away his religious privileges for a trifle; and then he is styled— "a profane person" (Hebrews 12:16; also Job 31:7,16; Philippians 3:19) …"

In Jimmy Swaggart's The Expositor's Study Bible, page 50, verse 31, Jimmy Swaggart gives us some details of the importance of the Birthright as well. "The birthright then dealt with spiritual things, of which Esau had no regard or concern. It had to do with earthily inheritance of Canaan but would take place hundreds of years in the future. It referred to the possession of the Covenant Blessing, which included his (Jacob's seed) being as the stars of the sky and all the families of the earth being blessed in him. As well, it was the progenitor ship of the Promised Seed (Jesus), which was the greatest Blessing (Jesus) of all and spoke of Christ. The firstborn was to receive the birthright, and Esau was the first born."

Not only do we see Esau's character in this passage (Genesis 25:27-34), but we see Jacob's character as well. Jacob's name means surplanter or deceitful. Primarily, Jacob is using Esau's weakness toward the flesh to get what he wants. People say of people like Jacob, "They will do whatever it takes to get what they want" or "The end justifies the means." This clearly defines Jacob in the beginning of his dealings with his brother, Esau and his father, Isaac. No doubt his mother, Rebekah, has shared with him the prophetical word of God over his life. In this interchange with Esau, he does get Esau to sell his Birthright for a "mess of pottage." The problem with Jacob in this situation with Esau and later when he deceives his father, Isaac, is in both instances Jacob is not trusting God to bring this about, but in his own cunning and trickery to not only get the Birthright, but also the Blessing of his father, Isaac. Even so, Jacob did value Divine favor and Blessing, unlike his brother, Esau.

Jimmy Swaggart's Expositor's Study Bible, page 50, verse 33 says this about Jacob. "Jacob, deplorable as was his character, valued Divine and eternal blessings; and had he placed himself in God's hand, the prophecy made to his mother before he was born would have been fulfilled to him, and without the degradation and suffering which his own scheming brought upon him."

The Birthright in my opinion is a type and shadow of being born again by the Spirit of God. Being born again into the family of God bring rights and privileges that worldings cannot enjoy. As we said before, Esau did not understand all this. No doubt his parents had talked about his prominent position to him but being a man of the field (a man of the world) it did not phase him or cause him to understand spiritual things. Therefore, we can understand Genesis 25:34. "And Jacob gave Esau bread and stew of lentils (beans, vegetables); then he (Esau) ate and drank, arose and went away. Thus, Esau despised his birthright." How pitiful Esau is. He has no idea of what he just gave up to Jacob.

Jacob is now the one with the Birthright. Here again is Jimmy Swaggart sharing his exposition of Esau from Jimmy Swaggart's Expositor's Study Bible, page 51. "The natural heart places no value on the things of God, as we see evidenced in the choices made by Esau. In the natural heart, God's Promises are a vague, valueless, powerless thing, simply because God is not known. Upon that which the unredeemed cannot see, they place no value. Thus, it was with Esau." Rev. Swaggart likens him to a natural man yet born in a spiritual family. "But the natural man does not receive the things of the Spirit of God, for they are foolishness to him; nor can he know them, because they are spiritually discerned." (1 Corinthians 2:14)

The thing about Esau, he did not even realize what he was giving away for just a bowl of stew. There are a lot of children born into families and their families are born again believers. But the children do not understand the parent's emphasis on spiritual things. They follow and judge after the natural things of the world and when they leave home their life continues after the natural appetites of the world, unless there is a Divine intervention by the Spirit of God. Parents should pray continually for such children that God will intervene in their lives.

Jacob Deceives His Father, Isaac

Neither son of Isaac and Rebekah were perfect or mature of character. Esau was looking at things naturally and Jacob was a deceiver, who would manipulate things to his advantage. But God saw in Jacob, beneath all that deception a heart that was seeking Him. In Romans 9:13, the Apostle Paul wrote, "As it is written, "Jacob I have loved, but Esau I have hated." God is looking at the heart of both sons and He sees in Jacob a heart that desires Him and one whose heart He can change. Whereas, God did not see that with Esau. Therefore, the Covenant of Promise and Blessing would come to Jacob and his descendants.

These are all steps that Esau took leading him away from God's best to a life governed by the flesh. Both Isaac and Rebekah must have seen all this coming to pass. The next verse that catches our attention is the verse that shows us where Isaac's and Rebekah's heart is. "And Isaac loved Esau because he ate of his game; but Rebekah loved Jacob." (Genesis 25:28) Now we have to look at the hearts of Isaac and Rebekah. As time goes on, Isaac's heart does not remember the prophetic word of God over the two sons, Esau and Jacob, even before they were born. He eats Esau's game or venison and his heart is turned toward his son because of his savory meat. The flesh is attracting Isaac's attention. This meat draws his heart and flesh toward Esau and away from Jacob, even though now Jacob has the Birthright.

Rebekah on the other hand because of the prophetic word of God is drawn to Jacob. The test will be will Rebekah and Jacob wait upon God and allow God to change the heart of Isaac? The Blessing that Isaac is going to bestow determines which son will receive the Covenant Promise of God. At this point, Isaac is leaning toward Esau and Rebekah is leaning toward Jacob.

In Genesis 27:1 is a description of Isaac as he is getting older. "Now it came to pass, when Isaac was old and his eyes were so dim that he could not see, that he called Esau, his older son and said to him, "My son." And he (Esau) said to him, "Here I am." Isaac in his state of being old has lost his physical sight and one would consider him blind. Not only is he physically blind but he is also spiritually blind. He does not remember what God said when Esau and Jacob were born and if he did he still believes now that the decision is his (Isaac) to make. The prophetic word of the Lord is "that the elder (Esau) shall serve the younger (Jacob)." (Genesis 25:23b) If he did, he is attempting to override God and do what he wants to do, which is to bless Esau and thus give him the Covenant Promises. Isaac has lost spiritual perception.

In Genesis 26:2-4 we find out what has caused Isaac's mind and spirit not to perceive spiritual things and hear the voice of God. We also see in these four verses (Genesis 26:1-4) that he has not even asked God which son should receive the Covenant Blessing. The two sons were born minutes apart and were twins. Isaac technically could have chosen either son since they both were born nearly at the same time. But Genesis 25:28 and Genesis 27:2-4 shows what guided Isaac's decision. "And Isaac loved Esau because he ate of his game (venison); but Rebekah loved Jacob." "And he (Isaac) said, "Behold now, I am old. I do not know the day of my death. Now therefore, please take your weapons, your quiver and your bow, and go to the field (the world) and hunt game (venison) for me. And make me savory food (meat) such as I love, and bring it to me that I may eat, that my soul may bless you before I die."

From the Scriptures we see the motivation of Isaac from the time his sons were growing up until he tells Esau what to do. Isaac's motivation at this time in his life is toward the flesh and the world. This is a warning. A person's motivation can change. He can start out in fellowship with God and then change. He isn't even asking God if he should give the Covenant Blessing to Esau. He did not ask because he already knew that God had chosen Jacob and loved him. Isaac was actually in rebellion against God at this point in his life. Why did not God intervene in this situation? I believe He wanted to see if Rebekah and Jacob would trust Him in this situation. As we shall see they did not trust God, but they would maneuver and manipulate to get the Covenant Blessing for Jacob.

Matthew Henry's A Commentary of the Whole Bible, Volume I Genesis to Deuteronomy, page 164 has some interesting thoughts about what Rebekah should have done instead of what she did. "If Rebekah, when she heard Isaac promise the blessing to Esau, had gone, at his return from hunting, to Isaac, and, with humility and seriousness, put him in remembrance of that which God had said concerning their sons, --if she further had shown him how Esau had forfeited the blessing both by selling his birthright and by marrying strange wives (the Hittite wives), it is possible that Isaac would have been prevailed upon knowingly and wittingly to confer the blessing upon Jacob and needed not to have been cheated into it. This would have been honorable and laudable, and would have looked well in history…"

It is possible that Isaac may have forgotten the prophetic word of the Lord like Matthew Henry conjectures. Like Matthew Henry suggests it would have been better if Rebekah in a humble spirit would have reminded him of that prophetic word, Rebekah and Jacob would not have suffered so much from what they did. God is ultimately going to get glory out of this, but it is going to cost them a lot for being deceivers. Without going into all of the details of Jacob's deception to get the Covenant Blessing, let us look at what it cost Rebekah and Jacob for their manipulation and deception. Since they both were in the plot to get the Covenant Blessing, they both would suffer loss as a result. This plot was not God's way of doing things. I believe God would have dealt with Isaac either before Esau bought the venison in to him or while he was eating it. If Rebekah and Jacob would have trusted God with it, God would have changed Isaac's heart and Jacob would have been blessed even more. Because sin was involved, we will never know what would have taken place.

The first thing that was lost was both Rebekah and Jacob lost their trust in God. It would take Jacob twenty years to regain that trust in God and he would have to wrestle God for it. He would meet one in Laban who really did know how to maneuver and manipulate people. He (Jacob) would be deceived by Laban many times. He would have to cry out to God about it until God told him to return home to Canaan. We never do find out about Rebekah's relationship to God after this. After Jacob leaves, nothing is recorded about her in Scriptures. The curse she said would be upon her (Genesis 27:13) is played out in that she never sees Jacob again.

The next thing Jacob and Rebekah lost was the close family relationship they had before this deception took place. Esau threatens to kill Jacob as soon as Isaac dies. Therefore, Rebekah talks to Isaac and asks him to send Jacob away, because she does not want two family members to die in one day. When Jacob does leave to go to Haran, Rebekah will never see Jacob again. This one deceptive act has torn apart a family. Esau hates Jacob. Can Isaac trust his son, Jacob, ever again? We don't know if Isaac found out that Rebekah was behind the whole thing. It will take twenty years or more for this family to get back together. But that is the high wages of sin and its aftermath in people's lives.

Esau hates Jacob. Genesis 27:41a says, "So Esau hated Jacob because of the blessing with which his father blessed him…." It will take twenty years for these two brothers to have restored love one toward another. Jacob comes back from Haran around the time Isaac passes away. Jacob and Esau bury him together. Therefore, for years Jacob thinks Esau would hunt him and kill him, if he got the chance. Even in coming home from Haran with Jacob's two wives and children, Esau comes to meet him with four hundred men. Genesis 32:6-7 says, "Then the messengers returned to Jacob saying, "We came to your brother Esau, and he also is coming to meet you, and four hundred men are with him." So, Jacob was greatly afraid and distressed, and he divided the people that were with him, and the flocks and herds and camels into two companies." He is greatly afraid of meeting his brother, Esau. I believe he lived in fear that his brother would kill him. That night before he faced his brother, he came face to face with God at Peniel (Face of God). He wrestles with God all night and Jacob would not let go of God until He blessed him. It is one thing to be blessed by your earthily father, which had taken place in Jacob's life. But it is another when your Heavenly Father blesses you and that night He did. He blessed Jacob and changed his name to Israel, which means Prince with God. "So, He said to him, "What is your name?" And he said, "Jacob." And He said, "Your name shall no longer be called Jacob, but Israel; for you have struggled with God and with men and have prevailed...And Jacob called the name of the place Peniel: "For I have seen God face to face, and my life is preserved." (Genesis 32:27-28,30) As we have said before, when a person's name is changed in the Bible, his character has been changed. God has done a work in his heart and in his life and he will never be the same. Plus, Jacob, now Israel, has seen God face to face and his life has been preserved. He did not die. At this point now, Jacob is able to face his brother, Esau. Jacob and Esau's relationship is restored. There is one thing I left out. Before Jacob's name could be changed, he had to admit who he was—Jacob, the deceiver, the surplanter. When he admitted that, God changed his name. God also weakened Jacob. For the rest of his life, he limped on his hip. (Genesis 32:32) "Therefore, to this day the children of Israel do not eat the muscle that shrank, which is on the hip socket, because He touched the socket of Jacob's hip in the muscle that shrank." To the end of the book of Genesis you will see Jacob is called Jacob and at other times he is called Israel. God was working in his heart to bring about change in his life and his character. He was restored to his brother and in the next step he will be restored to his father. This is a synopsis view of what it took to change Jacob's heart and life. I have jumped ahead, but let us return to Jacob's big lie.

Jacob's Big Lie

Jacob had lied to his father, Isaac. Genesis 27:24 says, "Then he (Isaac) said, "Are you really my son Esau?" And he (Jacob) said, "I am." That is an outright lie. Although it is not recorded in Scriptures, the relationship between Isaac and Jacob is strained because Jacob lied to his father, Isaac.

In Scripture, we never see or hear Jacob apologize to his father, Isaac for lying to him. Because of the possibility that Esau might kill Jacob, upon the urging of Rebekah, Isaac calls Jacob and asks him to leave. In Genesis 28:1-5, Isaac finally does give Jacob the Covenant Blessing and then sends him away. During all of this, nothing is recorded about the strained relationship but one knows it is there. Rebekah uses the fact that unlike Esau marrying Hittite women, she does not want Jacob to do so. Her real motive is the danger she feels Jacob is in with his brother Esau threatening to kill him. The whole family is in a strained relationship with Jacob being there in Canaan. But interesting to note is that in all of this Isaac does give the Covenant Blessing to Jacob in chapter 28 of Genesis and this time it is because it is what Isaac desires to do. Isaac sends Jacob away to Padan Aram to Laban, Rebekah's brother, with his blessing.

"Then Isaac called Jacob and blessed him, and charged him, and said to him: "You shall not take a wife from the daughters of Canaan. Arise go to Padan Aram, to the house of Bethuel your mother's father, and take yourself a wife from there of the daughters of Laban your mother's brother." Then Isaac precedes to give Jacob the Covenant Blessing of Abraham.

"May God Almighty bless you,
And make you fruitful and multiply you,
That you may be an assembly of peoples;
And give you the blessing of Abraham,
To you and your descendants with you,
That you may inherit the land
In which you are a stranger,
Which God gave to Abraham."

"So, Isaac sent Jacob away and he went to Padan Aram, to Laban the son of Bethuel the Syrian, the brother of Rebekah, the mother of Jacob and Esau." (Genesis 28:1-5)

Finally, Jacob is separated from all of his immediate family. This is because of the plot to get the Covenant Blessing and because Isaac and

Rebekah did not want him to marry any Canaanite or Hittite women. There is a chance that Esau would have murdered his brother, Jacob, if he had stayed in the land of Canaan. There is also a chance that he would have married a Canaanite or Hittite woman if he stayed in Canaan, which might have led him into idolatry.

Nearly every Biblical scholar that I have read about this incident in Isaac and Rebekah's life, says that Rebekah, who had engineered the plot to get the Covenant Blessing for Jacob also engineered Jacob leaving Canaan and going to Haran on the pretense of finding a wife at her brother Laban's house. Her real intent was to get Jacob away from Esau, so Esau would have no opportunity to kill him. In Genesis 27:43-45, Rebekah tells Jacob to make plans to leave for Haran for a few days. "Now therefore, my son (Jacob), obey my voice: arise, flee to my brother Laban in Haran. And stay with him a few days, until your brother's fury turns away, until your brother's anger turns away from you, and he forgets what you have done to him; then I will send and bring you from there. Why should I be bereaved also of you both in one day?" Notice Rebekah thought Jacob would only be gone a few days. She does not know that God has other plans for him away from her. Actually, what Jacob did was as much Rebekah's fault as Jacob's fault. Jacob will learn more about himself and God will be able to change Jacob's life away from his mother.

We see Rebekah's intent is to save Jacob from Esau. Jamieson, Fauset and Brown's Commentary of the Whole Bible, page 31 explains the question at the end of Genesis 27:45c; "Why should I be bereaved of you both in one day?" "This refers to the law of the Goeilison, by which the nearest kin would be obliged to avenge the death of Jacob upon his brother." She is afraid at the end of the day, both sons would be dead. A near kinsman would probably be a son of Ishmael. That would be tragic.

Maybe Rebekah has begun to see what she did with this plot and what she has done in bringing division to the family. She now sees that Esau wants to kill his brother. We now see the maneuverings and the manipulation of the two sons by her. Now she sees that she has to get Isaac on board of sending Jacob away to Haran to her brother, Laban. So, listen to what she tells Isaac, so he will send Jacob away with his blessing. "And Rebekah said to Isaac, "I am weary of my life because of the daughters of Heth; if Jacob takes a wife of the daughters of Heth, like those who are the daughters of the land, what good will my life be to me?" (Genesis 27:46) She says this to Isaac right after she has put the seed in the mind of Jacob to leave. She is manipulating the situation to get what she wants and Isaac not hearing what Rebekah said to Jacob sees that what she has suggested could happen; Jacob could take a wife of the Hittites. Notice that God lets her do all of this manipulating and maneuvering Isaac to get what she wants. In my opinion, God intentionally let Rebekah do this, so God could get what He wanted in getting Jacob away from his mother, Rebekah. This is what the Rev. Jimmy Swaggart said about this situation in the Jimmy Swaggart Expository Study Bible. "There is no doubt that Rebekah was concerned about the daughters of the land, and none of them being a suitable wife for Jacob; however, her real reason at this time for sending Jacob away was not that which she told Isaac, but rather that she feared for his (Jacob's) life as it regards the anger of Esau."

Jacob's Meeting with God

After Isaac calls Jacob and blesses him, he then sends him away with the charge not to take a wife of the daughters of Canaan. Another reason Rebekah got Isaac to send away Jacob, is because Isaac is the head of the household and only he is supposed to send Jacob away with his blessing on his leaving. Isaac is like the ruling Monarch of his house and it would be out of custom and tradition for Jacob to leave without his father's blessing. You would think after all has transpired with Jacob and Esau, that God would not be interested in Jacob as the next promised seed and He would not give Jacob the Covenant Promises and Blessings. After all, Jacob connived and deceived his father to get the Covenant Blessing and the Covenant in general, but God is still interested in him. The Covenant that God gave Abraham and then God blessed Isaac with it, is now passed on to Jacob. This happens when he leaves Beersheba and is headed toward Haran.

The Bible says in Genesis 28:11b, “So he (Jacob) came to a certain place and stayed there all night, because the sun had set…” This would be a night to remember. Jacob went sound to sleep. Then it happened. God spoke to him through a dream. “Then he (Jacob) dreamed, and behold a ladder was set up on the earth, and its top reached to heaven; and the angels of God were ascending and descending on it. And behold, the Lord stood above it and said: “I am the Lord God of Abraham your father and the God of Isaac; the land on which you lie I will give to you and your descendants. Also, your descendants will be as the dust of the earth; you shall spread abroad to the west and the east, to the north and the south; and in you and in your seed all the families of the earth shall be blessed. Behold, I am with you and will keep you wherever you go and will bring you back to this land; for I will not leave you until I have done what I have spoken to you.” (Genesis 28:12-15)

This is where God gives Jacob all of the Covenant Promises He had given to Abraham and Isaac. He tells Jacob the land where he slept last night is his and his descendants. God says Jacob and his descendants own all of it, north, south, east, and west. God tells Jacob, he and his descendants will be blessed with Covenant Blessings. He promises Jacob that He will be with him wherever he goes and that God will bring Jacob back to this place at some future date. Jacob had a “God moment” and he would never be the same after that night. God had extended His Covenant to him. Listen to what Jacob says to God in response. “Then Jacob awoke from his sleep and said, “Surely the Lord is in this place, and I did not know it.” And he was afraid and said, “How awesome is this place! This is none other than the house of God, and this is the gate of heaven!” Then Jacob arose early in the morning and took the stone that he had put at his head, set it up on a pillar, and poured oil on top of it. And he called the name of the place Bethel (the House of God); but the name of that city had been Luz (Separation) previously.” (Genesis 28:16-19)

This is the first time that Jacob has had an encounter with God in Scripture. Many Biblical scholars call this encounter is when Jacob receives salvation. But I believe it is much more than that. Here Jacob does receive salvation, but he is also presented with the Covenant of God that Abraham and Isaac received. God is promising to change his life completely. The place of his encounter with God is important also. The place or city was originally called Luz, the place of separation. It was a fitting place to sleep, because he had just been separated from his earthily family. The fact that Jacob changed the name of the place or city to Bethel, the House of God and the Gate of Heaven says that God had met him in this place of separation. Many times, God has to separate us from our family and friends so that He can talk to us. Family and friends are sometimes distractions. When we are separated unto God, then He has our full attention and can speak into our lives. Thus, it happened with Jacob in this place of separation. He encounters God and God changes his life.

Finally, Jacob makes a vow to the Lord. "Then Jacob makes a vow, saying, "If God will be with me, and keep me in the way I am going, and give me bread to eat and clothing to put on, so that I come to my father's place in peace, then the Lord shall be my God. And this stone which I have set as a pillar, shall be God's house, and of all that you will give me I will surely give a tenth (tithe) to you." (Genesis 28:20-22) Some Biblical scholars look at the phrase that starts this vow, "If God will be with me;" say it should read "Since God (will) be with me." Jacob is not doubting that God is going to be with him, rather it is an affirmation that God is with him. Notice, that this salvation and Covenant with God is not based on what Jacob has done thus far. Rather it is based on the grace of God and His love for Jacob. As it says in Romans 9:13a, "(God says) Jacob I have loved…" God saw in Jacob, someone who could change and that He could call forth that which is not, as though it was. Only God could change Jacob into the Patriarch He wants him to be. There are some character flaws in Jacob that God will change over the next twenty years. This encounter with God had started that change in his heart.

Jacob was believing that God would provide for him, both food and clothing. He believed God would eventually bring him back to his father's house in peace. In other words, Jacob believed his relationship with Esau could and would be restored. Jacob had learned from his father, Isaac, that Abraham had tithed to God. Possibly, Isaac had followed Abraham's example. This is the second mention of tithing in the Bible. Jacob planned to tithe to God all of the riches and wealth God gave him. All of these things mentioned in Jacob's vow, Christians should be doing in their response to what the Savior, Jesus Christ, has done for them. God extends the New Covenant in the New Testament (Covenant) to every believer in Jesus Christ. This Covenant is a Covenant of faith and must be received by faith, just like God's Covenant with Abraham, Isaac, and Jacob was received by faith.

Jacob and Laban

Jacob had been a deceiver and had tricked Esau into giving him his Birthright (Genesis 25:29-34) and then later he tricked his father, Isaac, into giving him his Covenant Blessing (Genesis 27:1-29). But for the next twenty years Jacob would be under a master trickster in Laban. At the time Laban is tricking Jacob, Jacob does not realize he is being tricked and maneuvered until close to the end of his laboring under Laban, his boss. It is interesting how God arranges for you to meet your match in another person, when there is something in your character that He wants to change in you. Hear Jacob's appraisal of Laban when he talks to Rachel and Leah about leaving and going back to the land of Canaan. "Yet your father has deceived me and changed my wages ten times, but God did not allow him to hurt me." (Genesis 31:7)

After a month's labor with Laban, Laban asks him the obvious. Up to that point Jacob had been laboring for his uncle for nothing. No doubt Jacob was doing what he did back home in the land of Canaan for his father; he was taking care of Laban's sheep. As a relative it was not the custom of the land for Jacob to work for nothing. Laban then asks Jacob what his wages will be. "Then Laban said to Jacob, "Because you are my relative, should you therefore serve me for nothing? Tell me what should your wages be." (Genesis 29:15) Jacob thought he would gain an advantage by waiting until Laban approached him. But Jacob did not know that he did not gain any advantage at all. Jacob asks for his younger daughter, Rachel, because he loved her and he offered to serve seven years for her. "I will serve you seven years for Rachel your younger daughter." (Genesis 29:18) By doing that Jacob actually gives the advantage to Laban. Plus, the fact that Laban does not explain the customs and traditions of Haran to Jacob. At the end of seven years, Jacob is given Leah instead of Rachel. He has to work another seven years for Rachel. Laban said it was the custom of their country, however, being a relative Laban could have made an exception. From Biblical Scholars sharing about that time, it really was not the custom that the older daughter had to be married first. Laban used that to deceive Jacob and gain seven more years of free labor from Jacob. But God wants to teach Jacob some lessons that he did not learn at home, especially that Jacob would be chastened for deceiving his own family and others.

Arthur W. Pink in his book, Gleanings in Genesis, page 260-261, we see his assessment of Laban and his treatment of Jacob and the consequences of Jacob's actions even in the long run. "In Laban's treatment of Jacob, we see the deceiver deceived. This principle that whatever a man soweth that shall he also reap is written large across the pages of Holy Scripture and is strikingly, nay marvelously, illustrated again and again.... The most striking example of what men term "poetic justice" is the case of Jacob himself. First, he deceived his father and was, in turn, deceived by his father-in-law. Jacob became the younger for the elder to deceive Isaac, and has the elder daughter of Laban given instead of the younger for a wife. Second, we may mark the same principle at work in Jacob's wife. In deceiving Jacob in the matter of Leah, Laban tricked Rachel; later we find Rachel tricking Laban (Genesis 31:35). Again, we note how a mercenary spirit actuated Jacob in buying the birthright from Esau for a mess of pottage; the sequel to this was the mercenary spirit in Laban which caused him to change Jacob's wages ten time (Genesis 31:40). Finally, what is most striking of all, that Jacob deceived Isaac by allowing his mother to cover his hands and neck with "the skins of the kids of the goats "(Genesis 37:31) and making him believe an evil beast had devoured him: note, too, that Jacob deceived Isaac in regard to his favorite son (Esau), and so was Jacob deceived in regard to his favorite son."

But what does this time with Laban teaching Jacob? That he can be out maneuvered and deceived by a master deceiver. God is using Laban to teach Jacob the law of sowing and reaping. "Do not be deceived, God us not mocked for whatever a man sows, that he will also reap. For he who sows to his flesh will of the flesh reap corruption, but he who sows to the Spirit will of the Spirit reap everlasting life." (Galatians 6:7-8) Actually, Laban was acting as God's mirror to Jacob of how Jacob was. Those twenty years under Laban taught him a lot. Jacob actually worked for Laban fourteen of the twenty years for Laban's two daughters to be his wives. That is a high price to pay for two wives. Plus, the fact that these two wives were squabbling over Jacob's affections and children they would give Jacob. The wives even end up giving Jacob their maid servants for wives to see which wife and maidservant would give him the most children. As Arthur W. Pink says the thirtieth chapter of Genesis illustrates "the fruitage and consequences of polygamy. The domestic discords, the envies and jealousies between Jacob's several wives, forcibly illustrate and demonstrate the wisdom and goodness of God's law that each man should have his own wife, as well as each woman her own husband..." (Gleanings in Genesis, page 262)

But Jacob's wives did produce the twelve children that became the twelve tribes of Israel. As we have stated before the parents of children waited and asked God to give them names for their children that would define their character and their lives or the parents lives at the time of giving birth. Many times, their names had prophetic implications on their lives. The Zondervan Pictorial Bible Dictionary, page 399 gives a good summary of the children of Jacob's wives, what they called the children, and what their names meant. "The conflict between Jacob and Esau had its counterpart in that between Leah and Rachel. Leah won favor from God and bore Reuben (See! A son!), Simeon (God heard), Levi (Added), and Judah (Praise) (Genesis 29:31-35). Rachel's desire for a son led her to give her maid to Jacob and she bore Dan (Judge), and Naphthali (Wrestling) (Genesis 30:1-8). Leah in turn gave her maid who bore Gad (Troop) and Asher (Gladness). She (Leah) herself also bore Issachar (Pay for Hire), Zebulum (Abiding) and Dinah (feminine for Dan or Judge). Rachel then bore a son, Joseph (Adding) (Genesis 30:22-27) ..." The last son to be born was Benjamin to Rachel, but in the process of child birth, Rachel dies. "Then they journeyed from Bethel. And when there was little distance to go to Ephrath, Rachel travailed in childbirth, and she had hard labor. Now it came to pass, when she was in hard labor, that the midwife said to her, "Do not fear; you will have this son also." And so, it was, as her soul was departing (for she died) that she called his name Ben-Oni (the son of my sorrow), but his father called him Benjamin (the son of my right hand). So, Rachel died and was buried on her way to Ephrath (that is, Bethlehem)." (Genesis 35:16-19) Names in the Bible are only important when it gives prophetic insight into the child's life or when God chooses to change the name of the person and thereby change the person for eternity. We will see this when Jacob's name is changed by God, when Jacob comes face to face with God. One can also see through the changing the name of the Patriarchs—Abraham and Jacob—that God under the Old Testament (Covenant) is calling them His children. They may not totally understand the name changing on earth, but they will when they pass the veil of death and spend eternity with God.

Jacob after he had worked for fourteen years for Leah and Rachel was thinking seriously of leaving Laban and returning to Canaan. He mentions this to Laban about returning home to Canaan. "And it came to pass, when Rachel had borne Joseph, that Jacob said to Laban, "Send me away, that I may go to my own place, and to my country. Give me my wives and children for whom I have served you, and let me go; for you know my service which I have done for you." And Laban said to him, "Please stay, if I have found favor in your eyes, for I have learned by experience that the Lord has blessed me for your sake." Then he said, "Name me your wages and I will give it." (Genesis 30:25-28) One must take note at this point Jacob does not have any sheep or cattle. His wages have been his wives and children. Also, one must see that Laban realizes he has been blessed by God because Jacob has been working for him. Laban has a compromised relationship with God, because he has idols in his house and is living in idolatry. Whereas, Jacob worships God only. The next few verses shows the shrewdness of Jacob as he negotiates a deal with Laban that will allow him to obtain a lot of cattle from Laban.

Arthur W. Pink in his book, Gleaning in Genesis, page 272, says this about Jacob's shrewdness. "The sequel would seem to show that Jacob accepted Laban's offer, and decided to prolong his stay. Instead, however, of leaving himself at the mercy of his grasping and deceitful uncle, who had already "changed his wages ten times" (Genesis 31:7), Jacob determined to outwit the one whom he had served for upwards of twenty years by suggesting a plan which left him the master of the situation, and promised to greatly enrich him. (See Genesis 30:31-42) Much has been written concerning this device of Jacob to get the better of Laban and at the same time secure for himself that which he had earned, and varied have been the opinions expressed. One thing seems clear: unless God prospered it, Jacob's plan failed, for something more than sticks from which a part of the bark had been removed was needed to make the cattle bear "ring streaked, speckled, and spotted" young ones. (Genesis 30:39)"

From this quote from Mr. Pink, and from what the Bible says, God had to be in the plan of Jacob for it to succeed. And God was in the plan for the last verse of Genesis 30 states how God prospered Jacob. "Thus, the man (Jacob) became exceedingly prosperous, and had large flocks, female and male servants, and camels and donkeys." (Genesis 30:43) When Jacob succeeded in becoming prosperous and Laban's livestock began to dwindle, because of the deal Laban made with Jacob, this became the turning point in Jacob and Laban's relationship. Jacob began to notice this not just the family of Laban but Laban, himself. "Now Jacob heard the words of Laban's sons, saying, "Jacob has taken away all that was our father's, and from what was our father's he has acquired all this wealth." And Jacob saw that the countenance of Laban and indeed it was not favorable toward him as before. Then the Lord said to Jacob, "Return to the land of your fathers, and to your kindred, and I will be with you." (Genesis 31:1-3) Now, Jacob acquiring most all of Laban's livestock occurred in a short period of time. This is why Laban and his sons were not favorable toward Jacob as before. Jacob had wanted to leave earlier. Now God wanted him to leave and He told Jacob that He would be with him. God's Covenant protection would enable Jacob to leave without a fight with Laban.

The fact that Laban was not able to succeed in hurting and deceiving Jacob about the livestock shows God's Covenant protection over Jacob and his family. Now Jacob must get his wives on board about leaving their father's house and the country they had lived in all of their lives. Therefore, he calls Leah and Rachel out to the field to tell them his plan. Jacob tells them how their father, Laban, has tried to deceive him and changed his wages ten times, yet he has worked with all of his heart to please Laban. He also told them that God had blessed him with the livestock of Laban. (Genesis 31:4-10) Finally, Jacob tells them that God wants them to leave that land and go back to Canaan and they agree with him. "Then the Angel of the Lord (Jesus) spoke to me in a dream, saying, 'Jacob.' And I said, 'Here I am." And He said, 'Lift up your eyes now and see, all the rams which leap upon the flocks are streaked and gray-spotted; for I have seen all that Laban is doing to you. I am the God of Bethel, where you anointed the pillar, and where you made a vow to Me. Now arise, get out of this land, and return to the land of your kindred." (Genesis 31:11-13) Leah and Rachel agree with him about leaving. They don't believe they have any inheritance any longer in that land. They consider themselves to be sold to Jacob and that all the riches God has given Jacob actually belong to them and their children. (Genesis 31:14-16)

Actually, in all of this, Laban is acting as God's mirror to show Jacob how he really is. I believe it caused Jacob to want to change his character of being a deceiver. There were still some changes that needed to take place in his life and even in his household. Jacob, his family and his livestock sneak away while Laban is shearing his sheep. He does not know they have left until after three days. Before Rachel leaves she steals her father's household gods that he worships. Unbeknownst to Jacob, Rachel has now verified she was living in idolatry. There may have been some more. Laban overtakes Jacob in the hill country of Gilead. God has already dealt with Laban about letting Jacob return to Canaan. What Laban is really interested in are the household gods that Rachel has stolen. Rachel hides them in a camel's saddle and sits on it, so he can not find them. Later, we will discuss why Rachel stole these household gods and what she hoped to accomplish with having them. Laban is forced to leave without them and makes a Covenant with Jacob. The essence of the Covenant is Laban will not go after Jacob into Canaan and Jacob will not return to Padan-

Aram. Thus, God has protected Jacob from Laban. Protection is one of the main characteristics of walking in Covenant Relationship with God.

Jacob's Name Is Changed

The Covenant of God with Jacob is actually bringing him to a place in his life, where Jacob wants change. He has faced Laban, a mirror image of Jacob's character, and now he sees the need for change. But when it comes to our nature and character, we cannot change them ourselves. We need God to bring us to that place of change and then for Him to change us. As soon as Jacob leaves Padan-Aram and comes into Canaan, he is met by the angels of God. (Genesis 32:1) Is it not interesting when Jacob comes back to Canaan, he is met by the very presence of God? The land of Canaan is the land of blessing and the very presence of God. But what happens next is going to scare him. When you leave where God wants you, you are leaving the very presence of God. When you come back, you come back to the presence of God.

Jacob sends messengers to the land of Edom, where his brother, Esau, lives. The messengers return and tell him that Esau is coming and four hundred men with him. "So, Jacob was greatly afraid and distressed; and he divided the people that were with him, and the flocks and herds and camels, into two companies." (Genesis 32:7) He prays to God in essence asking Him to protect him and his family and all that he has. Then after praying, Jacob decides to send his brother presents of flocks and animals, hoping that the presents will appease his brother. He gives the servants specific instructions about how to explain about the presents to his brother. One can see that Jacob is leaning on the arm of flesh rather than just trusting God in this situation. Even though he is in Covenant Relationship with God, it has been awhile since he has had to trust God with this situation with his brother, Esau.

Finally, Jacob takes all of his family across the ford of Jabbok and then he is left alone that night by himself. Jacob knows tomorrow he will see his brother, Esau, face to face. He has not seen him in twenty years. He has sent his flocks, his cattle, the children, his wives and concubines across the ford of Jabbok. Now, Jacob is all by himself and yet he is not alone. "Then Jacob was left alone; and a Man (God, Himself) wrestled with him until the breaking of day. Now when He saw that He did not prevail against him (Jacob), He touched the socket of his (Jacob's) hip; and the socket of Jacob's hip was out of joint as He wrestled with him. And He said, "Let me go, for the day breaks." But he (Jacob) said, "I will not let you go unless You bless me." And He (God) said to him (Jacob), "What is your name?" And he said, "Jacob." (Genesis 32:24-27)

Jacob is wrestling with God about all that he is and all that he wants changed. This time Jacob is not giving up. He wants to be blessed by God, but he can't in his present condition. God wants him to quit and give up, because it is nearly day and they have been wrestling all night over who Jacob is. But Jacob will not give up. So, God hurts him. Jacob is struggling to continue wrestling. Jacob's hip is out of joint, but he keeps wrestling. Finally, God asks Jacob who he is. And Jacob replies Jacob which means supplanter, deceiver, trickster. When Jacob says his name, he knows what God is trying to do. God wants Jacob to finally confess what he is and then God can change his name. That is what God wants from us. He wants us to confess what we really are in character and in nature; then God can change us and change our name.

"And He (God) said, "Your name shall no longer be called Jacob, but Israel; for you have struggled with God and with men, and have prevailed. Then, Jacob asked Him, saying, "Tell me your name, I pray." And He said, "Why is it that you asked about My Name? And He blessed him (Israel) there. And Jacob called the name of the place Peniel. For I have seen God face to face and my life is preserved. Just as he (Israel) crossed over Peniel the sun rose on him, and he limped on his hip." (Genesis 32:28-31) Only God can change our name. Notice Isaac and Rebekah called him Jacob. But God has the right to change our name. God told Jacob you are no longer to be called Jacob but Israel, which literally means Prince with God. When his name was changed, his nature and character begin to change. Change is something that is taking place, but is not completed immediately. I believe that is why in certain places after this chapter in Genesis, Jacob is called Jacob and other places he is called Israel. It is an ongoing process.

Look at Genesis 48 and you will see in certain places he is called Jacob (Genesis 48:2,3) and other places he is called Israel (Genesis 48:8,10,11, 14, 21). "But we all, with open face beholding as in a glass the glory of the Lord, are changed into the same image from glory to glory, even as by the Spirit of the Lord." (2 Corinthians 3:18 KJV) An old song I learned in Bible College went something like this. "From glory to glory He is changing me; He's changing me; He's changing me; His likeness and image drew perfect in me; the love of God shown to the world." On this earth the change is according to God; how He wishes to change us from glory to glory by the Holy Spirit of God. Just like Jacob to Israel; the same is true with us. Whatever our earthily fathers called us before, now God is calling us to be His sons and daughters.

The next day he met Esau face to face. Something had happened in Esau's life as well. God had been working on Esau too. "Then he crossed over before them and bowed himself to the ground seven times until he (Jacob) came near his brother (Esau). But Esau ran to meet him, and fell on his neck and kissed him and they wept." (Genesis 33:3-4) There was not much need for words, God has caused a restoration of their relationship that day. Covenant Relationship with God will bring a restoration of relationships with family and others.

Dinah's Sin

God has brought Jacob back to the land of promise, but Jacob's sons still have a lot of Laban, their grandfather's character and nature in them. This is seen when Jacob's daughter, Dinah, goes out to see the daughters of the land in the town of Shechem. "Now Dinah the daughter of Leah, whom she had borne to Jacob, went out to see the daughters of the land. And when Shechem the son of Hamor the Hivite, prince of the country, saw her, he took her, lay with her and violated her." (Genesis 34:1-2) Dinah, Jacob's daughter, is defiled by Shechem when she goes out to visit with the daughters of the land. Dinah actually brings this on herself by going out to visit with the daughters of the world without permission from her parents, especially her father. Daughters don't go out like that in far eastern countries unless they are in rebellion. Shechem, one of the princes of the land, immorally has relations with her and then wants her to be his wife. Hamor, the Hivite and Shechem's father, asks Jacob for her.

Now we will be able to see that being a deceiver runs in Jacob's family. The sons of Jacob's family tell Shechem and his father, Hamor, that they cannot allow Dinah to marry Shechem unless all of the men of Shechem are circumcised and become like the sons of Jacob. Genesis 34:13 says the sons of Jacob "spoke deceitfully." Genesis 34:14-19 describes the deceitful plan that they plotted with the men of Shechem. This all pleased Shechem and his father, Hamor, and they went to the city gate and convinced all the men and boys of the city to be circumcised. All were circumcised. But the sons of Jacob had no intention of allowing Dinah to stay there and/or marry Shechem. This was all done to make the men of the city weak, so Jacob's sons could come in and take Dinah out of the city by force and slaughter all the men there. They waited until the third day when all the men and boys were very weak.

"Now it came to pass on the third day when they (the men of Shechem) were in pain, that two of the sons of Jacob, Simeon and Levi, Dinah's brothers (all three had Leah as their mother), each took his sword and came boldly upon the city and killed all the males. And they killed Hamor and Shechem his son with the edge of the sword and took Dinah from Shechem's house, and went out. The sons of Jacob came and plundered the city, because their sister had been defiled." (Genesis 34:25-27) Jacob had another mirror experience of being deceitful and this time the mirror experience was watching his sons deceive Shechem, Hamor and the men of Shechem. He saw what had been in him—the Jacob nature, supplanter, deceitful—in them. He rebukes his sons for doing it, but he knows they inherited those character traits from him. "Then Jacob said to Simeon and Levi, "You have troubled me by making me obnoxious among the inhabitants of the land, among the Canaanites and Perizzites; and sense I am few in number, they will gather themselves together against me and kill me, I shall be destroyed, my household and I." But they said, "Should he treat our sister like a harlot." (Genesis 34:30-31)

Therefore, who is really at fault here—Dinah, Shechem, or Dinah's brothers? Rev. Jimmy Swaggart in his The Expositor's Study Bible, pages 68-69, says talks first about Dinah being at fault, Shechem had some fault and her brothers had some fault. Rev. Swaggart quotes The Pulpit Commentary, "Dinah paid the full penalty of her carelessness; she suffered the fate which Satan planned for Sarah and Rebekah in the land of Pharaoh and Abimelech; she was seen and taken by the son of the prince, forcibly, it seems against her will, but yet with the claims of her lover." There you see that both Dinah and Shechem both were to blame. If Dinah had not gone out into the world to the daughters of the world, she would not have been seen by Shechem. According to oustolerance.org on women in Old Testament (Covenant) times says this about women. "Unmarried women were not allowed to leave the home of their father without permission." It is most certain that Jacob did not give her permission to leave the home. Actually, Dinah was in rebellion against the traditional role of women of that time. Therefore, she is definitely at fault. Shechem was at fault too. In Old Testament (Covenant) times if a young man saw a woman he was interested in marrying, he talked to his father and his father dealt with the father of the woman. Most of the time the father and mother decided who the young woman is going to marry. Shechem and his family were living in idolatry and probably did not follow traditional customs when it came to marriage and the fact that he and his father were part of the ruling family of that city, because the city was called by their name, Shechem. The King James Version in Genesis 34:2 says "...he defiled her (Dinah)" The New King James Version in Genesis 34:2 says "...(Shechem) violated her (Dinah)" Both describe the incident as being forced by Shechem on her and not by her consent. The brothers, Simeon and Levi, the Scriptures say acted deceitfully. They waited until the men of the city were sore and in pain before they came and killed all the men of Shechem. (Genesis 34:25) The Scriptures give the impression that they had no intent of allowing Dinah to marry Shechem. Rev. Jimmy Swaggart says this about what they did in his The Expositor's Study Bible, page 70. "There is nothing to justify what these men (Simeon and Levi) did...In fact, the annals of uncivilized warfare scarcely record a more atrocious crime."

The Bible does not color code anything. One sees the people in the Bible as they are. You see the good, the bad and the ugly. Notice the fear that Jacob has after his sons do this. Fear is apart of the old nature that must be destroyed at the Cross of Christ. He also did not say anything when Simeon and Levi made the proposal that all the men be circumcised. He only says something after this bloody incident. One might say that silence breeds consent. Jacob might have known what his sons were planning. When it happens, he sees a mirror of himself.

As far as fear is concerned, Jacob had nothing to fear. "And they journeyed, and the terror of God was upon the cities that were all around them, and they did not pursue the sons of Jacob." (Genesis 35:5) God had intervened in that area and the Covenant of God with Jacob protected them from the other cities. The sons were still under the Covenant their father had with God. God had not as yet reached out to any the sons of Jacob or Dinah in Covenant Relationship. As we shall talk later only Joseph will actually come into that Covenant Relationship. Part of this is due to the fact that Rachel, Leah, the sons of Jacob and Dinah are actually living in a compromised relationship with God. Rachel has the household gods of her father, Laban. Therefore, there is a compromise going on right in Jacob's house. Jacob knew about it. Because in Genesis 35 he tells his family to get rid of the household gods. Evidently there are more than the one god that Rachel stole from her father, because he speaks of "gods" plural in Genesis 35:2.

The Household gods

It has been about ten years since Jacob and his family have returned to Canaan. God speaks in Padan-Aram asked him to return to Bethel. In Genesis 31:13 God says to Jacob, "I am the God of Bethel, where you anointed the pillar and where you made a vow to Me. Now arise and get out of the land, and return to the land of your kindred." God actually wanted him to go straight to Bethel, but instead he and his family went to Shechem. He might have avoided the problem with Dinah if he had followed God to Bethel. God during all this time is dealing with Jacob out of grace and mercy.

Now God gives him specific instructions. “Then God said to Jacob, “Arise, go up to Bethel and dwell there; and make an altar there to God, who appeared to you when you fled from the face of Esau your brother.” (Genesis 35:1) As we said before, Jacob had become aware that there were household gods among his family members, starting with Rachel. Others must have joined her in her idolatrous behavior for Jacob talks of more than one household god. God all this time has been dealing with Jacob out of grace. Jacob did not come immediately to Bethel as God had asked him to do in Padan-Aram. Now his household is worshipping household gods. But God does not say anything about it to Jacob. Jacob knows that Rachel is worshipping the household god that she had stolen from Laban, her father. But God does speak to Jacob about returning to Bethel to worship Him.

Immediately, God reminded Jacob of the time when He extended His Covenant to Jacob. That too was a hard time in Jacob’s life when he was fleeing from Esau. Even though now Jacob’s relationship with Esau has been restored, he does not want to live close to him. Arthur W. Pink in his book, Gleanings in Genesis, page 303 says this about Jacob’s life at this point. “That God’s Word to Jacob recorded in Genesis 35:1 was a reproof is further evidenced by the immediate effect which it had upon him. Not only had Jacob failed to go to Bethel, but what was worse, while Jehovah had been his (Jacob’s) personal God, his household was defiled by idols. Rebekah’s stolen “teraphim” had proven a snare to the family. At the time Laban overtook them Jacob seems to have known nothing about these gods; later, however, he was evidently aware of their presence, but not until aroused by the Lord appearing to him, did he exert his parental authority and have them put away. It is striking to note that though God, Himself said nothing, directly, about the “teraphim” yet, the immediate effect of His words was to stir Jacob’s conscience about them—"Then Jacob said unto his household and to all that were with him, ‘Put away the strange gods that are among you, and be clean, and change your garments.” (Genesis 35:2). These words show that Jacob was aware of the corrupt practices of his family, and had only too long connived at them.”

A lot of what was happening to Jacob and his family was the result of compromising about idolatry in the home. God had been gracious and had taken care of Jacob and his family despite the compromise of family members. But now it was time to get rid of all the household gods and worship Jehovah God only. As Rev. Pink said this had pricked Jacob's conscience. "And Jacob said to his household and to all who were with him, 'Put away the foreign gods that are among you, purify yourselves, and change your garments. Then let us arise and go to Bethel and I will make an altar there to God, who answered me in the day of all my distress and has been with me in the way I have gone.' So, they gave Jacob all the foreign gods which were in their hands, and all the earrings which were in their ears and Jacob hid them under the terebinth tree which was by Shechem." (Genesis 35:2-4)

In actuality, Jacob was asking Rachel and all the others in his family who worshipped the household gods, to let those things die and to worship his God, Jehovah. She had stolen those gods from Laban, possibly to give all the wealth of Laban to Jacob. Fred. H. Wright talks about this in his book, Manners and Customs of Bible Lands, page 119-120. "When Jacob left the home of Laban in Haran, Genesis says, "Rachel stole the teraphim (gods) that were in her father's (house)." (Genesis 31:19) Laban was very much agitated over the theft. He pursued Jacob's party and said to him, "Wherefore has thou stolen my gods?" (Genesis 31:30) But why was Laban so concerned about discovering those lost teraphim? Sir Charles Leonard Wodley, in charge of excavations in Ur of the Chaldees, tells of a tablet of that region which reveals a law that throws light on Rachel's theft. Dr. Wodley puts the law thus: "The possession of the household gods conferred the privilege of primogeniture." ("Primogeniture means the state or condition of being the first-born or eldest child of the same parents; the right of the eldest child." American Heritage Dictionary, page 1040) Thus Rachel must have stolen her brother's birthright when she took her father's teraphim, and she was thereby seeking to make Jacob the legal heir to the wealth of Laban. The ancient form of idolatry was virtually linked to family affairs. It would seem that Rachel brought forth those stolen teraphim (gods) when the family was about to move from Shechem to Bethel. Jacob said to his family at this time, "Put away the foreign gods that are among you and purify yourselves." (Genesis 35:2, A.R.V.) The presence of these relics of former days would indicate an effort to combine the superstitions and heathen charms of an idolatrous worship along with the worship of the true and living God..."

What Jacob was telling Rachel and everyone else in his household, I don't need those gods and neither do you. He wanted them to put the past behind and worship the true and living God. God would provide for them. From all indications Biblically, Jacob was already well off financially. What we see next is that Jacob's wives, concubines, children and servants were willing to trust their father and patriarch of the family. They turned all of their household gods to him and he hid them under a terebinth tree at Shechem. He left all those gods there, with all the hard memories of what his sons had done to rescue Dinah at Shechem. This would be a new era for his family, for they had turned to God from idols and chose to follow Him. The Apostle Paul said it this way in the book of Philippians. "But what things were gain to me, these I have counted loss for Christ. But indeed I also count all things loss for the excellence of the knowledge of Christ Jesus my Lord, for whom I have suffered the loss of all things, and count them as rubbish, that I may win Christ and be found in Him, not having my own righteousness, which is from the law, but that which is through faith in Christ, the righteousness which is from God by faith." (Philippians 3:7-9)

After that we see Jacob obeying God and doing what God had instructed him to do. "So, Jacob came to Luz (that is Bethel) which is in the land of Canaan, he and all the people who were with him. And he built an altar there and called the place El Bethel (God of the House of God), because there God appeared to him when he fled from the face of his brother." (Genesis 35:6-7) After being back in the land of Canaan seven or eight years, at God's insistence, he finally decided to obey God and return to Bethel as he had promised God. If you are going to abide in the Covenant of God that He has given you; you must obey God. Notice that Jacob and his family had been through some trials, but when he finally obeys God, he is blessed. A simple definition of faith is doing what God tells you do, when He tells you to do it. Jacob was not significantly blessed until he returns to Bethel.

Before we discuss what happened to Jacob at Bethel, there is one other event that took place right after he gets to Bethel. It is the death of Deborah, Rebekah's nurse. "Now Deborah, Rebekah's nurse, died, and she was buried before Bethel under the terebinth tree. So, the name of the place is called Allon Bachuth (Terebinth of Weeping)." (Genesis 35:8). This mention of Rebekah's name is the first time since Jacob and his family returned to Canaan. Because she is not mentioned or talked about at all, Bible scholars believe Rebekah had died. There is no mention of Rebekah except for this one place in chapter 35 from chapter 30 to the end of the book of Genesis except Genesis 49:31 where it is mentioned that Rebekah was buried next to Jacob. Therefore, most Bible scholars believe Rebekah never saw Jacob again, after he was sent away from the family by Isaac. This is a high price to pay for not seeking God about the promised Blessing of Isaac. Doing it your way, instead of God's way, has high consequences.

Evidently, Jacob saw his father, Isaac, and obtained Rebekah's nurse, Deborah, from him. Deborah is with Jacob and his family as they travel to Bethel. On the way there she dies and is buried under a terebinth tree. This seems to be the last remembrance of his mother and her influence in his life. Rebekah had told Jacob about the prophetic word over his life, but showed him the wrong way of acquiring that word. No doubt Jacob loved his mother in all this. It was probably hard to see her nurse, Deborah, pass. (Matthew Henry Commentary, Volume I, Genesis to Deuteronomy, page 205)

Jacob at Bethel

Probably, while Jacob is mourning the loss of Deborah, he has a fresh Revelation of God at Bethel. God knows just when to arrive on the scene and reveal Himself to Jacob. "Then God appeared to Jacob again, when he came from Padan Aram and blessed him. And God said to him, "Your name is Jacob; your name shall not be called Jacob anymore, but Israel shall be your name." So, He called his name Israel. And God said to him.

"I am God Almighty. Be fruitful and multiply; a nation and a company of nations shall proceed from you, and kings shall come from your body. The land which I gave to Abraham and Isaac I give to you; and to your descendants after you I give this land. Then God went up from him in the place where He talked with him." (Genesis 35:9-13)

If you read Genesis 28:10-22 and then read Genesis 35:9-13, you will see that God is renewing His Covenant Promises to Jacob. God has guided Jacob's steps from the beginning until now when he is at Bethel. Jacob may have lost sight of the Covenant Promises at times, but God is telling him they are still true. Once God has conferred and confirmed His Covenant with us, we can walk in it. Let us be sure to understand that the Canaanites and Hittites still seem to control and possess the land while Jacob was there. But this is a Covenant of faith that like Abraham and Isaac, you have to trust God to bring it about.

The next two events in Jacob's life show the closeness he had with his wife, Rachel, and then with his father, Isaac. After seeing God by revelation and then making an altar to God, he makes and offers a drink offering and an offering of oil to God. After worshipping God at Bethel, Jacob decides to move his family to Ephrath, which means fruitfulness. Ephrath is also called Bethlehem. When the family is on the journey to Ephrath (Bethlehem) his wife, Rachel, who is pregnant with child has hard labor and dies. But as Rachel dies, she gives birth to her second child, Benjamin. Rachel calls this child Benoni meaning son of suffering, but Jacob after Rachel dies changes his name to Benjamin meaning the son of my right hand. Names in the Old Testament (Covenant) were very significant. Parents prayed about naming their children believing that God would have a hand in naming each child they had. Jacob loved Rachel more than Leah and he did not want to remember Rachel in sorrow when he looked at the son that had just been born, so he changed the name to Benjamin, the son of my right hand. That is the reason for the change in names. Rachel thus had two sons; Joseph and Benjamin. Later toward the end of the book of Genesis, we shall see that Joseph was the favorite of Jacob. There are many reasons, but one of the reasons is Joseph's mother was Rachel and that love for Rachel carried over to the two sons, especially

Joseph. These two sons, Joseph and Benjamin are sons of Jacob's latter days. These two sons did not participate in what the older sons did like in Shechem. Although Jacob did still call them sons of his, he did not like what they did. We will talk about Isaac, his father, but we need to see how Jacob's fatherly Blessing plays out with his sons.

The important reason to take note of the fatherly Blessing or Covenant Blessing is not always given to the first-born child of the father as it was with all three Patriarchs. Isaac was born after Ishmael to Abraham, but God chose and preferred Isaac to Ishmael. Esau was considered to be the first-born of Isaac, but God chose and preferred Jacob to Esau. As Esau was disqualified because he sold his birthright to Jacob and then despised it, Jacob was given the birthright which was the Covenant Promise and Blessing. This also takes place with Jacob's first-born, Reuben.

We will discuss why Reuben is disqualified and Joseph and Joseph's two sons born in Egypt are chosen instead to inherit the Birthright and the Covenant Promise of Jacob. Jacob had a concubine named Bilhah. A concubine in Old Testament (Covenant) times was "(a woman) who was regarded as socially or sexually subservient, mistress (among polygamous people) a secondary wife of inferior rank." (Wikipedia-Concubine) This may have happened while Jacob was visiting his father Isaac. To be blunt, Reuben had immoral (sexual) relations with Bilhah. "Then Israel journeyed and pitched his tent beyond the tower of Eder. And it happened, when Israel dwelt in that land, that Reuben went and lay with Bilhah his father's concubine; and Israel heard about it." (Genesis 35:21-22) Maybe Rueben thought he would get away with it, but he did not. His father, Jacob, heard about it. This would disqualify Reuben from receiving the Covenant Birthright and the Covenant Blessing. As we have said before Jacob/Israel was the Patriarch of his family and he was considered to be the King of his family. He has the right to bypass Reuben, even though he is the firstborn of the family. Reuben was born to Leah (Genesis 35:23). For such sins against the family, Reuben lost his first-born son's Covenant privileges and blessings. Notice the prophetic word that Jacob/Israel delivers to Reuben on Jacob's death bed. "Reuben you are my firstborn, My might and the beginning of my strength, The excellency of dignity and the excellency of power. Unstable as water, you shall not excel, because you went up to your father's bed, then you defiled it---He went up to my couch." (Genesis 49:3-4). Matthew Henry's Commentary, Volume I, page 259, says this about this word Jacob spoke over Reuben. "He (Jacob) begins with him (Reuben)(v.3-4), for he was the firstborn, but by committing uncleanness with his father's wife, to the great reproach of the family to which he ought to have been an ornament, he forfeited the prerogative of the birthright; and his dying father (Jacob) here solemnly degrades him, though he does not disown or disinherit him; he shall have all the privileges of a son, but not of a firstborn." It is important to follow God and live according to his standards if you want to receive your Covenant Inheritance and Blessings. Jacob/Israel never rejected Reuben as a son, but he did lose the birthright he would have received. From that point on he lived beneath his inheritance and blessings as a son. This is a good example of what happens to Christians who don't live close to God and who fail to walk according to God's standards.

The last event in Genesis 35 is the death of Isaac. It is interesting to note that Jacob came and visited his father, Isaac, before his death. "Then Jacob came to his father Isaac at Mamre or Kirjath Arba (that is Hebron) where Abraham and Isaac had sojourned." (Genesis 35:27) Isaac had returned to Hebron to live out the rest of his days where his father, Abraham, had lived before him. This is the place that Jacob came to visit with his father, Isaac. Maybe Jacob apologized for deceiving him some thirty years earlier. We do not know. This is just a Biblically recorded incident that Jacob came to visit his father. We know that they had fellowship this last time.

Then the Bible records what happened when Isaac died. "Now the days of Isaac were one hundred and eighty years. So, Isaac breathed his last and died and was gathered to his people, being old and full of days. And his sons, Esau and Jacob buried him." (Genesis 35:28-29) Isaac actually lived longer than Abraham. He lived a very solitary life. Once God told him to stay in Canaan, Isaac never left. One thing is sure, when he died, both of his sons, Esau and Jacob, honored him by burying him together. This shows that the rift between Esau and Jacob was healed, and that they had a restored relationship. Covenant Relationship with God will cause one to walk in peace with others, even if the other person is not walking in close relationship with God. The Apostle Paul stated it this way, "If it is possible as much as depends on you, live peaceably with all men." (Romans 12:18)

Joseph is Jacob's Favorite Son

The last thing we wish to discuss about Covenant Promise and Blessing is that Jacob passed over Reuben and the other sons and chose Joseph as his favorite son. The father of a family in the East could bypass the firstborn and give the promised blessing to the son he considered to be his favorite. Jacob already knew about Reuben's infidelity at his expense since it was one of his wives, Bilhah. Also, Joseph reported on his brothers when they did something wrong. (Genesis 37:2) This is what the Bible says about Joseph in Genesis 37:3-4. "Now Israel loved Joseph more than all his children, because he was the son of his old age. Also, he made him a tunic of many colors. But when his brothers saw that their father loved him more than all his brothers, they hated him and could not speak peaceably to him." From this passage we can see that Joseph did not use wisdom in dealing with his brothers. They did not like him because he would tell the evil things that they were doing, to Jacob. Joseph was a tattle tale. Another reason they did not like him is because Jacob showed that he loved Joseph more than them. When Jacob, his father, awarded him the coat of many colors that meant for sure he would probably get the birthright and the promised blessing. It also helped that Joseph was one of the sons that Rachel produced and Jacob loved Rachel more than Leah and the other concubines.

Then, God begins to favor Joseph as well by giving him prophetic dreams about Joseph's future. The dreams of the sheaves show Joseph's brother's sheaves bowing down to his sheaf. (Genesis 37:6-8) This was the reaction of his brothers. "...So, they (Joseph's brothers) hated him (Joseph) even more for his dreams and his words." (Genesis 37:8b) The second dream he had he told his father, Jacob, and brothers. "Looked I have dreamed another dream. And this time, the sun, the moon, and the eleven stars bowed down to me." (Genesis 37:9b) This dream caused his father to rebuke him. "What is this dream that you have dreamed? Should your mother and I and your brothers indeed come to bow down to the earth before you." (Genesis 37:10) The Bible goes on to say that "his brothers envied him, but the father kept the matter in mind." (Genesis 37:11) From these Scriptures we can see that Joseph is not dealing wisely with his brothers. In the New Testament (Covenant) Jesus said this about that. "Do not give what is holy to the dogs, nor cast your pearls before swine, lest they trample them under their feet, and turn and tear you in pieces." (Matthew 7:6) Joseph's brothers already hated him and an opportunity was coming to the brothers to get even with Joseph.

Jacob does not see the hurt, the envy, and the hate in his son's eyes toward Joseph. If he had, he probably would have cautioned Joseph about what he was doing and saying to his brothers. Jacob only sees the bad that his older sons have done, therefore, he deals with them in that manner. Jacob sees what Reuben has done behind his back. He sees what Simeon and Levi did at Shechem to get Dinah back. He considers them brothers of cruelty. The rest of the older brothers plundered Shechem. Jacob told them they were making him look bad in the eyes of all the inhabitants of the land. In the midst of all that is Joseph, who has been so good. Therefore, Jacob gives Joseph a coat of many colors. What is significant about this coat of many colors? Got questions.com/coat of many colors? Has this insight about that coat. "As to the coat of many colors itself, the most common outer garment of this type was nothing more than a long cloth with a hole in the middle. After draping the long cloth over the shoulders, a rope or a belt was fastened around the waist. Some expositors argue that this particular coat was especially valued because sleeves were sown into the garment. Others believe the coat was ornamental by many colors. The real issue of course has nothing to do with the colors or sleeves. Jacob presented the specialized coat to Joseph as a sign that Joseph was esteemed above his brothers. The coat signified Joseph as being Jacob's choice as the future head of the clan—an honor normally bestowed upon the firstborn son."

There is the significance of the many-colored coat. Reuben, as firstborn, was out because of his sin against his father and of course his sin against God. Jacob was letting them know who the new leader of the family would be. So, of course the brothers wanted to do away with him anyway they could. That is why when the opportunity came to sell him into Egyptian bondage, they took it. The brothers got together and dipped that coat of many colors with lamb's blood, so their father would think Joseph had been killed by a wild animal. The older brothers believed that as a slave to the Egyptians they would never see Joseph again. But they were wrong!

The prophetical dreams were not just for Joseph's brother's benefit, but God was telling Joseph to trust Him no matter what happened. What happens when we are given a prophetical word from God? The enemy, the devil, tries to engineer circumstances, so that we will drop that prophetical word and also that we cease to trust God. But Joseph still trusted God when he was sold into slavery and again when Potiphar's wife falsely accused him. When he was put in prison for the lies of Potiphar's wife, Joseph was still looking up to God for the answer. Joseph never lost his trust in God. God saw him through all of that to victory.

One can see as one reads the life of Joseph in Genesis chapters 39 to 41 while he is in slavery, that he is being trained for leadership. Each step he takes with Potiphar, the chief officer of the prison and with Pharaoh, himself, is training him how to deal with the Egyptians. Potiphar's house trains him in finances and how to resist an immoral woman. That is something Reuben failed in doing. In prison, Joseph is given complete control of the prison and the prisoners. God has already given him the gift of interpreting dreams and this will become handy in the Egyptian prison. He interprets the chief butler's dream and the chief baker's dream and they both come to pass just like Joseph interpreted them. (Genesis chapter 40) It is this gift that God has given him to interpret dreams that opens the door for Joseph to understand and interpret Pharaoh's dream in Genesis chapter 41. With the interpretation of Pharaoh's dream of seven good years of harvests and seven bad years of harvest put him in the office of Governor of Egypt, second behind Pharaoh, himself. All of those events leading up to that moment were training him to bring Egypt and other countries out of the severe famine that would be coming to the world later. (Genesis chapter 41:37 to chapter 50)

Joseph's eleven brothers and his father do end up bowing to Joseph and come under his rule in Egypt, because he is second in command behind Pharaoh and Governor of all of Egypt. The prophetic dreams from God that he had as a youth did come to pass. What does all this mean? It means that in 1 Chronicles 5:1, Jacob ultimately honors Joseph in giving Joseph's sons the Covenant Birthright and the Covenant Blessing. God had already put His stamp of approval and favor upon Joseph. God had honored him as a fruitful son. In 1 Chronicles 5:1-2 we see who gets the Birthright. "Now the sons of Reuben the firstborn of Israel—he was indeed the firstborn, but because he defiled his father's bed, his birthright was given to the sons of Joseph, the son of Israel, so that the genealogy is not listed according to birthright; yet Judah prevailed over his brothers, and from him came a ruler (Jesus), although the birthright was Joseph's— (the right of the firstborn)"

The Bible is the best commentary on the Bible. How does this all make sense? Out of Judah would come the Ruler—Jesus Christ—but that was in the future. If one looks at the prophecies over Jacob's sons, Judah receives profound prophetic words for the future. The whole prophecy is about Jesus and how He will reign during the Millennium. "Judah you are he whom your brothers will praise; Your hand shall be on the neck of your enemies; Your father's children shall bow down to you. Judah is a lion's whelp; From the prey, my son, you have gone up. He bows down, he lies down as a lion; And as a lion, who shall rouse him? The scepter shall not depart from Judah, nor a lawgiver between his feet, Until Shiloh comes, And to Him shall be the obedience of people. Binding his donkey to the vine, And his donkey's colt to the choice vine. He washed his garments in wine, And his clothes in the blood of grapes. His eyes are darker than wine, And his teeth whiter than milk." (Genesis 49:8-12) Therefore, the prophetic word that Jacob gave for Joseph and his two sons were in the immediate future. But for Judah, the prophetic word was concerning the Lord Jesus Christ and his millennial reign at the end of days for a thousand years.

In Summary…

I wanted to show the other Patriarchs other than Abraham—Isaac and Jacob—and how they responded to the Abrahamic Covenant. Isaac and Jacob did not have their own Covenant with God, but rather received the Abrahamic Covenant with the Covenant Promises and Blessings. God shared with each father starting with Abraham which son was going to inherit those Promises and Blessings. The Bible shows their good points and character flaws of both Isaac and Jacob. It is God's intent and purpose to remove the flaws and to bring each family into Covenant Relationship with Him.

Sometimes with Jacob as a good example, it takes a wrestling with God to the breaking of the day to change Jacob. But Jacob would not let go of God until God changed Jacob's name to Israel and receive the blessing of God, Himself. (Genesis 32) Listen to what Jacob said about that place in which he came face to face with God. "And Jacob called the name of the place Peniel. "For I have seen God face to face and my life is preserved." (Genesis 32:30)

Then, one might look at Isaac, who every day, spent time in the presence of God. Every day, he wanted to dig a little deeper with his wells, to find the grace and blessings of God. The wells he dug are a picture or type of the Word of God. He obeyed God by staying in the Promise Land where God's Holy Presence was. Of course, his flesh liked the venison that Esau cooked. It nearly deceived Isaac into giving the wrong man (Esau), the Covenant Promises and Blessings of God. We don't know how God would have changed that situation, because Rebekah and Jacob used the arm of the flesh to get those Covenant Promises and Blessings. It would cost Jacob to be separated from his mother the rest of his life and her separated from her son the rest of her life. (Genesis 27:1-27; 28:1-9) Family relations were broken also between Jacob and Esau. Although, it is not mentioned in Scripture, this act of deception by way of the flesh possibly separated Jacob and his father, Isaac. But that is what sin does to families whether they are believers or unbelievers.

In Covenant Relationships with men, God is trying to break those sinful ties to the flesh. God wants man to trust Him and allow him to bring Covenant Promises and Blessings to everyone who has accepted His Covenant. The further into history man has gone, the more deceptive man is. God in His grace and mercy has to work to bring man back to a place of honesty and faith toward Him.

Now Jacob's twelve sons would become the nation of Israel. They would grow and multiply in Egypt. Because of the famine that God allows the nation would not grow in Canaan, the Promise Land, but in the land of Egypt (the world). Egypt is a type and picture of the world. The Covenant Blessings and Promises are given to Joseph by God. Under Joseph's leadership Israel and Egypt is preserved from the famine. As prophesied earlier in the Book of Genesis, Israel will be in bondage for four hundred and thirty years or four generations. Then He (God) said to Abram. "Know certainly that your descendants will be strangers in the land that is not theirs, and will serve them and they will afflict them four hundred years. And also, the nation whom they serve I (God) will judge: afterward, they shall come out with great possessions. Now as for you (Abraham), you shall be buried in a good old age. But in the fourth generation they shall return here; for the iniquity of the Amorites is not complete." (Genesis 15:13-16)

This prophecy of God was given to Abraham years before it happened. (Hebrew Calendar) BibleCalendarproof.com. says the actual starting of this prophecy starts at Genesis 21:12 and explains who would be the seed of Abraham. "But God said to Abraham, Do not let it be displeasing in your sight because of the lad (Ishmael) or because of the bondwoman (Hagar). Whatever Sarah has said to you, listen to her voice; for in Isaac your seed shall be called," This verse puts God's stamp of approval on Isaac as Abraham's seed by Abraham sending Hagar away. This is the point at which the 400-year prophecy begins; five years after Isaac's birth. This is when God tells and Abraham knows that his seed is in Isaac and no other. Also, it was the scoffing of Isaac by Ishmael that initiated that affliction. The 25 years, plus 5 years total 30 years, the difference between 400 years and 430 years."

Many Bible scoffers, scoff at the Bible because of the prophecy given to Abraham and then they read in Exodus 12:40-41 and Genesis 15:13-15 and they say that these two Bible texts contradict. "Now the sojourn of the children of Israel who lived in Egypt was four hundred and thirty years. And it came to pass at the end of the four hundred and thirty years—on the very same day—it came to pass that all the armies of the Lord went out of Egypt." (Exodus 12:40-41) All of this was calculated by Don Roth, an engineer, proved by the Hebrew Biblical Calendar. His work shows no contradiction between these two Scriptures. You can check it out yourself on either BiblicalCalendarProof.com. or endarproof.com.

This leads us to the next great Covenant of God, generally called the Mosaic Covenant. Many Biblical scholars call it the Mosaic Covenant, when in actuality it is God's Covenant with the nation of Israel. Moses was the servant of God, who delivered the Covenant to the nation of Israel. Four books of the Bible center around this Covenant—Exodus, Numbers, Leviticus, and Deuteronomy. Thus, God changed His Covenant Relationship with individual men to a Covenant Relationship with a whole nation—the nation of Israel. The foundation for the Mosaic Covenant is the Abrahamic Covenant. One cannot obey the Covenant of Law without faith. One cannot really obey any Covenant without faith and God has given every man, woman and child a measure of faith. "...as God has dealt to each one a measure of faith." (Romans 12:3c) Chapter 7 will begin our study of the Mosaic Covenant. We conclude this chapter with this Scripture. "But without faith it is impossible to please Him, for he who comes to God must believe that He is, and that He is a rewarder of those who diligently seek Him." (Hebrews 11:6)

Chapter 7
The Mosaic Covenant

The foundation of the Mosaic Covenant is the Abrahamic Covenant. The use of altars, clean animals for sacrifice, a particular place like Bethel to worship in the Abrahamic Covenant are identified and followed up in the Mosaic Covenant. The major difference is the Abrahamic Covenant is identified with the man Abraham; while the Mosaic Covenant is identified with Moses and in particular the children of Israel as a nation. Moses is the channel through which the Mosaic Covenant comes to the nation of Israel. This Covenant is for the nation of Israel. The Mosaic Covenant is written in its entirety by Moses and is recorded in the books—Exodus, Leviticus, Numbers and Deuteronomy.

God's word gives us a good picture of Israel coming out of Egypt, but Israel does not know how to approach God. God in His mercy extends His Covenant to His people. In Egypt, Israel had grown into such a multitude of people that Pharaoh wanted to stop them from growing. He tried to get the midwives to kill the baby boys at birth, but they feared God more than they did Pharaoh. (Exodus 1) We must see this as we approach the Mosaic Covenant. Then Pharaoh made the children of Israel serve with bitter, hard bondage. "But the more they afflicted them (Israel) the more they multiplied and grew. And they (Egypt and Pharaoh) were in dread of the children of Israel." (Exodus 1:12)

One can read how Moses' life was spared time and again by God in Exodus chapter 1 through chapter 2. God calls him to deliver his people in Exodus chapters 3 and 4. Moses tries to get his people released and God sends plague after plague on Egypt as Pharaoh continually hardens his heart against God in Exodus chapters 5 through chapter 12. We are not really studying the plagues and how Israel was delivered from Egyptian bondage. Our purpose is to understand the Mosaic Covenant and how and why God gave this Covenant to Israel. But you may want to read Exodus chapters 1 through chapter 12 to get a background for this Mosaic Covenant.

Only after ten plagues, which included the death of the firstborn of Egypt, did Pharaoh allow the children of Israel to leave. As Israel is escaping to the Red Sea, Pharaoh attempts to recapture them. (Exodus chapter 14) This would result in the death of all his mighty men in the Red Sea. All of Israel had walked on dry land through the midst of the Red Sea and were now on the other side. "Then the Lord said to Moses, "Stretch out your hand over the sea, that the waters may come back upon the Egyptians, on their chariots, and on their horsemen." And Moses stretched out his hand over the sea: and when the morning appeared, the sea returned to its full depth, while the Egyptians were fleeing into it. So, the Lord overthrew the Egyptians in the midst of the sea. Then the waters returned and covered the chariots, the horsemen and all the army of Pharaoh that came into the sea after them. Not so much as one of them remained. But the children of Israel had walked on dry land in the midst of the Red Sea, and the waters were a wall to them on their right hand and on the left." (Exodus 14:26-29)

From this passage we see that Israel has been delivered as God had promised Abraham, before Abraham's death. This is stated in Genesis 15:13-14. "Then He (God) said to Abram(ham): know certainly that your descendants will be strangers in a land that is not theirs, and will serve them, and they will afflict them four hundred years. And also, the nation whom they serve I will judge: afterward they will come out with great possessions." One thing we did not share is that the Israelites asked the Egyptians for articles of silver, gold and clothing. This is what it says in Exodus 12:36. "And the Lord had given the people (Israel) favor in the sight of the Egyptians, so that they granted them what they requested. Thus, they plundered the Egyptians."

God had redeemed Israel and plundered the Egyptians, but Israel still did not know how to approach God. Always before, God made a Covenant with Noah, Abraham, Isaac, and Jacob. God is a Covenant keeping God. Today, we have been redeemed by the blood of Jesus Christ. His blood has washed away all of our sins. Just like in the Old Testament (Covenant) we depend on other people to approach God for us—prayer warriors, ministers, evangelists. We are under a New Covenant, a better Covenant, but we don't understand it. May God help us to understand the New Covenant that God has given us. May we pray the prayer that the Apostle Paul prayed for the Ephesian believers. May we adopt that prayer as our prayer. "(T)hat the God of our Lord Jesus Christ, the Father of glory, may give to you the spirit of wisdom and revelation in the knowledge of Him, the eyes of your understanding being enlightened; that you may know what is the hope of His calling, what are the riches of His inheritance in the saints, and what is the exceeding greatness of His power toward us who believe, according to the working of His mighty power which He worked in Christ when He raised Him from the dead and seated Him at His right hand in the heavenly places, far above all principality and power and might and dominion and every name that is named, not only in this age but also in that which is to come." (Ephesians 1:17-21) May God give us a revelation of the Covenant Relationship we have in Christ Jesus. Even New Testament (Covenant) believers, God wants us to walk in Covenant Relationship with Him. From the Old Testament (Covenant) we can learn a lot about walking in Covenant Relationship with Him.

When the children of Israel got to Mount Sinai, they were to encounter God in a new way. They had lived in slavery for over four hundred years. The nation of Israel actually needed the Covenant that God was going to spell out for them. As the Apostle Paul said in the New Testament (Covenant), it is important especially for unbelievers to have laws. Listen to what he says in 1 Timothy 1:8-11. "But we know that the law is good if one uses it lawfully, knowing this: that the law is not made for the righteous person but for the lawless and insubordinate (disobedient) for the ungodly and for sinners, for the unholy and profane, for murderers of fathers, and for murderers of mothers, for manslayers, for fornicators, for sodomites, for kidnappers, for liars, for perjurers, and if there is any other thing that is contrary to sound doctrine, according to the glorious gospel of the blessed God which was committed to my trust."

Now we come to a place in the Wilderness of Sinai where God will meet with Moses. This is a significant time, because this is the first mention of a Covenant in the book of Exodus. This meeting is described in Exodus 19:1-8. I am going to quote all eight verses so you may get a picture of Moses meeting with God. Notice it is not the people meeting with God, but Moses alone is meeting with God. Because, of the thunder and smoke the children of Israel are actually afraid to meet with God. Later, they tell Moses to meet with God and then Moses can tell them what God has said. Moses would be the intermediary between God and the people. This is why they sent Moses to speak for them.

"In the third month after the children of Israel had gone out of the land of Egypt, on the same day, they came to the wilderness of Sinai. For they had departed from Rephidim, had come to the desert of Sinai, and camped in the wilderness. So, Israel camped there before the mountain. And Moses went up to God, and the Lord called to him from the mountain saying, "Thus, you shall say to the house of Jacob and to the children of Israel. 'You have seen what I did to the Egyptians, and how I bore you on eagle's wings and brought you to Myself. Now therefore, if you will indeed obey My voice and keep My covenant, then you shall be a special treasure to Me above all people, for all the earth is Mine. And you shall be to Me a kingdom of priests and a holy nation. These are the words you shall speak to the children of Israel.' So, Moses came and called for the elders of the people, and laid before them all these words which the Lord commanded him. Then all the people answered together and said, "All that the Lord has spoken we will do." So, Moses brought back the words of the people to the Lord." (Exodus 19:1-8)

We must insert here that the Elders of the people were a result of Jethro's suggestion to Moses. Jethro was Moses father-in-law by marriage and he had just brought Moses' wife, Zipporah, and his two sons to Moses from the desert. This suggestion was made to Moses in the eighteenth chapter of Exodus. Jethro observed that Moses did not have any help to judge the people. Jethro suggested that Moses appoint Elders to judge small matters and that Moses could judge hard matters and cases. Biblical scholars believe there were seventy men who carried the burden and weight of that responsibility. It is these seventy men that Moses shared the first thought of the Mosaic Covenant. They must have shared that with the people of Israel, because the Scripture says that all the people answered and said they would do what God commanded. Some Bible scholars believe this is when the Mosaic Covenant or Covenant of Law started. Others believe it started with the Passover Feast in Egypt. This Covenant, regardless of when it started, was very important to the nation of Israel. Israel needed a framework of laws to govern its people and God provided it.

In Exodus 24:1-8, the Mosaic Covenant is ratified by Moses, the Elders and the people of Israel. God call Moses, Aaron, Nadab, Abihu, and the seventy Elders up to the mountain to worship. God told Moses that he alone would come up and the rest could not come up. Moses comes down and tells all the people the Lord's words and judgments. Then the people of Israel said, "All the words which the Lord has said, we will do." (Exodus 24:3) Moses wrote all these words down. The next morning, Moses gets up early and builds an altar with twelve stones representing the twelve tribes of Israel. Then he and the young men of Israel offer burnt offerings and peace offerings to the Lord on that altar. This is what Moses did with the blood and what he did with the Book of the Covenant. "And Moses took half of the blood and put it in basins, and half of the blood he sprinkled on the altar. Then he took the Book of the Covenant and read it in the hearing of the people. And they said, 'All that the Lord has said we will do and be obedient. And Moses took the blood, sprinkled it on the people, and said, "Behold the blood of the covenant, which the Lord has made with you according to all these words." (Exodus 24:6-8) Thus, the Mosaic Covenant was ratified with Moses and the people of Israel.

The Beginning of the Mosaic Covenant

John Hagee in his Prophecy Study Bible, page 90 actually gives one a framework of the Mosaic Covenant under God's Covenant with Moses and under the subtitle Covenant for Relationships. "The Mosaic Covenant, found originally in Exodus and expanded in Deuteronomy, governed three areas of Israel's life. The commandments governed the personal lives with the Israelites in their relationship with God (Exodus 20:1-26, Commonly called The Ten Commandments). The judgments governed their social lives in their relationships with one another (Exodus 21:1—24:11). Finally, the ordinances governed the religious life so that the Israelites would know how to approach God (Exodus 24:12—31:18). Some of the Mosaic law exists in the form of moral or legal principles, such as the Ten Commandments. Most of it could be called case laws; specific situations that are addressed with specific measures. Many of the case laws are not grouped by subject: students have to compare related studies from several passages to understand the total perspective of the law on a given subject."

From this definition of the Mosaic Covenant by John Hagee one can see how important it was for the Israelites. They had lived in a pagan society of the Egyptians for over four hundred years. Now they were free from that pagan society. Therefore, they needed religious and moral laws to go by as a Theocratic Government. This Covenant by itself would not save them from their sins and its consequences. John Hagee went on to explain that too. "The Mosaic Covenant was not given for salvation. Keeping the law does not save. Rather the law keeps and prepares a person for salvation by faith. 'For if there had been a law given which could have given life, truly righteousness would have been by the law. Therefore, the law was our tutor to bring us to Christ, that we might be justified by faith.'" (Galatians 3:21,24)

God promises everything on this conditional covenant. "If you will indeed obey my voice and keep my covenant…then you will be a special treasure to Me above all the peoples of the earth;" (Exodus 19:5a) What most people don't understand and even Biblical scholars, is that fallen man always fails when it comes to a conditional Covenant. Like the Apostle Paul said in Romans 7:18. "For I know that in me (that is, in my flesh) nothing good dwells; for to will is present with me, but how to perform what is good (the law) I do not find."

Do the children of Israel realize what they are ratifying, when they tell Moses, "All that the Lord has spoken we will do"? (Exodus 19:8b) At first it seems like they know what they are doing, but later when failure after failure takes place on the part of Israel, I do not believe so. They have acted out of the emotion of the moment. They would like to do what is good, but they end up disobeying God. I believe this is because of their fallen nature as well as it being the emotion of the moment. It is true of us today. We are at a high emotional state at a service for God. We decide about our spiritual life in the height of the spiritual moment only to fail later. This is true of many Christians today. They are trying to obey the law, but they end up not obeying the law, even the Ten Commandments. The fallen nature of man gets in the way.

Therefore, what is the answer? I believe it is the revelation that Paul had in Romans 7:24-25. "O wretched man that I am! Who will deliver me from this body of death? I thank God—through Jesus Christ our Lord! So then, with the mind I myself serve the law of God, but with the flesh the law of sin." From this Scripture we get a revelation of our old wretched man. Jesus Christ is the only One Who can deliver us from our old wretched man, the fallen nature. Then God reveals to us, that it is through Jesus we can serve the law of God, which means we are serving God.

The nature of man, the fallen nature, apart from Jesus Christ is morally corrupt. The only way to be free from the morally corrupt sin nature is through the Cross of Jesus Christ. Accepting and receiving the revelation of the death of our old sinful nature at the Cross of Jesus Christ enables us to kill the old nature and to live unto God by the Holy Spirit. We will talk at length about this when we get to the New Covenant. But for the time being you can be studying and looking at Romans chapters six, seven, and eight.

The Law

Arthur W. Pink in his book, Gleanings in Exodus, page 160 talks about three definitions of the word "the law" in the New Testament. I believe his clarification of these terms is very helpful in understanding "the law" and he also gives us Scriptures for each clarification. "...First, there is "the law of God." (Romans 7:22,25) Second, there is "the law of Moses." (John 7:2; Acts 13:39; Acts 15:5) Third, there is "the law of Christ." (Galatians

6:2) Now these three expressions are by no means synonymous, and it is not until we learn to distinguish between them, that we can hope to arrive at any clear understanding on the subject of "the law."

"The law of God" expresses the mind of the Creator, and is binding on all rational creatures. It is God's unchanging moral standard for regulating the conduct of all men. In some places "the law of God" may refer to the whole revealed will of God, but usually it has reference to the Ten Commandments...The law has never been repealed and in the very nature of things cannot be. For God to abrogate the moral law would be to plunge the whole universe into anarchy."

"'The law of Moses' is the entire system of legislation, judicial, and ceremonial, which Jehovah gave to Israel during the time they were in the wilderness. "The law of Moses" as such is binding upon none, but Israelites. "The law of Moses has not been repealed for it will be enforced by Christ during the Millennium. "Out of Jerusalem shall go forth the Law, and the Word of the Lord from Jerusalem. (Isaiah 2:3) That "the law of Moses "is not binding on Gentiles is clear from Acts 15."

"'The law of Christ' is God's moral law in the hands of a Mediator. It is the law that Christ Himself was "made under." (Galatians 4:4) It is the law which was "in His heart." (Psalms 40:8) It is the law which He came to fulfill. (Matthew 5:17)"

Actually, governments today use some of the Mosaic laws, like the Ten Commandments to govern their people. Examples of this are the United States, Great Britain, Canada and a lot of Commonwealth nations throughout the world. The nation of Israel has just recently reconstituted itself under the Mosaic Laws; this includes having all businesses closed on the Sabbath day (Friday evening until Saturday evening), observing all the Feasts that are found in the Pentateuch (Genesis to Deuteronomy), making Jerusalem the capital of the nation, and Hebrew the national language. Therefore, in a real sense the Mosaic Covenant does have a real influence on our world today through Israel.

The Ten Commandments

Probably, the most noted part of the Mosaic Covenant is the Ten Commandments as listed in Exodus 20:1-17.

"And God spoke all these words, saying, "I am the Lord your God, who brought you out of the land of Egypt, out of the house of bondage. You shall have no other gods before me."

"You shall not make for yourselves any carved image, or any likeness of anything that is in heaven above, or that is in the earth beneath, or that is in the water under the earth; you shall not bow down to them nor serve them. For I, the Lord your God, am a jealous God, visiting the iniquity of your fathers on the children to the third and fourth generations of those who hate Me, but showing mercy to thousands, to those who love Me and keep My commandments."

"You shall not take the name of the Lord your God in vain, for the Lord will not hold him guiltless who take His name in vain,"

"Remember the Sabbath day, to keep it holy. Six days you shall labor and do all your work, but the seventh day is the Sabbath of the Lord your God. In it you shall do no work: you, nor your son, nor your daughter, nor your manservant, nor your maidservant, nor your cattle, nor your stranger who is within your gates."

"For in six days the Lord made the heavens and the earth, the sea and all that is within them, and rested on the seventh day. Therefore, the Lord blessed the Sabbath day and hallowed it."

"Honor your father and mother that your days may be long upon the land which the Lord your God is giving you."

"You shall not murder."

"You shall not commit adultery."

"You shall not steal."

"You shall not bear false witness against your neighbor."

"You shall not covet your neighbor's house, you shall not covet your neighbor's wife, nor his manservant, nor his maidservant, nor his ox, nor his donkey, nor anything that is your neighbors." (Exodus 20:1-17 NKJV)

There are different ways of looking at the Ten Commandments as they relate to the Mosaic Covenant and how that Covenant relates to the lives of the Israelites. First, we are going to look at what Ralph Smith took from Roy Sutton's ideas, James Jordan's ideas, and Gary North's ideas about the five-point covenant outline in their books. I believe this will be very helpful in understanding The Ten Commandments as it relates to the Mosaic Covenant.

"Also, the (T)en Commandments, according to North, Sutton, and Jordan are structured as a twofold repetition of the five-point covenant outline.

1. The first commandment, by teaching that God alone is to be worshipped, calls us to honor the transcendent Creator and Redeemer. By forbidding murder, the sixth commandment protects the image of the transcendent God.

2. The second commandment and the seventh are related throughout the Bible in the connection between idolatry and adultery. Both sins are perversions of submission to the God-ordained order.

3. The third section of the covenant, ethics, has to do with boundaries, which is also the point of the eighth commandment: "Thou shalt not steal." The third commandment demands that we wear the name of God righteously—a call to obey His law whereby we show the glory of His name in our lives.

4. The fourth and the ninth commandments are both concerned with sanctions since the Sabbath is a day of judgment in which man brings his works to God for evaluation; the command not to bear false witness views us in the courtroom participating in the judicial process.

5. The fifth and ten commandments correspond to the fifth part of the covenant, inheritance/continuity. In the fifth, children, the heirs to be, are told how to obtain an inheritance in the Lord. In the tenth, we are forbidden to covet, a sin that leads to the destruction of the inheritance in more ways than one."

This was taken from Ralph Smith's book, The Covenantal Structure of the Bible, page 8 as he quoted Sutton, Jordan and North. All three were showing how this relates to the Mosaic Covenant. They were attempting to show how this related to the Israelites daily life in the boundaries of the Mosaic Covenant and in specific, The Ten Commandments.

Arthur W. Pink in his book, Gleanings in Exodus, on page 161 gives us the reasons for the order that they are arranged. "The order of the Commandments was significant. The first four concern human responsibility Godward. The last five our obligations man wards. While the fifth suitably bridges the two, for in a certain sense parents occupy to their children the place of God. We may also add that the substance of each commandment is in perfect keeping with its numerical place in the Decalogue. One stands for unity and supremacy so is the first commandment the absolute sovereignty and pre-eminency of the Creator is insisted upon. Since God is who He is, He will tolerate no competitor or rival. His claims upon us are paramount."

Not only did the Ten Commandments establish the foundation of law for Israel, but was the foundation of law for nations to come. Actually, the Ten Commandments would provide a basis and an ethic that Israel needed to oppose the sinful nature and character of the nations that surrounded them. All the nations around them believed in many gods and many times ruled by force rather than law.

Ralph Smith in his book, The Covenant Structure of the Bible, describes how The Ten Commandments, page 34, revelation showed Israel how to live in the midst of an unholy environment of nations around them. "The revelation provided in the Ten Commandments and in the case-law commentary (Exodus chapters 21-24; Deuteronomy chapters 6-26) which expounded the fuller religious, civil and cultural meaning of the Ten Commandments, gave Israel a distinct ethic that would be the essence of their wisdom in the world (Deuteronomy 4:5-6). The law was a unit. The real meaning of the Ten Commandments could not have been seen apart from the broader application given in the detailed laws from Exodus to Deuteronomy. The law revealed God's righteousness in its commandments and His grace in its sacrifices. It surpasses all previous revelations. Israel was given an ethical revelation—priestly in its central concern, but applicable in every aspect of life—that would guide her in wisdom so that she could lead the world unto God (Deuteronomy 4:1-8)."

The Law of Moses

Rev. Smith and Rev. Pink agreed that the term, the Law of Moses, included all the Law that God had given Moses. This included the Ten Commandments, the individual case studies about the Ten Commandments, the sacrificial system God had set up in the Book of Leviticus, the Tabernacle that God instructed Moses to build, the laws concerning the Prophets and the Priests, the laws concerning marriage, the dietary laws, and finally the blessings if they obeyed God's laws and the curses if they disobeyed God's laws.

In Deuteronomy 4:1-2, God makes it clear to the Israelite nation what He expected from them. "Now, O Israel, listen to the statutes and the judgments which I teach you to observe, that you may live, and go in and possess the land which the Lord God of your fathers is giving you. You shall not add to the word which I command you, nor take anything from it, that you may keep the commandments of the Lord your God which I command you."

One has to understand that the reason God did not take Israel into the Promise Land immediately, is because they were not ready for the Promise Land. They are called "children of Israel" for a reason. They had not matured enough to enter the Promise Land. "But before faith came, we were kept under guard by the law, kept for the faith which would afterward be revealed. Therefore, the law was our tutor to bring us to Christ, that we might be justified by faith." (Galatians 3:23-24) It was in the Wilderness of Sinai that Israel started becoming a nation. God wanted to test Israel after He gave Moses the law to see if they would obey Him and do what He said. In the Wilderness of Sinai under the direction of Moses, they built the Tabernacle. They learned all the dietary and social laws that God gave Moses. The Israelites learned to trust God for their food and water. This was like a boot camp to see who would obey and who would not obey the Law of Moses. God taught Moses His Law and then Moses taught the children of Israel God's Law.

It is interesting what Rev. Ralph Smith says about the Law of Moses in his book, The Covenantal Structure of the Bible, page 35. "The Law of Moses, like every other covenant administration, included the threat of the curse for disobedience and the promise of blessing for obedience, but it was not, nor could it have been, a legislative covenant. The Pharisaic interpretation of the law was, as both Jesus and Paul taught clearly, a perversion of the law's true meaning. The law was given as a blessing for Israel to lead her in the way of joy, prosperity and peace. (Deut. 6:10-11, 24; 8:7ff; 10:13; 12:7,12, 18; 14:26; 16:11, 14, 15; 26:11; 29:9; 30:5,9,15) The greatest blessing of the law was the Tabernacle, a God-given sanctuary, His dwelling place among his people. The promise of the Covenant that God would be with His people found complete fulfillment in the gift of the Tabernacle sanctuary. However, this too was clearly temporary, since the law looked forward to a more permanent sanctuary to be established in the future in an unspecified location. (Deut. 12:5, 11, 14, 18, 21, 26; 14:23-25; 16:11, 15, 16; 17:8, 10)"

One of the problems the Israelites had was trying to obey the law of Moses in their own strength, instead of trusting God to enable them to do so. We see this when they are in the Wilderness of Sinai and they time and again complained about how hard it was to do what God had asked them to do. They would go out and gather food on the Sabbath day, when they were told not to do that. (Exodus 17:19-30) Even while Moses was on Mount Horeb receiving the Ten Commandments, the Israelites willfully disobeyed God and made a golden calf to worship rather than God. They knew that was wrong, but they did it anyway. (Exodus 33:1-6) Finally, they get to Kadesh Barnea and God tells Moses to choose twelve men as spies and to spy out the land. They spy out the land of Canaan and ten come back with a bad report while Joshua and Caleb (the other two spies) come back with a good report. The children of Israel believe the bad report. In unbelief the nation of Israel disqualifies themselves from entering the Promise Land. There report is that there are giants in the land and they don't believe they can overcome them. The ten men who brought the bad report die immediately and God says to the rest of the children of Israel that they will die to as they wander for forty years in the Wilderness of Sinai. (Numbers chapters 13 and 14) God told them, He would wait until a new generation of Israelites come forth who are willing to believe God and take possession of Canaan.

In Numbers 14:20-26 tells of the judgment of God on those who would not believe Him and go in and take possession of the Promise Land. "...Because all these men who have seen My glory and the signs which I did in Egypt and in the wilderness and have put Me to the test now these ten times and have not heeded my voice, they certainly shall not see the land of which I swore to their fathers, nor shall any of those who rejected Me see it..." (Numbers 14:22-23) The ten spies who brought an evil report died that day and only Joshua and Caleb who brought a good report lived. When all the men of that Israelite generation died off in the Wilderness, then God renewed the Mosaic Covenant of Law with that new generation. This is what the book of Deuteronomy is all about—the renewal of the Mosaic Covenant.

In Numbers chapter 20 gives the account of when Moses sinned against God. The nation of Israel was complaining about no water again. The glory of God appeared and God told Moses to speak to the rock, but he did not do that. Evidently, he had lost patience with Israel and this is what happened. "So, Moses took the rod from before the Lord, as He commanded him. And Moses and Aaron gathered the congregation together before the rock; and he said to them, "Hear now, you rebels! Must we bring water for you out of this rock?" Then Moses lifted his hand and struck the rock twice with the rod; and water came out abundantly, and the congregation and their animals drank. Then the Lord spoke to Moses and Aaron, "Because you did not believe Me, to hallow Me in the eyes of the children of Israel, therefore, you shall not bring this congregation into the land which I have given them." (Numbers 20:9-12)

Notice the punishment was upon both Moses and Aaron, even though only Moses spoke. God told Moses to speak to the rock and not hit it. This had happened before in the Wilderness journey and God told Moses to hit the rock, but this time He told him to speak to the Rock. In many Scriptures in the Old Testament (Covenant) God is seen spiritually as "the Rock" especially in the Psalms. In Psalms 18, the Scriptures calls God the rock. "The Lord is my rock and my fortress and my deliverer…" (Psalms 18:2a) "…And who is a rock, except our God?" (Psalms 18:31b) "The Lord lives! Blessed be my Rock! Let the God of my salvation be exalted." (Psalms 18:46) However, in the New Testament (Covenant) in 1 Corinthians 10:4 Paul talks about this Rock in the wilderness that Moses hit. "…and all drank the same spiritual drink. For they drank of that spiritual Rock that followed them, and that Rock was Christ." Most Bible scholars believe the first time God told Moses to hit the rock that signified Jesus trip to the Cross. The second time God told Moses to speak to the Rock that typified Jesus resurrection. Whether you go into typology or not, Moses and Aaron disobeyed God and when you disobey God that is unbelief at work in you. Just do what God says and everything turns out well. They were dishonoring God when they hit the Rock.

In the Hebrew-Greek Key Study Bible, by Dr. Spiros Zodhiates on page 217 he gives these comments about Moses actions and God's word to Moses. "Moses was excluded from the number of those entering Canaan. This was God's judgment on him for his attitude and action when providing water from the rock for Israel. At Horeb (Exodus 17:9) God had commanded Moses to strike the rock but, on this occasion, only to speak to it (v.8). In verse 10 he displayed a presumptuous attitude in striking the rock and apparently assumed for himself and Aaron the power to perform such a miracle and excluded the Lord. Here his sin is indicated as unbelief and in Numbers 27:14 as rebellion while in Deuteronomy 32:15 it is breaking faith with God and not holding Him in reverence before the people. Israel was also blamed for his sin (Deuteronomy 1:37; Psalms 106:32). Certainly, Moses and Aaron did not doubt God's power, but perhaps fearing a revolt of the proportions and nature of the one in (Numbers 14) they were asserting themselves before the people."

Moses' sin, although not related to the Covenant of Law, was about not doing what God asked him to do. When we disobey God, we are saying in essence we don't believe Him. It is a lack of faith. The Congregation of Israel did not believe they could conquer the giants in the land. They were trusting their own strength and not God's strength. Both Moses, Aaron, and the Israelites were not allowed to enter the Promise Land as a result. They were under the Covenant of Law, but they did not inherit the Promise Land that was a part of that Covenant just because they did not believe and trust God and do what He said to do.

If you look back over the life of Moses as he was leading Israel to the Promise Land, this is the only time he did not obey God's specific instructions. As a result, he did not enter the Promise Land. Unbelief is what stops us from getting God's best. God instructs Moses and Aaron to move the Children of Israel from Kadesh to Mount Hor right after this willful disobedience. He tells Aaron to climb Mount Hor and that he is going to be gathered to his people and die. Listen to what God says to Moses and Aaron. "Aaron shall be gathered to his people for he shall not enter the land which I have given to the children of Israel, because you rebelled at My word at the water of Meribah. Take Aaron and Eleazar his son, and bring them up to Mount Hor; and strip Aaron of his garments and put them on Eleazar his son; for Aaron shall be gathered to his people and die there." (Numbers 20:24-26) This shows Moses and Aaron that God was not changing his mind about that. Moses did what God commanded him to do and Aaron died that day. When God says something to us, He means what He says. Moses knew it was going to happen in the future. He would not be able to talk God out of what He said. Obedience is a necessary ingredient of staying in Covenant Relationship with God.

Rev. Ralph Smith believes that the Mosaic Covenant was given by God to Moses and the children of Israel to establish the priesthood and to gain the inheritance of the Promise Land. This is what he says on page 35 of his book. "The law established an elaborate system for the continuation of the priesthood and the inheritance of the land. Also, it emphasized the central concern of inheritance—inheritance of faith—by commanding parents to educate their children in the covenant, including this duty as an expression of parent's loyalty and love to God. "Hear, O Israel: The Lord our God (is) one LORD: and thou shalt love the LORD thy God with all thine heart, and with all thy soul, and with all thy might. And these words, which I command thee this day, shall be in thine heart: And thou shalt teach them diligently unto thy children, and shalt talk of them when thou sittest in thine house, and when thou walkest by the way, and when thou liest down, and when thou risest up." (Deuteronomy 6:4-7)

Rev. Smith believes what caused the Mosaic Covenant to fail was when Eli and his sons defiled the priesthood. (page 36) He believed the priesthood failed after all that happened in 1 Samuel chapters 3 and 4. He also believed the Tabernacle system failed when the Ark of the Covenant was taken into battle and captured by the Philistines in 1 Samuel chapter 4. (The Covenantal Structure of the Bible, page 36)

But one needs to look into the Scriptures to see if that is the truth. The Philistines gave back the Ark of the Covenant in 1 Samuel chapter 7. It is true the Tabernacle was not in the same place until Samuel became both the prophet and priest of Israel. Before King Solomon built the Temple that would house the Ark of the Covenant, the Mercy Seat, the Candelabra, the Table of Shewbread, and the Brazen Altar, there was a Tabernacle mentioned in 1 Kings 2:29a. "And King Solomon was told, "Joab has fled to the Tabernacle of the Lord; there he is at the altar..." Therefore, Rev. Smith is wrong in believing the Ark of the Covenant and the Tabernacle were no longer in existence. David earlier before thought of building a Temple for the Lord, had a Tabernacle which they called the Tabernacle of

David. This Tabernacle that is mentioned in 1 Kings 2:29a is that same Tabernacle. There were priests and High Priests in the days of King Saul, King David and King Solomon. Abimelech was the High Priest in the days of King Saul and Saul had him killed along with many of the priests. However, one escaped to stay with David and his name was Abiathar. He later became High Priest under King David's rule. Zadok became High Priest under King Solomon. Therefore, the priesthood continued after Eli died and his sons were slain in battle. Rev. Smith is wrong about the priesthood and about the Tabernacle. Later, the Tabernacle was replaced by the Temple which King Solomon built. But with the Temple the same worship took place. Then both Israel and Judah went into bondage for around seventy years. Under Cyrus and Darius, the Temple of God is rebuilt. God put into the heart of Cyrus to rebuild the Temple. "Thus, says Cyrus king of Persia: All the kingdoms of the earth the Lord God of heaven has given me. And He has commanded me to build Him a house at Jerusalem which is in Judah. Who is there among you of all His people? May his God be with him! Now let him go up to Jerusalem, which is in Judah, and build the house of God of Israel (He is God), which is in Jerusalem. And whoever remains in any place where he sojourns, let the men of his place help him with silver and gold, with goods and livestock, besides the freewill offerings for the house of God which is in Jerusalem." (Ezra 1:2-4) There is a struggle to build this Temple (the second Temple) because there is opposition to it. Later Darius I makes a search and it is discovered that Cyrus wanted it build and Darius I goes along with it. (Ezra chapter 5) Thus, the worship of God according to the Mosaic Covenant is started again with animal sacrifices and the Passover being celebrated. Also, there is a regathering of the Jewish people to the land of Canaan. Even in the New Testament era, the Mosaic Covenant was being practiced and all the feasts of Israel. Roman occupation was practiced, but the Roman emperors were allowing the Jewish people to practice the Mosaic Covenant.

The Mosaic Covenant among Jewish people is still in effect in Israel. There are some parts of that Covenant that cannot be practiced today because the second Temple has been destroyed. This happened thirty years after Jesus ascended to Heaven. The second Temple was in existence when

Jesus Christ was living in Palestine, was crucified and arose from the dead. Jesus prophesied that this second Temple would be destroyed a few days before His crucifixion. "Then Jesus went out and departed from the Temple, and His disciples came to Him to show Him the buildings of the Temple. And Jesus said to them, "Do you not see all these things? Assuredly, I say to you, not one stone shall be left here upon another, that shall not be thrown down." (Matthew 24:1-2) This was probably hard for the Apostles to accept. They were showing Jesus the Temple and how beautiful and magnificent it was, when Jesus prophesied this over the Temple. Jesus was saying it was going to be destroyed completely and not one stone would be left on another stone. At this time in history, the Jews were living in semi-harmony with the Romans, but after Jesus ascension to Heaven, the Jews would rebel against the Roman occupation. This rebellion started in 66 A.D. Roman General Titus was dispatched to quell the rebellion and his army destroyed Jerusalem and the second Temple in 70 A.D. This happened approximately thirty years after Jesus prophesied the Temple's destruction.

What did this mean to Judaism and the Mosaic Covenant? The Temple in Jerusalem was marked by God as the place to offer sacrifices according to the Mosaic Covenant. In Deuteronomy 12:5-7 the Mosaic Covenant specifies a place found for God's habitation and where sacrifices were to be made. "But you shall seek the place where the Lord your God chooses, out of all your tribes, to put His name for His habitation, and there you shall go. There you shall take your burnt offerings, your sacrifices, your tithes, the heave offerings of your hand, your vowed offerings, your freewill offerings, and the firstlings of your herds and flocks. And there you shall eat before the Lord your God, and you shall rejoice in all (all that you undertake) which you have put your hand, you and your households, in which the Lord your God has blessed you."

Because the second Temple was destroyed, there was no place for God's dwelling. God had chosen this place actually during the time of David and the first Temple was built during the time of Solomon, David's son. Cyrus and Darius I, had had the second Temple built for the Jewish people, but now it was destroyed by the Romans. There was no place for God to dwell and no place for the sacrifices of God to be made. The place designated by God was destroyed.

But with the revelation that the Apostle Paul received by the aid of the Holy Spirit, New Testament (Covenant) Jewish believers were able to move past the destruction of the Temple in Jerusalem and understand that God was moving them into the New Testament (Covenant). The Apostle Paul used the term "temple"; one the Jews were very familiar with in describing the individual believers as temples of the Holy Spirit. He said that of individual believers as well as the Church at Corinth. "Do you not know that you are the temple of God and that the Spirit of God dwells in you? If anyone defiles the temple of God, God will destroy him. For the temple of God is holy, which temple you are." (1 Corinthians 3:16-17)

Therefore, now we are the temple of God. That second Temple in Jerusalem was destroyed, so that we individually and corporately as the Church can worship God under the power of the Holy Spirit. We do not have to offer many sacrifices as the Jews did in the past in Jerusalem. Jesus Christ, God's Son, made one sacrifice for all, to pay for all of our sins once and for all. "But this Man (Jesus Christ), after He had offered one sacrifice for sins forever, sat down at the right hand of God, from that time waiting till His enemies are made His footstool. For by one offering He has perfected forever those who are being sanctified." (Hebrew 10:12-14) The Mosaic Covenant was fulfilled in Jesus Christ and now He is the resurrected Christ, living in us, but also seated at God the Father's right-hand making intercession for us. "Now He (Jesus Christ) who searches the hearts knows what the mind of the Spirit is, because He makes intercession for the saints according to the will of God." (Romans 8:27)

Is it not interesting that Jesus prophesied about the destruction of the second Temple and approximately thirty years later it happened? I believe God was trying to say something to Israel by its destruction. God was doing away with the physical, natural Temple with all of its sacrifices. God was pointing to His Son as the only sacrifice needed to take away our sins and the substitutionary death of Jesus Christ, taking our place for the judgment of Adam. "For if when we were enemies we were reconciled to

God through the death of His Son, much more having been reconciled, we shall be saved by His (Jesus) life." (Romans 5:10) This took place during the feast of the Passover on the exact day of Passover that Israel observed every year. What is amazing is that at the exact moment Jesus died on the Cross, the veil was rent from the top to the bottom. "And Jesus cried with a loud voice, and gave up the ghost. And the veil of the temple was rent from the top to the bottom." (Mark 15:37-38 KJV) You may say what is amazing about that? This is what is amazing is the veil was thirty feet long, the veil was fifteen feet high to block anyone's view of the two cherubim, and the veil was as thick as a handbreadth thickness or four inches thick. (Liberty Gospel Tracks Questions) Therefore, it would have been impossible for a man or a group of men to have rent the veil into two parts. There is no one fifteen foot tall to do that. No man has the strength to tear a veil in to two pieces, like it was done when Jesus was crucified. The Jewish priests would not have done it, for it would have desecrated the Temple and they were afraid God would strike them dead. Only the Holy Spirit could have done that, so Jesus, our High Priest, could enter within the veil and sprinkle that Holy blood of His on the Mercy Seat, therefore, cleansing away all our sins past, present, and future. All this information came from Liberty Gospel Tracts>questions. They got their information from the Works of Josephus. "But Christ came as High Priest of the good things to come with the greater and more perfect tabernacle not made with hands, that is, not of this creation. Not with blood of goats and calves, but with His own blood (perfect blood) He entered the Most Holy Place once for all, having obtained eternal redemption. But if the blood of bulls and goats and the ashes of a heifer sprinkling the unclean, sanctifies for the purifying of the flesh, how much more shall the blood of Christ, who through the eternal Spirit offered Himself without spot to God, purge your conscience from dead works to serve the living God?" (Hebrews 9:11-14)

The Feasts of the Lord

Jesus Christ, our High Priest, at the feast of Passover, became our Passover Lamb. At this Jewish feast, Jesus not only took care of all our sins on the earth, but entered Heaven itself and took care of our sins and our sin nature before God, in the Holy of Holies there. Now there is no veil between us and God, our Father. We can come boldly to the Throne of Grace with our needs and wants. "Let us therefore come boldly to the throne of grace, that we may obtain mercy and find grace to help in time of need." (Hebrews 4:16)

There are some who object to Jesus dying at the Feast of Unleavened Bread or Passover. They ask why He didn't die on feast day called the Day of Atonement? They question whether He could atone for our sins by dying at Passover. Got Questions? /org. Jesus Passover—atonement answers this question in a profound way. "An objection sometimes arises that the paschal sacrifice was not considered atonement; rather, atonement was provided for the Jews via the sacrifices on Yom Kippur (The Day of Atonement) Ergo. Jesus who was killed at Passover and who is called "our Passover" (1 Corinthians 5:7) in the New Testament, could not have been an atonement for sin...There are two ways to counter this objection. The first is simply to show how Jesus also fulfilled the symbolism of Yom Kippur. Jesus bore our sins in His own body. (1 Peter 2:24) and tasted death for every man (Hebrews 2:9) in doing so. He offered a better sacrifice than those of Yom Kippur—better because Christ's sacrifice was permanent, was voluntary, and did not cover sin but removed it altogether. (Hebrews 9:8-14).

The second counter is to point out that Jewish tradition did indeed view the Passover sacrifice as being expiatory; that is the lamb removed sin from God's view. The Passover lamb died under God's outpoured wrath, thus covering over the sins of the one offering it. Here's what Rashi, a well-respected mediaeval Jewish commentator, has to say. "I see the Paschal blood and propitiate you...I mercifully take pity on you by means of the Paschal blood and the blood of circumcision and I propitiate your souls." (Ex. R. 15, 35b, 35a)

During the tenth and final plaque in Egypt, the Passover sacrifice literally saved individuals from death (Exodus 12:23). On the basis of this redemptive offering of the Passover blood, the firstborn lived. Again, Rashi commented. "It is as if a king said to his sons: "Know you that I judge persons on capital charges and condemn them. Give me therefore a present, so that in case you are brought before my judgment seat I may set aside the indictments against you. So, God said to Israel. 'I am now concerned with death penalties, but I will tell you how I will have pity on you and for the sake of the Passover blood and the circumcision blood I will atone for you." (Ex. R. 15. 12, on Exodus 12:10)

This gives us some powerful reasons, why Jesus Christ became our Passover Lamb. "Christ our Passover has been sacrificed for you." (1 Corinthians 5:7) He bore our sins in His own body. (1 Peter 2:24) He tasted death for every man. (Hebrews 2:19) He removed our sins. (Hebrews 9:8-14) John the Baptist, Jesus' forerunner, said, "Behold the Lamb of God who takes away the sin of the world." (John 1:29) Finally, Jesus was silent before His accusers. (Isaiah 53:7)

I have touched on two important feasts of the Lord—The Feast of Unleavened Bread and the Day of Atonement. But in Old Testament (Covenant) there were three feasts that required all Jewish men to make a pilgrimage to Jerusalem every year according to the Mosaic Covenant. Wikipedia.com gives a good description of these three feasts. "The three pilgrimage festivals in Hebrew are Shalosh Regalim are three major festivals in Judaism—Pesach (Passover), Shavuot (Week of Pentecost), and Sukkot (Tabernacles, Tents or Booths)—when the ancient Israelites living in the Kingdom of Judah would make a pilgrimage to the temple in Jerusalem as commanded by the Torah (the Book of the Law)... After the destruction of the Second Temple and until the building of the Third Temple, the actual pilgrimages are no longer obligatory upon Jews, and no longer take place on a national scale... Jews around the world go to their nearest synagogue and the rabbis read from the Torah describing the holiday that is being observed. Those living in Israel go to the Western Wall and attend prayer services there. The Scripture that the Jewish men observe in doing this is taken from Deuteronomy 16:16-17. "Three times a year all your males shall appear before the Lord your God in the place which He chooses (Jerusalem Temple): At the Feast of Unleavened Bread (Passover), at the Feast of Weeks (Pentecost), and at the Feasts of Tabernacles (Booths or Tents, temporary dwellings they lived in for forty years wandering in the Wilderness); and they shall not appear before the

Lord empty handed (tithes and offerings). Every man shall give as he is able, according to the blessing of the Lord your God which He has given you."

Today, Jewish men do not have to journey to Jerusalem because currently there is no Temple there. A Third Temple is to be built in Jerusalem as prophesied in three places in the Bible; Daniel 9:27; 2 Thessalonians 2:3-4; and Revelation 11:1-2. Daniel 9:27 refers to sacrifices being made in a Temple. In 2 Thessalonians 2:3-4 refers to the Anti-Christ sitting in the Third Temple of God and exalting himself as a god. "Let no one deceive you by any means, for that Day will not come unless the falling away comes first, and the man of sin (the Anti-Christ) is revealed, the son of perdition, who opposes and exalts himself above all that is called God or that is worshipped, so that he sits as God in the temple (Third Temple) of God, showing himself that he is God." (1 Thessalonians 2:3-4) In Revelation 11:1-2 the Apostle John is asked to measure the Temple of God (the Third Temple). "Then I was given a rod like a measuring rod. And the angel stood, saying, 'Rise and measure the temple of God (the Third Temple), the altar and those who worship there. But leave out the court which is outside the temple (the Third Temple), and do not measure it, for it has been given to the Gentiles. And they will tread the holy city for forty-two months." (Revelation 11:1-2) This Temple, John refers to is considered to be the Third Temple. The Anti-Christ will defile it, but Jesus Christ when He comes with ten thousands of His saints will sanctify it again and will reign in the Temple from Jerusalem for a thousand years (Revelation 20) over all the nations of the earth. No doubt God will reinstate that law of coming to the Temple in Jerusalem three times a year.

Jesus Christ and the Ten Commandments

There are three areas we must look at before we close the chapter on the Mosaic Covenant. We have looked at the foundation of all the laws of the children of Israel, which is the Ten Commandments. All of the other case studies are based on the Ten Commandments. The Ten Commandments were addressed by Jesus Christ in the Sermon on the Mount in Matthew chapters five, six and seven. The Apostle Matthew wrote his Gospel centered around reaching the Jewish people.

In Matthew chapter five, Matthew quotes Jesus on the commandments that deal with our relationships to one another. Jesus would quote one of the Ten Commandments and then dealt with people's hearts in relationship to that commandment. For instance, in the commandment about not murdering someone, listen to what He says. "You have heard that it was said to those of old, you shall not murder; and whoever murders shall be in danger of the judgment. But I say to you whoever is angry with his brother without a cause shall be in danger of the judgment. And whoever says to his brother 'Raca' shall be danger of the council. But whoever says, 'You fool' shall be in danger of hell fire." (Matthew 5:21-22) The word 'Raca' means empty-headed or foolish one. Back in those days it was a very, bad derogatory remark to say to anyone. Jesus was dealing with people's hearts—what was in their hearts towards other people.

Every time, Jesus talked about a commandment, He would go to the heart of the issue which made it more meaningful to His disciples. Jesus in chapter five went on to deal with such subjects as adultery, divorce, oaths, retaliation, and love. (Matthew 5:21-48) Before we leave this, we must consider the fact that at the beginning of Matthew five, Jesus taught His disciples that He came to fulfill the law and the prophets. "Do not think that I came to destroy the Law or the Prophets, I did not come to destroy but to fulfill. For assuredly, I say to you, till heaven and earth pass away, one jot or one tittle (The smallest stroke in a Hebrew letter) will by no means pass from the law till all is fulfilled." (Matthew 5:17-18) To understand this one must look at Romans 10:4. "For Christ is the end of the law for righteousness to everyone who believes." The Greek word telos means the final end, which the dominion of the law has found in Christ. These Scriptures can be hard to understand. But what Paul was sharing with the Roman Gentile believers is that Jesus Christ fulfilled the Law to its final degree. No person could fulfill the law to the degree to which Jesus did. We must rest in His fulfillment of the law. To understand this one must look at the Greek word for "fulfill" which is pleroo which means "to fully satisfy." When Jesus said that He came not to destroy the law or the prophets but to fulfill, He meant that He came not only to fulfill the types and prophecies by His actions and sufferings, but also to perform perfect obedience to the Law of God in His own person and fully to enforce and explain it by His doctrine (teaching). Thus, He has fully satisfied the requirements of the law." (Lexicon to the New Testament, by Dr. Spiro Zodhiates, page 1722) Jesus Christ did what man cannot do. He fulfilled the Law perfectly in every way, therefore, anyone who receives Him has the righteousness of the Law fulfilled in them. This is explained in Romans 8:3-4. "For what the law could not do in that It was weak through the flesh, God did by sending His own Son in the likeness of sinful flesh, on account of sin: He condemned sin in the flesh, that the righteousness of the law might be fulfilled in us who do not walk according to the flesh but according to the Spirit."

The Diet of the Israelites

We have discussed the Feasts of the Mosaic Covenant and the Law of the Mosaic Covenant. The third part of the Mosaic Covenant has to do with the food or diet of Israel as designated by God in the book of Leviticus. In Leviticus chapter eleven certain animals that chew the cud or have cloven hooves like rock badgers, the hare (rabbit), swine (pigs) were forbidden by God to be eaten. Living things in the seas were also forbidden by God. God gives the distinction in Leviticus 11:9-11. "These you may eat of all that are in the water: whatever in the water has fins and scales, whether in the seas or in the rivers—that you may eat. But all in the seas or in the rivers that do not have fins and scales, all that move in the water or any living thing which is in the water, they are an abomination to you. They shall be an abomination to you; you shall not eat their flesh, but you shall regard their carcasses as an abomination."

God also listed in Leviticus chapter eleven the birds that were not to be eaten by the Jews. They are the eagle, the vulture, the buzzard, the kite, the falcon, the ostrich, the owl, the seagull, the hawk, the jackdaw, the carrion vulture, the stork, the heron, the hoopoe, and the bat. These are all listed in Leviticus 11:13-19.

God went on to say what insects the Jews were not to eat in Leviticus 11:20,23. "All flying insects that creep on all fours shall be an abomination to you…But all other flying insects which have four feet shall be an abomination to you." All other insects could be eaten and God provided a list of those in Leviticus 11:21-22. "Yet these you may eat of every flying insect that creeps on all fours: those which have jointed legs above their feet with which to leap on the earth. These you may eat: the locust after its kind, the destroying locust after its kind, the cricket after its kind, and the grasshopper after its kind." God was really specific about what could be eaten and what could not be eaten.

All clean animals or unclean animals that were dead that a Jew saw, he was not to touch them. If he or she did happen to touch them, God considered that person unclean until the priest had the regular evening sacrifices. Creeping things on the earth like the mole, the mouse, lizards, the gecko, the monitor lizard, sand reptiles, and the chameleon were considered unclean and were not to be touched or eaten. (Leviticus 11:29-31)

At the end of Leviticus chapter eleven, God gives the purpose of the dietary laws for His people, the children of Israel. "For I am the Lord your God. You shall therefore, sanctify yourselves, and you shall be holy; for I am holy. Neither shall you defile yourselves with creeping things that creep on the earth. For I am the Lord who brings you up out of the land of Egypt, to be your God. You shall therefore be holy, for I am holy. This is the law of the beasts and the birds, and every living creature that moves in the waters, and every living creature that creeps on the earth, to and the animal that may not be eaten." (Leviticus 11:44-47)

One might ask, why God was so particular about food? Many of the heathen nations around Israel ate of those unclean animals, unclean sea creatures, unclean insects, and unclean birds that God forbade Israel to partake of in the Old Testament (Covenant). Some if not all of those animals were offered to idols and idolatrous people loved to eat these type of animals, birds, animals of the sea, and insects. They did not want God to tell them what to eat and what not to eat. Therefore, this set the Jews apart from other nations.

The final dietary law was the draining of blood from clean animals before cooking and eating them. God made it clear in the Mosaic Covenant with Israel that they were to drain the blood. "Therefore, I said to the children of Israel, 'No one among you shall eat blood, nor shall any stranger who sojourns among you eat blood.' And whatever man of the children of Israel, or of the strangers who sojourn among you who hunts and catches any animal or bird that may be eaten, he shall pour out its blood and cover it with dust, for it is the life of all flesh. Its blood sustains its life. Therefore, I said to the children of Israel, 'You shall not eat the blood of any flesh, for the life of all flesh is its blood. Whoever eats it shall be cut off. And every person who eats what died naturally or what was torn by beasts, whether he is a native of your own country or a stranger, he shall wash his clothes and bathe in water and be unclean until evening. Then he shall be clean. But if he does not wash or bathe the body, then he shall bear his guilt." (Leviticus 17:12-16)

All of these commandments and precepts concerning their laws of worshipping God and Him alone, the moral laws, the laws concerning ethics, the laws about the Feasts, and their dietary laws were a part of the Mosaic Covenant. If they failed to follow these laws, they were cut off from their people and were usually stoned to death. There was no compromise. If you disobeyed you were cut off from your family and they had to turn their back on you, otherwise they would be cut off as well as you. After Moses' death, the leaders of Israel, which included the Prophets, Priests and Kings who followed Moses determined who was breaking the law, God's law, and who should pay the price for it.

We need to look at one other situation that happened in the New Testament (Covenant) in the book of Acts concerning the diet of the Jewish people. Peter is confronted by God three times on his views concerning what is clean and unclean meat. Peter is a very conservative Jew, who had never eaten anything unclean. He is staying with Simon, the tanner and is on the roof top of his house praying. In New Testament (Covenant) times houses in Israel usually had a flat roof with stairs on the outside of the house that led up to the roof. While praying, Peter has a vision from Heaven in which he sees four-footed beasts. At this point, Peter is hungry and wants to eat. God has let down this sheet in a vision showing him these unclean animals that according to Jewish law it is unlawful to eat. Listen to the conversation between God and Peter on the roof top. "In it were all kinds of four-footed animals of the earth, wild beasts, creeping things, and birds of the air. And a voice (God speaking) came to him (Peter), "Rise, Peter, kill and eat. But Peter said, "Not so Lord! For I have never eaten anything common or unclean." And a voice (God) spoke to him again the second time. "What God has cleansed you must not call common." This was done three times. And the object was taken up into heaven again." (Acts 10:12-16) Here is Reverend Matthew Henry's view of that Scripture. This taken from The Matthew Henry Commentary, Volume 6, Acts to Revelation, page 128. "6. God by a second voice from heaven, proclaimed the repeal of the law in this case (v.15): "What God has cleansed, that call thou not common." He that made the law might alter it when He pleased, and reduce the matter to the first state. God had for reasons suited to the Old Testament dispensation, restrained the Jews from eating such and such meats, to which, while that dispensation lasted, they were obliged in conscience to submit: but He has now, for reason suited to the New Testament dispensation, taken off the restraints, and set the matter at large---has cleansed that which was before polluted to us and we ought to make use of, and "stand fast in, the liberty wherewith Christ has made us free, and not call that common or unclean which God has now declared clean."

I tend to agree with Matthew Henry about this. However, there are some people who are not even Jewish, who consider the meats, birds, and creeping things in the Old Testament (Covenant) that were forbidden to eat during that Mosaic Covenant time; they consider them to be unhealthy to eat. God should advise people on that, rather than man advise people. It is really, a subject that is not now so frequently judged. The Apostle Paul gave this conclusion in his letter to Timothy, one of his sons in the faith. "...forbidding to marry, and commanding to abstain from foods which God created to be received with thanksgiving by those who believe and know the truth. For every creature of God is good, and nothing to be refused if it is received with thanksgiving; for it is sanctified by the word of God and prayer." (1 Timothy 4:3-5)

What cleansed those animals, birds, insects, and sea animals? I believe it was the Cross of Jesus Christ. When He shed His blood, He cleansed all of mankind, but He also cleansed all of creation. One must come to the revelation that God has cleansed everything. That was what God was telling Peter. "What God hath cleansed (declared clean) you must not call common or unclean (Greek word, akathartos—unclean by legal or ceremonial uncleanness)" (KJV) Lexical Aids to the New Testament by Dr. Spiro Zodhiates. This takes place as it is recorded in Romans 8:19-22. "For the earnest expectation of the creation eagerly waits for the revealing of the sons of God. For the creation was subjected to futility, not willingly, but because of Him who subjected it in hope; because the creation also will be delivered from the bondage of corruption into the glorious liberty of the children of God. For we know that the whole creation groans and labors with birth pangs together until now.

Moses again in the book of Deuteronomy in chapter eighteen discusses again the Priests, the tribe of Levi, which God has set aside to do the work of offering sacrifices to God. That tribe will not have any land as an inheritance. "The priests, the Levites, indeed all the tribe of Levi, shall have no part nor inheritance with Israel, they shall eat the offerings of the Lord made by fire, and His portion. Therefore, they shall have no inheritance among their brethren; the Lord is their inheritance, as He said to them." (Deuteronomy 18:1-2) The children of Israel would in essence tithe to them giving them sheep and bulls to eat. The priest's part would be the shoulder, the cheeks, and the stomach. "The first fruits of your grain and your new wine, and your oil, and the first of your fleece of your sheep, you shall give them." (Deuteronomy 18:3-4) The priests and Levites duty along with offering sacrifices to the Lord, will also be to act as judges when wrongdoing or murder occurs (Deuteronomy 19) Later in the book of Joshua chapter 21 Joshua gave the Levites forty-eight cities as outlined in Numbers 35:1-8. It shows how the Levites were given cities to dwell in and they were given land around the cities to plant and harvest. Six of those cities were cities of refuge for people involved in slaying someone innocently. They were also involved in teaching the Law of God in those cities. These were the plans, but they were not carried out completely. Israel disobeyed God in these plans. Most all of the information was gathered from The Zondervan Pictorial Bible Dictionary, page 484-485 This dictionary also brought out the differences between priests and the Levites. "IV. Priests and Levites. The Mosaic legislation made a sharp distinction between the priests and the non-priests or ordinary Levites. 1. The priest must belong to Aaron's family; the Levites belong to the larger family of Levi. A priest was a Levite; but a Levite was not necessarily a priest. 2. Priests were consecrated (Exodus 29:1-37; Leviticus 8). Levites were purified (Numbers 8:5-22). 3. Levites were considered a gift to Aaron and his sons (Numbers 3:5-13; 8:19;18:1-7) 4. The fundamental difference consisted of this: only the priests had the right to minister at the altar and to enter the most holy place (Exodus 28:1; 29:9; Numbers 3:10,38; 4:15,19f; 18:1-7; 25:10-13) …" As previously stated, the nation of Israel never did do completely what God gave Moses for them to do. Moses shared it with them, but even Moses knew they were ultimately going to fail this Covenant. We will talk about that when we summarize the Mosaic Covenant.

There is a prophetic word about Jesus Christ in Deuteronomy the eighteenth chapter. God gives this to Moses right before Moses dies. Jesus is described as a Prophet that will come to the nation of Israel. "I will raise up for them a Prophet like you from among their brethren, and will put My words in His mouth, and He shall speak to them all that I command Him. And it shall be that whoever will not hear My words, which He speaks in My name, I will require it of him." (Deuteronomy 18:18-19) Earlier we saw that Jesus Christ Is our High Priest and now God declares through Moses that Jesus will be a Prophet and will utter prophetic words to His people. Later, when we get into the Davidic Covenant, we will see that Jesus will be the last King of Israel and is in genealogy from the house and lineage of David. Thus, Jesus fulfills all three Old Testament offices of Prophet, Priest and King. Before we leave the office of Prophet in the Mosaic Covenant, we must see that God also points out about the false prophet. Jesus Christ is seen as the true Prophet of God, but God also shows what the false prophet is about. God lets Israel know the difference in a true prophet of God and a false prophet. "But the prophet who presumes to speak a word in My name, which I have not commanded him to speak, or who speaks in the name of other gods, that prophet shall die. And if you say in your heart, 'How shall we know the word which the Lord has not spoken? ---when a prophet speaks in the name of the Lord, if the thing does not happen or come to pass, that is the thing which the Lord has not spoken; the prophet has spoken presumptuously, you shall not be afraid of him." (Deuteronomy 18:20-22) False prophets, God commanded to be put to death. No matter if it came to pass or not. If the intent was to take you away from God, he or she normally were stoned to death. Therefore, one had to really know that God had called them to be a prophet. For instance, listen to the call of Jeremiah by the Lord. "Then the word of the Lord came to me saying, "Before I formed you in the womb I knew you. Before you were born, I sanctified you and I ordained you a prophet to the nations." (Jeremiah 1:4-5) If one has that kind of call, one knows that God is in it.

The Palestinian Covenant

There is another Covenant of God in some ways is separate from the Mosaic Covenant, but in other ways it is dependent upon the Mosaic Covenant. They call this the Palestinian Covenant and say it is found in Deuteronomy chapter twenty-nine. This Covenant was given to the young adults that grew up as their parents were dying in the Wilderness of Sinai. The parents of these young adults died as a result of their unbelief in what God had promised, which is the Promise Land of Canaan. We discussed this before about their lack of faith in God to possess the Promise Land. (Numbers chapters 13 and 14).

Now, God is reaffirming to the younger generation, that they will possess the Land of Canaan under the leadership of Joshua. It is called the Palestinian Covenant, because God has again promised the land that John Hagee talked about in his Prophecy Study Bible, page 226. Reverend Hagee gives a good description of that Palestinian Covenant. "The covenant concerning the Promise Land, call the Palestinian Covenant is the third of the Old Testament covenants that spell out the rule of God over his people. The first two were God's covenant with Abraham (Genesis 12:1-3) and His covenant with Moses (Exodus 19:5-8). The Palestinian covenant first appears as a part of the Mosaic Covenant in Deuteronomy 27-30, but later stands alone as Israel struggles to understand her special relationship to the Promised Land. (Jeremiah 23:5-8; Ezekiel 20:42-44; 36:24-30; 37:11-14; 47:1---48:35; Zechariah 12:10---13:2)" (John Hagee said the Palestinian Covenant was the third Old Testament Covenant. I believe there were more than that, that were major Covenants from God: Edenic Covenant, Noahic Covenant, Abrahamic Covenant, Mosaic Covenant, Palestinian Covenant, and the Davidic Covenant. That is six Covenants, not counting the New Covenant which is the New Testament.)

At first this is what I understood, that the Covenant given through Moses to Joshua was a part of the Mosaic Covenant. But after reading especially Deuteronomy 29:1, I saw that God made a distinct Covenant with the young adults that Joshua would be leading. "These are the words of the covenant which the Lord commanded Moses to make with the children of Israel in the land of Moab, besides the covenant which He made with them in Horeb." (Deuteronomy 29:1) In this Palestinian Covenant, God lays out the Land that shall belong to the children of Israel. This Covenant lays out the boundaries of the land that the children of Israel are to have as their own.

"The descendants of Abraham, the patriarch of faith, had a claim on the territory "from the river of Egypt to the great river, the River Euphrates." (Genesis 15:18) The western boundary of the Promised Land was the Mediterranean coast (Joshua 15:12) and the eastern border included the highland plateau beyond the Jordan River, the territory of Basham (Joshua 13:8-12) and the Syrian region of Lebo Hamath (2 Chronicles 8:3-4). During the reign of David and Solomon, all of this territory was occupied by Israel or subject to it by treaty (1 Kings 8:65)" (John Hagee's Prophecy Study Bible, page 226)

Although, this Promise Land, Canaan, is promised to the children of Israel and is what is spelled out in the Palestinian Covenant, it is still tied conditionally to the Mosaic Covenant. All of the laws, ordinances, and commandments of the Mosaic Covenant had to be obeyed by the children of Israel in order to keep possession of the Promise Land, Canaan. The two Covenants are tied together even to this day. The Palestinian Covenant is conditioned on the Mosaic Covenant. That is why I left the Palestinian Covenant under the Mosaic Covenant.

"Israel was obligated by the conditional aspects of God's covenant with Moses to obey the commands, judgments, and ordinances of the law in order to enjoy the immediate blessings of the Palestinian covenant. (Deuteronomy chapters 27 to 29) "If you diligently obey the voice of the Lord your God…the Lord your God will set you high above all the nations of the earth." (Deuteronomy 28:1) The historical books of the Old Testament trace the record of Israel's failure to keep the Mosaic Covenant during the centuries of the judges and the united and divided kingdoms. The dispersion of the Jews triggered by the destruction of Jerusalem by the Roman commander Titus lasted until 1948 when the modern secular state of Israel emerged on a sliver of the Promise Land." (John Hagee's Prophecy Study Bible, page 226)

As one can see that both the Mosaic Covenant and the Palestinian Covenant were conditional Covenants. They were conditioned on the children of Israel being obedient to the Mosaic Covenant and as a result they were made partakers of the Palestinian Covenant. In Deuteronomy 28:1-2 one can see the conditionalism of the two Covenants. "Now it shall come to pass, if you diligently obey the voice of the Lord your God to observe carefully His commandments which I command you today, that the Lord your God will set you high above all nations of the earth. And all these blessings shall come upon you and overtake you, because you obey the voice of the Lord your God." Moses shared the Mosaic Covenant with the Israelites who came out of Egypt. They failed to believe God, when He told them to go in and possess the land. Therefore, that generation died in the wilderness as God had promised.

The new generation of Israelites that rose up under the leadership of Moses and then Joshua, were given the Palestinian Covenant. But it too was a conditional Covenant. This Covenant promised the young adults of

Israel the land of Canaan if they obeyed the commandments, the ordinances and laws that God had already laid out in the Mosaic Covenant. For a while the generations after Joshua obeyed God and thus to a degree were able to conquer the Promise Land and live in it. There is a summation of the generation that followed God when Joshua and the Elders around him lived. Then in Judges chapter two it tells what happened when a new generation took over. "So the people served the Lord all the days of Joshua, and all of the days of the elders who outlived Joshua and who had seen all the great works of the Lord which He had done for Israel...When all the generation had been gathered to their fathers (Joshua's and the elder's generation), another generation arose after them who did not know the Lord nor the work which He had done for Israel. Then the children of Israel did evil in the sight of the Lord, and served the Baals (a foreign god)" (Judges 2:7,10-11) One final Scripture from the book of Judges gives the mindset of the children of Israel during the period of the Judges. The period of the Judges was that period immediately after the life of Joshua and the Elders who outlived Joshua. During the life of Joshua and the Elders who outlived Joshua, they did obey the Mosaic Covenant and to a degree received the land of the Palestinian Covenant. The final Scripture of Judges tells what happened after that. "In those days there was no king in Israel; everyone did what was right in his own eyes." (Judges 21:25)

What can one learn from the Scripture in Judges 2:7,10-11 and Judges 21:25? During the period of the Judges, Israel disobeyed the Mosaic Covenant time and time again. They worshipped other gods which was a violation of the First Commandment of the Ten Commandments. "You shall have no other gods before me" (Exodus 20:2). Therefore, in actual practice and life, the children of Israel broke the Mosaic Covenant and therefore, forfeited the Palestinian Covenant.

Moses actually prophesied over them before his death on the mountain, that they would fail later to obey God. In Deuteronomy chapter 28, Moses sets before them the blessings and the curses of the Mosaic Covenant. From Deuteronomy chapter 28:1-13 he lists all the blessings. In Deuteronomy 28:15-68, Moses tells Israel about all of the curses that will fall on them for disobeying God and the Mosaic Covenant. In

Deuteronomy 30:1-3, Moses declares what Israel will do when they are driven to foreign countries and are no longer in the land of Canaan. Notice, Moses is speaking prophetically. God has shown him the future, and this will take place. "Now it shall come to pass, when all these things come upon you, the blessings and the curses which I have set before you, and you call (cause them to refresh in your heart) them to mind among the nations where the Lord drives you, and you return to the Lord your God and obey his voice, according to all that I command you today, you and your children, with all your heart and your soul, that the Lord your God will bring you back from captivity, and have compassion on you, and gather you again from all the nations where the Lord your God has scattered you." (Deuteronomy 30:1-3)

Since God knows the end from the beginning about what is going to take place, it is no surprise to Him that Israel is a failure in both Covenants and thus goes into exile. The younger generation fails to follow the Mosaic Covenant and as a result does not meet the conditions of the Palestinian Covenant. As we have said before, these two Covenants are conditioned on each other. Failing to follow the Mosaic Covenant causes the nation of Israel to split into two nations; Israel and Judah. They both go into exile and thus lose the land. Even with Prophets like Isaiah and Jeremiah under the inspiration of God foretelling their future, they both go into bondage. For disobeying the Mosaic Covenant, Israel fell in 722 B.C. to Assyria. Israel split at the end of Solomon's reign. With the fall of Israel, only Judah remained. Judah would fall in 587 B.C. to Babylon because they also disobeyed the Mosaic Covenant. Both nations' failure revolved around not obeying the First Commandment of the Ten Commandments. "Thou shalt have no other gods before me." (Exodus 20:2 KJV) As is stated in the New Testament (Covenant), when you break one commandment, you have broken them all. "For whoever shall keep the whole law, and yet stumble at one point, he (or she) is guilty of all." (James 2:10).

Yet God did not say they would stay in bondage. Through the prophecies of Isaiah, Jeremiah, Ezekiel, and Daniel, God promised to restore the nation of Israel and Judah as one nation. God plans to make them one nation again. In Jeremiah 29:10-11, Jeremiah lets the people of

Israel know they will return. "For thus says the Lord: After seventy years are completed at Babylon, I will visit you and perform My good word toward you, and cause you to return to this place. For I know the thoughts that I think toward you, says the Lord, thoughts of peace and not of evil, to give you a future and a hope."

In chapters thirty and thirty-one of Jeremiah, he prophecies about their restoration. "For behold the days are coming, says the Lord, that I will bring back from captivity My people Israel and Judah, says the Lord. "And I will cause them to return to the land that I gave to their fathers and they shall possess it.'" (Jeremiah 30:3) Some Bible scholars believed this prophecy came to pass at the end of seventy years that Israel and Judah were in captivity to other nations. Others see the fulfillment of this at the end of time when Jesus Christ returns with ten thousand of His saints and restores Israel to its former glory and even greater glory during the thousand-year reign of Jesus Christ on earth from Jerusalem. Their interpretation comes from Daniel 9:24-27 and Revelation chapters 19: 15-21; 20:1-6.

Reverend Clarence Larkin in his book, The Book of Revelation, pages 48-50, clarifies the issue as far as I am concerned. "The Prophet Daniel had been sixty-eight years (B.C. 538) in Babylon and by a study of the Prophecy of Jeremiah (Jeremiah 25:11), he (Daniel) discovered that the "Seventy Years" Captivity of his people were nearing its end, and so he set his face, to seek by prayer and supplication (Daniel 9:3) to know the exact time of its ending, and while he was praying the Angel Gabriel appeared to enlighten him (Daniel 9:20-23). Daniel was concerned about the expiration of the "Seventy Years" of the Captivity, and the restoration of his people to Palestine and the rebuilding of the City of Jerusalem and of the Temple. But the Angel Gabriel came to disclose to him something more important than that. While he doubtless informed Daniel that God would fulfill His promise as to the "Seventy Years" of the captivity, which, as we know, He did, He also made known to Daniel that that would not end the troubles of Israel. That while the Jews were to return to Jerusalem at the end of the "Seventy Years" of Captivity, there was a longer period to elapse before the Kingdom would be restored to them, a period of SEVENTY WEEKS."

Therefore, Rev. Larkin shares the difference between "Seventy Weeks" and "Seventy Years." The "Seventy Weeks" is during "The Tribulation" period at the end of time. Daniel sees that at the end of the "Seventy Years" Israel's kingdom will not be restored, but this will come at the end of time when Jesus Christ, God's own Son, will come as King of Kings and Lord of Lords and will begin destroying the devil's kingdom. The beast and the false prophet will be cast into the Lake of Fire. The devil will be bound for a thousand years. (Revelation 19:26; 20:2-3)

One may ask, what has this to do with the Mosaic Covenant and the Palestinian Covenant? That is a good question. When Jesus Christ, God's Son, rules and reigns from Jerusalem the Mosaic Covenant will be fulfilled. The Mosaic Covenant's laws, ordinances, and feasts will again be established in Israel with Jesus Christ, the King, enforcing them. The sacrifices of that Covenant were all fulfilled in the sacrificial death of our Lord and Savior, Jesus Christ approximately two thousand years ago. Therefore, sacrifices at the Third Temple will no longer be necessary. The Palestinian Covenant will be fulfilled in that the Jewish people will be living on all the land of Israel that God promised them, during the thousand-year reign of God's Son, Jesus Christ. As Jeremiah promised the Jewish people, they will have a new heart and a new mind to do all that God commanded them to do. "Then, I will give them a heart to know Me, that I am the Lord, and they shall be My people, and I will be their God, for they shall return to Me with their whole heart." (Jeremiah 24:7)

The laws of God could not be obeyed until Israel's people had a new heart. One's heart must change, in order to obey God. The Israelites in the Wilderness, those who came into Canaan and with God's help conquered it; many of them still did not have a heart changed by the Spirit of God. Since Jesus is the complete fulfillment of the Mosaic Covenant, and He is coming back to complete that Covenant during His thousand-year reign. There is the need of a New Covenant that is shared in the New Testament (Covenant). In fact, Jesus went through out the land of Israel proclaiming "the Kingdom of God (Heaven)". This is what is shared in Matthew 4:23. "Now Jesus went about all Galilee, teaching in all their synagogues, preaching the Gospel of the Kingdom, and healing all kinds of sickness and all kinds of disease among the people." Before Jesus came, Jeremiah had prophesied that a New Covenant would come that would change the hearts and minds of the people of Israel. "But this is the covenant that I will make with the house of Israel after those day, says the Lord: I will put My law in their minds and write it on their hearts (inward parts); and I will be their God, and they shall be my people." (Jeremiah 31:33) We know that did not happen when Jesus came the first time. He was planting the seed of the Kingdom of God. When He comes the second time that seed will germinate and the Kingdom of God will be born with Jesus being the reigning King of the whole earth there in the Temple of God in Jerusalem.

Right now, the Mosaic and the Palestinian Covenants are broken. The Jewish people of Israel cannot even half way fulfill those two Covenants because there is no Temple built in Jerusalem. No sacrifices can be made now until a new Third Temple is built. The Jewish people must come back to the same place they were at two thousand years ago when they rejected Jesus Christ as their Messiah and Lord. It is a spiritual law that God always brings people back to the same place where and when they have rejected Him and His Word. Then the Jewish people will look on Him, Whom they have pierced. "Behold, He is coming with clouds, and every eye will see Him, and they also who pierced Him. And all tribes of the earth will mourn because of Him. Even so, Amen. (So be it)." (Revelation 1:7)

In Summary…

Why did God give the Mosaic Covenant and later the Palestinian Covenant to the nation of Israel? We do get some clues from the Pentateuch, the first five books of the Bible, as to why God gave these Covenants to Israel. We must remember that the Mosaic Covenant and the Palestinian Covenant are interrelated. By that I mean they are dependent upon one another. One reason God placed Israel under the Mosaic Covenant was Israel had been in bondage to the Egyptians for 430 years in an environment of idolatry. Egypt worshipped many gods and even worshipped Pharaoh, their ruler. The Apostle Paul makes this clear when writing the church at Corinth. "But with most of them (Israelites) God was not well pleased, for their bodies were scattered in the wilderness. Now these things became our examples, to the intent that we should not lust (evil desires) after evil things as they also lusted. And do not become idolaters as were some of them. As it is written, '" The people sat down to eat and drink, and rose up to play.'" (1 Corinthians 10:5-7) This Scripture in 1 Corinthians 10 is talking about their sexual immorality. God gave them the Ten Commandments in Exodus 20:1-17. This was to curb their lustful appetites and their sinful nature. It was to show Israel that God was a Holy God and would not tolerate sin on their behalf. The Ten Commandments addressed these sins.

This Mosaic Covenant also showed God's ability to test and correct a race of people, whereas before He was only dealing with individuals when God dealt with Noah, Abraham, Isaac, and Jacob. In the beginning when Moses led them out of Egypt and across the Red Sea, he tried to lead them all by himself. He had Aaron as his spokesman, but he made all of the decisions himself. God used Jethro, Moses father-in-law, to point out to Moses the importance of having God appointed leadership between Moses and the people. Jethro gave Moses sound advice about delegating responsibility. (Exodus 18) Otherwise, Moses would have worn out before getting to the border of the Promise Land.

Israel's failure to enter the Promise Land of Canaan under the leadership of Moses was due to a lack of faith on the Israelites part. God commanded them to go in and take possession of the land and He would be with them. In Deuteronomy 1:21-23 Moses tells Israel to go in and possess the land, but the Israelites wanted to send spies first. "Look, the Lord your God has set the land before you; go up and possess it, as the Lord God of your fathers has spoken to you; do not fear or be discouraged. And every one of you came near to me and said, 'Let us send men before us, and let them search out the land for us, and bring back word to us of the way by which we should go up, and of the cities into which we shall come. And the plan pleased me well; so, I took twelve men, one man from each tribe."

From this Scripture we can see that the idea of sending twelve spies started with the Israelites and not with Moses or God. The Israelites were hoping to find out how strong these city kingdoms were before they sent any of their warriors there. Therefore, from the outset it was not a step of faith, but rather of fear. Ten of the twelve spies came back with a bad report about the land and how strong the people were in the land. Only Joshua and Caleb, the other two spies, had a good report about the land and the inhabitants of the land. According to the Israelites "…we were like grasshoppers in our own sight, and so were in their sight." (Numbers 13:33) They did not even count on God or have faith in God to help them overcome what they considered to be giants in the land. It is no wonder Moses had this to say about them in Deuteronomy 1:26. "Nevertheless, you would not go up, but rebelled against the command of the Lord your God…" Moses goes on to say that the Israelites murmured in their tents against God and later against Moses. Finally, Moses wrote that God said this about all those men who had a bad report and all the Israelites. "And the Lord heard the sound of your words, and was angry, and took an oath, saying, 'Surely not one of these men of this evil generation shall see that good land which I swore to give to your fathers, except Caleb the son of Jephunneth; he shall see it, and to him and his children, I am giving this land on which he walked, because he wholly followed the Lord…but Joshua the son of Nun, who stands before you, he shall go in there. Encourage him, for he shall cause Israel to inherit it." (Deuteronomy 1:34-36,38) The ten spies died immediately and all those men God mentioned that were an evil generation, He caused them to die in the Wilderness.

We have shared how all of the first generation out of Egypt died in the Wilderness because of their unbelief. Notice, nothing is said about the Mosaic Covenant, about disobeying the Ten Commandments. Nothing is said about them not participating in the Feasts of the Lord, or not about obeying any case studies that surround the Ten Commandments. So, why did they not inherit the Promise Land of Canaan? If you read closely, it was because of their unbelief in God and not doing what He told them to do. He told them to go in and possess the Promise Land. They refused and therefore, they were cut off. Why did Moses share this with the new generation of Israelites that were growing up? Even Moses was not allowed to enter the Promise Land, because when God told him to speak to the rock to get water out of it for Israel, he hit the rock. He too was disobedient to God. He explained what he did and Moses died on Mount Nebo not entering the Promise Land. He shared all this with them, so they would not follow the same example of unbelief. Unbelief can cause you to break the Covenant Relationship that God has for you. Thankfully, the next generation of Israelites did go in and possess the land under the leadership of Joshua.

Another thing that sticks out to me, that even as Israel was embracing the Mosaic Covenant in the Wilderness, God was testing them. "And Moses said to the people, 'Do not fear, for God has come to test you, and that his fear may be before you, so that you may not sin." (Exodus 20:20) God could have led them right into the Promise Land. It would have taken only eleven days from Egypt and the Red Sea to Canaan. But instead God had led them to Mount Horeb instead of Canaan, because He wanted to test them to see what was in their hearts toward Him. God set boundaries about what Israel could do and what they could not do with the Ten Commandments and related case studies about the Ten Commandments in the books of Exodus and Deuteronomy. God had them spend time in the Wilderness to see if they would obey Him or not.

The Mosaic Covenant and the Palestinian Covenant had their foundation in the Abrahamic Covenant. In Deuteronomy 4:29-31, God shows Moses that foundation. "But from there you will seek the Lord your God, and you will find Him if you seek Him with all your heart and soul. When you are in distress, and all these things come in the latter days, when you turn to the Lord your God and obey His voice (for the Lord your God is a merciful God). He will not forsake you nor destroy you, nor forget the covenant of your fathers (Abraham's covenant that was extended to Isaac and Jacob) which He swore to them." The Covenant that Moses was referring to was the Abrahamic Covenant. God promised Abraham, Isaac, and Jacob, that He would bless and provide for their descendants. God promised to be with them and help them to be victorious over all the inhabitants of Canaan. They only had to obey God and do what He commanded them to do.

One can see that the Palestinian Covenant was for the new generation of Israelites who had grown up during the Wilderness wanderings and now stood with Joshua before God ready to go into the Promise Land. Moses in chapter 28 of Deuteronomy had just given them the blessings of following God and the curses, if they chose not to follow God in succeeding generations. Then in Deuteronomy the 29th chapter, Moses gives the Palestinian Covenant, which has also its foundation in the Abrahamic Covenant. This Palestinian Covenant like the Abrahamic Covenant promises the land to Israel and states that God will intervene and cause Israel to be victorious against all the inhabitants of the land. Listen to the preamble of this Covenant. "All of you stand today before the Lord your God: your leaders and your tribes and your elders and your officers, all of the men of Israel, your little ones and your wives—also the stranger who is in your camp, from the one who cuts your wood to the one who draws your water—that you may enter into covenant with the Lord your God, and into His oath, which the Lord your God makes with you today, that He may establish you today as a people for Himself, and that He may be God to you, just as He has spoken to your fathers, to Abraham, Isaac, and Jacob. I make this covenant and this oath, not with you alone, but also with him who stands here with us today before the Lord your God, as well as with him who is not here with us today." (Deuteronomy 29:10-15)

Actually, before Moses died, he went over all the Mosaic Covenant with this younger generation of Israelites. They had seen how their parents had died in the Wilderness because of disobedience to God and they did not want to be like their parents. This new Palestinian Covenant promised all the land that God had promised Abraham. In Reverend John Hagee's Prophecy Study Bible, on page 226, he goes over all the land promised in the Covenant. Unlike the Mosaic Covenant, which was conditional on Israel's obedience to that Covenant, the Palestinian Covenant had conditional aspects of that Covenant and unconditional aspects of that Covenant.

"The covenant concerning the Promise Land, called the Palestinian Covenant, is the third of the Old Testament Covenants that spell out the rule of God over His people...The Palestinian Covenant first appears as a part of the Mosaic Covenant in Deuteronomy (chapters) 27-30, but later stands alone as Israel struggles to understand her special relationship to the Promise Land. (Jeremiah 23:5-8; Ezekiel 20:42-44; 36:24-30; 37: 11-14; 47:1—48:35; Zechariah 12:10—13:20) The descendants of Abraham, the patriarch of faith, had a claim on the territory, "from the river of Egypt (Nile River) to the great river, the River Euphrates (Genesis 15:18). The western boundary of the Promise Land was the beyond the Jordan River, the territory of Bashan (Joshua 13:8-12) and the Syrian region of Lebo Hamath (2 Chronicles 8:3-4). During the reigns of David and Solomon all of this territory was occupied by Israel or subject to it by treaty (1 Kings 8:65). Israel was obligated by the conditional aspects of God's Covenant with Moses to obey the commands, judgments, and ordinances of the law in order to enjoy the immediate blessings of the Palestinian Covenant (Deuteronomy chapters 27 to 29) ...The future of the Promise Land resides under the unconditional aspects of the Palestinian Covenant."

The unconditional aspects of the Palestinian Covenant started coming to pass on May 15, 1948, when Israel again became a nation and was recognized by the United Nations. This was a fulfillment of Isaiah 66:8. "Who has heard such a thing? Who has seen such things? Shall the earth be made to give birth in one day? Or shall a nation (Israel) be born at once? For as soon as Zion prevailed, She (Israel) gave birth to her children." When this happened, the Palestinian Covenant became unconditional as Reverend John Hagee points out in his Prophecy Study Bible on page 839. "As long as God's covenant with Israel concerning Palestine was tied to His covenant with Moses, its blessings were a highly conditional matter. Occupation of the land, security from external foes, regular rains, freedom from locusts and good harvests all depended on keeping the law. However, since the Palestinian Covenant is rooted in God's covenant with Abraham (Genesis 12:1; 13:14-15), its final fulfillment ultimately is unconditional...When the modern state of Israel was organized in 1948 under the terms of Britain's League of Nations mandate, various groups and individuals interpreted the event in light of the Palestinian Covenant. Jewish Zionist view modern Israel as the beginning of the fulfillment of Biblical prophecy and work actively to expand the borders of Israel to encompass more and more of the Promise Land...Tel Aviv was the capital of Israel in 1948. Jerusalem was an international city. In the seven-day war of June 1967, Israel took control of Jerusalem and against world protest eventually made it their capital…"

One can see that the prophetical value of the Palestinian Covenant is coming to pass. Israel is gaining more and more land today as Muslim nations and world leaders protest. On December 6, 2017, President Donald Trump recognized Jerusalem as the capital of Israel and moved the United States embassy to Jerusalem. In the last seven months, Israel has decided that no work will be done on the Sabbath Day (Friday evening to Saturday evening) and recognized all of the Jewish feasts of the Old Testament to be celebrated in Israel. A lot of Jewish people are returning to their homeland from all over the world. Hebrew is now the official language of Israel. These are just some of the unconditional aspects of the Palestinian Covenant coming into existence in Israel today.

There is one last evidence of God's unconditional love to Abraham and His seed. This is recorded in Psalms 89:30-34. "If his sons (Abraham's sons) forsake My law and do not walk in My judgments; If they break My statutes and do not keep My commandments, Then I will visit their transgression with the rod, and their iniquities with stripes. Nevertheless, My lovingkindness I will not utterly take from him, nor allow My faithfulness to fail. My covenant I will not break. Nor alter the word that has gone out of My lips."

I believe the prophetical value of the two Covenants, the Mosaic Covenant and the Palestinian Covenant, will come to pass when Jesus Christ, the Son of God, reigns from Jerusalem. Then, all the land God promised Abraham, Isaac, and Jacob, will be a part of Israel. Jerusalem is and will be the capital of Israel and Jesus will reign from the Temple in Jerusalem. All nations will bow before Him and He is and will be the King of Kings and the Lord of Lords. What the Israelites could not do because of the hardness of their heart; God will change their hearts and give them a heart of flesh in exchange for the heart of stone, as recorded in Ezekiel 36:26. "I will give you a new heart and put a new spirit within you; I will take the heart of stone out of your flesh and give you a heart of flesh."

Chapter 8
The Davidic Covenant

The Davidic Covenant is about the Covenant that God extended to David, when David was King over all Israel. At that point in David's life most all of Israel's enemies had been put down or were in the process of being put under servitude or completely wiped out. He had just conquered Jerusalem and taken it from the Jebusites. "And the king (David) and his men went to Jerusalem against the Jebusites, the inhabitants of the land and spoke to David saying, "You shall not come in here; but the blind and the lame will repel you" thinking "David cannot come in here." Nevertheless, David took the stronghold of Zion (that is the city of David) …So David dwelt in the stronghold, and called it the city of David. Then David built all around from Millo and inward. So, David went on and became great, and the Lord God of host was with him." (2 Samuel 5:6-7, 9-10)

The Prophecy About A King in Deuteronomy

We are actually getting ahead of ourselves. Did Israel in the Mosaic Covenant have precedence for a king to reign over Israel? Actually, Moses foretells of this as he is sharing with the young adults what is going to take place when they come into the Promise Land of Canaan. This is right before Moses passes off the scene and Joshua takes over as the leader of Israel. Moses gives definite instructions to whoever becomes King of Israel in Deuteronomy 17: 14-20. "When you come to the land which the Lord your God is giving you, and possess it and dwell in it, and say, 'I will set a king over me like all the nations that are around you; you shall surely set a king over you whom the Lord your God chooses; one from among your brethren you shall set as a king over you; you may not set a foreigner over you, who is not your brother. But he shall multiply horses for himself, nor cause the people to return to Egypt, to multiply horses, for the Lord has said to you, 'You shall not return that way again.' Neither shall he multiply wives for himself, lest his heart turn away; nor shall he greatly multiply silver and gold for himself. Also, it shall be, when he sits on the throne of his kingdom, that he shall write for himself a copy of this law in a book, from the ones before the priests and the Levites. And it shall be with him, and he shall read it all the days of his life, that he may learn to fear the Lord his God, and be careful to observe all the words of this law and these statutes, that his heart may not be lifted above his brethren, that he may not turn aside from the commandments to the right hand or to the left, and that he may prolong his days in his kingdom, he and his children in the midst of Israel." (Deuteronomy 17:14-20)

This was a prophetic word that God gave Moses to share with His people Israel. God let Israel know that after they settled in the land, they would choose a King to rule over them. Even while they were settling in the land, God appointed Judges to rule over them. This is what Eerdmans Bible Dictionary on page 609 characterized "Judges" as. "The term (Judge) derives from Semitic (language speaking), which means basically "to exercise authority" and thus "to govern" (e.g. MT, 1 Kings 3:9; 2 Kings 15:5). The twelve persons recorded in the book of Judges as having "judged" Israel (the noun sopei is not used) are depicted as "saviors" (mosi) empowered by Yahweh to lead one or more tribes in resolving a particular crisis..."

The Period of the Judges

If one reads the book of the Judges, one sees that these Judges were called by God to save Israel time and again from idolatry. To give an example of how the Judges ruled Israel, one can look at Judges chapter three. Judge Ehud delivered Israel from the Moabites and according to Judges 3:30 the land had rest under his leadership. Before Ehud became Judge over Israel, Israel was worshipping idols. As soon as he delivered Israel from Moab, Israel had rest from idolatry for eighty years (Judges 3:30). When Ehud died, Israel went right back into idolatry (Judges 4:1-2). Therefore, in essence Ehud ruled like a King over Israel. This happened over and over again during the period of the Judges. When Judges ruled in Israel, Israel was free from idolatry. As soon as they died, unless the Judge had a son who took over as Judge, Israel went right back into idolatry.

John Hagee's Prophecy Study Bible on page 264 gave this unique description of the Judges who ruled after Joshua died. "The Hebrew title is Shophetim, meaning "judges," "rulers," "deliverers," or "saviors." Shophet not only carries the idea of maintaining justice and settling disputes, but it also used to mean "liberating" and "delivering." First, the judges deliver the people; then they rule and administer justice…"

One can see that the Judges with God's permission ruled like Kings. This was getting them ready when the people would ask for a King to rule over them like the other nations. This finally happened when Samuel was both Priest and Judge of Israel. Samuel's sons were much like the previous Priest's sons; Eli and his sons. (1 Samuel 3) In 1 Samuel 8:3 it says, "But his (Samuel's) sons did not walk in his (Samuel's) ways; they turned aside after dishonest gain, took bribes and perverted justice." Samuel had tried to make them judges in Israel when this happened. (1 Samuel 8:1-5) The Elders of Israel asked Samuel for a King like the other nations. Samuel tried to present God as the King over them, but the Elders rejected that recommendation. (1 Samuel 8:6-9) Samuel does warn them of what a King will demand from them, as God had instructed him to do, but the Elders of Israel still wanted a King. (1 Samuel 8:10-22)

This introduction lays the foundation of why a King was chosen by Israel and why Israel wanted to rush into finding a King. Nothing Samuel would or could say would change their minds. At this point God chooses Saul, but He does apply some tests to Saul in which he fails miserably. Ralph A. Smith has this description of Saul in his book, The Covenantal Structure of the Bible, on page 17. "Just as God's people were oppressed by a Pharaoh "which knew not Joseph" at the end of the patriarchal era, so they were oppressed by a king who apparently knew not the LORD at the end of the Mosaic era. Saul was a transitional figure—the first king of Israel, and, yet, because of his sin, not altogether a "true king"—not as evil as Pharaoh in many ways, but from the prospective, even worse than Pharaoh, for he sinned against greater light. Furthermore, as king of Israel he massacred eighty-five priests and destroyed the priestly city of Nob, killing men, women and children (1 Samuel 22:18-19), though he had spared the pagan king, Agag (1 Samuel 15). He also sought to slay David whom he knew to be God's anointed one." This gives a good description of Saul as he reigned over Israel.

Saul, the King of Israel

In the beginning, Saul was called and anointed by God to be the King of Israel. He was humble in the beginning after Samuel anointed him King and for a brief time obeyed the spiritual instructions of Samuel. But one day Saul got impatient with Samuel when he did not show up on time according to Saul. This was to do the priestly duties of sacrificing to God before Saul and his men went into battle. This is all recorded in 1 Samuel 13:5-11. In verses 9 and 10 of chapter 13 of 1 Samuel, Saul takes it upon himself to offer the burnt offering since Samuel was not there. Immediately, after Saul offers the burnt offering, Samuel appears and asks Saul what he is doing. This is Saul's reply to Samuel. "When I saw that the people were scattered from me, and that you did not come within the days appointed, and that the Philistines gathered together at Michmash, then I said, The Philistines will now come down on me at Gilgal, and I have not made supplication to the Lord. Therefore, I felt compelled, and offered a burnt offering." (1 Samuel 13:11-12) All this sounds reasonable to the natural mind, but there are a few things that are clear mistakes by Saul. He blames Samuel for being late and he intrudes into the spiritual office of priesthood which God did not want him to do. Listen to Samuel's response to him. "You have done foolishly. You have not kept the commandment of the Lord your God, which He commanded you. For now, the Lord would have established your kingdom over Israel forever. But now your kingdom shall not continue. The Lord has sought for Himself a man after His own heart, and the Lord has commanded him to be commander over his people, because you have not kept what the Lord commanded you." (1 Samuel 13:13-14) The big sin of Saul in the beginning of his being King over Israel is that he intruded into an office that was not his. The Priesthood had not been given to him, therefore, he should not have offered the burnt offerings. Samuel was the Priest of the Lord in Israel. This was the beginning of the end for Saul. To put an exclamation mark on this sin, listen to what happens after Samuel tells Saul this information. "Then Samuel arose and went up from Gilgal to Gibeah of Benjamin. And Saul numbered the people who were present with him, about six hundred men." (1 Samuel 13:15) Samuel did not seek the Lord for Saul as the Priest of God. Instead he left him there. Saul did not repent of what he had done, instead he acted as if what he did was alright with God and Saul numbered the people.

Dr. Spiro Zodhiates wrote this note about Saul in The Hebrew-Greek Key Study Bible, on page 383. "Saul showed himself to be a man without regard to God's will. Samuel had told Saul that he should wait for him in Gilgal for seven days. Saul seeing that Samuel had not arrived, took the priestly responsibility upon himself, which apparently, he had no right to do, and offered the burnt sacrifice. This is all summed up by Samuel as disobedience to the commandment of the Lord. Though Samuel affirmed that, because of Saul's disobedience, the kingdom would pass from him to another. Saul did not repent. He continued to disobey according to his own whims. Later Samuel stated that It is better to obey than to sacrifice. (1 Samuel 15:22)"

As we have said before, one can see the contrast between a person with a Covenant Relationship with God and one who does not have a Covenant Relationship with God. Just like Abraham and Lot, there is a marked contrast between Saul and David. Immediately, one can pick up on the fact that Saul after this experience with Samuel, was going to try to have his own way about being King. He was not listening to Samuel anymore and he was not even trying to listen to God. He willfully went against what Samuel had said. Samuel told him to wait until he got there. Saul was impatient and he saw that his soldiers were leaving and he was afraid he was going to lose his army. Fear began to motivate his life. Saul was completely depending on his five senses to battle the enemies of Israel. After this run in with Samuel, he quit going to Samuel for spiritual instruction in how to run the Kingdom of Israel. I believe his thought was: I have been anointed King of Israel therefore, I will take complete control of Israel as King. 1 Samuel 14:47 says, "So Saul established his sovereignty over Israel, and fought against all his enemies on every side, against Moab, against the people of Ammon, against Edom, against the Kings of Zobah, and against the Philistines. Wherever he turned he harassed them...Now there was fierce war with the Philistines all the days of Saul. And when Saul saw any strong man or any valiant man, he (Saul) took him for himself (Saul)." (1 Samuel 14:47, 52)

You might ask what is wrong with what Saul is doing? To begin with he has never repented of intruding into the office of the Priesthood. Therefore, he has unconfessed sin in his life. There aren't any Scriptures that says he ever repented of that sin. Saul from that point on, never consults Samuel, his spiritual authority, about anything he was doing. Since, Saul has no Covenant Relationship with God, he should be talking to Samuel like he did in the beginning when he was first anointed King of Israel. From all indications of the Scriptures, Samuel does have a Covenant Relationship with God. That Covenant Relationship Samuel had was a very close friendship with God. God was constantly talking to Samuel and telling Samuel what he wanted and what was going to happen in the future. An example of this is God telling Samuel to go to the home of Jesse and anoint David as the next King of Israel. (1 Samuel 16)

Usually, God gives individuals more than one chance to follow Him. God wants to see if we will be obedient or not. When we are obedient, then God will extend His Covenant to us. Then we start walking in Covenant Relationship with Him. Abraham waited until he was out from under his father, Terah's authority. When Terah died, then Abraham walked in obedience to what God wanted him to do—move to Canaan. In Canaan, Abraham received the Covenant that God had for him. God honored Abraham's obedience to Terah. But when Abraham was no longer under Terah, he obeyed God. God had to test Saul one last time to see if he would truly obey Him.

Because Saul is walking independent of Samuel and God, he is only using what his natural eyes can see. The last verse we looked at in 1 Samuel 14:47 and 52, tells us that Saul was looking for Israelites who were strong and valiant (brave) to fight for him. In these verses we sense that he drafted them into his army. He did the same thing to David after he killed Goliath. "Saul took him (David) that day, and would not let him go home to his father's house anymore." (1 Samuel 18:2) Saul is depending more and more on the arm of flesh. Notice Saul was the tallest Israelite and physically strong, but he did not volunteer to fight Goliath. He was afraid of Goliath.

With all this in mind, God sends Samuel to Saul one more time to give him a second chance. God wants to see if he will be obedient. This was Samuel's instructions to Saul. "Samuel also said to Saul. "The Lord sent me to anoint you king over His people, over Israel. Now therefore, heed the voice of the words of the Lord. Thus, says the Lord of hosts: 'I will punish Amalek for what he did to Israel, how he laid wait for him on the way when he came up from Egypt.' 'Now go and attack Amalek, and utterly destroy all that they have, and do not spare them. But kill both man and woman, infant and nursing child, ox and sheep, camel and donkey.'" (1 Samuel 15:1-3)

There is one other thing you must notice about this command. Saul on a daily basis before this is no longer talking or consulting with Samuel. Since the first failure of Saul, he has not approached Samuel at all. Samuel had to find Saul and give him these instructions from the Lord. To me this shows that Saul has become increasingly independent of God and Samuel. Before these instructions were given to Saul, Saul would speak to God and ask questions, but he receives no answer from God. I will give you an example in 1 Samuel 14:37. "So Saul asked counsel of God, "Shall I go down after the Philistines? Will you deliver them into the hand of Israel?" But He (God) did not answer him that day." Saul does not realize that his independence from Samuel, his spiritual authority, has caused God not to answer his prayers and his questions.

But now Samuel has come to Saul with definite instructions from God. Notice God is only speaking through Samuel to Saul. God wants him to kill all the Amalekites; men, women, children, babies and all their animals. No one is to be left alive of that nation. Those are pretty plain instructions to follow. Will Saul do what God has said? "But Saul and the people spared Agag and the best of the sheep, the oxen, the fatlings, the lambs, and all that was good, and were unwilling to utterly destroy them. But everything despised and worthless, that they utterly destroyed." (1 Samuel 15:9)

God was specific in what He wanted done. He wanted the Amalekites wiped out completely and all their animals destroyed. Saul must have thought that God did not mean it. At best one Biblical writer calls Saul's work as "incomplete obedience." To be in Covenant Relationship with God, one must obey God fully and do exactly what God has told one to do. One may say, that is in the Old Testament (Covenant). It does not apply to the New Testament (Covenant). I would have to disagree. One only has to look at the book of Acts chapter five. Acts 5:1-11 gives an account of Ananias and Sapphira lying to the Holy Spirit and giving only a portion of their goods to God after they sold their land. They promised to give all, but held back a portion for themselves thus lying to the Holy Spirit. God expects complete obedience on our part, if we are going to walk with Him in Covenant Relationship.

This was a willful choice on the part of Saul. As a result, God expresses His displeasure in making Saul the King of Israel. "Now the word of the Lord came to Samuel saying, "I greatly regret that I have set up Saul as a King, for he has turned his back from following Me, and has not performed my commandments. And it grieved Samuel, and he cried out to the Lord all night." (1 Samuel 15:10-11)

Incomplete obedience is a common sin among believers. This sin is only doing a part of what God has commanded you. What it means to the believer is he or she will never come into the fullness of the blessing of the Lord and God will not extend His Covenant to them. If He has extended His Covenant to you and you are living in sin or incomplete obedience, He will chastise you and life will be miserable until you repent and come back under His Covenant and His Covenant Blessing. An example of this is David after his sin of adultery with Bathsheba and murdering Uriah the Hittite. Of course, David repented as we shall see. His prayer of repentance is Psalm 51. What it says about believers who are in incomplete obedience is they are not interested in following God closely, but only at a distance. In the New Testament it is called grieving the Holy Spirit. "And do not grieve the Holy Spirit of God, by Whom you were sealed for the day of redemption." (Ephesians 4:30) Peter in the New Testament (Covenant), was guilty of following Jesus at a distance during the hour of the Cross and even denied he knew Jesus three times. (Luke 22:54-62) One can be restored into full fellowship with Jesus. One has to repent of the sin and determine to follow Jesus no matter what. Peter did this in John's Gospel chapter 21:15-23.

Notice when Samuel confronts Saul of his incomplete obedience, Saul still believes he has done what God has commanded. To get the full significance of Saul's sin and what he did and did not do, one should read the entire chapter of 1 Samuel 15. But in verses 20 and 21, Saul lists the excuses for not obeying the Lord fully. "And Saul said to Samuel, "But I have obeyed the voice of the Lord, and gone on the mission on which the Lord sent me, and brought back Agag king of the Amalek; I have utterly destroyed the Amalekites. But the people took the plunder, sheep and oxen, the best of the things which should have been utterly destroyed, to sacrifice to the Lord your God in Gilgal." People who suffer from incomplete obedience hear what they want to hear from God. They also have a tendency to blame others for their incomplete obedience like Saul did in this passage. But Samuel identifies Saul's problem. "Then Samuel said: Has the Lord as great delight in burnt offerings and sacrifices, as in obeying the voice of the Lord? Behold to obey is better than sacrifices, and to heed than the fat of rams. For rebellion is the sin of witchcraft (divination) and stubbornness is as iniquity and idolatry. Because you have rejected the word of the Lord, He has rejected you from being King." (1 Samuel 15:22-23)

This was not the end of it. Saul tries to make amends. He confessed what he did to Samuel. But was that confession to God? "Then Saul said to Samuel, "I have sinned, for I have transgressed the commandment of the Lord and your words, because I feared the people and obeyed their voice. Now therefore, please pardon my sin, and return with me, that I may worship the Lord." (1 Samuel 15:24-25) If you noticed, this confession is to Samuel and not to God. Only God can forgive sin. Samuel refused to go with Saul to offer sacrifices to God. Samuel tried to leave, but Saul tore

Samuel's robe. Then Samuel gave Saul this final word of prophecy. "The Lord has torn the kingdom of Israel from you today, and has given it to a neighbor of yours, who is better than you. And also, the Strength of Israel will not lie nor relent (repent). For He is not a man that He should relent (repent)." (1 Samuel 15:28-29)

Saul continues to say, "I have sinned." (1 Samuel 15:30a) But does he really mean it or has he just been caught? Samuel does go with him and worships the Lord with Saul. At the end of the worship, Samuel asks for Agag, the king of the Amalekites to be brought to him. From reading the Scriptures you will see that King Agag thinks Samuel will do nothing to him, but he is wrong. "But Samuel said (to Agag), "As your sword has made women childless, so shall your mother be childless among women." And Samuel hacked Agag in pieces before the Lord in Gilgal." (1 Samuel 15:33) Then Samuel went home to Ramah and verse 35 of 1 Samuel 15 says Samuel did not "see Saul again until the day of his death." That means that both Samuel and God were done with Saul. The biggest mistake of Saul's life is when he did not listen to Samuel, who had a close Covenant Relationship with God. As we shall see, Saul did have the Spirit of the Lord upon his life, because he had received the Spirit when Samuel anointed him King of Israel. If he had listened and obeyed the Lord speaking through Samuel, he might have come into Covenant Relationship with God.

Saul and David

Now we will look at David and how he is anointed King over Israel. Already, Samuel knows that Saul will not leave the throne of Israel willingly. When God tells Samuel to go to the town of Bethlehem to anoint one of the sons of Jesse the Bethlehemite to be King of Israel, he tells God he is afraid that if Saul hears of it, he will kill him. Even the elders of Bethlehem were afraid of Samuel and ask him if he came in peace. God told Samuel to disguise this meeting in the town of Bethlehem as a sacrifice to the Lord, but to be sure and invite Jesse and all of his sons to the feast after the sacrifice. In the process of the sacrifice, Samuel sanctifies (separates) Jesse and his sons. Samuel thinks it is all the older sons that are qualified to be King, but God corrects him of that reasoning with this statement. "...For the Lord does not see as man sees for man looks at the outward appearance, but the Lord looks at the heart." (1 Samuel 16:7b) God passes over all the sons of Jesse, because none of them are acceptable to him. Samuel finally asks Jesse if all of his sons are present and Jesse has to admit that the youngest son, David, is out in the field being a shepherd to the sheep. Notice what happens next. "So, he (Jesse) sent and brought him (David) in. Now he (David) was ruddy, with bright (beautiful) eyes and good looking. And the Lord said, "Arise anoint him (David) for this is the one. Then Samuel took the horn of oil and anointed him (David) in the midst of his brothers; and the Spirit of the Lord came upon David from that day forward. So, Samuel arose and went to Ramah." (1 Samuel 16:12-13)

The anointing of God comes upon David as soon as Samuel pours the oil upon him. All of his brothers and family knew that he has been anointed to be King over Israel. Notice, this happens to David right before his encounter with Goliath (1 Samuel 17). While David was experiencing the fullness of the Spirit, Saul experienced the Holy Spirit's departure from him. This comes immediately after David is filled with the Holy Spirit in the very next verse—1 Samuel 16:14. "But the Spirit of the Lord departed from Saul, and a distressing spirit from the Lord troubled him (Saul)."Notice, God gave Saul ample opportunity to repent, to change his ways, and determine to follow God at all costs. But Saul did not do that. He became independent of Samuel and God. He did not repent, even when the Spirit of the Lord left him. He did not turn to God, therefore, the Spirit of God left him (Saul).

Another example of the Holy Spirit leaving someone in the Old Testament (Covenant) is found in the life of Samson. (Judges chapters 14-16) Samson played fast and loose with carnal passions. Delilah deceived him into telling her about his spiritual strength that involved the Nazarite vow from birth that included him not to cut his hair all the days of his life. She made a deal with his arch-enemies, the Philistines. Delilah was also a Philistine. While he was asleep on her lap, the Philistines cut his hair. Listen to what happens to Samson in Judges 16:20. "And she (Delilah) said, "The Philistines are upon you, Samson!" So, he awoke from his sleep and said, "I will go out as before, at other times, and shake myself free!" But he (Samson) did not know that the Lord had departed from him."

A good question is what is this "distressing spirit from the Lord" that was troubling Saul? Matthew Henry in A Commentary of the Whole Bible, Volume II, Joshua to Esther, on page 368 says this. "Now God took (H)is mercy from Saul (as it is expressed in 2 Samuel 7:15) for, when the Spirit of the Lord departs from us, all good goes. When men grieve and quench the Spirit, by willful sin, (H)e departs, and will not always strive. The consequence of this was an "evil spirit from God troubled him." Those that drive the good Spirit away from them of course become prey to the evil spirit. If God and (H)is grace does not rule us, Satan will have possession of us. The devil by divine permission, troubled and terrified Saul, by means of the corrupt humorous of his (Saul's) body and passions of his (Saul's) mind. He grew fretful, and peevish, and discontented, timorous and suspicious, ever and anon starting and trembling; he was sometimes, says Josephus, as if he had been choked or strangled and a perfect demoniac by fits. This made him unfit for business, precipitate in his counsels, the contempt of his enemies, and a burden to all about him."

I agree with Matthew Henry about the state of mind and being of Saul after the Spirit of the Lord left him. God had permitted satan to torment him. Saul had a way out which was to repent and turn the Kingdom of Israel over to David, but he did not take it. He could have called all of Israel together and given the Kingdom to David. After David killed Goliath and a few battles after that, Saul in his heart knew David was suppose to be King of Israel, but he refused to accept it. There would be more steps in a downward spiral for Saul and his family. His decisions after David kills Goliath and then David marries his daughter, Michal, and then the victories David experienced in the battle field instead of destroying David, only proves more and more that David should be King. King Saul tried in every step to maneuver David into a place where David would be destroyed, but it always backfired on him, because God was with David every step of the way. These things only trained David to be the King of Israel. Saul could not keep the Kingdom for himself and his family. As Ralph Smith said earlier, Saul killed eighty-five priests and destroyed the priestly city of Nob. All of these would add up against Saul and would prove to be his downfall for both him and his sons.

In the beginning, David tried to help King Saul by playing music on his harp. This actually drove the evil spirit away. As Matthew Henry says, David is made a physician to Saul. God had uniquely prepared David for all of this. The last verse of 1 Samuel 16 says it better than I could. "And so, it was, whenever the spirit from God was upon Saul, that David would play the harp and play it with his hand. Then Saul would become refreshed and well, and the distressing spirit would depart from him." (1 Samuel 16:23)

What puzzles many individuals is why God did not kill Saul immediately and put David on the throne? One must remember that David was still a youth when he started playing the harp for King Saul. What would begin David's adventure to becoming the next King of Israel is when he defeated Goliath in 1st Samuel 17. This would show all Israel that God was with David. Matthew Henry in his Commentary said that Goliath was eleven feet four inches tall. Others believe he was over nine feet tall. Whichever is true about Goliath; he was a very tall giant of a man. The only man on Israel's side that was tall like Goliath was King Saul. Most believe Saul was six feet tall. According to 1 Samuel 9:2b it says of Saul, "From his shoulders upward he was taller than any of the (Israelite) people." So, if anyone on Israel's side should have accepted Goliath's challenge, it should have been Saul. But the Bible is clear, he was afraid to fight Goliath. "When Saul and all Israel heard these words of the Philistine (Goliath), they were afraid and greatly dismayed." (1 Samuel 17:11) Why was Saul afraid of Goliath? Saul knew that God was no longer with him. The Spirit of the Lord had left him. (1 Samuel 16:14)

The only one that could and would defeat Goliath was David. He was anointed by God and full of the Spirit of God to do just that. It was not by accident that Jesse sent David to see about his brothers, bring food, and find out about the battle. All of David's brothers were part of Saul's army. When David heard the challenge of Goliath, he was more than eager to face that challenge. That is when he told King Saul, he would fight the giant. David knew that the Lord was with him. He told Saul that as the shepherd of his father's sheep, he had killed both a lion and a bear. He gave all the credit to the Lord. "Moreover, David said, "The Lord who delivered me from the paw of the lion and from the paw of the bear, He will deliver me from the hand of this Philistine (Goliath)." And Saul said to David, "Go and the Lord be with you." (1 Samuel 17:37) A mark of a person coming into a Covenant Relationship with God is they are filled with the Holy Spirit and that God is with them in every endeavor.

If you read 1st Samuel 17, you will find out David could not use Saul's armor or his sword. He was just a youth; some believe around 14 to 16 years of age. But his trust in God was beyond his brothers, for they did not volunteer to fight Goliath. His faith in God was beyond the whole army of Israel. Even Jonathan, Saul's son, who had exercised faith in a previous chapter (1 Samuel 14) did not volunteer for this assignment. Finally, Saul who knew God had left him and would not volunteer willingly to fight the giant.

God used a shepherd boy, David, with a rock and a sling to defeat the giant. Notice, David had not said anything to anyone, including Saul about his being anointed by Samuel, the prophet, to be the next King of Israel. Even his brothers, apart of Saul's army, had not said anything to anyone about David being anointed King. Maybe David told his brothers to keep all that quiet. Perhaps, the Holy Spirit had cautioned him about saying anything. We do not know. The Scriptures are quiet about that. That day David killed the giant, Goliath, and brought his head to Saul, he was never allowed to return home to shepherd the sheep anymore. For the time being he became a commander and warrior for King Saul.

For the next thirty-nine years David is trained by God to be the next King of Israel. God uses the Training School of Adversity to prepare David for the throne. It isn't that God is not with us when he is preparing us for leadership and Covenant Relationship. If you want to follow the training of David to be the King of Israel, read 1st Samuel chapters 17 to 31. Saul becomes jealous of David and tries to kill him over and over again over those thirty-nine years. Therefore, David has to deal with a jealous spirit. Saul gives Michal, his daughter, to him in marriage, hoping she would entrap him. That failed because Michal really loved David. Then he takes Michal away from him and gives her to another man. He sends David out against the Philistines, hoping they will kill him, but he is victorious over them. He slanders David's good name and David even has to move his own family to the Philistines country. For years he lives with 600 men in caves and hideouts throughout all Israel. He is constantly on the run from Saul and his men. In all of this, he will not allow his men to kill Saul because he considers him to be the anointed of the Lord. Saul continued to pursue David and his men, until he moved all of them and their families to the country of Gath. (1 Samuel 27)

One could go into every detail of Saul's and David's life. One would see in Saul's life that he no longer has the Spirit of the Lord guiding his steps. He becomes a natural man. He has no possibility of a Covenant Relationship with God. On the other hand, David mostly on the run is led by the Spirit of God which ultimately leads him to becoming the King of Israel and eventually into a Covenant Relationship with God. From these two lives spelled out in Scripture, one can see how important the Holy Spirit of God is in one's walk with the Lord. Saul because of his willful disobedience and sinning against truth and God, the Holy Spirit leaves. This leaves him wide open for the devil to invade his life. Jealousy and a hatred for David is the result of that invasion. On the other hand, one can see how David by the power and tutoring of the Holy Spirit in the beginning is able to avoid the traps of the devil. Later, in David's life the Holy Spirit leads him into a Covenant Relationship with God.

David actually fulfilled the prophetic word that had been spoken by Moses in Deuteronomy 17:14-20. One might say David did slip and fall when he committed adultery with Bathsheba and then later had her husband, Uriah, the Hittite, killed in battle. (2 Samuel 11) He tried to cover it up, but Nathan, the prophet, came on the scene and told him of his great sins and the chastisement, he would receive the rest of his life. The sword would never depart from David's house. (2 Samuel 12:9-12) David did repent of his sin (Psalm 51), but the child that Bathsheba bore in adultery died. "Then David said to Nathan, "I have sinned against the Lord." And Nathan said to David, "The Lord has put away your sin: you shall not die. However, because by this deed you have given great occasion to the enemies of the Lord to blaspheme, the child also who is born to you shall surely die." (2 Samuel 12:13-14)

One might say what is the difference between Saul's sin and David's sin? There is one major difference. Saul did not have a truly repentant heart. He only said he had sinned to Samuel hoping that Samuel would bless him and be for him before God. There is no record in Scriptures of him ever repenting to God. David on the other hand had a truly repentant heart. In Psalms 51 David's prayer of repentance is recorded for all to see. David knew that God could cast him away from His Presence and also take God's Holy Spirit from him. He only had to look at the life of Saul to see that. Listen to what he says in Psalms 51:10-11. "Create in me a clean heart, O God, and renew a steadfast (or right KJV) spirit within me. Do not cast me away from Your presence and do not take Your Holy Spirit from me." David saw what happened in the life of Saul. He saw the Holy Spirit taken from Saul. David knew what the fear (respect) of the Lord is. "The fear of the Lord is the beginning of knowledge, but fools despise wisdom and instruction." (Proverbs 1:7)

A second question comes to my mind. Why would God allow David to continue in Covenant Relationship with Him, since he committed such grave sins of adultery and murder? That is a good question. Notice that David did not escape the chastisement of the Lord. What Nathan, the Prophet, prophesied did come to pass. Listen to the Prophet Nathan. "Why have you despised the commandment of the Lord, to do evil in His sight? You have killed Uriah the Hittite with the sword: you have taken his wife to be your wife, and have killed him with the sword of the people of Ammon. Now therefore, the sword shall never depart from your house, because you have despised Me, and have taken the wife of Uriah to be your wife. Thus, says the Lord: "Behold I will raise up adversity against you from your own house: and I will take your wives before your eyes and give them to your neighbor and he shall lie with your wives in the sight of the sun. For you did it secretly, but I will do this thing before all Israel, before the sun...However, because by this deed you have given great occasion to the enemies of the Lord to blaspheme, the child also who is born to you shall surely die." (2 Samuel 12:9-12,14) Thus, you see what God outlined as chastisement for David. Did all of this come to pass as stated by the Prophet Nathan? It most certainly did. First, the child he had with Bathsheba in adultery died, even though David prayed the child would not die. (2 Samuel 12:15-23) Before I go further, let me make this clear. David suffered all these adverse things in his life because of sin. Individuals who come into a Covenant Relationship with God and then sin will experience God's correction and chastisement. (Hebrews 12:5-11)

Immediately, the sword began to invade David's house. It starts with the sin of incest in 2 Samuel 13. This started with Tamar, David's lovely sister, and David's son, Amnon. Tamar did not do it willingly; Amnon forced her to do it. Absalom, who is the brother of Tamar plots and kills Amnon. This is just the beginning of the sword that invades David's house. Absalom goes away for a while, but returns some years later and plots and causes insurrection against David and the Kingdom of Israel. This insurrection brings Absalom to the place of trying to kill David and take over the Kingdom. For a while Absalom has control of Jerusalem and goes into his father's concubines before all Israel. David's men regain control and Joab, one of David's top generals, kills Absalom against David's wishes. (2 Samuel chapters 14-18)

Then Sheba, the son of Birchri, a Benjamite, rebels against David. He causes all Israel to desert David. Only Judah from the Jordan to Jerusalem remains loyal to David in the beginning of this rebellion. But as time advances, David is able to bring most all the people back under his reign. He sends Joab out after Sheba and they chase him to Beth Maachah. A wise woman in Israel who lives in that city is able to negotiate with Joab. He asks for Sheba's head and she has it tossed over the wall of the city to Joab. Thus, that rebellion is put down. (2 Samuel 20)

Finally, at the end of David's life, Adonijah, the son of Haggith, attempted to take over Israel. This happened when David was old and weak. Adonijah gathered some the chief men of Israel such as Joab,

David's chief general, and Abiathar, the priest, followed him and tried to make him King over Israel. But before this happened the other major men in Israel, like Zadok the priest, Nathan, the Prophet, gathered all the mighty men of Israel together and they approach Bathsheba, David's wife, and they approach David about the matter. David proceeded to crown Solomon as King in his stead, so he could put down this rebellion as well. (1 Kings chapters 1 and 2)

In all of these adverse conditions, David has a repentant heart. He knew he was the cause of these adverse conditions in his family and even outside his family. But God did not give up on him and continued with his Covenant toward His servant, David. David was "a man after God's own heart." (1 Samuel 13:14) David wrote many of the Psalms that are in the book of Psalms. Even though David sinned, God did not remove His Covenant from David.

The Davidic Covenant

The Davidic Covenant is shared with David by Nathan the prophet. We need to get the setting behind Nathan sharing this with David. Notice, unlike Saul, David relied on the prophetic voice to the Kingdom of Israel. Saul lived independently of Samuel, the prophet at that time. Evidently, Saul did not trust the prophetic voice in his kingdom. As a result, Saul never heard from Samuel again after he told Saul what to do with the Amalekites. The Spirit's voice was not heard. In many churches today, they have silenced the voice of the Holy Spirit because they don't want to hear what the Spirit is saying to them through the Prophet.

Here is the setting after David had defeated most of Israel's enemies. David had approached Nathan about building a house or temple for God to dwell in, in Jerusalem. At first Nathan tells David to do all that is in his heart and Nathan goes home to his dwelling place. But that night God speaks to Nathan, and tells him to tell David that he cannot build Him a house. In 2 Samuel 7:11-16 Nathan goes on to tell David the Davidic Covenant that God is extending to David. In this passage, however, it does not tell why David cannot build a House or Temple for God. But this is given in 1 Chronicles 22:7-9. "And God said to Solomon, "My son, as for me, it was in my mind to build a house to the name of the Lord my God; but the word of the Lord came to me, saying, "You (David) have shed much blood and have made great wars; you shall not build a house for My name, because you have shed much blood on the earth in My sight. Behold a son (Solomon) shall be born to you, who shall be a man of rest; and I will give him rest from all his enemies all around. His name shall be Solomon, for I will give peace and quietness to Israel in his days."

There are several ideas this Scripture gives us. First, it reveals why David was not allowed to build a House or Temple for God. God considered it good, that it was in David's heart to do that. God also told David, who He wanted to rule over Israel next, which would be his son, Solomon. Therefore, at the end of David's life, he was not acting on his own to make Solomon King of Israel. God had chosen Solomon to be the next King over Israel.

Now, we can get to God's Covenant with David. God does allow David and his family in succeeding years to reign over Israel. This is discussed in 2 Samuel chapter 7. This Covenant with David is the fourth Theocratic Covenant pertaining to the rule of God over Israel. There are some interesting thoughts that Ralph Smith in his book, The Covenantal Structure of the Bible, pages 37-38, that one must look at before proceeding into the promises that God made to David. "The Kingship was spoken of in the law of Moses, (Deuteronomy 17:14-20) but no king was provided…This was in part because of the curse of God on the seed of Judah, most of whom were the children of bastards (cf. Genesis 38) and, therefore, not qualified for kingship until the tenth generation (cf. Deuteronomy 23:2). Even if the family of Judah had been qualified, however, Israel was not, during the Mosaic era, mature enough for the institution of kingship. Only when she had developed, culturally and spiritually, would the kingship, central government, and a central place of worship be established. Thus, the same covenant (Davidic Covenant) that established the family of David as the royal family also gave to Israel a central place of worship, the city of David, Jerusalem. The law of Moses alluded to a central sanctuary (Deuteronomy 12:1-7), but only with the

Davidic Covenant was it actually provided. Planned by David and built by Solomon, the temple system brought important changes in the law and worship of Israel...The ceremonial aspects of the Mosaic system, though not the ethical ones, are significantly revised to fit the new covenant situation. In addition to fulfilled certain promises of the Abrahamic and Mosaic covenants, the Davidic Covenant further developed the important aspects of the promise of the covenant, the doctrine (teaching) of the Messiah. The Abrahamic covenant had promised that the seed of Eve who would save the world would be of the family of Abraham. The prophecy of Jacob had pointed to the tribe of Judah (Genesis 49:8-11). The Mosaic covenant had foretold of a prophet like Moses (Deuteronomy 18:15). Now, the new Kingly (Davidic) Covenant developed the promise further by declaring the Messiah would be a royal descendent of David through his son Solomon (2 Samuel 7:8-29; Psalms 89)."

Ralph Smith gives us a basic summary of how Israel reached the place where the Israelite people thought they needed a King. They could have continued to have Prophets and Priests running the country with God speaking through them, telling them what to do. That is called a Theocratic Government, where God is in control using Prophets and Priests. But the Elders and the children of Israel wanted a King. They asked God long enough until He gave them what they wanted. Since, God knows the end from the beginning, He prophetically told them what was going to happen.

John Hagee in his Prophecy Study Bible, page 345, points out the three primary features of this Covenant. "...There were three primary features of God's Covenant with David. The first aligned the Davidic covenant with the Palestinian covenant. David's dynasty could rule over the Promised Land (2 Samuel 7:10). Second, the Davidic dynasty would be permanent (2 Samuel 7:11, 16). Third, the Kingdom established under the rule of David's heirs would last forever (2 Samuel 7:13,16)."

Why Sacrifices Probably Happened

One thing we must talk about is the fact that not all Biblical scholars see Nathan's prophetic words over David as a Covenant of God. Their main complaint is the fact that there are no sacrifices mentioned in this setting. The Bible does not record any sacrifices before or after Nathan gives the prophetic word to David. Before we address this complaint, I want everyone to view what the Word of God says and hear what Nathan told David that God had shared with him. This is a long passage of Scripture taken from 2 Samuel 7:4-17. I am going to quote it in its entirety. I personally believe that this is a Covenant that God extended to David and it is an unconditional Covenant based on the faithfulness of God.

"But it happened that night that the word of the Lord came to Nathan saying," Go and tell my servant, David, "Thus says the Lord, "Would you build a house for Me to dwell in? For I have not dwelt in a house since the time that I brought the children of Israel up from Egypt, even to this day, but have moved about in a tent and in a tabernacle. In all the places where I have walked with all the children of Israel, have I ever spoken a word to anyone from the tribes of Israel, whom I commanded to shepherd my people Israel, saying, why have you not built Me a house of cedar? Now therefore, thus shall you say to My servant David, thus says the Lord of Hosts: I took you from the sheepfold, from following the sheep, to be ruler over My people, over Israel. And I have been with you wherever you have gone, and have cut off all your enemies from before you, and have made you a great name, like the name of the great men who are on the earth. Moreover, I will appoint a place for My people Israel, and will plant them, that they may dwell in a place of their own and move no more; nor shall the sons of wickedness oppress them anymore, as previously, since the time that I commanded judges over My people Israel, and have caused you rest from all your enemies. Also, the Lord tells you, who will come from your body, and I will establish his kingdom (Solomon). He shall establish a house for My name, and I will establish the throne of his kingdom forever. I will be his Father, and he shall be My son. If he commits iniquity, I will chasten him with the rod of men and with the blows of the sons of men. But My mercy shall not depart from him, as I took it from Saul, whom I removed from before you. And your house and your kingdom shall be established forever before you. Your throne shall be established forever. According to all these words and according to all this vision, so Nathan spoke to David." (2 Samuel 7:4-17)

Actually, this Davidic Covenant is based on the Mosaic Covenant and the Palestinian Covenant. The Mosaic Covenant included sacrifices for sin in it and even praise and blessings were a part of that Covenant. However, there were initial sacrifices of animals to begin the Mosaic Covenant. (Exodus 24:1-8) It went into effect when Moses and all the children of Israel said they would obey that Covenant in Exodus 19:5-8. But the Mosaic Covenant was ratified in Exodus 24:5-8 when they offered oxen to the Lord. After Moses put it basins and sprinkled half of it on the altar. Then Moses took the Book of the Covenant and read it to the people. "And they said, "All that the Lord has said we will do. And Moses took the blood and sprinkled it on the people, and said, "Behold the blood of the Covenant which the Lord has made with you according to all these words." (Exodus 24: 7b-8) One can read Exodus chapters 19 and 24 to see the background of this Covenant of Law. Therefore, the Davidic Covenant is based on the Mosaic Covenant of Law, because a King is foretold in that Covenant of Law. Also, the King of Israel was suppose to copy the Covenant of Law all the time that he is King, so he will not forget the Law of God.

The Palestinian Covenant that Moses shared with the young Israelite adults does not have an initial sacrifice of animals. One can read Deuteronomy chapter 29 and see there are no initial sacrifices associated with this Covenant. The Palestinian Covenant is based on the oath of the people who are standing before God with Moses promising to obey the Covenant. There are no recorded sacrifices with the Palestinian Covenant, and the Davidic Covenant. Instead the people involved vocally agreed to the Covenants with God. But the priests offered sacrifices every day both in the morning and the evening, therefore essentially the Palestinian Covenant was with blood sacrifices every day thus ratifying the Covenant with a blood sacrifice. If one reads through 2nd Samuel, one will see David offering sacrifices or having the priests offering sacrifices for him. David essentially is under the Mosaic Covenant when he receives the Davidic Covenant. So, that Davidic Covenant did have blood sacrifices applied.

Why Is Nathan's Prophecy Considered to Be A Covenant—the Davidic Covenant?

Another objection to the Davidic Covenant being considered a Covenant is that there is no mention of the word "Covenant" in the prophetic word that Nathan shares with David. However, Arthur W. Pink in his book, The Divine Covenants, pages 215-216, answers this argument of Biblical scholars. "It is pitiful that any should quibble that because there is no express mention here of any "covenant" being made, therefore we are not warranted in so regarding this event. It is true we have no formal account of any sacrifices being offered in connection with it, no express figurative ratification of it, such as we find attending every similar transaction of which mention is made in Scripture. But the silence observed on this point is no proof that no such formality took place...However, that it was a true covenant is evident from the distinct mention of it under this very designation in other passages."

Mr. Pink goes on to reference some of the Scriptures which describes this as a Covenant between God and David in the same book, The Divine Covenants, on pages 213-214. "That the great transaction narrated in 2 Samuel 7 was thus regarded by David himself as a covenant is clear from his own declaration: "Although, my house be not so with God, yet he has made with me an everlasting covenant, ordered in all things, and secure; for this is all my salvation; and all my desire." (2 Samuel 23:5) When was it that God made this everlasting covenant with David, if not in the place which we are now considering? But what is still more to the point, the Lord Himself refers to the same as a covenant, as we may see from His response to Solomon's prayer: "If thou wilt walk before me, as David thy father walked, and do according to all that I have commanded thee, and shalt observe my statutes and my judgments; then will I establish the throne of thy kingdom according as I have covenanted with David, thy father, saying, There shall not fail thee a man to be ruler in Israel." (2 Chronicles 7:17-18). With these statements before us, we cannot doubt that this divine transaction with David was a true covenant, even though there is no record of its ratification."

The Covenant showed David that the Temple would be built, because God promised that it would. The Covenant also showed David that his successor, Solomon, would reign in his place and that it would be a peaceable reign without any wars or battles. God promised David that Solomon like David, would have a father-son relationship with God. God told David that Solomon might be chastened at times, but Solomon would not be removed as King, like Saul had been. Finally, God said, "your house and your kingdom will last forever." In other words, at the end of time, the Messiah—Jesus Christ—will reign forever and ever. Every promise that God is making to David is a Covenant Relationship promise that is going to come to pass. As Reverend Pink quoted out of second Chronicles the seventh chapter it has all to do about Covenant Relationship. Therefore, how can Biblical scholars say this is not a Covenant?

David and Solomon's Sins

There is something else to consider after God makes all these Covenant Promises to David. Nearly immediately after this, David commits the sins of adultery and murder in 2 Samuel 11. God could have withdrawn His Covenant Relationship with David because David broke two of the Ten Commandments. David later in his life also sinned in numbering the children of Israel. God never wanted that done. (1 Chronicles 2) However, God chastised David, but the Covenant and the Covenant Promises remained intact. Even in sin, David had a tender repentant heart toward God.

Because of the latter Kings after Solomon, it would seem that this Covenant would be broken, because of their wickedness. This is what Ralph Smith says about the kings starting at the end of Solomon's reign in The Covenantal Structure of the Bible, page39. "The office of the King was to be inherited by David's descendants, eventuating in the Messiah. But Solomon's idolatry destroyed the United Kingdom, dividing the land into north and south. (1 Kings chapters 11 and 12) The northern kingdom from the beginning worshipped the true God of Israel through an idol, as the Israelites in the wilderness had. (1 Kings 12:16-33) They eventually fell into the grossest forms of idolatrous perversity. The north (Israel) never enjoyed a single Godly King. The southern kingdom (Judah and Benjamin), by the grace of God, had some Godly Kings, but in the end, was overcome with wickedness and idolatry worse than the north (Israel). Because of the sins, the house of David appeared to have lost the Messianic promise. God cursed the royal line, swearing that no one from the descendants of Coniah would ever rule the land (Jeremiah 22:28-30) The inheritance of the kingdom was lost, apparently forever."

What Reverend Smith says is true about the inheritance of Coniah. However, God's promise is to the seed of David. Coniah was the son of Jehoiakim and his actual name is Jeconiah and it was abbreviated to Coniah. He was taken to Babylon in chains. Jeconiah according to Matthew's Gospel did have a son in Babylon. That child was in the lineage of Jesus and was Shealtiel. (Matthew 1:12) Listen to what https://carm.org>Isaiah-Malachi says. "Matthew 1:12 states that Jeconiah bore Shealtiel in the lineage of David to Jesus). If Jeremiah 22:30 is true then how could a childless man have a child? Quite simply the context tells us what is meant by Jeremiah's term "childless." He tells us that none of his (Coniah's) descendants will have proper sitting on the throne of David. In Matthew's genealogy, Jeconiah is included. But Matthew gives the legal line through Solomon to Joseph. Luke gives the biological lineage from Mary through Nathan, brother of Solomon, upwards. Therefore, no descendants of Coniah (Jeconiah) has ever sat on the throne of David."

Thus, we have an explanation of how Jeremiah could call Coniah a father who had no children. Actually, he did have children in Babylon. If you read 2 Kings 25:27-30 shows that Evil-Merodach (the Man of Mardak), who was King of Babylon then, took Jehoiachin and released him from prison and gave him a more prominent seat than those of the Kings who were with him in Babylon. "He (Evil-Merodach) spoke kindly to him and gave him a more prominent seat than those of the Kings who were with him in Babylon." (2 Kings 25:28) No one knows if Jehoiakim ever repented of his sins. Only time will tell. But he is in the lineage of David through to Joseph, Jesus Christ's step-father.

The Davidic Covenant was set up by the permission of God, so that it would end with Jesus Christ, as the King of Kings. This was God's ultimate intention. Looking at what happened after David's and Solomon's reign, it looks as if God's plan has been derailed. Even with the Gentile Kings giving the Jews the right to return to Israel and build the Temple again and restore the City of Jerusalem.

This is what Reverend Ralph Smith says about that in his book, The Covenantal Structure of the Bible, pages 42-43. He gives this insight about the restoration of the Temple and Jerusalem. "Civil rule had been taken from the Jews and given to the Gentile empires (Syria, Babylon, and Rome) but the Gentiles were appointed as protectors not persecutors. So long as the Jews were faithful to God, they would find that the Gentile rulers favored them above the other nations, as, for example, the king of Persia favored the Jews in the days of Ezra, Nehemiah, Esther, and Mordecai. The temple had a new priesthood examined and approved by Ezra. (Ezra 2:62) Jerusalem was rebuilt no longer as a civic center but, which was far more important, as the world center for the true worship of God. Also, sometime near the beginning of the era, the scribes and the Pharisees apparently developed as a "prophetic" ministry of law experts to teach the Jewish people God's word. In the beginning, they were, no doubt faithful to God...During this era the most conspicuous leaders of the nation (Israel) were the prophets and teachers of the law. If these men had been faithful to God, they would have led the nation in righteousness and the Gentile kingdoms would have shown favor to the Jews..."

Therefore, we understand that the nation of Israel was no longer under the Kings from the House of David. They were rather under Gentile Kings who let them return to Israel, rebuild the Temple and the city of Jerusalem. As long as they followed the Mosaic laws, ordinances and worshipped God only, they were blessed and the Gentile nations favored them. The large word "if" is presented by Reverend Smith as he describes that at the beginning, they were faithful to God and had a faithful priesthood. But that did not last long. The last book of the Old Testament (Covenant), Malachi, describes what happened during the time of Malachi and his prophetic utterances.

John Hagee's Prophecy Study Bible, page 106, describes this period of Jewish unfaithfulness to God. "Although an exact date cannot be established for Malachi, internal evidence can be used to deduce an approximate date. The Persian term for governor, pechah, (Malachi 1:8 cf. Nehemiah 5:14, Haggai 1:1, 14; 2:21), indicates that the book was written during the Persian domination of Israel (539-333 B.C.). Sacrifices were being offered in the Temple (Malachi 1:7-10; 3:8), which was rebuilt in 516 B.C. Evidently, many years had passed since the offerings were instituted, because the priests had grown tired of them and corruption had crept into the system. In addition, Malachi's oracle was inspired by the same problems that Nehemiah faced; corrupt priests (Malachi 1:6—2:9; Nehemiah 13:10-13), neglect of tithes and offerings (Malachi 3:7-12; Nehemiah 13:10-13), and intermarriage with pagan wives (Malachi 2:10-16; Nehemiah 13:23-28) …"

The reason I shared this was to show how far Israel had gotten away from the Mosaic Covenant, the Palestinian Covenant, and the Davidic Covenant, by the time Malachi shared his prophetic utterances. This is what God says to the leaders of Israel and the priests of Israel in the book of Malachi. "But you have departed from the way; You have caused many to stumble at the law. You have corrupted the covenant of Levi, says the Lord of Hosts. Therefore, I also have made you contemptible and base before all the people, because you have not kept my ways but have shown partiality in the law." (Malachi 2:8-9)

Nathan's Prophecy to David

How could the prophet, Nathan, back during the time of David have prophesied that there would always be a King from the House of David on the throne of Israel? "And your house and your kingdom shall be established forever before you. Your throne shall be established forever." (2 Samuel 7:16) One has to look at the prophetic utterance of Nathan with the eyes of the Spirit of God. You cannot look with natural eyes at this prophecy. This was pointing to a time in the future, I believe during the Millennial reign of Jesus Christ on the earth.

There had to be another branch of David's sons to fulfill this prophecy. This is spelled out in John Hagee's Prophecy Study Bible, page 343 down at the bottom of the page in the Bible. "...Joseph (Jesus' stepfather), the legal, but not physical, father of Jesus traces his lineage to David through Jeremiah (Matthew 1:1-13). David had another son, Nathan (Luke 2:23-38). Notice the care and the extent to which God goes to keep His Word and preserve it for Jesus, but also to fulfill the Davidic Covenant. Jesus describes His "blood right" to David's throne through His earthily mother, Mary, and His "legal right" to David's throne through His adoptive earthily father, Joseph. The virgin birth guarantees that one of David's lines will sit on David's throne and rule forever, while at the same time preserving intact the curse and restriction on the line of descent of Jeconiah."

What this means is that Jesus Christ was the fulfillment of the prophetic word that Nathan spoke over David at the time when David was approaching God about building a Temple in Jerusalem. This quotation was taken from The Christian's Guide to the New Life. This quotation was not John Hagee's writing in his Prophecy Study Bible, but was an added source within the Bible itself that he included on page 343 of the Bible.

John Hagee had this to say about the Davidic Covenant in conclusion under the sub-title, The Last King, on page 345 of his Prophecy Study Bible. "For David's throne to continue after the Babylonian captivity, another branch of the dynastic tree would have to come into play. From this time on, David's son Solomon (2 Samuel 7:12-13) functioned as a symbol of his future descendent who would restore the Davidic kingdom and throne which ended with the Babylonian destruction of Jerusalem (586 B.C.) and has not been restored to this day. The promise of a son from David who would establish an eternal throne over an eternal kingdom (2 Samuel 7:13,16) pointed into the future in two ways. First, it alluded to the spiritual reign of the Messiah over all who possess the faith of Abraham (Galatians 3:6-9,14). Second, it guaranteed a time still further in the future when Messiah, the spiritual sovereign on David's throne in Jerusalem during the millennial reign (Isaiah 11:1-16)."

One should read all of Isaiah chapters 11 and 12 to get a sense of Jesus' millennial reign in Jerusalem. As a descendent of David, Jesus Christ takes His crusade to the nations in Revelation 19:11-21. All nations who oppose the Lamb of God will be destroyed and they will see Him as the King of Kings and the Lord of Lords. The Beast and the False Prophet will be captured and cast alive in the lake of fire. The devil and satan will be captured, bound and thrown into the bottomless pit for a thousand years. (Revelations 20:1-3) While the devil is bound and in the bottomless pit for a thousand years, Jesus Christ, the Son of God, will reign with the saints from Jerusalem for a thousand years. (Revelation 20:4-6) Again satan is loosed and gathers all the nations against Jesus Christ and all the saints at Jerusalem, but God sends fire down from Heaven and destroys all of them. At this point satan is cast into the lake of fire forever and ever, and Jesus reigns forever and ever thus fulfilling Nathan's prophecy and the Davidic Covenant. (Revelation 20:7-10) The Davidic Covenant represents Jesus Christ's royal rule over all of His saints. Revelation chapters 20 to 22 shows the complete fulfillment of that Covenant. Jesus Christ is the last King and there is no need for another King to reign over His people. The last part of Revelation 20:11-16 shows the judgment on those who refused to accept Jesus as their Savior, Lord and King. All of them are cast alive into the lake of fire and will burn forever and ever. Therefore, Nathan's prophecy and God's Covenant will finally be fulfilled with Jesus Christ being the reigning Monarch and King over Israel at the end of time.

Before this takes place there is only one condition that was presented to David by Nathan. This is found in 2 Samuel 8:14-15. "I will be his (Solomon's) Father, and he shall be my son. If he (Solomon and his descendants) commit iniquity, I will chasten him (Solomon and his descendants) with the rod of men and with the blows of the sons of men. But my mercy shall not depart from him, as I took it from Saul, whom I removed from before you." This is the only condition of the Covenant and it did come to pass just as God had said. The late Dr. C. Scofield says this about that condition in The First Scofield Reference Bible, on page 362. "And this fourfold covenant has but one condition: disobedience in the Davidic family is to be visited with chastisement, but not to the abrogation (nullification, to abolish or annul by authority) of the covenant (2 Samuel 7:15; Psalms 89:20-27; Isaiah 24:5)."

This condition was enforced toward the end of Solomon's reign. Solomon started worshipping the pagan gods of his many wives and this resulted first in the division of the Kingdom of Israel and finally in both Israel and Judah going into captivity to foreign countries. Israel even rejected Jesus Christ as their Messiah and King, and suffered the loss of their Temple. Israel could no longer offer sacrifices to God as she had in ages past, because of the destruction of the Temple. The nation of Israel has suffered the loss of many of her people and many Muslim nations hating her. Yet, they have remained a nation and are now returning to their homeland.

The woman spoken of in Revelation chapter 12 is the nation of Israel. She gave birth to the Messiah, Jesus Christ, and has been persecuted by the devil ever since that birth. Listen to the last two verses of Revelation 12. "But the earth helped the woman (Israel), and the earth opened its mouth and swallowed up the flood (persecution by various groups of people) which the dragon (the devil) had spewed out of his mouth. And the dragon (the devil) was enraged with the woman (Israel), and he (the devil) went to make war with the rest of His offspring (the Jews), who keep the commandments of God and have the testimony of Jesus Christ (the Messianic Jews)." (Revelation 12:16-17)

What is Replacement Theology?

Today, there are some Christian denominations, churches and Christian groups who believe in replacement theology. They believe the church today has taken the place of Israel. Their reasoning is that Israel rejected Jesus Christ as the Messiah and are therefore, no longer God's chosen people. But if one were to believe this replacement theology, one would have to throw out a lot of Scriptures both in the Old Testament (Covenant) and the New Testament (Covenant). I will give some of the Scriptures that will show a totally different picture and say that God is a God of grace who offers a second chance to all. These are just some of the Scriptures: Psalms

89:20-37; Revelation chapter 7; 11:1-14; Revelation chapter 14. People who believe in replacement theology believe they can remove Israel's name from the prophecies of the Old Testament prophets and what the Holy Scriptures say about Israel in the New Testament (Covenant). There is actually a curse placed on people who change the Scriptures to make it say what they want it to say. This is found in Revelation 22:18-19. "For I testify to everyone who hears the words of the prophecy of this book: If anyone adds to these things, God will add to him the plagues that are written in this book; and if anyone takes away from the words of the book of this prophecy, God shall take away his part from the Book of Life, from the holy city, and from the things which are written in this book." Some will say, the Apostle John was talking about the book of Revelation. I believe the Apostle John under the inspiration of the Holy Spirit was talking about all the Scriptures. I further believe it is dangerous to change the Scriptures and that one-day people who do that will have to answer to God for it.

In conclusion, here is what I would like to end the discussion on replacement theology. I am not going to give any reasonings of my own on the subject. Instead, I am going to ask you to read Psalms 89:20-37. I would further ask you to read the last four verses of that Scripture. "My covenant (to David) I will not break. Nor alter the word that has gone out of my lips. Once I have sworn by My holiness; I will not lie to David; His seed shall endure forever, and his (David's) throne as the sun before Me; It shall be established like the moon. Even like the faithful witness in the sky. Selah." (Psalms 89:34-37) When God promises something, it is sure and steadfast. You can take it to the Bank and count on it.

You may ask, well where does the Gentile Church fit in all of this? Actually, John, the beloved Apostle talks about that in Revelation 11:1-2a. "Then I was given a reed like a measuring rod. And the angel stood, saying, "Rise and measure the temple of God, the altar, and those who worship there. But leave out the court, which is outside the temple, and do not measure it, for it has been given to the Gentiles…"

There is also the traditional view that the church is the Bride of Christ. This is found in Revelation 19:7-9. It is a combination of both Jews and Gentiles. "Let us be glad and rejoice and give Him glory, for the marriage of the Lamb has come, and His wife has made herself ready. And to her it was granted to be arrayed in fine linen, clean and bright, for the fine linen is the righteous acts of the saints. Then he said to me, "Write: Blessed are those who are called to the marriage supper of the Lamb!" And he said to me, "These are the true sayings of God." (Revelation 19:7-9)

I believe we will be so glad to be there in Heaven with God, our Father, and Jesus Christ, our Elder Brother, it will not matter how it all fits together. We will be so glad to be in the Family of God. Praise God from Whom all blessings flow! Praise Him all you heavenly host! Praise Him; Father, Son and Holy Ghost!

In Summary…

In most everything God does, He tells you He is going to do it and then He does it. This is a principle of God. God told Moses about a King to rule over Israel. Moses told Israel about a King being placed over them in Deuteronomy 17:14-20. Then God sets the stage for a King. Judges are first used to prepare Israel for the rule of one person over them administering justice and righteousness.

Samuel, the last Priest and Judge of Israel, tries to talk Israel out of having a King reign over them. One must see that Israel is determined to have a King and rushes into it without much thought or prayer. Is that not the way we are when God shares a rhema word with us? We are determined to make it happen. A lot of times it is without much prayer or thought. Usually, what happens to us next is what happened to Israel. At this point in Israel's history, the nation of Israel is under the Mosaic Covenant. Samuel is probably the only one walking in a Covenant Relationship with God. God is talking to Samuel and he is listening and obeying the Lord.

Saul, Israel's first King, when looking according to the natural eye, appears like the vey King they needed. He is taller than any man in Israel, a muscular man, and turns out to be a man of war. Who could ask for anything more? Evidently, God was asking more out of him than he was willing to give. It might have helped if Saul had listened and obeyed Samuel, his spiritual authority at the time he became King of Israel. Saul tried to take Samuel's place as a Priest in sacrificing animals because he was impatient with Samuel's arrival time for a sacrifice before Saul and his men went off to battle. Samuel pointed out the fact that Saul was not a Priest and he had disobeyed the commandment of the Lord. (1 Samuel 13:13-14) It might have also helped if Saul could have obeyed God and did exactly what God said to do. For instance, when God told him to kill all the Amalekites and all the animals of the Amalekites. Saul should have done that. His willful disobedience to God caused him in the end to lose Israel and his position as King of Israel. (1 Samuel chapter 15) He became more and more independent of God and Samuel. As a result of his attitude and disobedience toward God, God took His Spirit from Saul. (1 Samuel 16:14) If Saul had listened and obeyed God and Samuel in the directions, they gave him, God would no doubt have extended not only the Kingdom to Saul but brought him into a Covenant Relationship with Himself. (1 Samuel 13:13-14; 15:26-29) Listening and obeying God and the servants of the Lord is very important in bringing you into a Covenant Relationship with God.

David is the second one to be chosen and anointed as King of Israel. Because David obeyed God from the heart, God let His Holy Spirit rest upon David. "Then Samuel took the horn of oil and anointed him in the midst of his brothers, and the Spirit of the Lord came upon David from that day forward...So Samuel arose and went to Ramah." (1 Samuel 16:13) After David being anointed King of Israel, some of his early accomplishments was killing Goliath as a youth about thirteen or fourteen years old. He also defeated the Philistines in all the battles that King Saul sent him to. David also "behaved wisely in all his ways, and the Lord was with him...But all Israel and Judah loved David, because he went out and came in before them." (1 Samuel 18: 14,16) All of this was happening while Saul was trying to kill David, because he knew God wanted him to be King of Israel. David is being trained by adversity for Kingship for 39 years. Most all of this time he is trying to escape Saul's hand. Twice David is given the opportunity to kill Saul, but chooses not to touch God's anointed. "...Do not touch my anointed ones, and do my prophets no harm." (Psalms 105:15)

As King David begins to bring all the enemies of Israel under control, it looks like nothing could go wrong. This seemed like a perfect picture, but that is when satan likes to move in and see what chaos he can create. But we are a little ahead of ourselves. As Saul lost all fellowship with God, David moved into closer relationship with God. We usually draw closer to God when we are in adverse circumstances. Adversity and the Holy Spirit teaches us to draw closer to God. A lot of the book of Psalms is written by David and shows how close he was to God. David knew he was going to be King of Israel, but he waited on God and His timing. In our walk with God, we need to let God bring about the things He has promised us. Getting impatient as Saul did, will not bring those promises to pass.

After Saul and all his sons were killed by the Philistines at the battle of Mount Gilboa, it was only a matter of time until David was King of all Israel. Even becoming King of all Israel took time, but David did not rush the matter. One of Saul's sons was still alive. Abner, the commander of Saul's army, made that son, Ishbosheth, King over Israel. That was approximately 10 tribes of the nation of Israel. On the other hand, David was anointed King over Judah and reigned seven years in Judah. When Ishbosheth was murdered by two of his own men (2 Samuel 4:1-8), David had those two men executed (2 Samuel 4:9-12). Then all the men of Israel chose David to be their King. "In Hebron he (David) reigned over Judah seven years and six months, and in Jerusalem he reigned thirty-three years over all Israel and Judah." (2 Samuel 5:5) All of this took time and patience on the part of David. He knew God wanted him to be King over all Israel, but he had to wait on God to bring all of that about in God's good time. Many times, people rush in to do what they believe God has told them to do. They don't wait on the timing of God and it never comes to pass. It is possible that God wants them to do that mission objective or that ministry objective, but one must wait on the timing of God. That is what David did.

It is another step in the direction of coming into a Covenant Relationship with God.

After David brought most all of the enemies of Israel under his control or they were destroyed, he sought to bring the Ark of the Covenant to Jerusalem where he was living. First, King David did it by incorrect means and Uzzah was killed. Then, King David brought the Ark by correct means and the Ark of the Covenant stayed at Jerusalem until Solomon built the Temple and placed it there. (2 Samuel chapter 6) After David was successful in bringing the Ark to Jerusalem, he began to entertain the idea of building a Temple for God. He approaches Nathan about building a Temple. From 2 Samuel 7:1-3, one can see that Nathan, the Prophet, did not know what God wanted about the Temple. He told David, "Go, do all that is in your heart, for the Lord is with you." (2 Samuel 7:3b) But during that night God spoke to Nathan, that David's son, Solomon, would build a Temple for Him. It is at this time that God extends His Covenant to David. Unlike Saul, David predecessor, David listened and obeyed what Nathan said. He did not try to build a Temple, but David did accept that Covenant relationship with God. (2 Samuel 7:4-17) Sometimes, we push ahead doing what is in our heart and mind, even when we know God is not in it. We really need to listen to the still, small voice of God and only do what He says. That is what being in Covenant Relationship with God is all about.

In this Davidic Covenant, God through the Prophet Nathan outlines not only David's life before him, but also Solomon's life. Finally, God tells David he will always have a man on the throne of Israel forever. "And your house and your kingdom shall be established forever." (2 Samuel 7:16) Then David comes into the Tabernacle and sits before the Lord in humility and accepts the Covenant that God has extended to him. He concludes his prayer with these words. "Now therefore, let it please You to bless the house of your servant (David), that it may continue forever before You; for You, O Lord God, have spoken it, and with your blessing let the house of your servant (David) be blessed forever." (2 Samuel 7:29)

For a while, everything David did prospered and he ruled over Israel in righteousness. He even took in some of Saul's family, Jonathan's son,

Mephibosheth, and made him like one of his sons to eat at his table every day. Everywhere David turned he was victorious. A lot of time the Covenant Blessing of God tends to go to our heads. We become proud and God has a way of unmasking the sin that is in our character and nature. It is at this point we need to humbly seek God, otherwise what happened to David may happen to us. Maybe not the same two sins that break the Ten Commandments, but they maybe even worse. If we humbly seek God in our Covenant Relationship, God will see us through those trials and troubles.

At this high point in David's life with God, he commits adultery with Bathsheba and attempts to cover it up by having her husband, Uriah the Hittite, killed in battle. Evidently, David thought he could get away with disobeying God's law under the Mosaic Covenant. He then marries Bathsheba and it looks like it is all swept under the rug. (2 Samuel chapter 11) But it is not. Nathan, the Prophet, appears and calls him out and describes David's sinfulness. God uses Nathan to tell David the consequences of his sins, which actually take place for the rest of David's life. (2 Samuel chapter 12) All of this is fully described in 2 Samuel chapters 13 to 24 and 1 Kings 1:1-9. There are rebellious plots against David for the rest of his life.

Both King Saul and King David had sinful tendencies. Both were approached by the Prophet of the day and were told their consequences. King Saul had the Kingdom of Israel stripped from him by God and the Spirit of the Lord left him. Because the Spirit left him, he could never have a Covenant Relationship with God. The Holy Spirit must be in control of your life in order for you to have a Covenant Relationship extended to you by God. King Saul was also double minded. At times he wanted to kill David and other times he wanted to spare David. David could not trust him and had to move to a Philistine city until Saul and his sons were killed. (1 Samuel chapters 16 to 31)

What is the difference between King Saul and King David? The sins of both persons are bad. King Saul's sin was intruding into the office of a Priest for which he had not been called. Only Priests could offer sacrifices.

His second sin was willfully being disobedient to God. These two sins stripped him of being King of Israel. He never repented to God for these sins. He told Samuel he was sorry for his sins, but there is no confession in the Scriptures to God. David's sins were grievous too. David committed adultery with Bathsheba and premeditated the killing of Uriah the Hittite, Bathsheba's husband. God was not happy with David either. At the end of chapter 11 of 2 Samuel 27b it says this about what David had done. "But the thing that David had done displeased the Lord." Why did God not strip the Kingdom of Israel from David? Why did God not strip David of the Covenant He had just made with him? David had a repentant heart all the days of his life. When one reads Psalms chapter 51 one sees the heart of David as he is confronted with these sins. David starts Psalms 51:1 asking God for mercy. "Have mercy upon me, O God, according to your lovingkindness, according to the multitude of your tender mercies, blot out my transgressions." In the middle of Psalms 51 David says this, "Create in me a clean heart, O God, and renew a steadfast (right) spirit within me. Do not cast me away from your presence, and do not take your Holy Spirit from me." (Psalms 51:10-11) David had seen what happened to Saul when he sinned. He did not want the same thing to happen to him. God's Presence had left Saul and God would not talk to Saul. David did not want that to happen to him. David had a fear and respect for God in his life. He knew what God could do. One should read all of Psalms chapter 51 to get a clear picture of David's repentant heart. God saw that and forgave David. But David did experience the consequences of his sin. These consequences extended throughout the rest of his life. It is never a good idea to knowingly sin. If you are a born again and a Spirit-filled Christian, the consequences could be devastating. One only has to look at the lives of King Saul and King David to see that.

God used David's house and lineage to fulfill the prophecy concerning Jesus Christ, His Son. Jesus prophetically fulfills the prophecy of Nathan being the last King of Israel that will reign forever and ever. Already, the nation of Israel is preparing for that reign today. As we stated in the last chapter on the Mosaic Covenant and the Palestinian Covenant, Israel is following those two Covenants today. They are beginning to celebrate the Feasts of the Mosaic Covenant. They now observe the Sabbath as it was and is in the Mosaic Covenant in Israel. Hebrew is now the national language of Israel. Jesus Christ returning to earth as the King of Kings and the Lord of Lords would be the crowning moment in history.

Before we close this chapter on the Davidic Covenant, we need to look at the last words of David before he passed and then see what Jesus said about David. This passage is in 2 Samuel 23:1-7. "Now the last words of David. Thus, says David the son of Jesse; "Thus, says the man raised up on high, The anointed of the God of Jacob, And the sweet psalmist of Israel." "The Spirit of the Lord spoke by me, And His word was on my tongue. The God of Israel said, The Rock of Israel spoke to me; He who rules over men must be just, Ruling in the fear of God. And he shall be like the light of the morning when the sun rises, A morning without clouds, Like the tender grass springing out of the earth, By clear shining after rain, Although my house is not so with God, Yet He has made with me an everlasting covenant, Ordered in all things and secure. For this is all my salvation and all my desire; Will He not make it increase? But the sons of rebellion shall all be as thorns thrust away, Because they cannot be taken with hands. But the man who touches them must be armed with iron and the shaft of a spear, And they shall be utterly burned with fire in their place." (This is a song of David and thus set differently than regular speech.)

This was David's farewell message to Israel before he died. He then placed the crown upon Solomon and made him King of Israel in his place before he passed. Dr. Spiro Zodhiates said this about these seven verses in his Hebrew-Greek Key Study Bible, on page 445. "This song was much more than a simple farewell. It was like the final blessing of Jacob in Genesis (chapter) 49. It was an inspired prophecy of the Messiah to come and of the Mediator's new covenant of salvation. This song was patterned along the same lines of Balaam's (Numbers 24:15-24)" Dr. Zodhiates gives a cross reference in Jeremiah 23:56. "Behold, the days come, saith the Lord, that I will raise unto David a righteous Branch, and a King (Jesus) shall reign and prosper, and shall execute judgment and justice in the earth. In His (Jesus) days Judah shall be saved, and Israel shall dwell safely. And this is His name whereby He shall be called, THE LORD OUR RIGHTEOUSNESS."

It is verse 5 of 2 Samuel 23, I want to draw your attention to in closing. In verses 2 to 4 of this chapter, David describes how God used him by the Spirit of the Lord. Then he contrasts in verse 5 how David's house had not been wholly righteous before God. "Yet He made with me an everlasting covenant." David is acknowledging the Covenant that God has made with him. He acknowledges that it is ordered by God and secure. He goes on in the last two verses of this song to acknowledge that there will be sons of rebellion to follow him (David), but their destruction is sure. David prophecies that his Kingdom and his house will last forever. With the death and resurrection of Jesus Christ, it is a sure fact that He will be King of Kings and Lord of Lords. With the ascension of Jesus Christ into glory, it is a sure thing that He will return and be victorious over all who oppose Him in Revelation 19:11-21 and Revelation 20:7, 10. Therefore, Jesus, the last and eternal King will reign over not only Judah and Israel, but over all the world. Thus, the prophecies given by Nathan to David will be fulfilled and the Covenant Promises to David are sure and steadfast. God's Covenant to David will become a reality just as God promised.

Chapter 9
Before And During The Silent Years

One might believe that there is nothing but silence between the Old Testament (Covenant) and the New Testament (Covenant), which is brought into being with the coming of Jesus Christ, the Son of God. But there is one final chapter before one see Jesus coming on the scene. Jeremiah had prophesied that Israel would remain in captivity for 70 years. "In the first year of his (Darius, the Mede) reign I, Daniel, understood by the word of the Lord, given through Jeremiah the prophet, that He would accomplish seventy years in the desolation of Jerusalem." (Daniel 9:2)

Judah had not obeyed God's law concerning the land lying dormant every seven years. This is brought out in 2 Chronicles 36:20-21. "And those who escaped from the sword he (King Nebuchadnezzar) carried away to Babylon, where they became servants to him and his sons until the reign of the Kingdom of Persia, to fulfill the word of the Lord by the mouth of Jeremiah, until the land had enjoyed the sabbaths. As long as she lay desolate, she kept Sabbath, to fulfill seventy years." This was according to the Law of Moses given in Leviticus 25:3-5. "Six years you shall sow your field, and six years you shall prune your vineyard, and gather in its fruit; but in the seventh year there shall be a sabbath of solemn rest for the land, a sabbath to the Lord. You shall neither sow your field nor prune your vineyard. What grows of its own accord of your harvest you shall not reap, nor gather the grapes of your untended vine, for it is a year of rest for the land." God goes on to say that any food gathered from the fields was to be eaten by the owners of the field and the servants of the field. But it was not to be sold or given to anyone else. Judah and Israel had neglected to obey God's law in this matter, thus the seventy years in captivity would allow the land to rest as 2 Chronicles points out.

At the end of the 70 years exile, the Lord stirred up Cyrus, King of Persia, to send the Jews back to rebuild the Temple in Jerusalem. This was a fulfillment of Jeremiah's prophecy that the Jews would return to

Jerusalem and rebuild the city and the Temple. "Now in the first year of Cyrus king of Persia, that the word of the Lord stirred up the spirit of Cyrus king of Persia, so that he made a proclamation throughout all his kingdom, and also put it in writing, saying, 'Thus says Cyrus king of Persia: All of the kingdoms of the earth the Lord God of heaven has given me. And He has commanded me to build Him a house at Jerusalem which is in Judah…" (Ezra 1:1-2) Ralph Smith calls this the Restoration Covenant. He says this is "the last era of Israel's history as the people of God and the climatic period of the old covenant." (The Covenantal Structure of the Bible, page 41) Reverend Smith goes on to say that Israel would no longer be a great civil power but would only serve God "as a prophetic witness to the world." (page 42) I disagree with Reverend Smith. I still believe Israel is God's chosen people for the very fact that the Apostle John writes about them in the book of Revelation and the fact that some of the Old Testament (Covenant) prophecies in Isaiah, Jeremiah, Ezekiel and Daniel about the Jewish people have yet to come to pass. From 1943 to the year 2019 Israel has become a civil power in the world. These are facts that cannot be ignored.

Ralph Smith goes on to say this under the subtopic "hierarchy" (organized ecclesiastical authority) of the Jews in his book, The Covenantal Structure of the Bible, page 42. This is a good description of that period of time. "Civil rule had been taken from the Jews and given to the Gentile empires, but the Gentiles were appointed as protectors, not persecutors. So long as the Jews were faithful to God, they would find that Gentile rulers favored them above the other nations, as, for example the king of Persia favored the Jews in the days of Ezra, Nehemiah and Esther and Mordecai. The temple had a new priesthood examined and approved by Ezra (Ezra 2:62). Jerusalem, was rebuilt no longer as a civil center but, which was far more important, as the world center for the worship of the true God. Also, sometime near the beginning of this era, the scribes and the Pharisees apparently developed as a "prophetic" ministry of law experts to teach the people God's word. In the beginning, they were, no doubt, faithful to God."

With Ezra and Nehemiah returning to the land of Canaan and especially Jerusalem to be rebuilt; the city of Jerusalem and the Temple, the Israelites who returned with them began to hear and listen to the Law of God again. Ezra enacted reforms so the Jewish people could understand the Law and then he went further in reestablishing the Priesthood again. During Ezra's and Nehemiah's lifetime the people of Israel lived in Canaan and returned to the Mosaic Covenant and obeyed the laws of Moses.

They did have many adversaries who wanted them to stop building the second temple in Israel's history. These enemies were Bishlam, Mithredath, Tabeel, and their friends who wrote to Artaxerxes, the King of Persia. They let him know how rebellious the Jews had been in times past. This is what they said about Jerusalem. "Let it be known to the king that the Jews who came up from you have come to us at Jerusalem and are building the rebellious and evil city, and are finishing its walls and repairing the foundations. Let it now be known to the king that if this city (Jerusalem) is built and the walls completed, they will not pay tax, tribute, or custom and the king's treasury will be diminished. Now because we receive support from the palace, it was not proper for us to see the king's dishonor; therefore, we have sent and informed the king, that search may be made in the book of records of your fathers. And you will find in the book of the records and know that this city (Jerusalem) is a rebellious city, harmful to kings and provinces, and that they have incited sedition within the city (Jerusalem) in former times, for which this city (Jerusalem) was destroyed. We inform the king that if this city (Jerusalem) is rebuilt and its walls are completed, the result will be that you will have no dominion over the region beyond the river." (Ezra 4:12-16)

Who were these men who were making accusations against the Jewish leaders and the city of Jerusalem? The Zondervan Pictorial Bible Dictionary, on page 273 describes the ones who were against the Jewish leaders and the rebuilding of the city of Jerusalem and the second temple in Jerusalem. "The Exile (70-year Exile) was brought to a close when the Babylonian Empire fell before Cyrus, King of Persia in 538 B.C. The way in which the expectations of the Jews respecting Cyrus were fulfilled is told in the opening remarks of the book of Ezra (Ezra chapter 1). The return from Exile did not bring with it political freedom for the Jews. They remained subjects of the Persian Empire. Jerusalem and the surrounding districts were under the control of a governor who sometimes was a Jew, but usually was not. Persian rule was in general not oppressive, but tribute was exacted for the royal treasury and the local governor. The hostile population surrounding them, especially the Samaritans, did all they could to make life miserable for them (the Jews), especially by trying to bring them into disfavor with the Persian authorities. Idolatry no longer tempted them (the Jews)—and never did again. The external features distinctive of the Jewish worship and the ceremonial requirements of the law were stressed. Prophecy became less important, scribes gradually taking the place of the prophets."

I quoted all of this from the Zondervan Pictorial Bible Dictionary, so you could see how the Jewish religion evolved into what it was when Jesus Christ came on the scene in the New Testament (Covenant) era. Ezra and Nehemiah got the King of Persia to reverse his ruling when they wrote a letter to make a search for that decree of Cyrus. King Darius did make a search for the decree and the decree was found. King Darius of Persia had made the Jewish leaders stop while the search was made for that decree by King Cyrus. In Ezra chapter 6:1-5 it records the finding of the scroll. "Then King Darius issued a decree, and a search was made in the archives, where the treasures were stored in Babylon. And at Achmetha, in the palace that is in the province of Media, a scroll was found, and in it a record was written thus. 'In the first year of King Cyrus, King Cyrus made a decree concerning the house of God at Jerusalem: Let the house be rebuilt, the place where they offered sacrifices; and let the foundations of it be firmly laid, its height sixty cubits and its width sixty cubits, with three rows of heavy stones and one row of new timber. Let the expense be paid from the King's treasury. Also, let the gold and silver articles of the house of God which Nebuchadnezzar took from the temple which is in Jerusalem and brought to Babylon, be restored and taken back to the temple, which is in Jerusalem, to its place; and deposit them in the house of God." With this finding King Darius issued a decree that Governor Tattenai do as the decree of King Cyrus said. King Darius went on to say that God had the right to destroy any King or people who lifted their hand to destroy this Temple of worship in Jerusalem

As a result of getting this decree from King Darius, Governor Tattenai complied with the decree of Darius. "Then Tattenai, governor of the region beyond the River, Shethar-Boznai, and their companions diligently did according to what King Darius had sent. So, the elders of the Jews built, and they prospered through the prophesying of Haggai the prophet and Zechariah the son of Iddo. And they built and finished it (the Temple), according to the commandment of the God of Israel and according to the command of Cyrus, Darius, and Artaxerxes king of Persia. Now the Temple was finished on the third day of the month of Adar, which was in the sixth year of the reign of King Darius." (Ezra 6: 13-15) The Temple of God in Jerusalem was finished in 515 B.C. If one reads the prophesies of Haggai and Zechariah one will find at times the Jewish people would slack off from building the Temple. During these times these two prophets had to continually to encourage the Jewish people to finish building the Temple. The reason they encouraged them to finish is found in the prophecy of Zechariah. The Messiah, Jesus Christ, is coming. "Rejoice greatly, O daughter of Zion! Shout, O daughter of Jerusalem! Behold your King is coming to you. He is just and having salvation, lowly and riding on a donkey, a colt, the foal of a donkey." (Zechariah 9:9) This prophecy of Scripture is fulfilled in Matthew 21:2-5. (Jesus said) "Go into the village opposite you, and immediately you will find a donkey tied, and a colt with her. Loose them and bring them to Me. And if anyone says anything to you, you shall say, The Lord has need of them, and immediately he will send them. All this was done that it might be fulfilled which was spoken by the prophet (Zechariah), saying: 'Tell the daughter of Zion, behold your King is coming to you, lowly, and sitting on a donkey, a colt, the foal of a donkey."

One has to understand, that the Jewish people that were being restored to their land, the land of Canaan, and had restored the city of Jerusalem and the Temple of God were still under the Mosaic Covenant. God had not changed His mind about Jerusalem or His Temple. He needed Jerusalem because He had chosen that place for His Temple. The Temple was important for the sacrifices to be made for the sins of the people and for the Feasts of the Lord. It would have been wonderful if the Jewish people after Ezra and Nehemiah had died, had remained faithful to God through the Mosaic Covenant that Ezra and the other scribes had taught them. Ezra made it clear to them that they were still under the Mosaic Covenant even though they were not in control of their government. The city of Jerusalem as well as the Temple of God had been rebuilt. They started offering the daily sacrifices and started having the Feasts of the Lord just as they did during the time of Moses and Joshua. They followed all the directions that were given in the book of Leviticus and the book of Deuteronomy for a while. They also followed all the dietary laws that are found in the Mosaic Covenant. They were faithful to do all of this for a while. But when the leadership that Ezra and Nehemiah had trained died and Ezra and Nehemiah died, they began to wander away from God. They started drifting from the teachings of the Mosaic Covenant. Not all remained faithful to God and the Old Covenant during this time.

One has to understand that the reason the Jewish people were in bondage 70 years in Babylon and then in Persia was because they had disobeyed the Mosaic and Palestinian Covenants. They broke the Covenants that God had made with them. When you break a Covenant with God, bad things are going to happen to you. God told Jeremiah that they would be in bondage for 70 years. Many of those Jewish people that went into bondage during those 70 years died and were buried in Babylon and Persia.

Now the same thing was happening again. The Jewish people had come back under the Mosaic Covenant and God had begun to honor that Covenant. But Ezra, Nehemiah and the scribes and priests that Ezra had trained, had died. The new scribes and priests were not following the Mosaic Covenant completely. The apostacy of the Jewish people is declared throughout the book of Malachi.

Zondervan Pictorial Bible Dictionary on page 504 describes this apostacy. One must understand that all of the old leaders have died off and are not present to straighten the new leadership of scribes and priests out.

"It is also clear that the early zeal for the rebuilding of the temple has now died out, and a situation of moral and religious declension has set in. The mixed marriages (Jews marrying Gentiles) (Malachi 2:10-12), failure to pay tithes (Malachi 3:8-10) and offering blemished sacrifices (not perfect lambs, goats, doves, pigeons, etc. according to human eyes) (Malachi 1:6-14) are conditions not unlike those referred to in the times of Ezra and Nehemiah (Ezra chapter 7; Nehemiah chapter 13). The fact that a Persian governor was ruling in Jerusalem indicates that Malachi prophecies happened after Haggai's and Zechariah's prophecies." The priests during this period of time often neglected their duties and sacrifices. The people also neglected the need for an inward faith toward God, moral righteousness and to be ritually clean. Therefore, the Jewish people as a whole no longer observed the Mosaic Covenant and did not listen to the prophetic voices like Malachi. The Jewish people were thus breaking the Mosaic Covenant. There would be some who would repent and follow God with their hearts toward Him, while the majority would break the Mosaic Covenant.

There is one final prophetic word that is shared in Malachi. Malachi shares the fact that the Messiah is coming soon and that He is going to purify and judge Israel. "Behold I send My messenger and he (John the Baptist) will prepare the way before Me (Jesus). And the Lord whom you seek, will suddenly come to His temple, even the Messenger of the Covenant, in whom you delight. Behold He (Jesus) is coming, says the Lord of Hosts." (Malachi 3:1) Not only were the Prophets looking for Him, but also the people.

As a result of the Jewish apostacy, God was silent for four hundred years. There are not anymore voices of the Prophets until John the Baptist comes on the scene. By then the nation of Israel is divided up into religious, political factions or sects: Pharisees, Sadducees, Essenes, with the Pharisees being the most influential.

The Mosaic Covenant does not change man's heart on the inside. It has no power to change the heart of man, only his outward performance. As we have seen, the Jews returned to Jerusalem and rebuilt it and the Temple.

They did observe the Ten Commandments, the sacrifices, the dietary laws, and the rituals for a while. But as the Apostle James said in James 2:10, if you disobey in one point of the law, you are guilty of all the law. "For whoever shall keep the whole law (the Mosaic Covenant), and yet stumble in one point, he is guilty of all." God's intent was to bring man and specifically His chosen people—the Jewish people—to the place where they understood they could not keep the Old Covenant. "Therefore, by the deeds of the law no flesh will be justified in His sight, for by the law is the knowledge of sin." (Romans 3:20) This is what God wants to bring man to—the knowledge of sin. Man cannot overcome sin himself. Which brings us to Romans 3:21-22. "But now the righteousness of God (Jesus) apart (separate) from the law (the Mosaic Covenant) is revealed, being witnessed by the Law and the Prophets; even the righteousness of God (Jesus) which is through faith in Jesus Christ to all (Jews and Gentiles) and on all (Jews and Gentiles) who believe. For there is no difference."

Therefore, the next step is to embark and study the New Covenant, that Jesus Christ brought into existence by the Cross of Jesus, the burial of Jesus, and the Resurrection of Jesus Christ. This New Covenant found in Jesus Christ is our only hope of salvation. We will see in the next chapter on the New Covenant, that this New Covenant is totally based on Jesus Christ, the Son of God. The Covenant of Law can only bring man to Jesus Christ. As we read this next chapter may God give us a revelation of Jesus Christ. "Therefore, the law (the Covenant if Law) was our tutor to bring us to Christ, that we might be justified by faith (the faith of Christ). But after faith (the faith of Christ) has come, we are no longer under a tutor (the Covenant of Law). For you are all the sons of God through faith in Christ Jesus." (Galatians 3:24-26)

Chapter 10
The New Covenant

The New Covenant is brought into existence with the coming of Jesus Christ, God's only Son. What many don't realize is that the New Covenant that God extended to all mankind is separate from the Old Mosaic Covenant and in fact all the Covenants of the Old Testament (Covenant). Many theologians and Bible scholars tend to mix the Old Mosaic Covenant and the New Covenant together. One must see them separately or one will be mixing the Old Covenant of law with the New Covenant of grace. One must ask the Holy Spirit at the beginning of the study of the New Covenant to cause a separation of the two Covenants in their mind and in their spirit.

Jesus Christ fulfills the Old Mosaic Covenant

What really causes individuals to error in the separation of these two Covenants, is they do not realize that Jesus came to fulfill the Covenant of Law or Mosaic Covenant all together. Jesus Christ came as the last Adam to completely fulfill what Adam in the Garden of Eden could not do, nor could anyone of us since the fall of man.

At the beginning of the Sermon on the Mount in Matthew 5:17-18 Jesus states the reason of His coming. "Do not think that I came to destroy the law (the Mosaic Covenant) or the Prophets. I did not come to destroy but to fulfill (to fully satisfy the Law). For assuredly, I say to you, till heaven and earth pass away, one jot or one tittle will by no means pass from the law (the Mosaic Covenant) till all is fulfilled." No Jew or Gentile can fully satisfy the law to the fullest degree. Only God's Son, Jesus Christ, could do that and He fully satisfied the demands of the Law with His sinless life, His teachings, miracles, and healings, and finally with His death on the Cross, His burial, and His resurrection.

This is further explained in the Apostle Paul's letter to the Romans. Listen to what Paul said in Romans 10:2-4. "For I bear them (the Jewish nation, Israel) witness that they have a zeal for God, but not according to knowledge. For they being ignorant of God's righteousness (Jesus Christ) and seeking to establish their own righteousness (according to the Law), have not submitted to the righteousness of God. For Christ is the end of the law for righteousness to everyone who believes." One has to look at the original language, Greek, to understand this passage and how it relates to the Old Covenant as well as the New Covenant.

The first word to look at is the word "righteous" which in the Greek language is dikaiosune, which means God's righteousness that He imputes or gives to man as man repents and accepts Jesus Christ as his Lord and Savior, making him a child of God. (The Hebrew-Greek Key Study Bible; Lexical Aids to the New Testament by Dr. Spiro Zodhiates) The Jews had self-righteousness according to Paul, following the old Mosaic Law. This is what Paul describes Israel as doing. The righteousness of God is that which comes by faith in Jesus Christ.

The second Greek word is the Greek word for "end" in verse four of this passage. The Greek word for "end" is telos which means "termination, the limit at which a thing ceases to be." This meaning came from The New Thayers Greek-English Lexicon of The New Testament on page 619. What Romans 10:4 is saying, "For Christ is the end of the Law (the Covenant of Law) for righteousness to everyone who believes." Jesus Christ has brought an end of the Covenant of the Mosaic Law. It now ceases to be for the believer. It does not cease to be for the unbeliever. Paul goes onto clarify this in 1 Timothy 1:9-10. "Knowing this, that the Law (the Mosaic Covenant of Law) is not made for a righteous person, but for the lawless and insubordinate, for the ungodly and for sinners, for the unholy and profane, for murderers of fathers, and murderers of mothers, for manslayers, for fornicators, for sodomites, for kidnappers, for liars, for perjurers, and if there is any other thing that is contrary to sound doctrine…" Therefore, we can say it is people who are walking and living in unbelief of God. These are people who are unbelievers. That is why Jesus said in Matthew 5:17-18 that the Law would not pass away until heaven and earth passes away. All of these lawless unbelievers are therefore under the Covenant of Law. They come under the Covenant of Grace when by simple faith they trust Jesus as their Lord and Savior.

One may ask how does one live in God's righteousness in an unrighteous society and a fallen world? The Apostle Paul gives us some keys to live by in Romans 8. "For the law of the Spirit of life in Christ Jesus has made me free from the Law of sin and death." (Romans 8:2) God's Spirit, the Spirit of Jesus Christ, lives in us and is constantly talking to us and teaching us how to live in this ungodly world. The Spirit of Jesus sets us free from the Law of sin and death, the Adamic nature we inherited from Adam in the Garden, and the flesh. God's Spirit, the Spirit of Adoption, is teaching us how to live in the Father's house with a godly life. One may look back at the Cross of Jesus and realize the old sinful nature has been crucified, as Paul stated in Galatians 2:20. "I have been crucified with Christ; it is no longer I who live, but Christ lives in me and the life which I now live in the flesh I live by faith in the Son of God, who loved me and gave Himself for me." (Galatians 2:20)

Let me say right here, when the Apostle Paul used the term "law" in the New Testament (Covenant) in most cases he is referring to the Old Covenant of Law or the Mosaic Covenant of Law. He is referring to that Old Covenant that he and the nation of Israel were under since the time of Moses. That is why it is called the Mosaic Covenant. God by revelation to Paul had showed him his deliverance from that Old Covenant and placed him under the New Covenant, which is in Jesus Christ. That deliverance took place at the Cross of Jesus. I may use anyone of those terms when speaking about the Law, but know I am referring to the Old Covenant of the Mosaic Law. One cannot get deliverance from the Law unless one has a Revelation of Jesus Christ and sees himself or herself in the New Covenant. Today, there are still a lot of Law Keepers in the church of Jesus Christ universally. Each church locally has their own set of rules and nearly immediately set new believers in Christ Jesus under their "laws." Many Christians have become proselyte Jews thinking coming under the Mosaic Covenant of Law will draw them closer to God and to Jesus. That is not what the Scriptures teach as we proceed into this study of the New

Covenant. I hope this has clarified everyone's understanding as we study the New Testament (Covenant).

This New Covenant was Prophesied about in the Old Testament (Covenant)

With these spiritual facts in mind, we need to see that the Old Covenant has been abolished at the Cross of Jesus Christ and that we as believers now live under a New Covenant of grace and love. The prophets in the Old Testament (Covenant) prophesied that God was going to bring in a New Covenant a thousand years or more before it happened. "Behold the days are coming, says the Lord, when I will make a new covenant with the house of Israel and with the house of Judah—not according to the covenant that I made with their fathers in the day that I took them by the hand to bring them out of the land of Egypt. My covenant (the Mosaic Covenant) which they broke, though I was a husband to them, says the Lord. But this is the covenant that I will make with the house of Israel after those days says the Lord: I will put my law (the Mosaic Law) in their minds, and write it on their hearts and I will be their God, and they shall be My people. No more shall every man teach his neighbor, and every man his brother saying, 'Know the Lord', for they shall all know Me from the least of them to the greatest of them, says the Lord. For I will forgive their iniquity, and their sin I will remember no more." (Jeremiah 31:31-34)

The late Dr. C.I Scofield in his The First Scofield Reference Bible on page 1297 had his own summary of the New Covenant which was interesting. It is located at the bottom of the page. "The New Covenant, Summary: (1) "Better" than the Mosaic Covenant, not morally but efficaciously (Hebrews 7:19; Romans 8:3-4) (2) Established on "better" (i.e. unconditional) promises. In the Mosaic Covenant God said, "if ye(you) will" (Exodus 19:5) in the New Covenant He says, "I will" (Hebrew 8:10,12) (3) Under the Mosaic Covenant obedience sprang from fear (Hebrews 2:2; 12:25-27), under the New Covenant; from a willing heart and mind (verse 10). (4) The New Covenant secures the personal revelation of the Lord to every believer (verse 11); (5) The complete oblivion of sins (verse 12); Hebrew 10:17; c.f. Hebrew 10:13); (6) (The

New Covenant) rests upon accomplished redemption (Matthew 26:27-28; 1 Corinthians 11:25; Hebrews 9:11-12, 18-23) (7) (The New Covenant) secures the perpetuity of future conversion and blessing of Israel (Jeremiah 31:31-40); see also "Kingdom" (Old Testament and 2 Samuel 7:8-17). The New Covenant is…thus speaking of resurrection and eternal redemption."

The late Dr. C.I. Scofield is just one of many Biblical scholars of the past that saw the complete separation of the New Covenant from the Old Covenant. Dr. Spiro Zodhiates in his Hebrew-Greek Key Study Bible on page 939, is another Biblical scholar that saw in Jeremiah's prophecy the separation of the two Covenants, the one from the other (Jeremiah 31:31-40). This is what he says. "From a Christian perspective, this is the most important passage in Jeremiah, because of the way the writer of Hebrews used it. It was quoted in its entirety in Hebrews 8:8-12, the longest quote of an Old Testament text in the New Testament. From the words "new covenant" the author argued that the covenant established at Jesus' death had superseded (taken the place of) the one made with Israel at Mount Sinai (Hebrews 8:6-8, 13). Later, on the basis of another meaning of the Greek word for "covenant," he develops the point that Jesus' death initiated the new covenant, because a "will" or testament goes into effect only upon the death of the one who made it (Hebrews 9:16-18). Hence, our term "New Testament" comes from the Hebrews writer use of Jeremiah 31:31." You have probably figured out by now that I also use the word "Testament" and "Covenant" interchangeably for what was just quoted. The Hebrew and Greek words for "Testament" are also translated "Covenant."

The New Covenant was to the Jews First and then to the Gentiles

The problem is that we tend to make up our own rules or attempt to go back under the Old Mosaic Covenant after receiving the kindness and love of God into our hearts upon accepting Jesus Christ as our Lord and Savior. We say we are under a New Covenant, but then live like we are under the Old Mosaic Covenant. Basically, it is because we do not understand the New Covenant that is in Jesus Christ. Another problem is some believers believe there is a New Covenant for Israel and another New Covenant for the Gentile Church. In actuality, the New Covenant was prophesied by a

Jewish Prophet, Jeremiah, to the Jewish nation of Israel. But God extended the New Covenant to the whole world through His Son, Jesus Christ. In fact, after Jesus death and resurrection Jesus commissioned His disciples to go into all the world and preach the Gospel. "All authority has been given to Me in heaven and on earth. Go therefore and make disciples of all the nations, baptizing them in the name of the Father and of the Son and of the Holy Spirit, teaching them to observe all things that I have commanded you; and lo, I am with you always, even to the end of the age." (Matthew 28:18b-20) "Go into all the world and preach the Gospel to every creature." (Mark 16:15) Notice before the Cross of Jesus, Jesus was sent to the lost sheep of the house of Israel. "These twelve Jesus sent out and commanded them, saying: Do not go into the way of the Gentiles, and do not enter a city of the Samaritans. But go rather to the lost sheep of the house of Israel." (Matthew 10:5-6) God sent Jesus to Israel first. But after His death, burial and resurrection, Jesus sent His disciples to the world and to all the nations of the world. Therefore, it does not matter whether we are Jews or Gentiles, the New Covenant is for all on the earth. The Apostle Paul expressed this concept through several of his letters, but we will discuss this later in this chapter.

Actually, the New Covenant is extended to all the Gentile world when Peter has an open sheet revelation while he was staying with Simon the tanner in Joppa. This revelation occurs in Acts 10:9-22 in 37 A.D. according to Bible Hub>timeline>Acts. The day of Pentecost when all the Jewish apostles and disciples were filled with the Holy Spirit in Jerusalem was in 30 A.D. Therefore, this revelation given to Peter and the subsequent meeting at Cornelius house was approximately seven or eight years after the day of Pentecost. Up to this point in the book of Acts, God had dealt with the Jewish people about His Son, Jesus Christ. From Acts 2, on the day of Pentecost Jews and Jewish proselytes were saved and filled with the Holy Spirit. The Apostles according to the word of the Lord went to the Jews first.

In his work, The Power to Overcome Prejudice under www.biblicaltheology.com>act, J.W. Carter describes what happened in chapter ten of the book of Acts. "Chapter ten in the book of Acts, illustrates a turning point in the basic view of Christianity as seen by the church. Up to that time the church considered Christianity to be fulfilled if Judaism (which it is), and consequently is limited to Jews (which it is not). They (the Jewish apostles and disciples) felt that in order for a Gentile or non-Jew to come to Christ, they first had to become Jewish. Otherwise, they were still ceremonially unclean because they did not adhere to Jewish customs and laws."

This was the position of the church in Jerusalem before Acts 10 happened. Cornelius was a Gentile centurion who was over the Italian regiment. But he according to Scripture was a man who feared and loved God. This is what the Scriptures say about him in Acts 10:2. "(Cornelius) a devout man and one who feared God with all his household, who gave alms generously to the people, and prayed to God always." This man is instructed by God through an Angel to send for Peter in Joppa. The Angel tells him his prayers and alms are "a memorial before God." (Acts 10:4) While Cornelius is having this vision of an Angel, Peter is having an open sheet vision or revelation. Peter is getting hungry because it is approaching the noon hour when this revelation or vision takes place. I call this an open sheet revelation from God.

This is what J.W. Carter says about this in The Power to Overcome Prejudice. "...The scripture states that Peter was hungry, so eating was on his mind. No doubt he could smell the preparation of the meal that was taking place before him. Note that noon was not a typical time to eat. Their (Jewish meal during the day) was in the late afternoon. Peter had full knowledge and understanding that the meal that was being prepared for him was ceremonially correct: it was "kosher." Just like every area in his life, it was maintained in a clean, or kosher manner. God was preparing Peter for what was about to take place when he came down from the roof. Just like food was divided into two groups, clean and unclean, Peter had divided the population of people into two groups, clean and unclean."

Peter is on the roof top having this open-sheet revelation of unclean animals and the Lord is telling him to kill and eat. He has lived under the Old Mosaic Covenant of Law all his life. Peter objects saying to the Lord,

"Not so Lord! For I have never eaten anything common or unclean." (Acts 10:14) But listen to what God tells Peter. "What God has cleansed you must not call common." (Acts 10:15) Some Biblical scholars believe that when Jesus died on the cross, He not only saved us from sins and our sin nature, but He also brought cleansing to the old creation (unclean animals, birds and insects) and therefore, we can partake of it now. This was done three times to Peter. Because it happened three times some believe it means growth and reproduction while other believe the Trinity was in agreement that common things were now clean. God was preparing Peter for an encounter with Gentiles. Immediately after this the Holy Spirit spoke to Peter. "Behold, three men are seeking you. Arise therefore, go down, and go with them, doubting nothing; for I have sent them." (Acts 10:19b-20) To me, because this happened to Peter three times, it possibly means resurrection or bringing to life something that was dead.

Peter leaves the next day with the three men and goes to Cornelius house, where he finds a house full of Gentiles. Cornelius thinks Peter is so close to God, he falls down to worship Peter. Peter has to reassure him that he is a man also. Peter finds that Cornelius has a house full of Gentiles. Listen to what Peter says to them. "You know how unlawful (the Old Mosaic Covenant of Law) it is for a Jewish man to keep company with or go to one of another nation. But God has shown me that I should not call any man common or unclean. Therefore, I come without objection as soon as I was sent for..." (Acts 10:28-29b)

Cornelius then shares with Peter about his vision with the Angel and that the Angel said Peter would tell him what he must do. Knowing that Peter is coming he gathers all of his Gentile friends and relatives to hear Peter. Peter immediately preaches the Gospel of Jesus Christ to them and while he is preaching the Gentiles receive the Gospel and are saved and filled with the Holy Spirit, thus a Gentile Pentecost and a Gentile Church is born. (Acts 10:38-48)

Dr. Spiro Zodhiates in his Hebrew-Greek Key Study Bible on page 1336 says this about the Holy Spirit baptism that Cornelius' house experienced. "...This is the third group to receive the baptism in the Holy Spirit, falling upon Cornelius and other Gentiles. As in the case of the Pentecostal occasion, it took place in the presence of at least some of the Twelve Apostles, and in the presence of Peter. The special manifestation of the Holy Spirit was to prove that God was visiting the Gentiles in equal gift (verse 17), the same as the Jews. The whole event of how salvation came unto Cornelius and the Gentiles is detailed in Acts (chapters 10 and 11). As in the case at Pentecost, so here as per Acts 10:44, the Holy Spirit fell upon all present. Those on whom the Holy Spirit fell were heard speaking in tongues or languages, glossais (1100). The people who spoke in these languages which were different than their own mother tongue were praising and glorifying God, and so they were understood and needed no interpreter. This spiritual baptism is a historical event is that attaches every genuinely repentant believer in the body of Christ. (1 Corinthians 12:13)."

It is my conclusion from this passage in Acts 10:44-48 that the Gentiles at Cornelius house and himself were saved and received the Baptism in the Holy Spirit at the same time. God is not in a box. He delights in tearing up our theology. I would not say this happens every time, but it did happen this time at Cornelius' house. Before Peter's preaching the Gospel of Jesus Christ to them, there are no Scriptures that say that they were saved from their sins. In fact, Cornelius was told that Peter would give them instructions from God. He would tell them "what they must do." (Acts 10:6) As Peter was sharing the Gospel with them, the Holy Spirit fell on them. "While Peter was still speaking these words, the Holy Spirit fell upon all those who heard the word. And those of the circumcision (the Jews) were astonished, as many as came with Peter because the gift of the Holy Spirit had been poured out on the Gentiles also. For (because) they heard them speak with tongues and magnify God. Then Peter answered, "Can anyone forbid water, that these should not be baptized who have received the Holy Spirit just as we have?" And he (Peter) commanded them to be baptized in the name of the Lord. Then they asked him (Peter) to stay a few days." (Acts 10:44-48)

My observations of this that started at Cornelius' house is that they were all saved and filled with the Holy Spirit in one operation of the Spirit. "For with God nothing will be impossible." (Luke 1:37) The impossible is made possible by the hand of God. As I said before you cannot put God in a box. The Gentiles were grafted into the body of Jesus Christ. It was no longer just a Jewish church in Jerusalem. God loves the Gentiles as well as the Jews. That is why Gentiles are in the body of Jesus Christ today. This was Pentecost again at a new Gentile church. Even Peter and his circumcised Jewish friends knew they, Cornelius' house, were apart of the church for God had given them the Holy Spirit.

After this Peter is asked to stay a few more days at Cornelius' house. Jews did not stay with Gentiles. Jews would have nothing to do with Gentiles much less eat with them. But now Peter, because of God, is eating their foods, drinking their drinks, and staying at their house. Peter will have a lot of explaining to do when he gets back to Jerusalem. James, the Lord's brother, who is a devout Jewish Christian will be asking him a lot of questions.

Let us look at Acts 11:1-3 and see what happens when Peter gets back to Jerusalem. "Now the apostles and brethren who were in Judea heard that the Gentiles had also received the word of God. And when Peter came up to Jerusalem, those of the circumcision (the Jews) contended with him, saying, "You went in to uncircumcised men and ate with them." (Acts 11:1-3) According to the Amplified Bible the Jewish brethren were really upset with what Peter had done. Let us look at the same passage in the Amplified. "Now the apostles (special messengers) and the brethren who were throughout Judea heard [with astonishment] that the Gentile (heathen) also had received and accepted and welcomed the Word of God [the doctrine concerning the attainment through Christ of salvation in the kingdom of God]. So, when Peter went up to Jerusalem, the circumcision party [certain Jewish Christians] found fault with him [separating themselves from him in a hostile spirit, opposing and disputing and contending with him]. Saying why did you go to uncircumcised men and [even] eat with them." (The Amplified Bible, page 1206-1207, Acts 11:1-3) From the Amplified Bible one can see that they were not happy with Peter going to Cornelius' house. Jews had no dealings, fellowship or friendship with Gentiles as well as Samaritans. The word contended is taken from the Greek word diakrino which means to separate from the rest.

From this they would not have anything to do with Peter until he made a full explanation of why he went to Cornelius' house because he was a Gentile and those in his house were Gentiles. (The New Thayer's Greek-English Lexicon, page 138)

At this point, Peter has to explain what happened when he went to Cornelius' house and how God moved there. Peter and the Jewish leaders were still Jews and they were not accustomed to talking, fellowshipping or eating with Gentiles. But at this point, Peter shares with them the Open Sheet vision and revelation he had received from the Lord. "I was in the city of Joppa praying: and in a trance I saw a vision, an object descended like a great sheet, let down from heaven by four corners; and it came to me. When I observed intently and considered, I saw four-footed animals of the earth, wild beasts, creeping things and birds of the air. And I heard a voice saying to me, 'Rise Peter, kill and eat. But I said, 'Not so Lord: for nothing common or unclean has at any time entered my mouth.' But the voice answered me again from heaven, 'What God has cleansed you must not call common.'" (Acts 11:5-9) He went on to share with the Jewish brethren that this happened three times. As we shared before three is the number of resurrection and also of the Trinity.

After this Peter explained how the Holy Spirit directed him to go with some men who were knocking at Simon the Tanner's gate. These were probably Gentile men as well that Cornelius had sent to get Peter. We do not know for sure, because the Scripture calls them brethren. The Spirit told him not to doubt but follow them. After going with these men and entering Cornelius' house, Peter begins to understand the vision he had and explained that to the Jewish leadership at Jerusalem. Cornelius' house was full of Gentiles, who had come to hear Peter speak. Then, Peter explained to the leaders how he preached the Gospel to them just like he did to the Jews on the day of Pentecost. He explains to them while he is still preaching the Holy Spirit fell on the Gentiles. "And as I began to speak, the Holy Spirit fell upon them, as upon us at the beginning. Then I remembered the word of the Lord, how He said, 'John indeed baptized with water, but you shall be baptized with the Holy Spirit.' If therefore God gave them the same gift (tongues) as He gave us when we believed on the

Lord Jesus Christ, who was I that I could withstand God? When they heard these things, they became silent: and they glorified God saying, "Then God has also granted to the Gentiles repentance to life." (Acts 11:15-18)

It is interesting to note that the Jewish leadership of the church in Jerusalem had to accept the fact that God had given salvation and life to the Gentile believers at Cornelius' house. God had also filled them with the Holy Spirit and given them the same gift, tongues, that He had given the Jewish believers on the day of Pentecost. The Gentiles were now a part of the New Covenant that God had instituted through His Son, Jesus Christ and they were a part of the Lord's Church.

Dr. Richard Longenecker in the Zondervan NIV Bible Commentary, Volume 2, New Testament, page 442 says this about the conversion of Cornelius and those in his house. "The conversion of Cornelius was a landmark in the history of the Gospel's advance from its strictly Jewish beginnings to its penetration of the Roman Empire. True, it did not settle any of the issues relating to Jewish-Gentile relations within the church, nor did Jewish believers take it as a precedent for a direct outreach to Gentiles. But it did show the sovereign God was not confined to the traditional forms of Judaism and that He could bring a Gentile directly into relationship with Himself through Jesus Christ, a part from any prior commitment to distinctive Jewish beliefs or lifestyle…"

I wanted to make sure everyone understands that with the outpouring of the Spirit at Cornelius' house, that the Gentiles were included in the New Covenant. The New Covenant was given to the Jews on the day of Pentecost when the church was born, but then was extended to the Gentiles there at Cornelius' house. To begin with the Old Mosaic Covenant of Law had to be taken care of and fulfilled by God through Jesus Christ. The Jewish nation, Israel, since the time they accepted the Mosaic Covenant, could not obey it and could not fulfill it. No Israelite from Moses until Jesus came was able to fulfill that Old Covenant. Even the sacrifices that looked perfect in man's sight, were not perfect in God's sight. Hebrews 10:1 describes this imperfection. "For the law (Mosaic Covenant of Law), having a shadow of the good things to come, and not the very image of the things, can never with these same sacrifices, which they offer continually year by year, make those who approach perfect." God must send a man, His own Son, Jesus Christ, who could fulfill all of the Old Mosaic Covenant of Law perfectly. That is what God's Son, Jesus Christ, did. As Jesus said in Matthew 5:17, "Do not think that I have come to do away with or undo the Law (Covenant of Law) or the Prophets; I have not come to do away with or undo but to complete and fulfill them." (Amplified Bible, page 1079)

A lot of Bible scholars have problems with the verb "to fulfill" (pieres). In Zondervan NIV Bible Commentary, Volume 2, New Testament, page 25, Dr. Donald Carson offers these comments on that word. "The nub of the problem lies in the verb "to fulfill" (pieres), for which a variety of interpretations have been offered. The best one says that Jesus fulfills the Law and the Prophets in that they point to Him, and He is their fulfillment. Therefore, we give "fulfill" exactly the same measure as in the formula quotations, which is the prologue (Matthew chapters 1-2) have already laid great stress on the prophetic nature of the Old Testament and the way it points to Jesus...In the light of the antithesis (vv. 21-48) the passage before us insists that just as Jesus fulfilled Old Testament prophecies by His person and actions, so He fulfilled Old Testament Law by His teaching. In no way does this "abolish" the Old Testament as canon, any more than the obsolescence (the process of becoming obsolete or no longer in use) of the Levitical sacrificial system abolished tabernacle ritual as canon. Instead the Old Testament's real and abiding authority must be understood through the Person (Jesus) and teaching of Him (Jesus) to Whom it points and Who so richly fulfills it."

God Is Pleased with Jesus

Therefore, Jesus in His life and teachings fulfilled the Old Mosaic Covenant of Law. We find also that God, the Father, twice confessed that Jesus was and is His Son and that He was pleased with His Son. The first place was when John the Baptist baptized Jesus in the River Jordan. Even when John the Baptist was questioning Jesus about his right to baptize Him, Jesus said this. "Permit it to be so now, for thus it is fitting for us to fulfill all righteousness." (Matthew 3:13) Again the word "to fulfill" is used to describe Jesus in His purity. When Jesus came up out of the water, God the Father's statement and witness was this. "This is My beloved Son, in whom I am well pleased." (Matthew 3:17)

The second time God the Father witnessed to the fact that Jesus was His Son, was when Jesus took His three disciples—Peter, James, and John—to a high mountain. Jesus is transfigured before them all. The Greek word for transfigured is metamorpho and it means to transform literally or figuratively, to change right before one's eyes. (AllAboutJesus Christ.org>transfiguration) Of course Peter starts saying a lot of things when probably he should keep his mouth shut. But sometimes we do that too. God the Father not only states that Jesus is His Son, but that He is pleased with Him again. He also tells Peter to listen to Jesus. "While he (Peter) was still speaking, behold, a bright cloud overshadowed them; and suddenly a voice came out of the cloud saying, "This is My beloved Son, in Whom I am well pleased. Hear Him." (Matthew 17:5) This shut Peter up and the Scriptures said he "was greatly afraid." (Matthew 17:6)

Only a Person, God's own Son, that pleased God could and was the Sacrifice for our sin from the beginning of time to the end of time. Jesus was and is the only appropriate Sacrifice for our sin. As John the Baptist said in John 1:28. "Behold the Lamb of God who takes away the sin of the world." It was John the Baptist's assignment to announce the Lamb of God (Jesus) who would take away the sin of the world. John was the prophetic forerunner of Jesus Christ. He had come in the spirit and power of Elijah. "He (John the Baptist) will also go before Him (Jesus) in the spirit and power of Elijah, to turn the hearts of the fathers to the children, and the disobedient to the wisdom of the just, to make ready a people prepared for the Lord." (Luke 1:17) This is what the Angel of the Lord had told Zechariah when he told Zechariah that they were going to have a child and to name him John.

The fact that John the Baptist fulfilled all of Malachi's prophecy about him actually shows that everything was lining up prophetically for Jesus to fulfill those Old Testament prophecies. The fact that John the Baptist said

Jesus was the Lamb of God that would take away the sin of the world says there could only be one sacrifice for sin to fulfill all the sacrifices that God called for in the Old Testament. (John 1:29)

Listen to what the Apostle Paul said about Jesus in Hebrews 9:12-15. "Not with the blood of goats and calves, but with His own blood He entered the Most Holy Place once for all, having obtained eternal redemption. For if the blood of bulls and goats and the ashes of an heifer, sprinkling the unclean, sanctifies for the purifying of the flesh, how much more shall the blood of Christ, who through the eternal Spirit offered Himself without spot to God, purge your conscience from dead works to serve the living God? And for this reason, He (Jesus) is the Mediator of the new covenant, by means of death, for the redemption of the transgressors under the first covenant (the Old Mosaic Covenant of Law), that those who are called may receive the promise of eternal inheritance."

Jesus' Sacrifice at the Cross Satisfies God

Old Testament (Covenant) sacrifices could never satisfy God. He must have a perfect Sacrifice. Those Old Covenant sacrifices only covered sins; they did not remove sins. Jesus blood, which was perfect blood from His Father completely removes all sins—past, present and future. Jesus Christ, God's Son, fulfilled all of the Old Covenant. He actually disposed of that Covenant at the Cross. No man of earthily origin could satisfy the judgment of God. Only God's Son could do that. Paul, the writer of Hebrews, says in Hebrews 10:2-4 that those offerings of the Old Covenant could not take away sins, they could only cover them until the next year when they were offered again. "For then would they not have ceased to be offered? For the (Old Testament) worshippers, once purged, would have had no consciousness of sins. But in those sacrifices, there is a reminder of sins every year. For it is not possible that the blood of bulls and goats could take away sins." This means the sacrifices covered the sin for a year, but the next year the same sacrifices would have to be made again. But look down at verse 12 of Hebrews 4. "But this Man (Jesus), after He had offered one sacrifice for sins forever, sat down at the right hand of God, from this time waiting till His enemies are made His footstool. For by one offering He (Jesus) has perfected forever those who are being sanctified." (Hebrew 10:12-14) All it took was one Sacrifice for sin, a perfect Sacrifice, that God would accept. None others would do. That is why the Old Mosaic Covenant has passed away and we are living under the New Covenant of Jesus Christ.

Paul, the Apostle, gives us word pictures of what Jesus did for us at the Cross. He describes how Jesus has made both Jews and Gentiles one at the Cross of Jesus. "But now in Christ Jesus you (Gentiles) who once were afar off have been made near by the blood of Christ. For He Himself is our peace, who has made both (Jews and Gentiles) one, and has broken down the middle wall of division between us, having abolished in His flesh the enmity that is, the law of commandments (the Old Mosaic Covenant of Law) contained in ordinances so as to create in Himself one new man (Jesus) from the two, thus making peace, and that He might reconcile them both (Jew and Gentile) through the Cross, thereby putting to death the enmity." (Ephesians 2:13-16)

Not only does the Cross of Jesus do away with the Old Covenant, but it brings both Jews and Gentiles together under a New Covenant. The Old Covenant (the Mosaic Covenant) required a perfect sacrifice. Even in Hebrews 8:13 after quoting Jeremiah 31:31-34 where Jeremiah prophesies about a New Covenant being made with the house of Israel and the house of Judah, the writer of Hebrews prophesies that the Old Covenant with its effect on the Jewish people was going to pass away. "In that He (God) says, "A new covenant," He has made the first obsolete (no longer useful). Now what is becoming obsolete (no longer useful) and growing old is ready to vanish away." (Hebrews 9:13) Most Biblical scholars believe the book of Hebrews was written before the destruction of Jerusalem and the Temple. Jews, that did not accept Jesus as the Messiah and the Son of God, were still making sacrifices in the Temple when this was written. It took the destruction of Jerusalem and the Temple for the Jewish sacrificial system to be destroyed. Thus, Hebrews 8:13 is a prophetic word describing the end of the Old Mosaic Covenant of Law, which actually happened in 70 A.D.

Jesus is Our High Priest

The Old Mosaic Covenant of Law had a High Priest that was sinful and first had to do sacrifices for himself as High Priest. This was described in Hebrews 9:6-10. "Now when these things had been thus prepared (during the time of Moses and Aaron), the priests always went into the first part of the tabernacle, performing the services. But into the second part (the Holy of Holies) the High Priest went alone once a year (the Day of Atonement), not without blood, which he offered for himself (because he was sinful) and for the people's sins committed in ignorance; the Holy Spirit indicating that the way into the Holiest of All was not yet made manifest (revealed) while the first tabernacle was still standing. It was symbolic for the present time in which both gifts and sacrifices are offered which cannot make him (the High Priest) who performed the service perfect in regard to conscience—concerned only with foods and drinks, various washings, and freshly ordinances imposed until the time of reformation (of setting things right—the New Covenant)." (Hebrews 9:6-10)

This is a description of the main duty of the High Priest. Once a year he entered the earthily Holy of Holies and sprinkled blood on the earthily Ark of the Covenant for the sins of himself and the Jewish people. Even though they were made from the best quality materials that the Israelites had, they were still earthily materials and flaws that God could see. Yet God accepted them under the Old Mosaic Covenant. The forgiveness of these sins was only temporary. "For it is not possible that the blood of bulls and goats could take away sins." (Hebrews 10:4) Since these sacrifices year after year could not take away sins and "without shedding of blood there is no remission (forgiveness)" (Hebrews 9:22b), therefore, the same sacrifice on the Day of Atonement would have to be made again next year on the next Day of Atonement. This would go on year after year. Sins were covered, but not removed. Not until Jesus Christ came and did it with one sacrifice for sin as we shared about earlier.

But the writer of Hebrews, the Apostle Paul, goes on to describe what happened with a New Covenant and a perfect High Priest, Jesus Christ. He did not have to atone for His own sins, because He had none. "For we do not have a High Priest who cannot sympathize with our weaknesses, but was in all points tempted as we are, yet without sin." (Hebrews 4:15) The writer of Hebrews goes on to describe what Jesus Christ did spiritually as High Priest in Hebrews with the greater and more perfect tabernacle not made with hands, that is, not of this creation… "For Christ has not entered the holy place made with hands (the Old Covenant) which are copies of the true but into heaven (God's abode) itself, now to appear in the presence of God for us; not that He should offer Himself (Jesus Christ) often, as the high priest enters the Most Holy Place every year with the blood of another (animals)—He (Jesus) then would have had to suffer often since the foundation of the world, but now, once at the end of the ages, He (Jesus) has appeared to put away sin by the sacrifice of Himself (Jesus)." Then, the Apostle Paul concludes with this remark that Christ only had to offer Himself once to take away all of our sins. "…so, Christ was offered once to bear the sins of many. To those who eagerly wait for Him He will appear a second time, apart from sin, for salvation." (Hebrews 9:28)

In the Temple, the day Jesus died the veil in the Temple was rent from top to the bottom. "And behold, the veil of the temple was torn in two from top to bottom, and the earth quaked, and the rocks were split." (Matthew 27:51) "In accordance with Matthew's fulfillment themes (Matthew 5:17-20; 11:11-13) the tearing of the veil signifies the obsolescence (becoming obsolete) of the temple ritual and the law governing it (cf. Hebrews 9:1-14). Jesus, Himself is the New Temple, the meeting place of God and humankind…; the old is obsolete. At the same time, the rent veil serves as a sign of the temple's impending destruction—a destruction conceived not as a brute fact but as a theological necessity." (Zondervan NIV Bible Commentary, Volume 2, New Testament, page 130)

As you have probably seen thus far, the book of Hebrews in the New Testament (Covenant) is actually a comparison of the Old Mosaic Covenant of Law with the New Covenant. In Hebrews 9:1-5 goes further in describing the old tabernacle that was erected in the wilderness. "Then indeed, even the first covenant (the Mosaic Covenant) had ordinances of divine service and the earthily sanctuary. For a tabernacle was prepared, the first part, in which was the lampstand, the table and the showbread, which is called the sanctuary; and behind the second veil, the part of the tabernacle which is called the Holiest of All, which had the golden altar of incense and the ark of the covenant overlaid on all sides with gold, in which the golden pot that had manna, Aaron's rod that budded, and the tablets of the covenant; and above it were the cherubim of glory overshadowing the mercy seat..." All of this is of the Old Mosaic Covenant of Law. When Jesus died and the veil was rent from top to bottom by God, Himself; God was saying I am finished with the Old Covenant. Now I have a New Covenant with a new sanctuary in Heaven. That veil rent desecrated the old sanctuary and rendered it null and void. That is why the Israelites today are hoping to rebuild the Temple and start animal sacrifices again. They cannot accept the fact that the Old Mosaic Covenant of Law is over and there is a New Covenant with a new and living way. "Therefore, brethren, having boldness to enter the Holiest (the Holy of Holies in Heaven) by the blood of Jesus, by a new and living way which He consecrated for us, through the veil, that is His flesh, and having a High Priest over the house of God." (Hebrews 10:19-21)

The New Covenant Requires a Sacrifice and a High Priest

We need to consider that the Old Covenant was fulfilled in Jesus Christ and through His death on the Cross, He actually fulfilled all the sacrifices once and for all. Therefore, in His burial, He buried the Old Covenant. Thus, it is in the past. But the New Covenant also needed a Sacrifice, the Sacrifice of Himself, Jesus Christ. This New Covenant and how it came about is in Hebrews 9. This is at the central core of the New Covenant. It talks about the New Covenant Sacrifice in Hebrews 9:12-14, which we have quoted before. It talks about how Jesus sacrificed Himself and then entered the Most Holy Place in the Heavenlies for us and has obtained eternal redemption for us. We were bought off the slave market of sin from the devil. He also purged or cleansed our conscience minds of dead works "to serve the living God. Since that sacrifice has been made, Jesus is in the Heavenlies before God as our Mediator (Lawyer, Negotiator). "And for this reason, He is the Mediator of the New Covenant, by means of death, for the redemption of the transgressions under the first covenant, and those who are called may receive the promise of the eternal inheritance. For where there is a testament (covenant), there must also of necessity be the death of the testator. For a testament (covenant) is in force after men are dead, since it has no power at all while the testator lives." (Hebrews 9:15-17)

Actually, Jesus Christ started a New Covenant with His death. Jesus did away with the Old Covenant with His death and then started a New Covenant with His death. Only God could do that. Dr. Leon Morris in writing the commentary on the book of Hebrews in the Zondervan NIV Bible Commentary, Volume 2, New Testament, page 981 says this about Hebrew 9:16-18. "The argument is not easy to follow in English because we have no single word that is the precise equivalent of diatheke. The Greek word is the normal word for a "last will and testament," but it is also used to refer to any covenant" God makes with people. These are not the result of a process of negotiation in which God and the person come to a mutually acceptable arrangement. God lays down the terms. The result is a covenant characterized by the same kind of finality we see in a testament. (One cannot dicker with a testator!) The author therefore moves easily from the idea of covenant to that of testament. It might help us follow him if we render the first clause in v. 15 as "he is the mediator of a new covenant or testament." This gives two translations for the one Greek word but helps us retain something of the continuity of thought. The death of the testator (Jesus Christ) is necessary for a will or testament to come into effect. The will may be perfectly valid, but it does not operate till death takes place."

Let us look at verses 17-18 by Dr. Morris. "The author uses a technical legal term to indicate that the will (diatheke) is" in force only" when death occurs. "It never takes effect" is another legal term. Only the death of the testator brings the provisions of a will into force. From this the author reasons to the necessity for Christ's death, since (H)e is bringing into force a new covenant (diatheke). It was not so to speak, an option God happened to prefer…"

I felt it necessary to quote Dr. Morris because he really shows the true understanding of these three verses. This is at the very heart of what God, the Father and God, the Son did for us. Not only did God wipe the slate clean as far as our old transgressions through the death of His Son, but through Jesus' death, He has brought us into a New Covenant with Him and with God, the Father. Just like in a last will and testament of a person on earth, it is not in effect until the person dies. Therefore, the "better promises" are given to us and we have boldness to enter the Holy of Holies in Heaven by the blood of Jesus. (Hebrews 10:19) My father left my three brothers all that he had at his death, but it did not become ours until he died, even though it was in the last will and testament. Until individuals realize what Jesus wrought at the Cross at His death, they will not enter into the New Covenant promises and position.

The new sanctuary and the new High Priest according to the New Covenant is described in Hebrews 8:1-2,6. "Now this is the main point of the things we are saying. We have such a High Priest (Jesus), who is seated at the right hand of the throne of the Majesty (God, Himself) in the heavens, a minister of the sanctuary and of the true tabernacle (in Heaven) which the Lord erected and not man...But now He (Jesus) has obtained a more excellent ministry inasmuch as He is the Mediator (the Arbiter, Agent) of a better Covenant (the New Covenant), which was established on better promises..." The promises of the New Covenant talked about here are based on the sacrificial death of Jesus Christ once for all. His blood washes away all of our sins, therefore, we do not need any additional sacrifices. "But if we walk in the light as He (Jesus) is in the light, we have fellowship one with another, and the blood of Jesus Christ cleanses us from all sin." (1 John 1:9) This one sacrifice of Jesus take care of all our sins. Jesus arose and sits as a Mediator in the presence of God for us. Jesus is our Lawyer before God.

This is what the Dr. Leon Morris says in the Zondervan NIV Bible Commentary, Volume 2, New Testament, on page 974 of Hebrews 8:6. "The ministry of priests in a sanctuary made according to the heavenly pattern is obviously one of great dignity. But the author's point is that Jesus' ministry in the heavenly architype is of comparably greater dignity and worth. He chooses to bring this out by using a comparison of the two covenants. Jesus is the mediator of a superior covenant. Mediator is a legal term for one who arbitrates between two parties. (Jesus) Christ mediates between people and God (His Father); it is He who establishes the new covenant. This new covenant is better than the old (covenant) because it is "founded on better promises"—it concentrates on spiritual things (e.g. the forgiveness of sins) and is unconditional in nature."

The New Covenant takes effect in the life of believers when they receive Jesus Christ's sacrifice as theirs, when they accept the blood of the New Covenant as theirs to remove all their sins, and when they are raised by faith to walk in newness of life. Does this sound familiar? Pastors says this when they baptize a new believer in Christ after they confess that Jesus is their Lord and Savior.

The Renewing of Our Minds

God wants to change our old conscience from evil to good thoughts. He talks about this in Hebrews 10:22. "…let us draw near with a true heart in full assurance of faith, having our hearts sprinkled from an evil conscience and our bodies washed with pure water. Let us hold fast the confession of our hope without wavering, for He who promised is faithful. And let us consider one another in order to stir up love and good works." As our minds become renewed to the New Covenant we are under, and our Covenant Relationship with God, it is going to change our minds from earthily things to the heavenly. Paul talks about this in Romans 12:1-2. "I beseech you therefore, brethren, by the mercies of God, that you present your bodies a living sacrifice, holy, acceptable to God, which is your reasonable service. And do not be conformed to this world, but be transformed by the renewing of your mind, that you may prove what is the good and acceptable and perfect will of God."

There are three words that stick out in this Scripture—transformed, renewing and prove. Paul says not to be conformed to the world. It is possible to return to your old frame of mind. Worldliness can grip your mind again through worldly people, television, and radio broadcasts. They will promote the world's system and beliefs for example like greed, lusts, and dishonesty. The devil does not give up trying to influence you, once you have received Jesus as your Lord and Savior. There is going to be a battle for your mind. You will have to yield to the Holy Spirit and allow Him to transform and renew your mind.

Let us look at the word "transformed" first. The Greek word for "transformed" is metamorpho. We get the word metamorphosis. "It refers to an invisible process in Christians which takes place or begins to take place already during this life in this age." (Lexical Aids to the New Testament from The Hebrew-Greek Key Study Bible, edited by Dr. Spiros Zodhiates, page 1171 word # 3339) A butterfly has a larvae stage, when it is a caterpillar until it changes to a butterfly. The caterpillar looks gross and ugly until it changes to a butterfly. The Christian has to undergo changes in thinking and attitude to become fully adopted into the family of God.

The second word is the "renewing" of the mind. The word "renewing" comes from the Greek word anakainosis and means qualitatively new. "Therefore, a renewing or a renovation which makes a person different than in the past. (Lexical Aids to the New Testament from The Hebrew-Greek Key Study Bible, edited by Dr. Spiros Zodhiates, page 1664 word # 342) All of this has to do with the redeeming of the mind as well as the spirit of man. All of this takes place in the Christian believer's mind when it is renewed in the Word of God. The change of the mind cannot take place unless one is daily in the Scriptures. Paul spent his time in the Old Testament Scriptures because the New Testament had not yet been written. "Bring the cloak that I left with Carpus at Troas when you come—and the books, especially the parchments." (2 Timothy 4:13)

The third word we need to look at is "prove." The Greek word for "prove" is dokimazo. This Greek word means "to prove, discern, distinguish, approve. It has the notion of proving a thing whether it be worthy to be received or not. It also means to prove to, bring forth the good in us…" (Lexical Aids to the New Testament from The Hebrew-Greek Key Study Bible, edited by Dr. Spiros Zodhiates, page 1683, word #1681) After carefully examining the Scriptures and listening to the Holy Spirit one is able to prove and distinguish what God wants the Christian believer to do in a given situation along life's journey.

Therefore, God accepts us as we are at salvation, but He wants to change us into sons and daughters of His, who can sit at His table with understanding of their position, responsibilities and the character that reflects the image and likeness of God. He told the Jewish nation, Israel, through the prophet, Jeremiah, that He would write "the commandments on their hearts" and "put My laws in their minds." (Jeremiah 31:33) You might say God is going to renew their minds and the Holy Spirit is going to be the One who will bring that about as Israel enters the New Covenant. The New Covenant is for both for Jews and the Gentiles. It is not just writing commandments in their hearts and writing His laws in their mind, but changing their spirit-man into His likeness and image. God wants the very Spirit of Jesus Christ to live and move in them bringing forth His character, His likeness in each child of God.

God is going to do something different to Israel with this New Covenant that He is bringing about in Gentile Christians as well. "None of them (Israel) shall teach his neighbor, and none his brother, saying, 'Know the Lord,' for all shall know Me, from the least of them to the greatest of them. For I will be merciful to their unrighteousness and their sins and their lawless deeds I will remember no more." (Jeremiah 31:34) It is God's will for the whole world to know Him in the Spirit and to forgive mankind. This is a part of the New Covenant that both Jews and Gentiles must accept. God is going to reveal Himself to all and wants to forgive us all, so that we can walk with Him in truth. The word "know" is an intimate knowledge that can only be acquired by relationship, Covenant Relationship with our God. Only He can bring us step by step into that relationship.

In 2 Corinthians 5:17 it states, "Therefore, if anyone is in Christ, he is a new creation; old things (the Old Covenant) have passed away; behold all things have become new (the New Covenant)." We were placed in Christ by God the Father. "For by Him (God the Father) you are in Christ Jesus, who became for us wisdom from God—and righteousness and sanctification and redemption—that, as it is written, "He who glories, let him glory in the Lord." (1 Corinthians 1:30) We were placed in Jesus at the Cross by God the Father. We didn't and don't put ourselves in Jesus. God put us there and we accept that spiritual fact by faith. Paul makes this abundantly clear in Romans 6:3-9. This Scripture is often used to explain physical baptism to new believers without really looking at the truth this Scripture conveys. May the Spirit of God reveal this truth to you—your position in Jesus. "Or do you not know that as many of us as were baptized (immersed) into Christ Jesus were baptized (immersed) into His death? Therefore, we were buried with Him through baptism (immersed) into death, that just as Christ was raised from the dead by the glory (eternal plan) of the Father, even so we also should walk in newness of life. For if we have been united together in the likeness of His death (the Cross) certainly we also shall be in the likeness of His resurrection, knowing (by revelation) this, that our old man (Adamic nature) was crucified with Him, that the body of sin (Adam) might be done away with, that we should no longer be slaves to sin (the Adamic nature). For he (us) who has died had been freed from sin (the Adamic nature). Now (right now) if we died with Christ, we believe that we shall also live with Him. Knowing (by revelation) that Christ, having been raised from the dead, (He) dies no more. Death no longer has dominion over Him." (Romans 6:3-9) You and I died with Jesus on the Cross and now you and I are living resurrected, eternal life in Jesus. You and I have been placed in a New Covenant with God the Father and with Jesus Christ, God's own Son. Gentiles don't use the words New Covenant, because those are far Eastern words. But God is a Covenant-keeping God and He wants to enlighten us about this New Covenant Relationship. Under this New Covenant Relationship, you are living resurrected, eternal life, because death no longer has dominion or control over our spirit-man.

There is one other thing about this New Covenant relationship we have with God. When Jesus died on the Cross, He became the last Adam. "And so, it is written, 'The first man, Adam became a living being.' The last Adam (Christ) became a life-giving spirit." (1 Corinthians 15:45) Jesus became the last Adam, in order to kill the last Adam, therefore, doing away with Adam's fallen race. In Jesus' resurrection He is thus bringing forth a new creature (creation) in Himself. We have become apart of that new creation in Jesus Christ. The new creation revolves around Jesus and not us.

The Cross of Jesus Christ and His death on the Cross was to do away with the old creation (Adam) and to end the Old Mosaic Covenant with all its laws and practices. Not all have received this revelation among Jewish believers and Gentile believers. To those who will not accept this revelation and truth, they remain under the Old Mosaic Covenant of law. Those under the Old Covenant cannot possibly live it or be set free by it; they are still under it and the condemnation that it brings. That is why Jesus Christ said in Matthew 5:18 these words. "For assuredly, I say to you till heaven and earth pass away, one jot or one tittle by no means pass from the law till all is fulfilled." The Jewish people, especially the Messianic Jews, have a hard time accepting the passing away of the Old Covenant of law. This is because they have lived under that Old Covenant of law for such a long time.

In Acts 10 we find the Revival that occurred at Cornelius' house. We have already discussed to some degree about Cornelius' house receiving the Gospel and the Holy Spirit being poured out there. This outpouring of the Holy Spirit happened approximately seven or eight years after the day of Pentecost when the 120 disciples were filled in the upper room with the Holy Spirit and spoke in tongues (Acts 2:1-4). This all happened at Cornelius' house while Peter was preaching. All that were in Cornelius' house were Gentiles. Peter had all of them physically baptized and he stayed with them a few days.

To the Jews First and Then the Gentiles

Briefly, I summarized what was shared earlier of the events that occurred in Acts 10. But what does all this mean to Jews and Gentiles alike? The first thing it means is that the Gospel went first to the Jews just as Jesus instructed His disciples earlier. He said the Gospel of the Kingdom of God must be preached first to the lost sheep of the house of Israel. This is recorded in Matthew 10:5-8. "These twelve Jesus sent out and commanded them saying. "Do not go into the way of the Gentiles, and do not enter a city of the Samaritans. But go rather to the lost sheep of the house of Israel. And as you go, preach, saying, "The Kingdom of Heaven is at hand. Heal the sick, cleanse the lepers, raise the dead, cast out demons. Freely you have received, freely give."

Notice when Jesus Christ ascended to Heaven and the Holy Spirit was sent on the day of Pentecost to the 120 apostles and disciples that for seven or eight years, they shared the good news of the Gospel with the Jews only. Maybe they remembered the words of our Lord Jesus Christ. "But you shall receive power when the Holy Spirit has come upon you; and you shall be witnesses to Me in Jerusalem, and in Judea and Samaria, and to the end of the earth." (Acts 1:8) Then Stephen was martyred in Acts 7. After that there began a great persecution of the church. "Now Saul (Paul) was consenting to his (Stephens) death. At that time a great persecution arose against the church which was at Jerusalem; and they were all scattered throughout the regions of Judea and Samaria, except the apostles…Therefore those who were scattered went everywhere preaching the word." (Acts 8:1,4) Jewish believers were scattered throughout Judea and Philip went to Samaria and preached the Gospel there. But the Apostles still stayed in Jerusalem. In the meantime, while all this is happening Paul (Saul) is converted to Jesus Christ on the road to Damascus in Acts 9. The Lord Jesus also tells Paul what his mission is going to be. He (Jesus) gives Ananias the mission for Paul to share with Paul (Saul). "Go, for he (Paul) is a chosen vessel of Mine to bear My name before Gentiles, kings, and the children of Israel. For I will show him (Paul) how many things he must suffer for My name's sake." (Acts 9:15-16) This is the beginning of Paul being called to be the Apostle to the Gentiles.

Approximately seven or eight years have passed since the day of Pentecost when God poured out His Holy Spirit on the Jews in Jerusalem. In Acts 10 Cornelius' house filled with Gentiles receives the Gospel from the Apostle Peter and were filled with the Holy Spirit as well. Jesus, at several times during His ministry, hinted at this. He heals the Roman Centurion's servant (Matthew 8:5-13) and the daughter of the woman of Syria (Matthew 15:21-28). In John's Gospel, Jesus had to go to Samaria to minister to the woman at the well and then stayed a few more days and preached to the Samaritans. (John 4) We actually do not know how many Gentiles, Jesus ministered to during His three and a half years of ministry.

The Apostle John says this at the end of His Gospel. "And there are also many other things that Jesus did, which if they were written one by one, I suppose that even the world itself could not contain the books that would be written. Amen." (John 21:25)

Even with the Samaritans experiencing the Gospel and the Baptism in the Holy Spirit it was obvious that the Gospel, the good news, was going to reach the Gentiles. Therefore, when Cornelius' friends and probably relatives received the Gospel while Peter preached and then the Baptism in the Holy Spirit, it was certain that God was extending His New Covenant to all the world. Even with God sovereignly moving among the Samaritans in Acts 8 and at Cornelius' house, we must remember that the Jewish believers in Jerusalem are still having problems accepting this fact. Their culture is totally against the Samaritans and the Gentiles and having anything to do with them. Let us look at the revival at Samaria first.

The Samaritan Revival

The revival at Samaria was a result of the Jews who practiced Judaism in Jerusalem persecuting the Jewish believers. All the Jewish believers were "scattered throughout the region of Judea and Samaria, except the apostles…Therefore, those who were scattered went everywhere preaching the word." (Acts 8:1b, 4) This happened around 31 A.D. according to Bible Hub>Timeline>Acts. The next verse says that Philip went down to the city of Samaria and preached Christ to them. Many Biblical scholars believe it was Sychar and they believe this is where Jesus preached in John 4. Before we get into what happened at Samaria during this revival, remember that the Jews have no dealings with the Samaritans. (John 4:9) This is what Blue Letter Bible says about them. "The Samaritans were half-Jew, half-Gentile. This race came about after the Assyrian captivity of the northern kingdom of Israel in 721 B.C. Certain people from the nation of Israel stayed behind. These people intermarried with the Assyrians producing the Samaritans…The Samaritans had their own temple, their own copy of the Torah—the first five books of the Old Testament—and their own religious system. There was an issue among the Jews and the Samaritans as to where the proper place to worship." (Blue Letter

Bible>don_stewart_1319 Who Were the Samaritans?) Thus, one can understand the Samaritan woman in John 4 when she asked Jesus where the proper place was to worship. All of this changed after the Cross of Jesus Christ, when the New Covenant was established.

From this explanation of Samaritans, one must come to the conclusion that the Samaritans were looked down upon by the Jews as Gentiles. Wikpedia.com had these observations about the Samaritans from the Jewish point of view. "They worshipped other gods besides Jehovah. They had their own versions of the Torah and the Talmud. They also believed Mount Gerizim is the original Holy Place of Israel. Therefore, the Jews considered the Samaritans as Gentiles."

Even though Jesus knew what His Jewish people thought about Samaritans, He did not avoid them. In John 4:4 it reads. "But He needed to go through Samaria." Jesus preached and taught in Samaria. There were some who believed in Jesus there. "Now we believe, not because of what you (the Samaritan woman) said, for we have heard for ourselves and know that this is indeed the Christ, the Savior of the world." (John 4:42) One of Jesus main parables (stories) was about a good Samaritan. Evidently, Jesus must have gone through Samaria several times (Luke 17:11).

With all this about the cultural divide between Jews and Samaritans, let us observe what happened in the city of Samaria (probably Sychar) when Philip went there to preach. "Then Philip went down to the city of Samaria and preached Christ to them. And the multitude with one accord heeded the things spoken by Philip, hearing and seeing the miracles which he did. For unclean spirits, crying with a loud voice, came out of many who were possessed; and many who were paralyzed and lame were healed. And there was great joy in the city." (Acts 8:5-8)

Notice that God loved the Samaritans as well as the Jews. God is no respecter of persons. He saved them just like He saved the Jews and now the Samaritans are entering the New Covenant. There is a person among them who has been practicing sorcery. Sorcery is black magic, witchcraft, and the occult. His name is Simon, but if you read all of Acts 8 you will find that he is exposed by Peter. Many in the city had been following Simon, but Peter will draw him out into the open and expose him. Notice this happens after he is saved. "But when they (the Samaritans of the city) believed Philip as he preached the things concerning the kingdom of God and the name of Jesus Christ both men and women were baptized. Then Simon himself also believed; and when he was baptized, he continued with Philip, and was amazed, seeing the miracles and signs that were done." (Acts 8:12-13) As is brought out in Mark's Gospel signs were following Philip's ministry. "And these signs will follow those who believe: In My name they will cast out demons; they will speak with new tongues; they will take up deadly serpents; and if they drink anything deadly, it will by no means hurt them; they will lay hands on the sick, and they will recover." (Mark 16:17-18) Philip was sharing the New Covenant with the Samaritans. He is a good example to follow in the New Testament.

Immediately, when this revival was heard about in Jerusalem, the church in Jerusalem wanted to verify it. They sent two Apostles, Peter and John to Samaria. Even with the fact that the Samaritans had received the Gospel of Jesus Christ, it must have been hard for the Jewish Christians in Jerusalem to accept the fact that the Samaritans had been saved, healed delivered and loved by Jesus Christ. Jesus had extended His New Covenant to them. Jesus is the New Covenant. When they received Him as their Lord and Savior, they received the New Covenant, which meant now they were apart of the Family of God.

Bible.org/Samaritans says this about this revival in Samaria, in which God used Philip to bring many to Jesus. They asked this important question. Why didn't the Samaritans receive the Holy Spirit when they were physically baptized by Philip? "In this context the divine withholding of the Spirit until the arrival of Peter and John, the two primary leaders in the Jerusalem church, is still the Lord's way of confirming to the Apostles that He had indeed extended the invitation of the (Holy) Spirit to the Samaritans and that there should be no division between the Jews and the Samaritans in the church, not between Peter and John and Philip." Bible.org/Samaritans also acknowledged the fact "that there was no love lost between Jews and Samaritans of the first century. This was indeed a move of God, that God had brought about, that went against all racial barriers."

Got Questions?>Acts8-receive-Holy Spirit says this about receiving the Holy Spirit. They believe there are several reasons why God waited until Peter and John got there. "First, it is good to remember the book of Acts is a history of how God started the church. It is the record of the transition between the Old (Mosaic) Covenant and the New Covenant, and much of what we see in Acts relates to that transition. The Samaritans manner of receiving the Spirit should be taken for what it is—an accurate account of what happened in this case...Second, we should note that the Spirit did come upon the Samaritans (Acts 8:14-17) but not until the apostles Peter and John were present before He sent the Holy Spirit upon the Samaritans. 1)Jesus had given Peter the "keys to the Kingdom" (Matthew 16:19). Peter was present—and was the main spokesman—at Pentecost (Acts 2), when the Spirit was given to the Jews. Peter was present in Samaria (Acts 8), when the Spirit was given to the Samaritans. And Peter was present in Cornelius' house (Acts 10) when the Spirit was given to the Gentiles. Jesus used Peter to "open the door" to each of these people groups. 2) The church was to be built on the foundation of the apostles and prophets (Ephesians 2:20). Philip, the Evangelist, had been a deacon in the Jerusalem church, but he was not one of the twelve apostles. Peter and John needed to be in Samaria for the "official" start of the Samaritan church...3) The presence of Peter and John kept the early church unified. Remember there was great animosity between Jews and Samaritans (John 4:9). If the church in Samaria had begun on its own, with no connection to the "Jewish" church, the church in Jerusalem would never have accepted it. The Samaritans were known historically as corrupters of Judaism (John 4:20). So, God made sure that Peter and John, apostles and Jews from Jerusalem, were present to witness the gift of the Spirit given to the Samaritans. The Samaritans were part of the same church that had been started in Jerusalem, and they were filled with the same Spirit (see Galatians 3:28). Their testimony was clear, what happened in Samaria was not a separate religious movement. In this way, God prevented the early church from immediately dividing into different sects."

This was a long quotation. But Got Questions?>Acts 8 gave an honest evaluation of the situation between the Jews and the Samaritans, an interesting insight between the Old Covenant and the New Covenant and finally, a great understanding of the creation of the Church by God in the New Testament era. It is truly a time of transition from the Old Mosaic Covenant to the New Covenant in Jesus Christ.

From what is recorded in Acts 8:14-18, there seems to have been a manifestation of the Holy Spirit especially one that Simon, the sorcer, saw when the Apostles, Peter and John laid hands on the Samaritans. "Then they (Peter and John) laid hands on them, and they received the Holy Spirit. Now when Simon saw that through the laying on of the apostles' hands the Holy Spirit was given, he offered them money." (Acts 8:17-18) Although the Scriptures don't say what manifestation was given by the Holy Spirit, it is certain that there was one because Simon, the Sorcer, saw the manifestation. Simon wanted to buy it from the Apostles, that on whomever he laid hands on they would receive the Holy Spirit. Peter by the Holy Spirit used the gift of discernment to tell where Simon was spiritually. "But Peter said to him (Simon), 'Your money perish with you, because you thought that the gift of God could be purchased with money! You have neither part nor portion in this matter, for your heart is not right in the sight of God. Repent therefore of this your wickedness, and pray God if perhaps the thought of your heart may be forgiven you. For I see that you are poisoned by bitterness and bound by iniquity.'" (Acts 8:20-23) Simon then asked for prayer to escape all that Peter had spoken over him. We don't hear about Simon anymore, but we do know that the manifestation gifts of the Holy Spirit were there since Simon and the Apostles saw them. Peter and John must have returned nearly immediately to Jerusalem, but on the way back home they did preach in many Samaritan villages the gospel. (Acts 8:25) Notice they did not stay to make sure the Samaritans were rooted and grounded in the faith of Jesus Christ. Philip, the Evangelist, has been sent by the Holy Spirit to witness to the Ethiopian. He explains the Gospel to him and Philip baptizes him before he went back to Africa. (Acts 8:26-39) Therefore, there is no one left with the Samaritans. Hopefully, enough of the Gospel was shared with them to keep them established in the faith.

Let me summarize briefly again what happened at Cornelius' house. In Acts 10 we discussed how Cornelius has a vision of an angel of God in his house and he is told to send for Peter in Joppa. At the same time this is happening Peter is having an Open Sheet Revelation from God. There are several reasons why I chose to talk about Peter and the Open Sheet Revelation in which he saw unclean animals. God told him to kill and eat those animals. We need to get the setting established in our minds. Peter was at Simon the Tanner's house in Joppa. Peter was hungry because it was the sixth hour of the day or noon. God showed him unclean animals, creeping things or insects, and birds. All of these according to the Mosaic Law were forbidden to be eaten. We discussed this in chapter 7, the Mosaic Covenant. God told him to kill and eat. Peter recognized it was the Lord telling him these things. (Acts 10:14) Peter had this vision or revelation three times. Three in Scriptures is the number of the Trinity; God in three persons—Father, Son and Holy Spirit. Because the Covenant of Law is so ingrained in Peter, he refuses to eat even though God told him to do so. Then the Lord told Peter that three men were seeking him downstairs at the gate. The Lord told him to go with them doubting nothing. (Acts 10:19-20)

Peter the next day follows these three men to Caesarea, a Gentile city named after Caesar. These men take him to Cornelius' house, a centurion of the Italian Regiment. No self-respecting Jew would enter such a Gentile house. But Peter did because God told him to do so. When he talks to Cornelius, he gives this explanation of the vision or revelation he had from God before he came. "Then he (Peter) said to them (Cornelius and those in his house), "You know how unlawful (the Mosaic Law) it is for a Jewish man to keep company with or go to one of another nation. But God has shown me that I should not call any man common or unclean." (Acts 10:28)

Cornelius then tells Peter and the Jewish people who came with Peter about the vision he had of the angel of God and how the angel told him to send for Peter. (Acts 10:30-33) Then Peter preached the Gospel to the Gentiles at Cornelius' house. This incident occurred approximately seven or eight years after the day of Pentecost, when the one hundred and twenty Jewish people in the upper room were filled with the Holy Spirit and spoke in tongues. (Acts 2:1-4) While Peter is preaching the Gospel, the Holy Spirit falls on Cornelius and all the Gentiles in his house. They are all saved and filled with the Holy Spirit. Then Peter had all of them physically baptized (immersed) in water. Peter went on to stay with them a few days. Notice if you read all of the book of Acts, you will find that like Samaria, Peter and those with him did not stay long with people that are considered Gentiles. The Jews who came with Peter to Cornelius' house are astonished when the Gentiles receive the gift of the Holy Spirit. "And those of the circumcision (the Jews) who believed were astonished, as many as came with Peter, because the gift of the Holy Spirit had been poured out on the Gentiles also. For they heard them speak with tongues and magnify God..." (Acts 10:45-46a) Peter stayed with them a few days. Those were probably days of teaching by the Apostle Peter. Nothing else is said about Cornelius or those in his house after this occasion. It is hard to say whether these Gentiles got anymore teaching. I must say that when referring to Gentiles in the book of Acts, or any other book in the New Testament (Covenant) it is referring to all nations and people who are not of Israel or apart of Judaism. That includes Samaritans as well, even though they were half-Jew and half-Gentile.

That is a brief summary of the events that occurred in Acts 10. But what does all this mean? The first thing we must be aware is that the Gospel of Jesus Christ went to the Jews first. Jesus in instructing His Apostles and disciples said the Gospel of the Kingdom must be preached first to the lost sheep of the House of Israel. This is recorded in Matthew 10:5-8. "These twelve Jesus sent out and commanded them saying, "Do not go into the way of the Gentiles, and do not enter a city of the Samaritans. But go rather to the lost sheep of the house of Israel. And as you go, preach saying, "The Kingdom of heaven is at hand. Heal the sick, cleanse the lepers, raise the dead, cast out demons. Freely you have received, freely give."

Notice after Jesus was crucified and then raised from the dead, He told His Apostles and disciples to wait in Jerusalem for the promised Holy Spirit. They waited in Jerusalem and the Holy Spirit came upon the Apostles and 120 disciples on the day of Pentecost. This outpouring of the Holy Spirit came to the Jews first. All of Judea heard the Gospel for the first seven or eight years. But then in Acts 10, God sees fit to share the Gospel with the Gentiles at Cornelius' house. Jesus hinted about this when He healed the Roman Centurion's servant and, on another occasion, He healed the woman's daughter who was of Syria. Jesus must have gone to Samaria several times and He even shared a parable that was centered around a Samaritan. Even Jesus' disciples wanted to send fire down from Heaven to destroy a Samaritan village because they would not receive Jesus and His passing through their village going to Jerusalem. Jesus rebuked them for that. Jews did not like Samaritans and would have no dealings with them, but Jesus did. These were huge hints that the Son of God cared for all people, even if they were not Jews.

With this second Pentecost happening among Gentiles at Cornelius' house, it was hard for Jews in Jerusalem to accept this. In Acts 11, Peter has to give an explanation when he comes back to Jerusalem. He has to defend his ministry among the Gentiles. The Jewish leadership and believers found fault with going into a Gentile home and after they are born again and filled with the Holy Spirit continuing to fellowship with them. It is evident that the Jewish Christians still believed and practiced the Old Mosaic Covenant, because Paul had not as yet began teaching and writing about the New Covenant. The Apostle Paul in his 14 letters including Hebrews will become the great architect of explaining the New Covenant to the Gentiles as well as the Jews. One has to remember that the New Testament (Covenant) had not been written as yet. Peter did give a good explanation and the Jewish leadership and believers did accept it for a while.

But there are going to be some who want to change that. Let us look at Acts 11:20-21. "But some of them were men from Cyprus and Cyrene, who when they had come to Antioch, spoke to the Hellenist (Jews who spoke Greek), preaching the Lord Jesus. And the hand of the Lord was with them, and a great number believed and turned to the Lord." What is happening is, not only Jews are being saved at Antioch, but also Gentiles and some were Hellenists. The Hellenists were Jews who spoke Greek. This is what Zondervan Pictorial Bible Dictionary, on page 397 says about the Hellenists. "Hellenists, non-Greeks who spoke Greek, a term used especially of Jews who made Greek their tongue, and with it often adopted Greek ideas and practices (Acts 6:1; 9:29) …" The very fact that the Hellenist (Greek speaking Jews) were joining the church at Antioch, did not set well with the Jewish leadership in Jerusalem, who had not left the Old Mosaic Covenant. They decided to send Barnabas there to find out what was going on at the church in Antioch. "Then news of these things came to the ears of the church in Jerusalem, and they sent Barnabas to go as far as Antioch. When he came and saw the grace of God, he was glad, and encouraged them all that with purpose of heart they should continue with the Lord." (Acts 11:22-23)

The Church at Jerusalem

We need to see a few things that are taking place. The first thing is that the Jewish leadership and believers at the church in Jerusalem have not left the Old Mosaic Covenant beliefs and practices. When the Jewish leadership at Jerusalem see these men from Cyprus and Cyrene come to Antioch and preach the Gospel to the Hellenist (Greek speaking Jews) they are alarmed and send Barnabas to find out what these men are sharing. Barnabas upon arriving in Antioch does not see anything wrong, but rather the grace of God has brought many into the fold.

Evidently, Barnabas needs help with this new church at Antioch, therefore, he goes and finds Saul (Paul). They come back to Antioch and they teach at that church for a whole year. Notice this last phrase in Acts 11:26b. "…And the disciples were first called Christians at Antioch." Notice there is not any reference to Judaism or the Mosaic Covenant of Law. From this point on there is a shifting change in emphasis from law to grace. With this change in emphasis from the Covenant of Law to the Covenant of Grace, the Jerusalem church will become alarmed. Among Jewish believers and leaders, not all will agree to this change or emphasis.

Barnabas and Saul (Paul) minister to the church at Antioch for a whole year as was previously stated. During this time, they must have been led by the Holy Spirit to have a fast among the leadership. "Now in the church that was at Antioch there were certain prophets and teachers: Barnabas,

Simeon who was called Niger, Lucius of Cyrene, Manaen who had been brought up with Herod the tetrarch, and Saul (Paul). As they ministered to the Lord and fasted, the Holy Spirit said, "Now separate to Me Barnabas and Saul (Paul) for the work to which I have called them. Then, having fasted and prayed, and laid hands on them, they sent them away." (Acts 13:1-3)

It is during this time of going out that Saul's name is changed to Paul. Paul begins to be the dominant member of the group, as they minister in several Gentile cities. At the end of Acts 14, Paul and Barnabas return to Antioch and report what God has done among the Gentiles. "From there they sailed to Antioch, where they had been commended to the grace of God for the work which they had completed. And when they had come and gathered the church together, they reported all that God had done with them, and that He (God) had opened the door of faith to the Gentiles. So, they stayed there a long time with the disciples." (Acts 14: 26-28) From this one sees that the church at Antioch was composed mostly of Gentile believers.

Paul, The Apostle to the Gentiles

It is possible that during this time, that Paul had his meeting with James, the brother of Jesus and Pastor of the church at Jerusalem, and Peter. It was during that meeting, that it was revealed that Paul was called by God to be the Apostle to the Gentiles and Peter was called to be the Apostle to the Jews. This is recorded in the book of Galatians. "But on the contrary, when they saw that the gospel for the uncircumcised (Gentiles) had been committed to me, as the gospel of the circumcised (Jews) was to Peter (for He (God) who worked effectively in Peter for the apostleship to the circumcised (Jews) also worked effectively in me toward the Gentiles), and when James, Cephas (Peter), and John who seemed to be pillars, perceived the grace that had been given to me, they gave me and Barnabas the right hand of fellowship, that we should go to the Gentiles and they to the circumcised (Jews). They desired only that we should remember the poor, the very thing which I also was eager to do." (Galatians 2:7-10)

This acknowledgement by Peter, James and John, that the Apostle Paul had been sent to the Gentiles is very important. For a crisis is coming in Acts 15 that will decide how the church in Jerusalem really looks at Gentile believers. Even today some Jewish Messianic believers are trying to do the same thing that happened in the book of Acts, wanting Gentile believers to be circumcised and come under the Old Mosaic Covenant of Law.

But before we get into the Jerusalem Conference that happens in Acts 15, we must look at some major events that took place during Paul and Barnabas' first missionary trip. Paul and Barnabas went to several Gentile cities and there were synagogues in these cities where Paul preached the Gospel. They went to a city called Antioch, but it was located in a region called Pisidia. Paul preached in the synagogue there, but notice the reaction of the Jews and Gentiles when he finished preaching. "And when the Jews went out of the synagogue, the Gentiles begged that these words might be preached to them the next sabbath." It seemed the Gentiles were really hungry for the Gospel of Jesus Christ. But some of the Jews were also hungry too. "Now when the congregation had broken up, many of the Jews and devout proselytes followed Paul and Barnabas, who speaking to them, persuaded them to continue in the grace of God." (Acts 13:43) But this hunger of the Jews did not continue. The next sabbath, Paul came back and preached again and this time the Jews were envious of Paul and Barnabas, therefore, they started contradicting them and opposing them. (Acts 13:45-46) Then Paul and Barnabas made this decision. "Then Paul and Barnabas grew bold and said, "It was necessary that the word of God should be spoken to you first; but since you reject it, and judge yourselves unworthy of everlasting life, behold, we turn to the Gentiles. For so the Lord has commanded us. "I have set you to be a light to the Gentiles, that you should be for salvation to the ends of the earth." Now when the Gentiles heard this, they were glad and glorified the word of the Lord. And as many as had been appointed to eternal life believed. And the word of the Lord was being spread throughout all the region." (Acts 13:46-49)

From this point on the Jews in that region stirred up the chief men and women against Paul and Barnabas to the point that they were expelled from that region. Paul and Barnabas were now dealing directly with the Gentiles and sharing the New Covenant of Grace and salvation with them. The Jews followed the same pattern in Lystra and Derbe while the Gentiles received the Gospel of Grace.

In Lystra, God used Paul in healing a crippled man. But then Paul and Barnabas had to stop the crowds from making Paul a god. Then the Jews came and stirred the crowds against Paul. He was stoned nearly to death, but the disciples of the Lord encircled him, prayed for him and he got up and walked back into the city of Lystra. They then returned to all the Gentile churches that had been established in Lystra, Iconium and Antioch in Pisidia strengthening them in the faith. They appointed elders in every church and commended them to the Lord and His grace. They then returned to the church who sent them out at Antioch. (Acts chapters 13 and 14)

Why are you sharing this? This passage shows that Paul had stopped preaching to the Jews and turned his attention and ministry to the Gentiles and establishing Gentile churches in Gentile cities throughout the Roman empire. This is not only a fulfillment of the prophecy by Isaiah that I quoted earlier, but it is a fulfillment of the word spoken over Paul when he was baptized in Acts 9:15-16. Ananias shared this word with Paul as he prayed for him. "But the Lord said to him, "Go for he is a chosen vessel of Mine to bear My name before Gentiles, kings, and the children of Israel. For I will show him how many things he must suffer for My name's sake." God's prophetic word is coming to past. Paul has been directly sharing the Gospel with the Gentiles. This first missionary journey of Paul's was approximately in 48 A.D., 18 years after the day of Pentecost, when the 120 were filled with the Holy Spirit.

The Council at Jerusalem in 48 A.D.

It looks as if everything is happening according to what the Lord Jesus Christ had commanded when He ascended to Heaven. "But you shall receive power when the Holy Spirit has come upon you; and you shall be witnesses to Me in Jerusalem, and in Judea and Samaria, and to the end of the earth." (Acts 1:8) Paul and Barnabas had just finished their first missionary adventure "to the ends of the earth." (Acts 1:8b) It was 48 A.D. (Bible Hub>teaches>Acts) and 18 years after the first Pentecostal revival. The Holy Spirit had fell on all those in the upper room. Of course, the devil is not happy about all this. Paul and Barnabas are back at their home church at Antioch in Syria. They have just returned from Antioch in Pisidia. Some men have come from Judea and are preaching and teaching a new doctrine (teaching). "And certain men came down from Judea and taught the (Gentile) brethren, "Unless you (Gentiles) are circumcised according to the custom of Moses, you cannot be saved." (Acts 15:1) It does not take a rocket scientist to discover what is happening. The devil is trying to bring division between the Jewish believers and the Gentile believers.

Immediately, these men have a confrontation with Paul and Barnabas. Both sides agree that this question must be taken to the Apostles and leadership in Jerusalem. Let us look at what happened next. A major decision about the New Covenant must be decided. Therefore, this is what the brethren did at the church in Antioch. They decided to send Paul and Barnabas along with some others, probably Judaizers (those who practice Judaism even though they believe in Jesus), to Jerusalem.

"Therefore, when Paul and Barnabas had no small descension and dispute with them, they determined that Paul and Barnabas and certain others of them should go up to Jerusalem, to the apostles and elders, about this question. So, being sent on their way by the church, they passed through Phoenicia and Samaria, describing the conversion of the Gentiles; and they caused great joy to all the brethren. And when they had come to Jerusalem, they were received by the church and the apostles and elders; and they reported all things that God had done with them. But some of the sect of the Pharisees who believed rose up, saying, "It is necessary to circumcise them, and to keep the law of Moses." (Acts 15:2-5)

When Paul and Barnabas arrive in Jerusalem, they immediately begin to share how the Gentiles on their first missionary trip have responded to the Gospel of Jesus Christ. One must remember that this missionary trip was after the revival at Cornelius' house in 37 A.D. (Bible

Hub>timeline>Acts>1.htm) This missionary trip occurs eleven years later in 48 A.D. So, now the Gentiles are beginning to organize and have churches of their own. Paul is also considered to be Apostle of the church in Galatia as well as to all the Gentile churches that Paul and Barnabas had established. The Judaizers evidently have been there to cause trouble too. Therefore, this was going to be a monumental conference. This conference would decide whether Gentiles would have to become Jews by being circumcised and whether they would have to obey the law of Moses. Earlier, when Paul had visited Jerusalem with Barnabas before this meeting, Paul was considered to be "the Apostle to the Gentiles." All of this was not known until Paul wrote this letter to the church at Galatia. I lean in the direction that he wrote this letter to the Galatian church while they were at this conference in Jerusalem. One reason I believe this is because in this letter to the church at Galatia, Paul mentions Barnabas being with him in the ministry to the Gentiles. (Galatians 2:7,9) After this conference in Jerusalem Barnabas separates himself from Paul over the issue of Mark, Barnabas' nephew, going with them again on another Missionary trip. (Acts 15:36-41)

In this letter to the church at Galatia Paul also talks about his trouble with Peter at Antioch. He talks about how Peter separates himself from Gentile believers after Jews come to Antioch. This is recorded in Galatians 2:11-16. "But when Peter had come to Antioch, I withstood (opposed) him to his face, because he was to be blamed; for before certain men came from James, he would eat with the Gentiles; but when they came, he withdrew and separated himself, fearing those (Jewish Christians) who were of the circumcision. And the rest of the Jews also played the hypocrite with him, so that even Barnabas was carried away with their hypocrisy. But when I saw that they were not straightforward about the truth of the gospel, I said to Peter before them all, "If you, being a Jew, live in the manner of the Gentiles and not as the Jews, why do you compel Gentiles to live as Jews? We who are Jews by nature, and not sinners of the Gentiles, knowing that a man is not justified by the works of the law but by faith in Jesus Christ, even we have believed in Christ Jesus, that we might be justified by faith in Christ and not by the works of the law, for by the works of the law no flesh shall be justified. But if, while we seek to be justified by Christ, we ourselves also are found sinners, is Christ therefore a minister of sin? Certainly not!" (Galatians 2:11-17)

We could quote the whole passage in Galatians 2, but what Paul has done has shown Peter his hypocrisy and that Peter is trying to come back under the Covenant of Law and still trying to trust Jesus at the same time. It cannot be done. To be saved one must trust Jesus only. Paul is showing Peter, Barnabas and the Jews that they are hypocrites by separating from the Gentiles in the area of eating and fellowship and living in fear of the Jews. Actually, Paul is opening Peter's eyes about the Covenant of Law and the Covenant of Grace. I believe this all happened before this Jerusalem Council takes place and as a result, we will see Peter take his stand with the Gentiles about this matter of circumcision and the Covenant of Moses.

Paul opened Peter's eyes to living by grace and not by the deeds that the law produces. With these examples in the book of Galatians, Paul is giving the Galatian believers examples of believers who come back under the Covenant of Law. Paul in turn had received much revelation knowledge of what happens to people who come back under the Mosaic Covenant. The Judaizers had mixed up the Galatian believers and Paul was endeavoring to straighten them out. Paul had visited some of the area of Galatia before this conference. The cities he visited were Lystra, Derbe, and the cities of Lycanonia. As we shall see, Paul goes back to these cities after the conference with a letter from James, Peter and the elders at Jerusalem.

I shared this from the letter to the Galatians to give you an idea of what Paul believed about the Mosaic Covenant of Law. One does see the change in Peter as he gets up to share at the Jerusalem Council in Acts 15. "So, the apostles and elders came together to consider this matter. And when there had been much dispute, Peter rose up and said to them: "Men and brethren, you know that a good while ago God chose among us, that by my mouth the Gentiles should hear the word of the gospel and believe. So, God, who knows the heart acknowledge (bore witness to) them, by giving them the Holy Spirit just as He did to us, and made no distinction between us and them, purifying their hearts by faith. Now therefore, why do you test God by putting a yoke on the neck of the (Gentile) disciples which neither our fathers nor we were able to bear? But we believe that through the grace of the Lord Jesus Christ we shall be saved in the same manner as they." (Acts 15:6-11)

Notice Peter has changed his attitude about law and grace. No doubt that confrontation with Paul earlier at Antioch had opened his eyes to the grace of God. Therefore, he sided with Paul and Barnabas and the Gentile believers. This would not be the only time that the New Covenant of Grace would be challenged. We shall see later that the church at Jerusalem later in the book of Acts would again slip back under the law. Today, this is still a problem with believers and churches here in America and around the world. Individuals after they are once saved by the grace of God, have trouble living out that salvation by grace through faith. "For by grace you have been saved through faith, and that not of yourselves; it is the gift of God, not of works, lest anyone should boast." (Ephesians 2:8-9)

Let us state here unequivocally, that one cannot live under both the Mosaic Covenant and the New Covenant simultaneously. One may have given his or her heart and life to Jesus and still try to live under the Mosaic Covenant. But in the end, one will become frustrated and confused because of the sin principle talked about in Romans 7 will surface and defeat them in the doing of the law. "For we know that the law is spiritual but I am carnal sold under sin. For what I am doing, I do not understand. For what I will to do (the Law), that I do not practice; but what I hate (sin principle), that I do...For I know that in me (that is in my flesh) nothing good dwells; for to will is present with me, but how to perform what is good I do not find...For I delight in the Law of God according to the inward man. But I see another law (sin principle) in my members, warring against the law of my mind, and bringing me into captivity to the law of sin which is in my members. O wretched man that I am! Who will deliver me from this body of death? I thank God—through Jesus Christ our Lord! So then, with the mind I myself serve the law of God, but with the flesh the law of sin." (Romans 7:14-15; 18; 22-25)

This is Paul's personal testimony about law and grace. As long as he put his faith and trust in the law, inevitably it resulted in Paul disobeying the law and committing a sin. But then Paul had a revelation of Jesus Christ and Jesus freed him from putting his trust in the law. He found himself putting his faith in Jesus Christ. Then as he followed Jesus Christ placing all his confidence in Jesus Christ, he automatically obeyed the law of God in the inward man. How is that possible? The Spirit of Jesus Christ will not disobey God's law. Or to put it another way, the Spirit of Jesus Christ will never lead a person into sin.

One of the errors of our thinking is that the Law of God is going to save sinful man. But the law could never save sinful mankind. Listen to what Paul says in Galatians 2:16. "…knowing that a man is not justified (saved) by the works of the law but by faith in Jesus Christ, even we have believed In Christ Jesus that we might be justified (saved) by faith in Christ and not by the works of the law; for by the works of the law no flesh shall be justified (saved)." The law cannot save us from sin, only Jesus can do that.

We have taken another look at the New Covenant or as some say the Covenant of Grace. The reason it is called the Covenant of Grace is because it is not based on man or man's ability to save himself. It is based on the finished work of Jesus Christ on the Cross and His resurrection from the dead. This was what Paul and Barnabas was preaching and teaching. But then the Judaizers (law keepers) who had also been saved by grace through faith, now wanted everyone to return to the law and be circumcised and keep the law of Moses. What all this amounted to was that the Gentile believers would become Jews—proselyte Jews. Peter was telling them, that it was too much of a burden or load to place on the Gentile believers. Peter ended up telling them, that even their Jewish forefathers were not able to completely obey the law of Moses and that God, Himself, had not told them to place the Gentiles under the Covenant of Law.

After hearing from the Apostle Peter and his stand with the Apostle Paul and Barnabas, immediately Paul and Barnabas get up and begin to share about the miracles, wonders and the many who have been miraculously saved by the Holy Spirit among the Gentiles. This is recorded in Acts

15:12. “Then all the multitude kept silent and listened to Barnabas and Paul declaring how many miracles and wonders God had worked through them among the Gentiles.” Notice this all was done without any mention of circumcision or the Covenant of the Mosaic Law. To this point no one had expressed to the Gentile believers that they needed to be circumcised and come under the Law of Moses. The church at Antioch, Paul and Barnabas' home church, was a mixed church. There were Jews and Gentiles in the same church. No one there had said anything about the Gentiles being circumcised or their coming under the Mosaic Covenant of Law. This only came up when the Judaizers came and began to share that in order to be saved the Gentiles would have to be circumcised and come under the Law of Moses. This was a ploy of the devil to bring division between the Jews and the Gentiles.

The last speaker at the Jerusalem Conference was the Pastor of the church at Jerusalem, James the half- brother of Jesus. He was highly respected by both Jews and Gentiles. Evidently, Jesus had appeared to him privately after He arose from the dead. In 1 Corinthians 15:7 Paul shares that appearing of Jesus to James. “After that He (Jesus) was seen by James, then by all the apostles.” The Apostle Paul had great respect for James as well as all the other Apostles. Everyone must have been extremely quiet when James spoke.

“And after they had become silent, James answered, saying, “Men and brethren, listen to me: “Simon (Peter) has declared how God at the first visited the Gentiles to take out of them a people for his name. And with this the words of the prophets agree, just as it is written: After this I will return and will rebuild the tabernacle of David which has fallen down. I will rebuild its ruins, and I will set it up. So that the rest of mankind may seek the Lord, even all the Gentiles who are called by My name, Says the Lord who does all these things.” (Amos 9:11-12) Known to God from eternity are all His works. Therefore, I judge that we should not trouble those from among the Gentiles who are turning to God, but that we write to them to abstain from things polluted by idols, from sexual immorality, from things strangled and from blood. For Moses has had throughout many generations those who preach him in every city, being read in the synagogues every Sabbath." (Acts 15:12-21)

The Four Decrees by the Church at Jerusalem

I quoted all of James' message at the Jerusalem council, so you could get a clear picture of where he stood concerning the Gentiles coming into the church. He names four things that James and the Jewish Apostles, Elders, and leadership count important that Gentiles need to abstain from if they are going to remain in fellowship with the Jewish believers. James doesn't want them to concern themselves about circumcision or the Mosaic Covenant of Law, but he does want them to stay away from these four things he mentioned in his address. James is asking for a letter to be written to them clarifying everything to the Gentiles.

Before we get into that letter that was sent to the Gentiles and who delivered it to the Gentiles, I want you to hear what the late Dr. C.I. Scofield says about this decision at the Jerusalem Conference. He believes that this is a very important decision that was made by the Jewish brethren, Apostles and Elders at the church in Jerusalem. "…It gives the divine purpose for the age (the age of grace), and for the beginning of the next. The taking out from among the Gentiles of a people for His name, the distinctive work of the present or church age. The church is the ecclesia—the "called-out assembly." Precisely this has been in progress since Pentecost. The Gospel has never anywhere converted all, but everywhere has called out some…The scope of this decision goes far beyond the mere question of circumcision. The whole question of the relation of the law to Gentile believers had been put in issue (Acts 15:5), and the exemption is declared in the decision (Acts 15:19,24). The decision might be otherwise stated in the terms of Romans 6:14. "Ye (you) are not under the law, but under grace." Gentile believers were to show grace by abstaining from the practices offensive to godly Jews. (Acts 15:20, 21, 28, 29; cf. Romans 14:12-17; 1 Corinthians 8:1-13)." (The First Scofield Bible, by Dr. C.I. Scofield, pages 1169-1170)

The late Dr. Scofield, an elder Christian statesman of the past, defines this moment in Christian History as one that extended grace from the Jewish brethren to the Gentile brethren. In his words, they are exempted from becoming Jews, therefore they do not have to be circumcised nor obey the Mosaic Covenant of Law. The Apostle James did mark out some practices from which the Gentile believers should abstain. They should abstain from things offered to idols, from sexual immorality, from animals strangled and from tasting or drinking blood. If the Gentile believers did practice these things then it would be a hindrance in fellowshipping with Jewish believers.

The Matthew Henry Commentary, Volume 6, Acts to Revelation, page 193 gives a synopsis of the Apostle James, the half-brother of Jesus. By the way, the book of Acts in this commentary was the last book that Matthew Henry wrote before he passed away. "He (James) gives his advice what was to be done in the present case, as the matter now stood with reference to the Gentiles (Acts 15:19)...Now his (James) advice is, (1) That circumcision and the observance of the ceremonial law be by no means imposed upon the Gentile converts: no, not so much as recommended nor mentioned to them..." Now this was the positive side. James did not think it wise to circumcise the Gentiles or to force the law of Moses on them.

But the Jewish brethren had some things which they wished they would abstain. Matthew Henry brings these up on page 194 of the same commentary. "...But the Jews who were willing to think the worst of those they did not like, suggested that there were things in which the Gentiles, even after conversion, allowed themselves, and the apostles of the Gentiles (Paul) connived at it. Now, to obviate this suggestion, and to leave no room for this calumny, James advises that, beside the private admonitions which are given them by their ministers they should be publicly warned to abstain from pollutions of idols and fornication—that herein they should be very circumspect, and should avoid all appearances of these two evils, which would be in so particular a manner offensive to the Jews. (2) From things strangled, and from blood, which, though not evil in themselves, as the other two, nor designed to be always abstained from, as those were, had been forbidden by the precepts of Noah (Genesis 9:4) before the giving of the law of Moses; and the Jews had a great dislike of them, and to all those that took a liberty to use them; and therefore, to avoid giving offense, let the Gentile converts abridge themselves of their liberty herein: 1 Corinthians 8:9,13…"

This brings us to an astute review of James, the Lord's brother, by Dr. Richard Longenecker in the Zondervan NIV Bible Commentary, Volume 2, New Testament, page 464-465. You must have a clear picture of the Apostle James, our Lord's half-brother in order to understand what he said at the Jerusalem Council. "James, the Lord's brother, presided at the Jerusalem Council. He was ascetic (self-disciplined) and scrupulous (conscientious) in keeping the law. The Judaizers within the church looked to him for support, knowing both his legal qualifications and his personal qualities. But while rigorous and scrupulous in his personal practice of his faith, James was more broadminded than many of his followers. After calling the council to order by using the formal mode of address," Men, brothers," he went on to sum up the emerging view of the council in a way that linked it to what had already been said."

Most Biblical scholars believe that Peter in the beginning was the under shepherd of the Jerusalem church from the day of Pentecost when the Holy Spirit fell on the Jewish believers. But later in the 30s A.D., James began to emerge as the Pastor of the Jerusalem church. That is why he spoke last at the Council. The Judaizers respected him as well as those who leaned toward the Gentile position. James actually at this meeting brought both sides together.

The Zondervan NIV Commentary, The New Testament, Volume 2, on page 464 shows how James brought the two opposing sides together. The Jewish leaders who were called Judaizers, even though they had been saved by the Lord Jesus and were baptized in the Holy Spirit, still leaned toward Judaism. This is the summary that The Zondervan NIV Commentary gives. "In summing up, James made no reference to Paul and Barnabas' report, probably more for political reasons than any other principle. After all, it was the work of Paul and Barnabas that was on trial, and James wanted to win his entire audience to the position he believed to be right without causing needless offense. Therefore, he begun by reminding the council of Peter's testimony and went on to show how he felt about the question at issue by speaking of believing Gentiles as a people whom God had taken "for Himself"—thus (1) applying to Gentile Christians a designation formerly used of Israel alone, and (2) agreeing with Peter that in the conversion of Cornelius God, Himself, had taken the initiative for direct Gentile ministry." (page 464 verse 14)

From this speech by James at the Jerusalem Council, one can see he does not want to bother the Gentile Christians with the Covenant of Law. James in this speech takes the position, that this is a fulfillment of prophecy that Isaiah and Amos had talked about a thousand or more years before Jesus came and the church was established. This is what is meant by the quote from Amos 9:11-12. "On that day I will raise up the tabernacle of David which has fallen down, and repair its damages; I will raise up its ruins, and rebuild it as in the days of old; That they may possess the remnant of Edom, and all the Gentiles who are called by My name. Says the Lord who was doing this thing." According to James this is a fulfillment of prophecy. The Gentiles calling on the Lord is in fulfillment of what Amos said and thus should not be challenged by any of the Jewish leadership or the Judaizers. James sides with Peter, Paul and Barnabas because of this. This is a major contribution by James in this situation.

Before we come to a final word about James' speech, let us look at Acts 15:18. "Known to God from eternity are all His works." Some Biblical scholars find this statement by James hard to interpret. The Zondervan NIV Commentary, New Testament, Volume 2, page 465 interprets it this way. "It seems better, however, to interpret the words here as a comment by James to this effect. We cannot be in opposition to the express will of God, as evidenced by Peter's testimony and the prophet's words—but only God, Himself, knows for certain how everything fits together and is to be fully understood."

James was not willing to question why God did things the way He did. The Gentiles had accepted Jesus as their Lord and Savior and they had received the Holy Spirit making them apart of the New Covenant relationship with God. James knowing that it was God who brought this about, he could not go against it. However, James believed there were some limits that must be put on the Gentiles, if they were to have fellowship with the Jewish Christians. Therefore, he put these stipulations on that fellowship between Gentiles and Jews. "Therefore, I judge that we should not trouble those from among the Gentiles who are turning to God, but that we write to them to abstain from things polluted by idols, from sexual immorality, from things strangled, and from blood." (Acts 15:19-20)

I agree with The Zondervan NIV Commentary, Volume 2, New Testament, page 465, when they state that the Apostle James did not agree with Paul and Barnabas about all their teaching on the New Covenant to the Gentiles. "He (James) may have not been prepared to endorse openly all the details of Paul's Gentile policy. Certainly, there is no indication that he expected the Jerusalem church to do that. But he could not be in opposition to the express will of God, and therefore his advice was that Jewish Christianity should not take any stance against the promotion of the Gentile mission. In so concluding, he (James) swept aside the obstacles that had risen to Paul's Gentile mission among believers at Jerusalem and left it free for further advances within the (Roman) empire."

James is giving practical advice to both Jew and Gentile Christians about the best way to have fellowship. "...the question of fellowship between Jews and Gentiles in the church and for tolerance for the scruples of others—James' advice was that a letter to be written to the Gentile Christians. This letter should request them to abstain "from food polluted by idols, from sexual immorality, from the meat if strangled animals and from blood." These prohibitions have often been views as a compromise between two warring parties, which nullified the effect of James' earlier words and made the decision of the Jerusalem Council unacceptable to Paul. But in reality, they should be viewed not as dealing with the principle issue of the council but as meeting certain practical issues...To sum up, we may say that two types of "necessary" questions were raised at the Jerusalem Council. The first had to do with the theological necessity of circumcision and the Jewish law for salvation and that was rejected. The second had to do with the practical necessity of Gentile Christians to abstain from certain practices for the sake of Jewish-Gentile fellowship in the church and the Jewish Christian mission throughout the Diaspora and that was approved." (The Zondervan NIV Commentary, Volume 2, New Testament, page 465)

A letter was written to all Gentile believers and Gentile churches. Usually, Gentile churches had both Jewish believers and Gentile believers in them at this time. This letter was composed and written in 48 A.D. Before we look at the letter that was composed by the Jewish Apostles, Jewish Elders and Jewish believers, let us consider this fact that this letter is not the New Covenant. Jesus Christ is the New Covenant that you and I have entered into when He saved us and made us a part of His Bride, the Church. We are a part of Him as stated in 1 Corinthians 12:12-13. "For as the body is one and has many members, but all the members of that one body, being many, are one body, so also is Christ. For by one (Holy) Spirit we were all baptized into one body—whether Jews or Greeks, whether slaves or free—and have all been made to drink into one (Holy) Spirit."

Jesus Christ fulfilled the Old Mosaic Covenant of Law by living a perfect life on earth for thirty-three and a half years and then offering Himself as our Sacrifice of Himself for us once and for all. As John the Baptist said when he saw Jesus for the first time, "Behold! The Lamb of God Who takes away the sin of the world." (John 1:29b) Once and for all Jesus Christ, God's only Son, took away our sins forever. "…so, Christ was offered once to bear the sins of many. To those who eagerly wait for Him (Jesus), He will appear the second time, a part from sin for salvation." (Hebrews 9:28) "But this Man (Jesus Christ), after He (Jesus) had offered one sacrifice for sins forever, sat down at the right hand of God, from that time waiting till His enemies are made His footstool. For by one offering, He (Jesus) has perfected those who are being sanctified." (Hebrews 10:12-14)

What can one add to Jesus' sacrifice? What can one add to Jesus' salvation? What can one add to the New Covenant, which is Jesus Christ?

It is forever full and complete in Him. Therefore, Jesus did away with the Old Mosaic Covenant of Law with one sacrifice. Now He has brought in the New Covenant by the same sacrifice at Calvary.

Paul says it this way in 2 Corinthians 5:17. "Therefore, if anyone is in Christ, he is a new creation; old things (the Old Covenant of law) have passed away; behold, all things (the New Covenant of Grace) have become new." Throughout Paul's letters he is describing and defining the New Covenant. In Romans 5:12-21, Paul describes what happened under Adam—sin, death, condemnation, judgment and disobedience. Then Paul goes on to describe what happens now that we are in Christ—grace, justification, righteousness, obedience and eternal life. Thus, one begins to understand the free gift of God through Jesus Christ. We will talk more later about this New Covenant we have entered into.

Therefore, let me say again that this letter that the Jewish Apostles, Jewish Elders, and Jewish believers composed at the church in Jerusalem is not the New Covenant. James and the Jewish brethren there added these instructions so that the Jewish brethren could have fellowship with the Gentile brethren throughout that area of the world, commonly known as Judea. Outside of Judea there were towns and cities in which Paul started or would start Gentile churches. Usually there were Jewish believers who would attend those churches. According to James and the others Jewish brothers in Jerusalem these areas would offend Jewish believers. Although James did not want to bring Gentile believers under the Covenant of Law, circumcise them, and make them follow all the dietary laws the Jews were under, he did want them to see that some of their life style and practices were offensive to Jewish Christians.

Let us now look at the letter that James and the Jewish brethren composed. "They (the Jewish leadership in Jerusalem) wrote this letter by them:

"The (Jewish) Apostles, the (Jewish) elders, and the (Jewish)brethren, To the brethren who are of the Gentiles in Antioch, Syria, and Cilicia: Greetings, Since we have heard that some who went out from us have troubled you with words, unsettling your souls, saying, 'You must be circumcised and keep the law'—to whom we gave no such commandment—It seemed good to us, being assembled with one accord to send chosen men to you with our beloved Barnabas and Paul, men who have risked their lives for the name of our Lord Jesus Christ. We have therefore sent Judas and Silas, who will also report the same things by word of mouth. For it seemed good to the Holy Spirit and to us, to lay upon you no greater burden than these necessary things: that you abstain from things offered to idols, from blood, from things strangled, and from sexual immorality. If you keep yourselves from these you will do well. Farewell." (Acts 15:21-29)

Idolatry, eating animals strangled, partaking of blood, and sexual immorality or commonly called fornication and adultery were common in cities like Corinth, Ephesus, and the surrounding areas around Judea. These were the areas of restraint that the Jewish brethren wanted them to practice. It is no wonder that they admonished the Gentile believers not to partake of these sinful practices. Notice they said they did not send the Judaizers to circumcise them or to bring them under the Mosaic Law. All of these admonitions were agreed upon by all the Jewish Apostles, Jewish Elders, and Jewish brothers in Jerusalem including Paul and Barnabas. At that time Paul was considered to be "the Apostle to the Gentiles."

Let us see if Paul, Barnabas, Judas and Silas obeyed the church at Jerusalem and delivered the letter to the Gentile churches. One must remember that these churches were filled with Jewish and Gentile believers. The first church they went to was Antioch, Paul and Barnabas' home church. This is the church that sent Paul and Barnabas out as missionaries or ambassadors for Jesus Christ. "So, when they were sent off, they came to Antioch (in Syria), and when they had gathered the multitude together, they delivered the letter. When they had read it, they rejoiced over its encouragement. Now Judas and Silas, themselves being prophets also, exhorted the brethren with many words and strengthened them." (Acts 15:30-32) The fact that the Gentile believers did not have to be circumcised and they did not have to follow the Old Mosaic Covenant of Law was an encouragement to them. Let me state at this point, that Paul the Apostle had received much revelation knowledge of the New Covenant and what the New Covenant was and is; it is Jesus Christ. The Apostle James and the Apostle Peter had not received as clear an understanding of the New Covenant that Paul had. James and Peter seemed to stay in the realm of the Covenant of Law and you can especially see this in how they acted toward Paul. The Apostle John had a great revelation of Jesus Christ, as the New Covenant, and one can tell that by the Gospel he wrote under the inspiration of the Holy Spirit. His epistles and the book of Revelation shows his further spiritual understanding of the New Covenant. Paul and John's writings revolve around the Lord Jesus Christ, who is the New Covenant.

Let us now look at the four restraints that the church at Jerusalem placed on Gentile believers. The first one we will look at is that of eating or drinking blood. "This condition call "haemochromatosis" can cause a wide variety of diseases and problems, including liver damage, buildup of fluids in the lungs, dehydration, low blood sugar, and nervous disorders…" (Is it Safe to Drink Blood—Live Science>15899) Also, God told the Jewish people not to eat and drink blood. "For the life of the flesh is in the blood, and I have given It to you upon the altar to make atonement for your souls; for it is the blood that makes atonement for the soul. Therefore, I said to the children of Israel, No one among you shall eat blood, nor shalt any stranger who sojourn among you eat blood." (Leviticus 17:11-12)

Eating animals that are strangled is the next restraint placed on Gentile believers. This is considered unhealthy because of the tension it places the animal in. As a result, according to sciene the animal loses its vitamin value. This edict or rule was considered along with the edict or rule about eating blood. Both were forbidden by God. "You shall not eat anything that dies of itself; you may give it to the alien who is within your gates, that he may eat it, or you may sell it to a foreigner, for you are a holy people to the Lord your God. You shall not boil a goat in its mother's milk." (Deuteronomy 14:21) These two are lumped together because they cause health concerns. We do well to heed the warnings here by God to eat meat that is properly bled out and prepared.

The other two restraints that the Jewish leadership were putting on Gentile believers and Gentile churches actually come from the Ten Commandments. The first one is about idolatry and relates to the first Commandment of God. "You shall have no other gods before Me." (Exodus 20:3) To think logically, how can one ask the Lord Jesus Christ into your heart and then worship something or someone else as well. One cannot. If you have given your heart and life to Jesus Christ, you cannot worship anything or anyone else. What the Apostle James and the brethren at the church at Jerusalem were asking was that one should not eat any food or meat that had been offered to an idol. "A new convert (to Jesus) should not eat food sacrificed to idols, because it will defile the conscience. Having left the pagan practices behind, they should not return to them…No Christian should eat food with an unbeliever if he (or she) knows it has been sacrificed to idols." (Reformed Health.net 7. What does it mean?) This means one is returning to his or her old life style of idolatry and eating things sacrificed to idols. Again, it must be said that Gentile Christians should refrain from this practice.

The final edict or rule was to abstain from sexual immorality. If one says that he or she is a Christian and yet is living an immoral life with another, the witness and testimony of Jesus Christ will suffer as a result. This was and is a violation of the seventh Commandment of the Ten Commandments. "You shall not commit adultery." (Exodus 20:14) Any sexual misconduct falls under this commandment. Although, the word "sexual misconduct" is also translated fornication. This was a prevalent sin during the New Testament era and still is today. This was especially true of the Gentiles during this time. The Apostle James and the Jewish leadership were hoping this edict (rule/decree) would change that among Gentile believers. One only had to look at the church at Corinth and the church at Ephesus to see why they wrote this edict. People in these two cities, Corinth and Ephesus, often practiced sexual immorality and justified it by saying they were doing it with prostitutes of the temple gods. Becoming a born-again believer meant you left those practices. Therefore, this edict or rule should have been practiced by Gentile Christians with the aid of the Holy Spirit.

One can see why the Apostle James and the Jewish leadership at Jerusalem were wanting this letter sent to the churches that Paul and Barnabas had established with the aid of the Holy Spirit. Paul and Barnabas not only brought the letter from the Jewish leadership in Jerusalem to the church at Antioch, their home church but later, Paul and Silas brought this letter to the other churches that Paul and Barnabas had started. Therefore, the edicts were delivered to all the churches. This is brought out in Acts 16:4-5. "And as they went through the cities, they delivered to them the decrees to keep, which were determined by the apostles and elders at Jerusalem. So, the churches were strengthened in the faith and increased in numbers daily."

Since, Paul was the "Apostle to the Gentiles" it was important for him, Silas, and Timothy to deliver the letter personally. Reverend Ronald Kosor in his book, Unveiling the New Covenant, page 90, defines the word "decree used in Acts 16:4. "Decree—an edict; an order or law; a predetermined purpose, a judicial decision; an authoritative order having a legal force." Rev. Kosor went on to define the word "abstain." "abstain: to hold oneself from, invariably, from acts of evil." Rev. Kosor goes on to share some timely information that we would do well to consider in our study of the New Covenant. "Always keep in mind that the New Covenant as we know it had not yet been compiled. There were many questions, decisions, and issues that the early church faced for which the apostles had to seek the Holy Spirit's guidance. The answers to these questions were written in the form of letters (Paul's Epistles, John's Epistles, Peter's Epistles, James' single Epistle, and Jude's single Epistle) to each area where there were churches. These must have been copied over and over, and circulated among the churches to give wisdom, guidance, and direction." (Unveiling the New Covenant, page 91)

Paul's Revelation of the New Covenant

The Apostle Paul had probably the clearest revelation of the New Covenant and understood what Jesus was establishing in the church as the New Covenant. This Covenant would change a person and is probably defined in a clearer manifestation in Romans chapters 6,7, and 8, 1

Corinthians chapters 1,2 and 3, 2 Corinthians chapter 3 and in Hebrews chapters 7,8,9 and 10. It would be of great benefit to each New Testament (Covenant) believer if he or she would do a verse by verse study of these chapters. Although, we will look at the differences between the Old Testament (Covenant) and the New Testament (Covenant), one must read about these differences and ask the Holy Spirit to make it a reality in one's life. One must have a revelation of Jesus Christ and allow that revelation to change one's life. Otherwise, you are getting second hand information and all that results in is head knowledge.

That being said, let us look first at Romans chapters 6, 7, and 8. Notice in Romans 6:6 that our old man is declared dead. This is the part of us that wants to sin. "...knowing this, that our old man (the Adamic nature) was crucified with Him (Jesus), that the body of sin might be done away with, that we should no longer be slaves of sin." (Romans 6:6) This is a progressive Spirit-revealed knowledge. It is that Adamic nature that bucks at obeying the Covenant of Law. Then down in verses 7-9 we see that we are raised up with Jesus when He arose from the dead and thus, we are freed from sin. "For he (us) who has died has been freed from sin. Now if we died with Christ, we believe that we shall also live with Him, knowing that Christ, having been raised from the dead, dies no more. Death no longer has dominion over Him." Therefore, sin and death no longer has dominion over us. We are a part of Jesus, since God placed us in Christ (1 Corinthians 1:30). Paul goes onto share in this passage in verse 10 that we are now living unto God. "For the death, that He died, He died to sin (the nature of sin) once for all, but the life that He lives, He lives to God." We are now living unto God because we have been united with Him. This all took place at the Cross, the day that Jesus died. When Jesus said, "It is finished." (John 19:30), He was saying that the Old Mosaic Covenant of Law was finished in Him that day. That Old Covenant only produces sin and death. It cannot produce eternal life. Under the New Covenant which is Jesus Christ, He gives us eternal life and the right to become sons and daughters of God. That is why in Romans 6:11 Paul makes this statement. "Likewise, you also, reckon (consider) yourselves to be dead indeed to sin (the sin nature), but alive to God in Christ Jesus our Lord." Reckon is an accounting term that one uses when one considers all the facts. We are to consider all the spiritual facts and realize that we died with Jesus, we were buried with Him and now we live to God through Jesus. At the end of this chapter, Paul sums it up this way. "For the wages of sin is death, but the (free) gift of God is eternal life in Christ Jesus our Lord." (Romans 6:23) We are in Jesus; thus, we have eternal life. This is all apart of the New Covenant we have in Christ Jesus.

In Romans 7:1-6 we see both the Old Covenant and the New Covenant as husbands to a woman. One husband must die before the other husband can be legally married to her. The first husband is the Old Covenant of Law. But in Romans 7:4 Paul states the situation that takes place, so we are allowed to marry our new husband, Jesus Christ. "Therefore, my brethren, you also have become to dead to the (husband—the Covenant of law) through the body of Christ that we should be married to another (Jesus Christ—the New Covenant), even to Him (Jesus) who was raised from the dead that we should bear fruit to God." As I have said before, Jesus Christ is the New Covenant and that is why we are married to Him. Paul sums it all up in Romans 7:6. "But now we have been delivered from the (Covenant of) law, having died to what we were held by, so that we should serve in the newness of the Spirit and not in the oldness of the letter."

The Apostle Paul goes on to state in the latter part of Romans 7 how it is impossible to serve the Covenant Law of God. It brings a Gentile believer as well as a Jewish believer into frustration and confusion which may lead them to give up the race altogether. Evidently, Paul went through this frustration and was therefore able to share his conclusions with the Roman Christians whether they were Jew or Gentile. Sin (the old nature) interacts with the Covenant of law as Paul states in this chapter and brings one into bondage to the law of sin and death. But then Paul had a revelation of Jesus Christ which delivered him from the Covenant of Law. This was possible through the teaching of the Holy Spirit and not Paul's will power. Listen to Paul's conclusions in Romans 7:23 to Romans 8:1. "But I see another law (the Covenant of law) in my members warring against the law (carnal reasonings) of my mind, and bringing me into captivity to the law of sin in my members. O wretched man that I am! Who will deliver me from the body of this death? I thank God—through Jesus Christ our Lord!

So then, with the mind I myself serve the law of God, but with the flesh the law of sin. There is therefore now no condemnation to those who are in Christ Jesus, who do not walk according to the flesh, but according to the Spirit."

This leads us to Romans 8 where Paul describes the walk in the Spirit. The Holy Spirit is the One Who guides us through this maze leading us every step of the way. With a revelation of Jesus Christ and walking in the Holy Spirit we are guided from one victory to the next victory. There is the possibility of becoming a "carnal Christian" if we begin to follow the dictates of the flesh. That will be a constant battle as is brought out in Romans 8:1-11. Paul tells us what has constantly helped him to lead the Spirit-filled life. This is found in Romans 8:2-6. "For the law of the (Holy) Spirit of life in Christ Jesus has made me free from the law of sin and death." The word "made" is the Greek word eleuthero which means deliver, make free. This is something the Spirit of God does for us. "For what the (Covenant of) law could not do in that it was weak through the flesh (our flesh), God did by sending His own Son (Jesus) in the likeness of sinful flesh(just like ours), on account of sin (the sin nature): He (God) condemned sin (our sinful nature) in the flesh, that the righteous requirement of the law (Covenant of law) might be fulfilled in us who do not walk according to the flesh but according to the Spirit." We must choose to walk according to the Spirit. We have a free will and we must choose to walk according to what the Spirit of God tells us to do. "For those who live according to the flesh set their minds on the things of the flesh, but those who live according to the Spirit, the things of the Spirit. For to be carnally minded is death, but to be spiritually minded is life and peace." God does not dictate to us like a dictator, but He allows the Spirit of God to teach us and we must choose to walk in the Spirit and to set our minds on spiritual things which brings life and peace to us.

The latter verses in Romans 8 under this New Covenant relationship brings us into a relationship with our Heavenly Father, where He adopts us into His Family. As we put to death the deeds of the flesh and choose to be led by the Spirit of God, the Spirit of Adoption begins to rule and reign in our lives and we become more and more like our Heavenly Father.

(Romans 8:12-17) We know that the Holy Spirit is constantly interceding for us and our Father is telling us what is going to happen next on our journey to the Father's House. We know of a certainty that we are loved by God and we want to love Him more and more.

Moving onto 2 Corinthians 3, Paul begins comparing the Old Covenant with the New Covenant. "...you are manifestly an epistle of Christ, ministered by us, written not with ink (the Old Covenant was written with ink) but by the Spirit of the living God, not on tablets of stone (the Old Covenant and in particular the Ten Commandments was written on stone) but tablets of flesh (God by His Spirit writing the word on our hearts) that is of the heart."

As you can see there are word pictures from the Old Testament (Covenant). From this one verse one can see comparisons from the Old Covenant to the New Covenant. Rev. Kosor gives a good example of this on page 56 in his book, Unveiling the New Covenant. "A good example of this is Adam. His creation and life are an example of "a type of Him who is to come." He is a "type" of Christ. The "shadow" is the comparison between Adam and Christ. Both entered the world through a special act of God as sinless man. Adam is the head of the old creation. Christ is the head of the new creation...Every book of the Old Covenant (Testament) contains a type and shadow of Jesus Christ. If it did not, Christ could not be "The Word" John spoke of in John 1:(1). Some aspects of Jesus is represented in every book of the Bible."

Therefore, Paul is using the language of the Old Testament (Covenant) to compare with the language of the New Testament (Covenant). He does this again in 2 Corinthians 3:5-8. "Not that we are sufficient of ourselves to think of anything as being from ourselves, but our sufficiency is from God who also made us sufficient as ministers of the new covenant not of the letter (of the law) kills, but the (Holy) Spirit gives life. But if the ministry of death, written and engraved on stones (the Old Covenant—the Ten Commandments) was glorious, so that the children of Israel could not look steadily at the face of Moses because of the glory of his countenance, which glory (the Old Covenant) was passing away, how will the ministry of the (Holy) Spirit (the New Covenant) be more glorious."

The Holy Spirit brings life whereas the law of God, engraved on stones when it is applied by the letter of the law brings death. The Apostle Paul calls the law, the Ten Commandments apart of the Old Covenant a ministry of death. This was a radical change especially to New Testament (Covenant) Jewish believers. This is what Reverend Kosor says about it on page 57 of his book, Unveiling the New Covenant. "Here we find the Old Covenant described as the ministry of death. These were and are very strong words for the Apostle (Paul) to use to discuss the Old Covenant. Please remember at that time, the New Covenant had not been fully written or compiled as we know it today. These views we now accept as scripture were merely letters at that time, shared among the brethren. To many, the teachings were heresy, and it is why the apostles and prophets were so severely treated. These apostles of Jesus Christ were "messing" with the teaching that were centuries old. They were presenting a new way of thinking, a ministry of the Spirit—a ministry of life—which could be far more glorious than the old."

Rev. Kosor presents some solid points that need to be considered. A lot has to do with the misconception by Christians today, that the New Testament (Covenant) had already been written right after Jesus Christ's resurrection and ascension to glory. The Gospels and the book of Acts were not written until 40 to 140 A.D. The letters that the Apostle Paul wrote were not written until 50 to 62 A.D. The Apostle Paul's letters identified and clarified the New Covenant that God was making with all people whether they were Jew or Gentile. Paul was writing down the revelation of the New Covenant that God had given him.

The Apostle Paul in writing to the church at Corinth was actually writing to a mixed congregation. Most of them were Gentiles, but there were a few Jews in the congregation. This is the second letter Paul wrote to the Christians at Corinth and he was contrasting the New Covenant with the Old Covenant. "For if the ministry of condemnation (the Mosaic Covenant) had glory, the ministry of righteousness (the New Covenant) exceeds much more in glory. For even what was made glorious had no glory in this respect, because of the glory that excels. For if what is passing away (the Mosaic Covenant of law) was glorious, what remains (the New Covenant) is much more glorious." (2 Corinthians 3:9-11) Here the Apostle Paul was making a distinction between the glory of the Old Covenant, stating that, that glory is passing away. Then he shows that the ministry of righteousness is remaining and will continue as he states later—forever. In the next few verses Paul describes what Moses established and what Jesus is now establishing.

"Therefore, since we have such hope, we use great boldness of speech—unlike Moses, who put a veil over his face so that the children of Israel could not look steadily at the end of what was passing away (the Old Covenant). But their minds were hardened. For until this day the same veil remains unlifted in the reading of the Old Testament (Covenant) because the veil is taken away in Christ." (2 Corinthians 3-12-14) Here again the Apostle Paul is contrasting the Old Covenant with the New Covenant. What Paul is presenting is something the Jewish people at that time did not want to accept, the New Covenant. To them, that God would move away from the Covenant of Law to the New Covenant—the Covenant of Grace was just too radical for them to accept. Notice what Reverent Kosor says about these verses. "The apostles knew what they were saying would seem radical, yet they felt very bold in speaking out what they knew as the Gospel. Although, what they had to say was more glorious than the old, they felt no need to shield their faces and cover the glory shining forth from what they had to say, because they knew unlike the old, this New Covenant would never pass away! Here it is! Look at it in all it's glory! No need to ever again be afraid of God's Word!" (Unveiling the New Covenant, page 58) Because God's Word is Jesus Christ! "In the beginning was the Word (Jesus), and the Word (Jesus) was with God, and the Word (Jesus) was God. He (Jesus) was in the beginning with God." (John 1:1-2)

Then Paul goes onto describe the hardness of heart and rejection of the Jewish people to this New Covenant. The veil that is on their minds and hearts cannot be taken away until they turn to the Lord (Jesus). Those Jews that have turned to the Lord (Jesus)have had the veil removed by the Lord (Jesus). Paul uses a lot of word images to describe the veil being removed. "For we know in part and we prophesy in part. But when that which is perfect (the New Covenant) has come, then that which is in part (the Old Covenant) will be done away. When I was a child (under the Old Covenant), I spoke as a child, I understood as a child, but when I became a man (under the New Covenant) I put away childish things (the practices of the Old Covenant). For now, we see in a mirror dimly (the Old Covenant), but then face to face. Now I know in part, but then I shall know just as I also am known (by the Lord)." (1 Corinthians 13:9-12)

This passage is known by most believers as apart of the love chapter. However, it is a clear picture of the passing from the Old Mosaic Covenant of Law to the New Covenant of Grace. Revelation was continuing to come to Paul of what was taking place as God revealed Himself and showed Paul the New Covenant. This New Covenant revolved around Jesus Christ, and would set both Jews and Gentiles free from their past sins and their sin-controlled lives. This abundant life was promised through Jesus Christ. "The thief (the devil) does not come except to steal, and to kill and to destroy. I have come that they may have life, and that they may have it more abundantly." (John 10:10) The New Covenant in Jesus Christ would give believers whether Jews or Gentiles eternal life and that life abundantly.

On the other hand, the majority of the Jewish nation, Israel, did not accept the New Covenant and the person it was centered around, Jesus Christ. Therefore, to this day they remain under the Old Covenant of Judaism. This has also placed them under the curse of the law. Paul talks about this in Galatians 3. "For as many as are of the works of the law are under the curse; for it is written, 'Cursed is everyone who does not continue in all things (the Old Covenant) which are written in the book of the law(the Mosaic Covenant), to do them."(Deuteronomy 27:26) "But that no one is justified by the law in the sight of God is evident, for 'the just shall live by faith.' Yet the law is not of faith, but 'The man who does them shall live by them. Christ has redeemed us from the curse of the law, having become a curse for us (for it is written, 'Cursed is everyone who hangs on a tree'), that the blessing of Abraham might come upon the Gentiles in Christ Jesus, that we might receive the promise of the Spirit through faith." (Galatians 3:11-14)

Paul's revelation of the New Covenant centered in Jesus Christ, brought the Gentiles out from under the curse of the law. His kinsmen, the Jews, rejected to large extent the message of life through Jesus Christ. Even during Jesus' life on earth, the Gentiles exhibited more faith than the Jews. When Jesus healed the Roman Centurion's servant, this is what Jesus said about the Centurion's faith. "Assuredly, I say to you, I have not found such great faith, not even in Israel." (Matthew 8:10b) Jesus went onto say prophetically that many Gentiles would be sitting in the kingdom of heaven with Abraham, Isaac, and Jacob, while the Jewish people would be cast out into outer darkness. (Matthew 8:11-12) Another, example of great faith by a Gentile woman is found in Matthew 15:21-28. She asked Jesus to heal her daughter who was demon possessed. After her persevering in talking to Jesus, Jesus finally does heal her daughter. This is what He said about her faith. "Then Jesus answered and said to her, 'O woman, great is your faith! Let it be to you as you desire!' And her daughter was healed from that very hour." (Matthew 15:28) Those are just some of the examples of great faith by Gentile believers.

We talked briefly earlier about the veil being over the hearts and minds of the Jewish nation, Israel. The day that Jesus was crucified, after He declared, "It is finished," and He surrendered His Spirit to His Father, the veil in the Temple in Jerusalem was rent from top to bottom. Considering the fact that Jesus had declared, "It is finished", first. What He was declaring was that the Old Mosaic Covenant was finished. Three days later when He arose, that was the beginning of the New Covenant. The next thing to consider is the veil being rent from top to bottom. That meant that everyone has access to God the Father. That was to show the Jewish people that there would be no longer a veil between them and God. Through Jesus sacrificial death, He had removed the veil. But many of the Jewish people that day and to this day refuse to accept the renting of the veil. They refused to accept Jesus as their Messiah and that He is the Son of God. If they did, they would have to move away from the Old Covenant to the New

Covenant in Jesus. "Now the Lord is the Spirit; and where the Spirit of the Lord is, there is liberty. But we all, with unveiled face, beholding as in a mirror the glory of the Lord, are being transformed into the same image from glory to glory, just as by the Spirit of the Lord." (2 Corinthians 3:17-18)

Notice that the Apostle Paul is writing to the Corinthian church. This is a mixed church of both Jews and Gentiles. That is why he talks about the liberty that the Holy Spirit brings. He also states what an unveiled face means. It means that one is seeing in the mirror of God the glory of the Lord and that glory is changing them, transforming them into the same image just by beholding the Lord—the Revelation of Jesus Christ. This is all done by the Spirit of the Lord, for every born-again Christian cannot change himself on the inside. This means that everyone can enter within the veil where God, our Father, is because of the blood of the everlasting Covenant. In Hebrews 13:20, the Apostle Paul calls the blood of Jesus, "the blood of the everlasting covenant." That blood has been sprinkled on the Mercy Seat in the Heavenlies by Jesus Christ, our High Priest.

The tabernacle on earth was made under the direction of Moses, was copied from the tabernacle in Heaven. This is the New Covenant's sanctuary in which Jesus Christ is the High Priest of that Covenant. "But Christ came as High Priest of good things to come with the greater and more perfect tabernacle not made with hands, that is, not of this creation." (Hebrews 9:11) Because Jesus is our High Priest, who is constantly making intercession for us, He is the Mediator (Counselor, Lawyer) of the New Covenant. "...to Jesus the Mediator of the New Covenant, and to the blood of sprinkling that speaks better things than that of Abel." (Hebrews 12:24) The word "Mediator" means lawyer and advocate. Jesus is our Mediator before the High Court of God. He is constantly representing us before His Father, especially when the accuser, the devil, is accusing us before God. Jesus has never lost a case. Your case is not to hard for Jesus Christ. The blood of Jesus still avails before our Father.

Now instead of sacrificing animals to receive forgiveness of sins; Jesus blood avails and we have total forgiveness forever. Now we bring a sacrifice of praise to God, because of what Jesus has already done. "Therefore, by Him let us continually offer the sacrifice of praise to God, that is the fruit of our lips, giving thanks to His name." (Hebrews 13:15) Why do we offer praise and thanksgiving to His name? It is because of God's great love for us and the fact that He has forgiven us of all our sins. "If we confess our sins, He is faithful and just to forgive us our sins and to cleanse us from all unrighteousness." (1 John 1:9) Another thing we can do as a sacrifice to God is to do good and share with others. "But do not forget to do good and to share, for with such sacrifices God is well pleased." (Hebrews 13:16) A lot of times this requires a sacrifice on our part monetarily or with goods that we have.

Paul Turns to The Gentiles

Notice that Paul, as the Apostle to the Gentiles, was still speaking in terms that Jewish people could understand. He has not totally given up on the Jewish people coming to Jesus Christ and receiving Him as their Messiah and their God. Paul realizes that this is the time for the Gentiles to turn in faith to Jesus. Everywhere Paul goes, he first preaches to the Jews in every town and then turns to the Gentiles. One can see that he obeys the Lord in preaching to the Jews first. Notice in Acts 18 when Paul comes to Corinth, he preaches that Jesus is the Christ in the synagogue trying to persuade both Jews and proselyte Gentiles. Then Paul makes a decision in Acts 18:4-6. "And he (Paul) reasoned in the synagogue every Sabbath and persuaded both Jews and Greeks. When Silas and Timothy had come from Macedonia, Paul was constrained in the (Holy) Spirit, and testified to the Jews that Jesus is the Christ. But when they (the Jews) opposed him and blasphemed, he shook his garments and said to them, 'Your blood be upon your own heads. I am clean. From now on I will go to the Gentiles."

If you read down further in Acts 18, you find Paul leaving the Jewish synagogue, the worship place of the Jews, and they enter the house of Justus, a worshipper of God, who lived right next door to the synagogue. Then Crispus, the Jewish ruler of the synagogue, believed in the Lord Jesus Christ and is converted along with all his family. Along with him, many

Corinthians after hearing of his conversion are saved and baptized as well. After this the Lord appears to Paul in a vision by night and tells him what to do next. "Do not be afraid, but speak and do not be silent. For I am with you, and no one will attack you, for I have many people in this city." (Acts 18:9b-10) Paul continued in Corinth for a year and a half. This was basically a Gentile church with a few Jewish believers.

Nearly, the same thing happens in Ephesus in Acts 19. He finds twelve disciples of John the Baptist at Ephesus. He preaches Christ to them and they are baptized in the name of the Lord. He also shares about the Baptism in the Holy Spirit with these twelve men and they receive the Baptism and are filled with the Holy Spirit and speak in tongues and prophesy. (Acts 19:1-7) Notice throughout the book of Acts, that every time people are filled with the Holy Spirit that there are spiritual gifts manifested and the main one is tongues. Individuals can use tongues for a prayer language (1 Corinthians 14:14-15) or they can speak in tongues in the congregation and then pray for the interpretation which is usually prophetical (1 Corinthians 14:13).

In Ephesus, Paul shares the Gospel of Jesus Christ in the synagogue for three months. The same thing happens in Ephesus that happened in Corinth. Listen to what Paul tells them. "But when some were hardened and did not believe, but spoke evil of the Way before the multitude (probably Jews), he departed from them and withdrew the disciples, reasoning daily in the school of Tyrannus (a public-school building). And this continued for two years, so that all who dwelt in Asia heard the word of the Lord Jesus, both Jews and Greeks." (Acts 19:9-10) Evidently, Paul was no longer allowed to teach in the Jewish synagogue, so he went to the school of Tyrannus. This is what Zondervan Pictorial Bible Dictionary, on page 878 says about the school of Tyrannus. "According to the commonly accepted text of Acts 19:9, Paul at Ephesus taught in the afternoon in "the school of a certain Tyrannus," which, since instruction was commonly given in the morning (Martial 9:68; 12:57; Juv. 7:222-6), would be vacant for his (Paul's) use later in the day…Tyrannus was a living Ephesian (Greek) schoolmaster. If another well-supported reading is followed, "in the school of Tyrannus." This would indicate a public building traditionally named thus, or a school founded by Tyrannus. The name was common enough. W. M. Ramsay discusses the question in The Church in the Roman Empire, page 152 and St. Paul the Traveler and Roman Citizen, page 271." Therefore, we see that Paul again had moved from a Jewish place of worship, the synagogue, to a public building belonging to a Gentile-Greek man named Tyrannus. This no doubt was where the Gentile church at Ephesus began. The church at Ephesus again was predominantly made up of Gentile believers with a few Jews who had put their faith in Jesus.

If you are following the trend in the book of Acts, you are noticing that Paul begins by trying to minister to the Jews, but when they reject the Gospel of Jesus Christ, he then turns to the Gentiles. The Gentiles if you have noticed are extremely open to the message of Jesus. Now this was accompanied with miracles, healings and signs following that message. Usually, that means Paul establishes a Gentile church in nearly every town along with ordaining Elders to carry on the ministry when he has to leave. There are probably Jewish believers in the church but they are in the minority. That is why Paul is called "the Apostle to the Gentiles."

Notice in Acts 19:13-16, there were some Jewish exorcists who tried to cast out demons like Paul did. Evidently, they were not believers in Jesus, because the demons answered them and said, "Jesus I know, and Paul I know, but who are you?" (Acts 19:15b) They must have thought they could duplicate what Paul had done, but they were mistaken. "Then the man in whom the evil spirit was leaped on them, overpowered them, and prevailed against them, so that they fled out of the house naked and wounded." (Acts 19:16) The Jewish people in these towns were so jealous of Paul and other Christian believers, that they thought they could do the same things using Jesus' name whom Paul had preached. But that never works. One must be anointed, filled with the Holy Spirit, and directed by the Spirit to do those things.

This had a positive effect on the believers in Ephesus, both Jews and Greeks. "This became known both to all Jews and Greeks dwelling in Ephesus, and fear fell on them all, and the name of the Lord Jesus was magnified. And many who had believed came confessing and telling their deeds. Also, many of those who had practiced magic brought their books together and burned them in the sight of all. And they counted up the value of them, and it totaled fifty thousand pieces of silver ($364, 000.). So, the word of the Lord grew mightily and prevailed." (Acts 19:17-20)

Paul Returns to Jerusalem

While all this was going on, Paul was used by God to remove diseases and evil spirits out of people. The Christian church in Ephesus was growing in numbers. It is about this time that the Holy Spirit began to call Paul back to Jerusalem for one last time. "When these things were accomplished, Paul purposed (felt directed) in the (Holy) Spirit, when he had passed through Macedonia and Achaia to go to Jerusalem, saying, 'After I have been there, I must also see Rome.'" (Acts 19:21) He goes to every Gentile church he has established as an Apostle in the faith and tells them goodbye. Paul is told on more than one occasion not to go to Jerusalem. When Paul says goodbye to the Ephesian Elders in Acts 20, he tells them what the Holy Spirit is saying. "And see, I go bound in the spirit to Jerusalem, not knowing the things that will happen to me there, except that the Holy Spirit testifies in every city, saying that chains and tribulation await me." (Acts 20:22-23) When Paul reaches Tyre certain disciples tell him the same thing; do "not go up to Jerusalem." (Acts 21:4b)

When Paul reaches Caesarea, he enters Philip's, the Evangelist, house. Philips lives there with his four daughters who are Prophetesses. After a few days, Agabus, a prophet from Judea comes to Philip's house. Agabus, upon entering Philip's house, takes Paul's belt and says this to Paul. "Thus, says the Holy Spirit, 'So shall the Jews at Jerusalem bind the man who owns this belt and deliver him into the hands of the Gentiles.'" (Acts 21:11) Everyone at Philip's house tries to get Paul not to go to Jerusalem but to no avail. Paul felt it was God's will for him to go to Jerusalem, therefore, everyone says, "The will of the Lord be done." (Acts 21:14b) Paul felt it was God's will, no matter what others thought.

There is a lot of controversy among Biblical scholars about why Paul decided to go to Jerusalem. People in Tyre and Agabus, the Prophet, told Paul not to go to Jerusalem. In both instances, it says that they spoke by the Spirit of God. If one goes back to Acts 19:21 where Paul sensed by the Holy Spirit he was to go to Jerusalem, it would seem like the Holy Spirit is giving contradictory directions. People telling Paul not to go to Jerusalem by the Spirit and then Paul sensing by the Spirit to go there. When I read those passages, I see that fear has entered into the motivation of the people of Tyre and Agabus' message to Paul. Paul cannot be governed by fear as he seeks to discern God's will.

The late Dr. C. I. Scofield in his The First Scofield Reference Bible, page 1178 states another motive why Paul decided to go to Jerusalem. "Paul's motive in going to Jerusalem seems to have been his great affection for the Jews (his people), (Romans 9:1-5), and his hope that the gifts of the Gentile churches, sent by him to the poor saints at Jerusalem (Romans 15:25-28), could open the hearts of the law-bound Jewish believers to the "gospel of the grace of God. (Acts 22:24)"

Dr. Scofield's point about Paul's love for his Jewish people is seen in what he writes in the book of Romans. Paul coming into a revelation of the New Covenant revealed to him that the Gospel was for the Jews as well as the Gentiles. Even though Paul was the Apostle to the Gentiles, he loved his people which is stated in the Scripture that is mentioned by Dr. Scofield, Romans 9:1-5. Even though Paul is writing to the Gentiles in Rome this letter, he lets them know of his great love for his people, the Jews.

"I tell the truth in Christ, I am not lying, my conscience also bearing me witness in the Holy Spirit, that I have great sorrow and continual grief in my heart. For I could wish that I myself were accursed from Christ for my brethren, my kinsmen according to the flesh, who are Israelites, to whom pertain the adoption, the glory, the covenants, the giving of the law, the service of God, and the promises; of whom are the fathers and from whom, according to the flesh Christ came, who is over all, the eternally blessed God. Amen." (Romans 9:1-5) Through these verses most everyone can see

Paul's heart and love for his own people. Though he was the Apostle to the Gentiles, he truly loved his people, the Jews.

In Romans 10:1-4, Paul goes on to talk about the Jews rejection of Jesus Christ, as the righteousness of God. "Brethren, my heart's desire and prayer for Israel is that they may be saved. For I bear them witness that they have a zeal for God, but not according to knowledge. For they being ignorant of God's righteousness (Jesus), and seeking to establish their own righteousness (according to the Covenant of Law), have not submitted to the righteousness of God (Jesus). For Christ is the end of the (Covenant of) law for righteousness to everyone who believes."

One must remember that Paul is writing to Roman Christians in which some are Jews and some are Gentiles. In this passage, Paul is showing a contrast between the two Covenants, the Covenant of Law and the Covenant of Grace. In this passage, one can see that Jesus Christ, God's Son, ended the Covenant of Law. We need to look at the word "end" in Romans 10:4. This is what The New Thayer's Greek-English Lexicon, on page 619 defines the word "end" in Romans 10:4. "It is the Greek word telos, which means termination, the limit at which a thing ceases to be; Christ has brought an end to the law." This is the context of the word "end" in Romans 10:4. Jesus Christ brought an end to the Covenant of Law. Every aspect of the Law is fulfilled in Jesus Christ. The Amplified Bible on pages 311 and 312 says it in terms that no one should mistake it's meaning. "For Christ is the end of the Law (the limit at which it ceases to be, for the Law leads up to Him (Jesus) Who is the fulfillment of its types, and in Him the purpose which it was designed to accomplish is fulfilled. That is, the purpose of the Law is fulfilled in Him) as the means of righteousness (right relationship to God) for everyone who trusts in and adheres to and relies on Him (Jesus)."From this we learn that Jesus Christ brought an end to the Old Covenant—the Mosaic Covenant of Law—and established a New Covenant in Himself. Does that mean we are free to disobey the Ten Commandments and the moral boundaries of God's law? No it does not. If you are obeying the Spirit of Jesus Christ, which is the Holy Spirit, you will automatically fulfill "the righteous requirement of the law," and this will "be fulfilled in us who do not walk according to the flesh but according to the Spirit." (Romans 8:4)

The Good Olive Tree Analogy

One must see that at this point in history when Paul is writing this Roman letter, that the majority of the Jews had rejected Jesus Christ as the Messiah and as the Son of God. From the writing of this Roman epistle until the present, this is considered the time the Gentiles have opportunity to receive the Gospel. But Paul goes onto say that Israel will be given a second chance by God. This is all taken up in Romans the eleventh chapter. Paul has stated that he is in deep sorrow about his people, the Jews, rejecting Jesus as the Messiah and the Son of God. He knows that the Roman Gentiles, who are Christians, maybe asking the question; is God casting away His chosen people forever? In this eleventh chapter of Romans, Paul answers that question, plus he answers the question about the Roman Gentile Christians becoming prideful about their standing before God now and in the future. Finally, Paul shares the fact that his people, the Jews, will be given a second chance. He uses an analogy that both Jews and Gentiles understand. It is the analogy of the good olive tree. The Jews believe that this olive tree stands for the Jews and the Mosaic Covenant. They believe they are the olive tree and get this understanding from the book of Jeremiah 11:16. However, one must look at verse 17 of the same chapter as well. "The Lord called your name, Green Olive Tree, Lovely and of Good Fruit. With the noise of a great tumult He has kindled fire on it, and its branches are broken. For the Lord of hosts who planted you, has pronounced doom against you for the evil of the house of Israel and of the house of Judah, which they have done against themselves to provoke Me to anger in offering incense to Baal." (Jeremiah 11:16-17) From this passage Messianic Jews (believers in Jesus) believe they are the Good Olive Tree spoken by Paul in Romans 11. Jeremiah claims that God was going to destroy that tree. So, what tree is Paul talking about? I believe the Good Olive Tree in Romans 11 is God, Himself. Notice Paul says some of the branches were broken, which are the Jews who rejected Jesus Christ. The Gentiles, who put their faith in Jesus, are the branches from a wild olive tree, that have been grafted into God, Himself. One reason I believe this is the right meaning because in John 15:1-6, Jesus declares Himself to be the vine and the believers in Him the branches. "I am the vine, and my Father (God) is the vinedresser. Every branch in Me that does not bear fruit He takes away, and every branch that bears fruit He prunes (cuts on it), that it may bear more fruit. You are already clean because of the word which I have spoken to you. Abide (Remain) in Me, and I in you. As the branch cannot bear fruit of itself, unless it abides (remains) in the vine, neither can you, unless you abide (remain) in Me. I am the vine; you are the branches. He who abides (remains) in Me and I in him, bears much fruit, for without Me you can do nothing. If anyone does not abide (remain) in Me, he is cast forth as a branch and is withered; and they gather them and throw them into the fire, and they are burned." God does not center things in people, nations or Covenants and religions or even Judaism of the past. It is all centered in His Son, Jesus Christ. This is why the New Covenant is in sharp contrast to what the Jews had before. The Jews ended up centering everything around the Covenant of Law and when God moved on to establish the New Covenant in Jesus Christ, they were not prepared for it, and thus rejected Jesus Christ. Notice that I used another word alongside of "abide." This is the Greek word meno which from the Strong's Greek Lexicon, page 45, means "to stay (in a given place, state, relation or expectancy), --abide, continue, dwell, endure, be present, remain, stand, tarry…" This also means staying where God put you. If you are going to bear fruit, you have to abide, remain, stay in the vine as a branch. You must bear fruit where God puts you and not run off somewhere else. Verses 7 thru 11 talks about receiving what Jesus is teaching you and obeying Him. This has to do with individual believers but also could be particular churches.

Let us now look at what Paul said in Romans chapter 11. As we shared before Paul is talking about his people the Jews. I am going to quote all of the ones I shared about, so you can see what Paul was saying. "I say then, has God cast away His people (Israel)? Certainly not! For I am an Israelite of the seed of Abraham, of the tribe of Benjamin. God has not cast away His people (Israel) whom He foreknew." (Romans 11:1-2a) Paul is stating that they are not cast away, but later in this chapter he is going to state their spiritual condition.

Then look at Romans 11:11-14. "I say then, have they (Israel) stumbled that they should fall? Certainly not! But through their fall (trespass), to provoke them in jealousy, salvation has come to the Gentiles. Now if their fall is riches for the world, and their failure riches for the Gentiles, how much more their fullness! For I speak to you Gentiles; inasmuch as I am an apostle to the Gentiles, I magnify my ministry, if by any means I may provoke to jealousy those who are my flesh and save some of them!" Throughout this passage, Paul is letting the Roman Gentile Christians and us know today that Israel for now has fallen into unbelief. But that will not last. In the next verses, Paul is describing what has happened and what will happen when Israel returns to the Lord. "For if they (Israel) being cast away is the reconciling of the world (the Gentiles), what will their (Israel's) acceptance be but life from the dead. For if their first fruit is holy, the lump is holy; and if the root (God and Jesus) is holy, so are the branches. And if some of the branches (Israel's branches) were broken off, and you (Gentiles), being a wild olive tree were grafted in among them (the Jews), and with them (Jew and Gentile) became a partaker of the root (Jesus) and fatness (God) of the Olive tree (God the Father, God the Son); do not boast against the (Jewish) branches. But if you (Gentiles) boast, remember that you (Gentiles) do not support the root (God and Jesus), but the root (God and Jesus) supports you (Gentiles)." (Romans 11:15-18) From this Scripture, whether Jew or Gentile, there is no room to boast about anything. Just as in the parable of the Vine and the Branches, if one does not look to God the Father and God the Son in a trusting relationship, one can be thrust out and burned. We need to reverentially fear God and respect Him.

Now let us take a look at some errors in interpreting these passages in Romans 11. Most Messianic Jews believe that the olive tree Paul is talking about is the nation of Israel. Therefore, if you are not a part of Israel, you are not a part of God's plan. Among those who believe this is Marvin P. Wilson. In his book, Our Father Abraham, on pages 14-15, he gives the view supported by Evangelical Christians and then the one supported by most Messianic Jews. Since he is a Messianic Jew, he supports the view on pages 14 and 15 of this book. "Second, one must accurately identify the root of the olive tree (Romans 11:16-18). Some have argued that the root represents the Messiah or the messianic movement. But this view confuses the expression "root of Jesse" (Isa 11:1cf. also 53:2) or "Root of David" (Revelation 5:5) with "root of the olive tree." The flow of the context supports the conclusion that the root represents the patriarchs: Abraham, Isaac, and Jacob, the faithful forefathers of the Jews, the stalwart founders of that original people of God…" However, looking at his explanation and view it in line with the revelation of the Holy Spirit. With that in mind let us look at the "root of Jesse" in Isaiah 11:1 and 53:2 a little closer. These verses are both Messianic prophetical Scriptures about Jesus. The Jews believe they get their root in themselves, so they see these verses as coming out of the natural. Jesus Christ was and is Divine and that is what gave the Jews life. Eternal life does not come out of natural beings, but rather out of the Life-giving Spirit of Jesus. In Revelation 5:5 the Scripture talks about the "Root of David" which points to Jesus Christ. All these Scriptures point back to Jesus Christ, not to Israel. There are those who see the olive tree correctly. Karl Barth in his book, Church Dogmatics, on page 285 to 287 says this about the olive tree. Actually, Marvin Wilson quoted Mr. Barth's view in his book, Our Father Abraham, even though he did not agree with it. "It should be noted that some of the (early) Church Fathers and more recently, Karl Barth interpreted the root (in Romans 11:16-18) as Christ."

It is my conclusion, that the olive tree is a picture of Jesus Christ, Himself. Just as is in John 15, Jesus is seen as the vine and His Father is the vinedresser. God in Romans 11 removed branches that did not bear the fruit of faith in Jesus Christ. One can see the proper perspective in Paul's writing in Romans 11 by comparing it to John 15. If you look at the next few verses in Romans 11, it becomes clearer. "You will say then, 'Branches were broken off (by God the husbandman) that I (Gentiles) might be grafted in. Well said. Because of unbelief they (the Jews) were broken off, and you (Gentiles) stand by faith. Do not be haughty (full of pride), but fear (God). For if God did not spare the natural (Jews) branches, He may not spare you (Gentiles). Therefore, consider the goodness and severity of God: on those who (Jews) fell, severity, but toward you (Gentiles), goodness, if you (Gentiles) continue in His goodness. Otherwise, you (Gentiles) also will be cut off." (Romans 11:19-22)

From this Scripture, one can see that God has extended His New Covenant to the Gentiles, but they will have it by faith and trust in Him to stay, continue in the goodness of the New Covenant, Jesus Christ. The basis of entering the New Covenant is by putting our faith in Jesus for salvation and we must continue to walk by faith in the Spirit to stay in this New Covenant. This is not a works-based Covenant, but continued faith in the finished work of Jesus Christ. I believe the "fear" that the Apostle Paul is talking about in this passage is a godly fear or reverence for God our Father and His Son Jesus Christ. We are not to become prideful of the salvation we have in Jesus and the Covenant Blessings, God our Father has extended to us. We are to rest in the goodness of our Father.

Then Paul converses about a time when Israel will be given a second chance to the Jewish people to trust Jesus Christ. Isaiah prophesies of a nation being born in a day, which is Israel. Isaiah 66:8 says, "Who has heard such a thing? Who has seen such a thing? Shall the earth be made to give birth in one day? Or shall a nation be born at once (speaking of Israel)? For as soon as Zion travailed, she gave birth to her children." Prophetically speaking, Romans 11 and the book of Revelation (Revelation 7:1-8; chapter 12) declares that Israel will be born in a day, and will acknowledge Jesus as the Son of God and the King of Israel.

The Times of the Gentiles

In writing Romans 11, the Apostle Paul is giving a warning to Gentile believers of all ages and declaring to Jewish believers that the nation of Israel will be given a second chance. Paul shares how this is possible in Romans 11:23-24. This is why the Replacement Theology is invalid and that Israel will not be replaced by the Gentile Church. "And they (Israel) also, if they (Israel) do not continue in unbelief, will be grafter in, for God is able to graft them (Israel) in again. For if you (Gentiles) were cut out of the olive tree (Adam's tree) which is wild by nature, and were grafted contrary to nature into a good olive tree (by God), how much more will these who are the natural branches, be grafted into their own olive tree (the Divine Tree that they originally were apart of)?" (Romans 11:23-24)

When one realizes that God can do anything, even things that are against nature, one understands then that God can give Israel a second chance of believing by faith on His Son, Jesus Christ. Right now, they are blinded by the Old Covenant of Law and do not realize it has side tracked them from God. The Old King James Version of the Bible in Romans 11:25 uses the word "blindness" to diagnose Israel's condition before God. The New King James Version uses the word "hardening" instead of "blindness" in that verse. The Greek word is porosis which means stupidity, callousness, blindness, and hardness. Let us look at that verse, Romans 11:25. "For I do not desire (Christian) brothers, that you should be wise in your own opinion (estimation), that hardening (stupidity, callousness, blindness, hardness) in part has happened to Israel until the fullness of the Gentiles has come in." Jesus Christ also prophesied about this before His death and resurrection. "And they (the Jews) will fall by the edge of the sword, and be led away captive into all nations. And Jerusalem will be trampled by Gentiles until the times of the Gentiles are fulfilled." (Luke 21:24) Got Questions?>times-of-the-Gentiles says this about those two Scriptures. "Looking again at Luke 21:24, we see Jesus mentions a time in which Jerusalem is under the dominion of Gentile authority." This actually started in 588 B.C. until May 14, 1948. This was God's time to reach the Gentile world with the Gospel.

The Gentile Christians have used a lot of the world's inventions and organizations to reach the Gentile world with the Gospel. But what about the theme in Romans 11? Got Questions?>times of the Gentiles goes on to explain the theme of Romans 11. "One theme of Romans 11 is that, when the Jewish people rejected Christ, they were temporarily cut off from the (Covenant) blessings of a relationship with God. As a result, the Gospel was given to the Gentiles and they gladly received it. This partial hardening of the heart doesn't preclude individual Jews from being saved, but it prevents the nation from accepting Christ as Messiah until His plans are finished. When the time is right, God will restore the entire nation, and they will come to faith in Him once again, ending "the time of the Gentiles. (Isaiah 17:7; 62:11-12; Romans 11:26)." The Gentile Christian Church has reached into nearly all the corners of the earth with the Gospel of Jesus Christ. Listen to what Jesus said in Matthew 24:14. "And this gospel of the kingdom will be preached in all the world as a witness to all nations, and then the end will come." What few understand is the Gospel also means the New Covenant relationship we have with God the Father and our Lord Jesus Christ. They are one and the same.

Let us finally look at Romans 11:26 in which the Apostle Paul quotes Isaiah declaring that Israel will be saved. "And so, all Israel will be saved, as it is written: 'The Deliverer will come out of Zion, and He will turn ungodliness from Jacob; For this is My Covenant with them, when I take away their sins." This prophetic word is confirmed by the Apostle John in Revelation chapters 7, 14, 19-22. Although, it hurt the Apostle Paul to a great extent during this period of time to see the majority of his people, Israel, rejecting Jesus Christ as the Messiah and the Son of God, but he knows they will return in faith to Jesus one day.

We have taken a detour by looking at Romans chapters 9, 10, and 11. But really it shows the Old Covenant and the New Covenant in contrast even in Paul's letter to the Roman Christians. It also shows Paul's great love for his own people, the Jews. This probably more than anything else along with God's Spirit moving him; he decided to go one final time to Jerusalem. From the prophetic words of Agabus and others along the way, he knew he would probably be opposed when he reached Jerusalem by the Jews.

One can see nearly immediately, when Paul reaches Jerusalem that false rumors and tales about Paul, have reached the ears of the Jewish Christian leadership in Jerusalem. The Jewish Apostles and Elders are cordial and listen to Paul as he shares about how the Gentiles have received the Gospel and his ministry. Notice it has been eight years since the Jerusalem Council decided that the Gentiles only needed to obey four decrees in order to have fellowship with the Jewish brethren. Notice that the four decrees are not the New Covenant, but are given to the Gentiles if they wish to have fellowship with their Jewish brethren. That Jerusalem Council had sent a letter by Paul, Barnabas, Timothy and Simon sharing those four decrees. One should read Unveiling the New Covenant, by Pastor Ronald David Kosor. Reverend Kosor shows throughout Paul's Epistles how Paul wrote agreeing with the four decrees. Those were the only instructions the Jerusalem Church gave to all the Gentile churches that Paul, under the leadership of the Holy Spirit, had established. Reverend Kosor shows how Paul, Barnabas, Simon and Timothy explained these four decrees to every Gentile church. One can pick up a copy of Unveiling the New Covenant by Rev. Kosor at Amazon.com.

Therefore, Paul was going to Jerusalem one final time, having fulfilled what the Jerusalem Church had told him to do in Acts 15. With it being eight years, many of the Gentile brethren, and some Jewish brethren like Agabus, Philip and his four daughters who were prophetesses had tried to convince Paul not to go to Jerusalem. I believe he went out of love for his Jewish brethren. In 1 Corinthians 9:19-20, we see another aspect of that love and a desire to share the Gospel with the Jews. "For though I am free from all men, I have made myself a servant to all, that I might win the more; to the Jews I became as a Jew, that I might win Jews, to those who are under the law (the Covenant of law), as under the law (the Mosaic Covenant of law), that I might win those who are under the law (the Mosaic Covenant of law)…" Paul became whatever they were in order to reach them. In verses 21 to 22, he became one free from the law in order to gain those who were without law. Paul also said he became weak in order to gain the weak. Finally, he says this in 1 Corinthians 9:23. "Now this I do for the Gospel's sake, that I may be a partaker of it with you." With all of these Scripture truths in mind, one can see why Paul went to Jerusalem to fellowship with those Jewish believers in the Jerusalem Church. Paul would set aside differences in order to fellowship with people who believed differently than he did. He believed true fellowship was "in Jesus."

"And when we (Paul, Luke, and Paul's Gentile and Jewish friends) had come to Jerusalem, the (Jewish) brethren received us gladly. On the following day Paul went in with us to James, and all the (Jewish) elders were present. When we had greeted them (the Jewish brethren), he (Paul) told in detail those things which God had done among the Gentiles through his ministry. And when they (James and all the Jewish Elders) heard it they glorified the Lord…" (Acts 21:17-20a)

In this account by Luke, the writer of Acts, gives a careful presentation of exactly what happened. Let us consider the fact that Luke is considered by most Biblical scholars to be a Gentile. Paul acknowledges Luke as "the beloved physician" in Colossians 4:14. Luke wrote the Gospel according to Luke and the book of Acts. Most Biblical scholars consider Luke to be the only Gentile writer in the New Testament. So, Luke and some of Paul's Gentile friends and believers accompanied Paul to Jerusalem. As we considered before that Jews had no dealings with Gentiles at all, it is a stretch of our imagination that these Jews would have anything to do with Luke or his Gentile friends. The reason they received Paul and his Gentile friends was because Paul is still considered to be an honored Jew among them and they know that God has called him to be the Apostle to the Gentiles.

After Paul shares about the great evangelistic work done among the Gentiles, Paul gives the Jewish Elders and brethren the offering he has brought from the Gentiles to the Jewish brethren and sisters there in Jerusalem. This is another sticky point of fellowship between Jews and Gentiles. Jews very seldom fellowshipped with Gentiles much less received money or goods from them. From this point on, Paul will find out why there is a distance in the relationship between him and the Jewish brethren. Paul wants to bring an end to that distance of their relationship. This is another reason; I believe why Paul came to Jerusalem.

What the Jewish Leadership Wanted Paul to Do

"And they (the Jewish leaders) said to him (Paul), 'You see brother, how many myriads (an extremely great number) of Jews there are who have believed, and they are zealous for (the Covenant of) law, but they have been informed about you (Paul) that you teach all the Jews who are among the Gentiles to forsake Moses (the Mosaic Covenant), saying they ought not to circumcise their children nor walk according to the customs (the Mosaic Covenant of Law). What then? The (Jewish) assembly must certainly meet, for they will hear that you (Paul) have come. Therefore, do what we tell you: We have four men, who have taken a vow (no doubt a Nazarite vow). Take them and be purified with them (according to the Law of Moses), and pay their expenses so that they may shave their heads, and that all may know that those things of which they were informed concerning you (Paul) are nothing, but that you yourself also walk orderly and keep the law (of Moses). But concerning the Gentiles who believe (are believers in Jesus), we have written and decided that they should observe no such things (the Mosaic Covenant of Law), except that they (the Gentiles) should keep themselves from things offered to idols, from blood, from things strangled, and from sexual immorality (the four decrees given in Acts 15:23-29 at the first Jerusalem Council).'" (Acts 21:20b-25)

I wanted you to see the complete answer James and the Jewish Elders gave Paul. They believe Paul is doing a great work among the Gentiles. However, in Paul's preaching and teaching the New Covenant, which is based on the finished work of Jesus at the Cross and His resurrection from the dead, it is sending a mixed message to the Jewish believers who attend the Gentile churches. Paul is telling the Gentile believers that they don't have to be circumcised, nor follow all the Jewish customs, dietary laws, and other laws contained in the old Mosaic Covenant of Law. The Jewish believers that are in the Gentile churches and among Gentile believers hear all of this and they decide to just take hold of the New Covenant, which is Jesus Christ, and leave the Old Mosaic Covenant behind. Therefore, the Jewish believers are forsaking the Old Mosaic Covenant of Law. That is upsetting the church in Jerusalem which is completely made up of Jewish believers.

The second major theme one receives from this meeting Paul and the Jewish leadership have in Jerusalem is that they have no intent of leaving the old Mosaic Covenant of Law. Thus, in reality they are trying to hold onto both Covenants. Eventually, that is an impossible situation. One only has to read Romans chapter 7 to see how impossible that is. According to BlueLetterBibles.com Paul wrote the book of Romans in 56 A.D. He was arrested in Jerusalem in 57 A.D. Most Bible scholars believe that James and the Elders at Jerusalem had access to Paul's letters. Therefore, they knew what Paul believed concerning the Old Covenant of Law and the New Covenant of Jesus Christ. Even if they were not able to read Paul's letter to the Romans, Judaizers were all around and could report what Paul was teaching in the Gentile churches. Believers in Christ today are trying to do the same thing. They are trying to live under both Covenants. Even though Paul throughout his letters was sharing how the Old Mosaic Covenant of Law was passing away. In Hebrews 8:13 Paul says this after introducing the New Covenant. "In that He says, "A new covenant, He has made the first obsolete. Now what is becoming obsolete and growing old is ready to vanish away." In context this refers to the Old Covenant of Law. If one reads all of Hebrews chapters 8 and 9, one has to come to the conclusion that this verse we quoted is talking about the Old Covenant, that is obsolete and "ready to vanish away." (Hebrews 8:13)

Paul wrote Romans chapter 7 to show the frustration of trying to live under both the Old Covenant of Law and the New Covenant of Grace. In Romans 7:1-6, Paul uses the illustration of marriage to show how an individual whether Jew or Gentile(proselytes)are in essence married to the Covenant of Law. The Covenant of Law, is the first marriage partner, and how through death the old marriage partner dies. In Romans 7:1b Paul talks about how "the Law (Covenant of Law) has dominion over a man as long as he lives." He is showing Gentile Romans believers and Jewish believers in Christ, how the Covenant of Law has dominion over them. They are married or joined to the Covenant of Law as long as that marriage partner is alive.

Then Paul uses the same illustration of marriage and death to show how one is released from that marriage partner, the Covenant of Law. "For the woman who has a husband is bound by the law to her husband as long as he lives. But if the husband (the Covenant of Law) dies, she is released from the law of her husband (the Covenant of Law)." (Romans 7:2) This is an illustration of how both Jews and Gentiles are bound to the Covenant of Law. As long as the Law is enforced and they both are alive, they are bound to one another. That Covenant of Law is in control of their lives. "So then if, while her husband (the Covenant of Law) lives, she (Jew or Gentile) marries another man, she will be called an adulteress; but if her husband (the Covenant of Law) dies, she (Jew or Gentile) is free from the (Covenant of Law), so that she (Jew or Gentile) is no adulteress, though she be married to another man (Jesus Christ)." (Romans 7:3)

Just like in this illustration one cannot be married to two different Covenants. In reality, the Jewish leadership in Jerusalem were trying to live under two different Covenants. The Apostle Paul is showing the way out of that dilemma. He points to the Cross of Jesus and shows that the Covenant of Law died there. When Jesus said "It is finished," He was talking about the Old Mosaic Covenant being finished. It's purpose and usefulness were gone. When Jesus arose the third day, He ushered in a New Covenant built on better promises. "But now He has obtained a more excellent ministry, inasmuch as He is also Mediator of a better covenant, which was established on better promises." (Hebrew 8:6)

"Therefore, my brethren, you also have become dead to the (Covenant of) law, through the body of Christ, that you may be married to another, even to Him (Jesus) who was raised from the dead that we should bear fruit to God." (Romans 7:4) One has to understand that Jesus Christ is the New Covenant. The New Covenant is centered in one man, Jesus Christ. If you read the book of Hebrews and the book of Romans, Jesus is the center of it all. The third person of the Trinity, the Holy Spirit, has to open our minds and reveal the Truth to us.

A lot of people hold onto the Covenant of Law, because they think they can obey it. It is only when they come to the end of themselves, they realize they cannot because it is against their flesh and their nature. In verse 4 of Romans 7, Paul points to the Cross of Jesus, where we died with Him to the Covenant of Law. When we died to the Covenant of Law through the body of Jesus Christ, we are now free to marry another, even the Lord Jesus Christ. This union will produce the fruit of the Spirit of God (Galatians 5:22-23). One cannot bear fruit to God married to the Law of God. Romans 7:7-24 shows the result of such a union of us to the Covenant of Law. Verse 5 shows what kind of fruit we will bear married to the Covenant of Law. "For when we were in the flesh, the passions of sins which were aroused by the (Covenant of) law were at work in our members to bear fruit to death." (Romans 7:5) The end result of that marriage to the Covenant of Law is death.

The devil likes it when we remain under the dominion of the Covenant of Law. This happens when individuals refuse to accept the fact that the Old Covenant of Law is dead and God wants them to walk and live in the New Covenant. One reason the devil likes it when people stay under the Covenant of Law, it is easy to draw them into sin and condemnation. A lot of people do not want to hear the beginning of the next verse—verse 6. The Covenant of Law cannot deliver us from sin and death, nor can it produce fruit to God. "But now we have been delivered from the (Covenant of) law, having died to what we were held by, so that we should serve in the newness of the Spirit, and not in the oldness of the letter." (Romans 7:6) The Holy Spirit must show us our new position "in Christ" and the New Covenant that we are under.

Romans seven does not make sense being stuck in between chapters six and eight, unless it shows how one must be freed from the Old Mosaic Covenant of Law and marry our new Husband, Jesus Christ, under the New Covenant of Grace. Romans six has to do with us dying with Christ at the Cross and how God put us in Jesus to take care and kill the "old man", our Adamic nature that we inherited from Adam, when he sinned in the Garden of Eden. Jesus Christ became "the last Adam" (1 Corinthians 15:45) so He could destroy Adam's fallen race. Romans seven has to do with getting free from the Covenant of Law. This marriage illustration does not make sense stuck here, unless it is relating to how we are freed from that Covenant of Law. Death is the only way we can be freed and that also happened at the Cross of Jesus Christ. Paul in Romans seven shows how difficult it is and how tenacious that husband of Law is. Only through the death of that husband are we freed to marry Jesus Christ and move into a New Covenant of Grace and Mercy. Romans 7:22-25 gives the picture of how this is all brought about. "For I delight in the law of God according to the inward man. But I see another law (Covenant of Law) in my members warring against the law of my mind, and bringing me into captivity to the law of sin which is in my members. O wretched man that I am! Who will deliver me from this body of death? I thank God—through Jesus Christ our Lord! So then, with the mind I serve the law of God, but with the flesh the law of sin." And then dropping down to Romans 8:1-2 we see the process fulfilled. "There is therefore now no condemnation to those who are in Christ Jesus, who do not walk according to the flesh, but according to the Spirit. For the law of the Spirit of life in Christ Jesus has made me free from the law of sin and death." After the death of the old husband, the Covenant of Law, we still have choices to make. We are free by choice to marry another, Jesus Christ, and walk and live in the Holy Spirit which day by day He will set us free from the law of sin and death. It is a choice we make daily. We can go back to the old husband who is dead and that will bring carnality, fleshly living, or we can choose to love, serve and honor our new husband, Jesus Christ. The choice is ours. This all comes by a revelation of the Spirit of God.

Most Bible scholars believe this book of Romans was written in 56 A.D. right before Paul came to Jerusalem. No doubt the Jewish leadership in Jerusalem had heard about what Paul wrote about the Old Mosaic Covenant of law. Rumors had circulated about what the Apostle Paul was teaching in the Gentile churches he had established. A lot of those Gentile churches had Jewish believers attending who wanted to hear what Paul shared. His presentation of the gospel of the New Covenant was going contrary to the Mosaic Covenant. Notice this last verse, "But now we have been delivered from the law…" (Romans 7:6a) The Jerusalem Council in Acts 15, had only put four restrictions on Gentile believers. But now it came down to what would they do with Paul.

Therefore, going back to Acts 21, they are now asking him to affirm his support for the Old Covenant of Law. Paul in essence had been preaching and teaching that we are delivered from that Old Covenant of Law. What would he say in response to them? James and the Jewish Elders say again that all they require of the Gentiles are the four decrees that they sent out by letter at that time with Paul and Silas. But they expected since Paul was Jewish, that he would keep the Covenant of Law. By Paul taking a Nazarite vow with four other men and purifying himself according to the Law of Moses, he would be saying in effect, that he was affirming the Covenant of Law for the Jews. I know this was a difficult decision for him. His motive is to reach his brethren in the flesh with the Gospel of Jesus Christ. That is why I believe he did it, even though it contradicted everything he has been preaching, teaching and writing.

If you remember what I quoted from 1 Corinthians 9:20, you will see what he planned to do even though it contradicted what Paul had been teaching, preaching and writing. "...and to the Jews I became as a Jew, that I might win the Jews, to those under the law, as under the law, that I might win those who are under the law..." (1 Corinthians 9:20) This Scripture gives us a clear understanding of why Paul submitted to the Jewish leadership there in Jerusalem. He was doing everything he could to win the Jews to Jesus Christ. Therefore, it is no surprise that Paul chose to do what the Apostle James and the Jewish Elders asked him to do. The Jerusalem leadership was still trying to live under both Covenants, just like many who are Christians do today. They have not had a revelation of Jesus Christ as the New Covenant life within them. "Then Paul took the men, and the next day, having been purified with them, entered the temple to announce the expiration of the days of purification, at which time an offering should be made for each one of them." (Acts 21:26)

What Happens to Paul in Jerusalem?

Paul was trying to be a witness and an example even to the Jewish men, who were considering becoming born again Christians. Many times, we do things in order to influence others to follow Christ. This would not play out as Paul; James and the Elders had hoped. There were Jews who had come from Asia, who saw Paul in the Temple and incited the crowds of Jews against Paul. They believed Paul had brought some Gentiles into the Temple, which was against the Mosaic Covenant of Law. They had seen Paul with these Gentiles earlier in the week and thought he had brought them there, but he had not. The Romans would take Paul into custody rather than allow the Jews to kill him. This happens right at the very end of the seven days of the Nazarite vow. That Nazarite vow had not finished and no sacrifice has been made for Paul. In reality the sacrifice had already been made 57 years earlier on an old wooden cross. The Cross of Jesus Christ and His offering for sin was sufficient. Paul did not need to make another sacrifice.

The Romans take Paul into custody and he is allowed to share his testimony one last time in Jerusalem before his kinsmen, the Jewish people. This is recorded in Acts 24:1-24. Paul shares his complete testimony in the Hebrew language from the time Jesus met him on the road to Damascus. He spoke in their Hebrew language, that is why all of his kinsmen, the Jews, listened. They listened until he told them that Jesus in a vision in the Temple told him to leave Jerusalem that day and go to the Gentiles. Because Paul said to go to the Gentiles, all the Jewish people at the Temple area wanted to kill him. It is that word "Gentiles" that turned them off and they again tried to attack Paul. Most all of them that had gathered there in the Temple were not Jewish believers. They were a part of the Jewish Sanhedrin and had not accepted Jesus Christ as the Messiah and the Son of God. One can see the great hatred the Jews had for the Gentiles in Acts 22:17-23.

"Then it happened when I return to Jerusalem and was praying in the temple, that I was in a trance and saw Him (Jesus) saying to me, 'Make haste and get out of Jerusalem quickly, for they will not receive your testimony concerning Me.' So, I said, 'Lord, they know that in every synagogue I imprisoned and beat those who believe on You. And when the blood of Your martyr Stephen was shed, I also was standing by consenting to his death, and guarding the clothes of those who were killing him.' Then He (Jesus) said to me, 'Depart, for I will send you far from here to the Gentiles.' And they listened to him until this word (Gentiles), and then they raised their voices and said, 'Away with such a fellow from the earth, for he (Paul) is not fit to live.' Then as they cried out and tore their clothes and threw dust into the air." (Acts 21:17-23)

From this passage, one can see the Jews animosity and hatred for the Gentiles. If the Roman soldiers had not rescued Paul he would have been killed by the Jewish mob. This would be one of the last times that Paul would present his testimony to a Jewish crowd. The next day, he would appear before the High Priest, the Pharisees and Sadducees. He would declare the resurrection from the dead and cause a division between the Pharisees and Sadducees because the Sadducees did not believe in a resurrection from the dead, while the Pharisees did. There would be one more time that he presents the Gospel before Felix, the Governor of the area, and the High Priest, Ananias, certain Jewish elders and an orator, Tertullus. Until Paul gets to Rome that would be his last time to present the Gospel to his kinsmen, the Jews. Every time, he presents it, they oppose him and his testimony of Jesus. But the Lord appears to Paul and tells him what is ahead. "Be of good cheer, Paul, for you have testified for Me in Jerusalem, so you must bear witness in Rome." (Acts 23:11b) Paul by this time has appealed to Caesar to try him. He does give his testimony before King Agrrippa and Bernice, his wife, before leaving for Rome. (Acts 26) After an eventful trip to Rome, in which Paul and his Roman guard are shipwrecked, he testifies on the ship as well. Everywhere Paul goes, he is a powerful witness. Even in chains Paul is a powerful witness of Jesus Christ. (Acts 27)

Paul's Testimony in Rome

When Paul finally reaches Rome, he has been granted a rent house, and a Roman guard. He then sends for the leaders of the Jews in Rome. He obeys Jesus command, "to go to the lost sheep of the house of Israel," first one more time. (Matthew 10:6) He tells them first what happened to him in Judea and Jerusalem and why he is in Rome. After they hear from Paul they decide on a day when Paul can present the Gospel (the New Covenant) to them. "So, when they had appointed him a day, many came to him at his lodging, to whom he explained and solemnly testified of the kingdom of God, persuading them concerning Jesus from both the law of Moses and the Prophets, from morning till evening. And some were persuaded by the things which were spoken and some disbelieved..." (Acts 28:23-24) The Gospel (the New Covenant) always causes a division, especially because the Jewish people have been under the Covenant of Law for a long time. But Paul did obey the Lord and shared the Gospel with the Jews first.

This was Paul's final word to the Jewish leaders in Rome. "So, when they did not agree among themselves, they departed from Paul after he shares this word with them. "The Holy Spirit spoke rightly through Isaiah, the prophets to our fathers, 'Go to this people and say, 'Hearing you will hear, and shall not understand; And seeing you will see, and not perceive:

For the heart of this people has grown dull. Their ears are hard of hearing, and their eyes they have closed, lest they should see with their eyes and hear with their ears, lest they should understand with their heart and turn, so that I (God) should heal them (Israel).' Therefore, let it be known to you that the salvation of God has been sent to the Gentiles and they will hear it." (Acts 28:25-28)

Although, from the Scriptures in Acts 28, it is certain that some Jews believed and received the Gospel (the New Covenant); we are also certain that a large number of the Jews in Rome did not believe the Gospel (the New Covenant). We see this from Paul's quoting of Isaiah 6:9-10 and from his final statement to the Jews in Acts 28:28. "And when he (Paul) had said these words (verses 26-28), the Jews departed and had a great dispute among themselves." (Acts 28:29) The Gospel (the New Covenant) will cause a division among individuals, especially the Jews.

Paul must have had to wait two whole years before his case was presented before Caesar. It is believed among Biblical scholars that he was acquitted and released for an unknown amount of time. But during those two years at Rome, Paul received everyone who came to see him. This is the final statement about Paul in Acts 28:30-31. "Then Paul dwelt in his own rented house, and received all who came to him, preaching the Kingdom of God and teaching the things which concern the Lord Jesus Christ with all confidence, no one forbidding him."

Why is all this important? Paul is not only the Apostle to the Gentiles, but he is the Apostle with the clearest revelation of the New Covenant by the Holy Spirit in the New Testament (Covenant). Paul's revelation of the Old Mosaic Covenant of Law in contrast to the New Covenant enlightens the believer's stand before God. This is made known through Paul's writing in the book of Romans, 1st and 2nd Corinthians, and the book of Hebrews. The believer's stand before God ceases to be a standing based on the Law and works, and becomes a standing based on the Cross of Jesus Christ and the grace of God. All of this is shared in these four books: Romans, 1st and 2nd Corinthians and Hebrews. In the prison epistles, which are Ephesians, Philippians and Colossians, Paul clarifies the revelation of the Church, the believer's position "in Jesus Christ," and the Revelation of Jesus Christ. Paul's writing of 1st and 2nd Timothy and Titus was Paul instructing his two sons in the faith of how to Pastor a New Covenant Church. Paul not only shared his revelation of the New Covenant in Christ, but he also shared the decrees the Jerusalem Church wanted to have established in the Gentile churches that Paul had established with the aid of the Holy Spirit. These four decrees were for the purpose of fellowship between the Gentiles and the Jews. One can read about their establishment by the Jerusalem Church in Acts 15:23-29 and reaffirmed in Acts 21:25. This took the Gentile churches and believers off the hook of obeying the Old Mosaic Covenant of Law as far as the Jerusalem Church was concerned. Today, very little is said or taught about those decrees that Paul, the Apostle to the Gentiles, agreed to do and taught. In many Gentile churches today, they have broken all these decrees as Reverend Ronald Kosor states in his book, Unveiling the New Covenant.

Because the book of Acts closes so abruptly, one cannot find out what happened to Paul from Acts. The NIV Bible Commentary, Volume 2, New Testament on page 517 gives us some ideas of what happened to Paul. They use some of Paul's Prison Letters in supporting the outcome they produce in this Commentary. We cannot be certain about it all until we reach Heaven and God tells us for sure. But this outcome is plausible. "With Acts ending so abruptly, we must look elsewhere for information about Paul's imprisonment and it's aftermath. According to the Prison Letters as having been written during this time, we may surmise that Paul fully expected to stand before Caesar's court and that while we cannot be certain about the outcome, he did expect to be released (cf. Philippians 1:19-26; Philemon 22). We may date such a release around 63 (AD). Accepting the Pastoral Letters as genuine, after Paul's release from this imprisonment, he continued evangelizing the eastern portion of the (Roman) empire (at least in lands surrounding the Aegean Sea)—perhaps even fulfilling his desire to visit Spain (Romans 15: 23-24). And since 2nd Timothy 4:16-18 speaks of a second trial in a tone of resignation, we may conclude that Paul was rearrested about 67 (AD) and, according to tradition, beheaded at Rome by order of Nero."

Matthew, Mark, Luke, John and 1st Corinthians

One might have the question that why is the word "Covenant" and the word "New Covenant" not used much throughout the New Testament (Covenant)? The word "Covenant" is an ancient word that was used among ancient tribes, nations and peoples, like the Hebrew people (the Jews). It was still being used in New Testament (Covenant) times. God used words and phrases that to His people (the Jews) were familiar. Outside the book of Hebrews, the word is seldom used in the New Testament (Covenant). One reason for that is the book of Hebrews was written to the Jewish people to try and convince them that Jesus was and is the Messiah and the Son of God. This book was written to especially contrast the Old Covenant with the New Covenant and why the New Covenant is a better Covenant based on the person of Jesus Christ and His better promises. The book of Hebrews takes things the Jewish people are and were familiar with like the High Priest, the Altar, the Holiest place (the Holy of Holies), the veil, etc. and compares them to the scene in Heaven where Jesus is our High Priest forever. The book compares the one sacrifice Jesus made with those of the Old Covenant. The whole book of Hebrews is written to the Jewish people especially those Jews who had stepped into the Christian faith and become Christians. Some of those Jews were thinking about leaving the New Covenant, which was faith in Jesus Christ. Hebrews was attempting to convince them to stay in Jesus. John Hagee in his Prophecy Study Bible on page 1504 shares the reason for the writing of the book of Hebrews. "Many Jewish believers, having stepped out of Judaism into Christianity wanted to reverse their course in order to escape persecution by their countrymen. The writer of Hebrews (Paul) exhorts them to "go on to perfection" (Hebrews 6:1). His appeal is based on the superiority of Christ over the Judaic system…"

Thc Apostle Paul wrote mostly to Gentile churches and believers of that era in and around Palestine. Thirteen of those letters, some say it says very little about the New Covenant and yet everything in those letters are a part of the New Covenant that God has made with believers. These letters were to Jews and Gentiles who had trusted Jesus Christ as their Lord and Savior. Some of those letters are letters of correction like 1st and 2nd Corinthians and Galatians. Other letters of Paul are to bring believers into a deeper relationship with Jesus Christ like Ephesians, Colossians, and Philippians. Another group of letters by Paul deal with end-time events when Jesus will return for His church like 1st and 2nd Thessalonians. The letters to Timothy and Titus are training letters for men who have become Pastors and/or Elders who are shepherding (pastoring) churches. Wherever Paul went he was an Apostle and an Evangelist. He led Philemon to the Lord in prison and then began to discipline him as one of his sons in the faith. If you look, really look, you can see the New Covenant in all of these letters.

Notice that during the time that Jesus was on earth, He introduced some new words that had never been talked about before in the area of Judea. For ages Jewish men would attach themselves to teachers. What is interesting is that after Jesus called His disciples and later made them Apostles, He introduced the new idea of the Church. The word "Church" was not introduced until Jesus introduced it. The Greek word for Church is ecclesia and means the called-out ones. In Matthew 16 Jesus starts asking them who they thought He was. As soon as Peter acknowledges Him as the Son of God listen to what Jesus said. "And I also say to you that you are Peter (a small stone) and on this rock (a very large, massive, living rock) I will build my church, and the gates of Hades shall not prevail against it." (Matthew 16:18) I believe that massive living stone was not Peter, but the revelation Peter had of Jesus, Him being the Son of God. The church, this new word, would be built on that revelation of Jesus Christ. A second idea was introduced in the last Passover that Jesus partook with His disciples. That was the idea of Holy Communion. Jesus changed the course of that meal by declaring and presenting the broken bread as His body that would be broken for His disciples and us and the wine representing the blood that He would shed for His disciples and us. (Matthew 26:26-29) These two are just a few of the new words and symbols that Jesus Christ introduced that never were talked about or mentioned before He did it. There are probably other words that you will discover that are different from the Jewish background.

Going back to the books or letters that Paul wrote as an Apostle to the Gentiles, you might be wondering why I left out Romans and Hebrews. Romans was written to the Christians in Rome, whether Jew or Gentile. It is a masterful theology book that covers the basic doctrines (teachings) of the Christian faith. I believe Paul wrote the book and used words like "law," "faith," and "righteousness." Paul explains the two Covenants, the Old Covenant and the New Covenant, in Romans 7. We covered that earlier. One must understand that chapter 7 in order to understand and contrast the two Covenants. That revelation by the Spirit of God will free one from the Old Covenant and the enjoyment of the New Covenant. I covered Hebrews earlier and will not repeat myself here. It would be good for both Jew and Gentile believers to understand the book of Hebrews. Although at the time, it was written to Jewish believers. To really understand the New Covenant that we have in Jesus Christ, one must do a thorough study of both Romans and Hebrews. I have only scratched the surface of those two books.

What about the Gospels? The first two Gospels, Matthew and Mark, were written by Jews to get Jews interested in the Gospel of Jesus Christ. Throughout, the Gospel of Matthew, Matthew uses Jewish terms, phrases and understanding to get the attention of the Jewish people. In John Hagee's Prophecy Study Bible on page 1141, it says this about the Gospel of Matthew. "Matthew is the gospel written by a Jew to Jews about a Jew. Matthew is the writer, his countrymen are the readers, and Jesus Christ is the subject. Matthew's design is to present Jesus as the King of the Jews, the long-awaited Messiah. Through a carefully selected series of Old Testament quotations, Matthew documents Jesus Christ's claim to be (the) Messiah. His genealogy, baptism, messages, and miracles all point to the same inescapable conclusion: Christ is King. Even in His death, seeming defeat is turned to victory by the Resurrection, and the message again echoes forth: The King of the Jews lives…"

The words "new covenant" does appear one time in the book of Matthew when Jesus takes Communion with His disciples. "Then He took the cup, and gave thanks, and gave it to them saying, 'Drink from it, all of you. For this is My blood of the new covenant, which is shed for many for the remission (forgiveness) of sins.'" (Matthew 26:27-28) Notice Jesus said this was and is His blood of the New Covenant. There is no mention of the Old Mosaic Covenant or animal sacrifices. We participate in this when we participate in the Lord's Supper (or some call it the Last Supper). It is a renewing of the New Covenant in ourselves. The Gospel of Matthew is a perfect bridge from the Old Testament (Covenant) to the New Testament (Covenant). Matthew, throughout his presentation of the Gospel of Jesus Christ, illustrates how Jesus Christ fulfilled all the Biblical prophecies of the Old Testament (Covenant). Not only did Jesus fill full the Law, but He also completely fulfilled the prophet's words about Him. "Do not think that I came to destroy the Law or the Prophets. I did not come to destroy, but to fulfill (but to complete and fulfill them). (Matthew 5:17) (last parenthesis was the Amplified Bible version) Jesus Christ was and is the fulfillment of the Old Mosaic Covenant of Law.

Moving on to the Gospel of Mark. Mark was a cousin of Barnabas, but was most probably led to the Lord by Peter. Peter regarded Mark as one of his spiritual sons. "She who is in Babylon, elect together with you; and so, does Mark my son." (1 Peter 5:13) John Mark was a Jewish brother who wrote his gospel from a different perspective. Most Biblical scholars believe Mark got most of his primary information from his close relationship and association with Peter. John Hagee's Prophecy Study Bible states on page 1194 Mark's emphasis in this book. "Mark portrays Jesus as a servant on the move, instantly responsive to the will of the Father. By preaching, teaching, and healing, He ministers to the needs of others even to the point of death. After His resurrection, He commissions His followers to continue His work in His power—servants following in the steps of the perfect Servant."

Most Biblical scholars date this book about 70 A.D. Mark uses many quotations from the Old Testament (Covenant) to illustrate that Jesus is indeed the Messiah, the promised one of God, just like Matthew did. A list of those can be found in some Bibles. When Jesus Christ is asked by Pilate if He is the King of the Jews, notice Jesus answer. "Then Pilate asked Him (Jesus), "Are You the King of the Jews?' And He (Jesus) answered and said to him, 'It is as you say.'" (Mark 15:2) Jesus said the same night when

He was tried by the Sanhedrin. "Again, the high priest asked Him (Jesus), saying to Him (Jesus) 'Are You the Christ, the Son of the Blessed?' and Jesus said, 'I Am. And you will see the Son of Man sitting at the right hand of the Power (God, Himself) and coming with the clouds of heaven.'" (Mark 14:61b-62) Of course according to Mark's Gospel they rejected Him. Both in Matthew's Gospel and Mark's Gospel they show Jesus definitely saying, I Am the Messiah, the Son of Man sitting on the right hand of the Father. Pilate gave him up to the Jews and letting Him be crucified, thus rejecting Jesus, the New Covenant that God was instituting through His Son. One has to accept the Jesus Christ, the New Covenant in order for it to become binding on their life.

Finally, at the Lord Supper, Jesus Christ makes reference to this New Covenant in Mark 14:23-25. "Then He (Jesus) took the cup, and when He had given thanks, He gave it to them, and they all drank from it. And He said to them, 'This is my blood of the new covenant, which is shed for many. Assuredly, I say to you, I will not drink of the fruit of the vine until that day when I drink it new in the kingdom of God.'" Jesus did not use the term New Covenant until they had Communion together. Jesus Christ will not drink wine again until He drinks it in the Kingdom of God. That is when He rules and reigns as King of Kings and Lord of Lords from Jerusalem during His millennial reign in Israel. He will rule over the whole earth then.

Notice, Jesus did not make any reference to the Old Mosaic Covenant of Law. From that day forward He was establishing the New Covenant. The Church of Jesus Christ is not under the Old Covenant of Law, but under the New Covenant of Jesus Christ. Do not think that being under the New Covenant of Grace you are free to kill, to steal, to commit adultery, to lie or cheat people. Under the New Covenant of Jesus Christ, you are under King Jesus and the Holy Spirit will convict you of known sin in your life. The Holy Spirit will not lead you into sin and His convicting power will make you feel miserable if you do not follow His leading. He will make you confess known sins in your life.

Let us look next at the Gospel of Luke. In Reverend John Hagee's Prophecy Study Bible on page 1227, in the introduction to the Gospel of Luke, Biblical scholars describe Luke's background as the writer of this Gospel. "Luke may have been a Hellenistic Jew, but it is more likely that he was a Gentile. (This would have been the only Gentile contributor to the New Testament.) In Colossians 4:10-14, Paul lists three fellow workers who are "of the circumcision" (vv. 10-11) and then includes Luke's name with two Gentiles (vv. 12-14). Luke's obvious skill with the Greek language and his phrase "their own language" in Acts 1:19 also imply that he (Luke) was not Jewish…" Therefore, most all Biblical scholars believe Luke was a Gentile who wrote the Gospel of Luke and the Book of Acts. Biblical scholars also believe this Gospel was written in the early 60s A.D.

The emphasis of the Gospel of Luke was on the humanity of Jesus Christ. John Hagee's Prophecy Study Bible on page 1227 gives a fairly accurate picture of this Gospel. "Luke, a physician, writes with the compassion and warmth of a family doctor as he carefully documents the perfect humanity of the Son of God, Jesus Christ. Luke emphasizes Jesus ancestry, birth and early life before moving carefully and chronologically through His earthly ministry. Growing belief and growing opposition (to Jesus Christ) develop side by side. Those who believe are challenged to count the cost of discipleship. Those who oppose will not be satisfied until the Son of Man hangs lifeless on a cross. But the resurrection ensures that His purpose will be fulfilled: "to seek and to save that which was lost." (Luke 19:10)

It seems fairly accurate that when Luke was not traveling with Paul, he went throughout Canaan and Galilee to get eye witness accounts of Jesus and His life. Luke being a physician and a Gentile, he wanted to find first hand information about Jesus that included His genealogy, His birth, and early childhood, His public ministry throughout Jerusalem, and Galilee. No doubt He knew as a physician the land around Galilee. Luke knew the Hebrew and Aramaic languages and the Greek language. "He (Luke) probably assumed responsibility for publishing the Gospel of Luke and the Book of Acts, so that they would be available to Gentile readers. Luke translates Aramaic terms with Greek words and explains Jewish customs and geography to make his Gospel more intelligible to his original Greek readership." (John Hagee's Prophecy Study Bible, page 1227, The Time of Luke)

Luke acknowledges that there are other writers who had decided to write an account of Jesus' life, ministry, death and resurrection in Luke 1:1-2. But he decided he would write an account also that Gentile readers who had entered the New Covenant of Jesus Christ could understand. His attention to details and chronological order of His life shows not only the fact that he was a doctor, but also that he wanted to appeal to Gentile believers. "…It seemed good to me also, having had perfect understanding of all things from the first, to write to you an orderly account, most excellent Theophilus (friend of God), that you may know the certainty of those things in which you are instructed." (Luke 1:3-4) Notice the person that Luke seems to be writing to—Theophilus. This comes from the Greek and means a friend of God. It is not really known whether this was an actual person. Perhaps, Luke was writing to all the Gentile friends of God throughout the world, who had put their trust in Jesus Christ as their Lord and Savior. Luke addresses the same person, Theophilus (Friend of God), in both the Gospel of Luke and the Book of Acts. No doubt, Luke sent these two books to all of the Gentile churches Paul had established. Luke also took quotations from the Old Testament (Covenant) to show the validity of Jesus' life, ministry, death and resurrection. They are seen throughout the text from the beginning of the Gospel of Luke to the very end of the Gospel, when Jesus ascends to heaven. Most good study Bibles list the quotations and where they are found in the Old Testament (Covenant).

Where does Luke actually use the words "New Covenant" in the Gospel of Luke? He does write what Jesus said at the Last Supper. "Likewise, He (Jesus) also took the cup after supper saying, "This cup is the new covenant in my blood, which is shed for you." (Luke 22:20) Again there is no mention of the Old Mosaic Covenant of Law. His blood—the blood of Jesus Christ—would bring to pass a New Covenant established on better promises. The fact is that God is doing away with the Old Mosaic

Covenant and He is bringing in a New Covenant that will extend grace to Gentile believers as well as Jews.

It is interesting to note that Luke, the physician, a Gentile believer, wrote this Gospel for all believers, but it probably influences Gentile churches and believers, more than Jewish churches around Galilee. As we stated when looking at the Book of Acts. Peter was questioned about his presenting the Gospel to Cornelius' house and Gentile friends. Paul was criticized in Acts 21:17-26 about how he presented the Gospel to mixed congregations that had both Jews and Gentiles. The Jewish leadership at the Jerusalem church including the Apostle James, believed Paul was teaching the Jews in those mixed congregations not to observe the law of Moses. From his letters to the church in Corinth, the church at Galatia, and the church at Rome probably in essence he was telling the Jews that they no longer had to stay under the Old Mosaic Covenant of Law, but were in actuality under a new and better Covenant—the New Covenant. Today, Messianic Jewish congregations are going after Gentile believers and telling them they need to be circumcised and come under the Mosaic Covenant and they are getting converts. But one must look at the New Testament (Covenant) and really get a Spirit revealed revelation of the New Covenant. I believe then Gentile believers will see as they did in the New Testament (Covenant) era, that this is not necessary. Once a person by revelation sees that he or she is in Christ by the new birth and that their lives revolve around Jesus Christ, they will see that they do not have to come under the Old Mosaic Covenant of Law. They will automatically do that which is right because the Spirit of God lives on the inside of their temple and will not lead them astray. "Do you not know that you are the temple of God and that the Spirit of God dwells in you. If anyone defiles the temple of God, God will destroy him. For the temple of God is holy, which temple you are." (1 Corinthians 3:16-17)

The last Gospel is the Gospel according to John. It is different from the other three Gospels. Luke presents Jesus as the Son of Man while John presents Jesus in all His Deity, the Son of God. John Hagee's Prophecy Study Bible say this about John's Gospel on page 1278. "Just as a coin has two sides, both valid, so Jesus Christ has two natures, both valid. Luke presents Christ in his humanity as the Son of Man; John portrays Him in His Deity as the Son of God. John's purpose is crystal clear; to set forth Christ in His Deity in order to spark believing faith in his readers. John's Gospel is topical, not primarily chronological, and it revolves around seven miracles and seven "I Am" statements." The Apostle John was one of Jesus closest disciples. Throughout this Gospel, John is identified as the disciple "whom Jesus loved." "His knowledge of Palestinian geography and Jewish customs makes it clear that he was a Palestinian Jew, and his meticulous attention to numbers …and names…indicates that he was an eye witness (of Jesus throughout His life, ministry, death and resurrection)." (John Hagee's Prophecy Study Bible, page 1278) John was a part of Jesus inner circle of disciples which also included Peter and James. He was the disciple who stood with Jesus when He was on trial before the Sanhedrin. (John 18:15) He was also the disciple who told Peter it was the Lord at the Lord's breakfast for His disciples after Jesus was raised from the dead. (John 21:1-14) Throughout the Gospel of John, John presents Jesus as the divine Son of God. In fact, all three persons of the Trinity are presented in this Gospel; (John 1:1, 14; 14:16-18, 26) Father, Son and Holy Spirit.

Does John like the other Gospels show Jesus sharing the wine as a symbol of the New Covenant in His blood? No, it is not like the other Gospels in this regard. There is a mention of the supper in John 13:2. "And supper being ended, the devil having already put it into the heart of Judas Iscariot, Simon's son, to betray Him." The other three Gospels—Matthew, Mark and Luke—describe the breaking of the bread (His body) and the giving of the wine (the New Covenant in His blood). It is not necessary, I believe, to have it in all four Gospels. Three out of four Gospels witness to the Lord's Supper and the wine representing the blood of the New Covenant. John saw some things that were different and recorded what the other three Gospels did not, like the washing of the disciples' feet (John 13:2-20), and evidently, John the beloved got a clue as to who was going to betray Jesus—Judas Iscariot. (John 13:21-30) Jesus tells them the commandment that will set them apart from the world—loving one another. (John 13:31-35) Jesus lets them know He is coming back for them, just like a bridegroom comes back for His bride. (John 14:1-20) Jesus also teaches them about the Holy Spirit who is going to come and teach and guide them. (John 14:26; 16: 7-15) There is a lot of teaching that the other Gospels did not present, but John did from John chapters 13 to 16. Finally, John hears Jesus interceding to His Father and our Father for His disciples and all the other believers that will follow, including us (John 17).

How was it that Paul knew about the Lord's Supper and the New Covenant? He was not one of the original eleven Apostles, nor had he been around to hear what the early disciples and Christians shared about the Lord's Supper. Evidently, Paul received a revelation from Jesus Christ about the Lord's Super and its relationship to the New Covenant. He shared this revelation with the church at Corinth. "For I received from the Lord that which I also delivered to you on the same night in which He was betrayed took bread; and when He had given thanks, He broke it and said, 'Take eat; this is My body which is broken for you; do this in remembrance of Me.' In the same manner He also took the cup after supper, saying, 'This cup is the new covenant in My blood. This do, as often as drink it, in remembrance of Me.' For as often as you eat this bread and drink this cup, you proclaim the Lord's death till He comes." (1 Corinthians 11: 23-26)

Paul, the Apostle, is proclaiming the New Covenant in the blood of Jesus just like Matthew, Mark, and Luke did. Bull, lambs and goats' blood did not bring anyone to the New Covenant. The precious, divine blood of Jesus Christ is the only blood that could bring us to the New Covenant. There is no mention of the Old Mosaic Covenant. Why was that? Because according to the book of Hebrews the Old Covenant was ready to vanish away. "In that He (Jesus) says, 'A new covenant,' He has made the first (covenant) obsolete. Now what is becoming obsolete (the Old Covenant) and growing old (the Old Covenant) is ready to vanish away." (Hebrews 8:13)

Paul would go onto write about the New Covenant and what it brought about in all of his epistles. He would contrast the Old Covenant of the Jews with the New Covenant we have today in the book of Hebrews. I believe twice Peter was showed that the Gentiles were to receive this New

Covenant which included the Gospel of salvation and the Baptism in the Holy Spirit, when he went to the Samaritans in Acts 8 when the Apostle John and him laid hands on them and they received the Holy Spirit after Philip had led them to Jesus. But he only stayed a few days and then went back to Jerusalem. Then God showed Peter again when he went down to Cornelius' house and shared the Gospel of Jesus Christ with the Gentile friends of Cornelius. God moved on the Gentiles by saving them and filling them with the Holy Spirit. (Acts 10) But again, he only stayed a few days and then he went back to Jerusalem. He had to convince his Jewish brethren including James, the Lord's brother, that God had sent him there. (Acts 11:1-18) That is when God chose Paul to be the Apostle to the Gentiles. Even though God had told His eleven disciples to go into all the world and preach the Gospel to every creature, for awhile they were contented to stay in Jerusalem and minister there. Even though believers left Jerusalem and carried the message of Jesus to the world, it would take some years before the Apostles would choose to do so. Maybe, it was seeing Paul carrying that message to Gentile cities and establish Gentile churches, that spurred them onto doing what Jesus commanded His disciples and Apostles to do, when He ascended into Heaven. Foxe's Book of Martyrs by John Foxe verifies that, because in chapter 1 of the book it takes up every disciple of the Lord and tells where they died as a martyr. Matthew died in Ethiopia, Andrew died as a martyr in Edessa, John Mark died as a martyr in Alexandria, Peter died as a martyr in Rome, Paul died as a martyr in Rome, Jude was crucified in Edessa, Bartholomew died as a martyr in India, Thomas died as a martyr in Calamina, India, Luke, the physician died as a martyr in Athens, Greece. James, the son of Zebedee died as a martyr in Jerusalem, James (the Less), the brother of Jesus, died as a martyr in Jerusalem and Stephen died as a martyr in Jerusalem. These last three did not leave Jerusalem, but they still died as a martyr for the Lord. Only John, the beloved, did not die a violent death. He died at Ephesus in 98 A.D. (Foxe's Book of Martyrs, pages 2-8) I am trying to show you that ten of the eleven original disciples did not die in Jerusalem but did follow the Lord's command and went to the known world with the Gospel of Jesus Christ. John, the beloved disciple, who went into the judgment hall with Jesus before the High Priest, Caiaphas, and the Sanhedrin and who stood at the Cross of Jesus with Jesus' mother, Mary;

he did not die a violent death. John thus fulfilled Jesus' prophetic word. "For whoever desires to saves his life will lose it, and whoever loses his life for My sake will find it." (Matthew 16:25)

Why Didn't Jesus Use the Words New Covenant in His Teaching?

Why did Jesus Christ not use the words "New Covenant" in His teaching to His disciples and the multitudes? It is possible that the early disciples only understood the Old Mosaic Covenant of Law and it might have been confusing to them if He used the word "New Covenant." Jesus was using words, parables, signs and miracles that they understood. If the disciples did not understand that Jesus needed to die and be raised from the dead the third day, how would they understand that Jesus was beginning and establishing a "New Covenant" with them and those who believe on Him? He also told them that there were many things they would not understand until the Holy Spirit came and would give them understanding in all things. Toward the end of His ministry on earth, this is what He shared with His disciples. "These things I have spoken to you in figurative language; but the time is coming when I will no longer speak in figurative language, but I will tell you plainly about the Father." (John 16:25) One needs to remember that these were unlearned fisherman, tax collectors, and some practice other trades. This is probably the reason they did not understand until after His death and resurrection some of the things He taught. The Apostle Paul was probably the most learned man among the eleven disciples. He knew and understood both the Hebrew and Greek languages. In 2 Corinthians 12:1-5, we learn that Paul had been transported into Heaven itself and received many revelations from the Lord. Although Paul refused to identify himself as the man Paul talks about; it is obvious that it was him. Most Biblical scholars believe that in his later life, Paul wrote the book of Hebrews which compares the Old Covenant of Law with that of the New Covenant. Thus, Jesus prophetic word about the Holy Spirit came to pass; that the Holy Spirit would teach any hungry soul all things. "However, when He, the Spirit of truth, has come, He will guide you into all truth; for He will not speak on His own authority, but whatever He hears He will speak, and He will tell you things to come. He will glorify Me, for He will take of what is Mine and declare it to you. All things that the Father has are Mine. Therefore, I said that He will take of Mine and declare it to you." (John 16:13-15) Therefore the original disciples were not ready for the teaching on the New Covenant, nor how it revolved around Jesus Christ. Even Peter, after Paul began to teach and write about these things concerning the New Covenant that it is centered in Jesus Christ, had this to say about Paul's writing. "Therefore, beloved, looking forward to these things, be diligent to be found in Him in peace, without spot and blameless; and account that the longsuffering of our Lord is salvation—as also our beloved brother Paul, according to the wisdom given to him, has written to you, as also in all his epistles, speaking in them of these things, in which are some things hard to understand, which those who are untaught and unstable twist to their own destruction, as they do also, the rest of the Scriptures..." (2 Peter 3:14-16) Peter said that what Paul was sharing was hard to understand. There are two ingredients that you must have. You must be hungry for a Covenant walk with God and you must allow the Holy Spirit to lead you into that walk. One cannot pursue this without the aid of the Holy Spirit. The final ingredient is to understand the Word of God by revelation. Only the Holy Spirit can lead you into that walk. But God is listening to you and wants to hear the desires of your heart. Do you wish a Covenant walk with God? Let God befriend you in Jesus' name. Amen.

Finally, why did Paul say you would proclaim the Lord's death until He comes by partaking of the Lord's Supper? Because those two things, the bread and the wine, symbolize His death. The bread typifies a broken body and will of Jesus when Jesus said, "O My Father, if it is possible, let this cup pass from Me, nevertheless, not as I will, but as You will." (Matthew 26:39b) No sacrifice but the sacrifice of Jesus' body would be acceptable to God. Jesus was and is our sacrifice for sin. As John the Baptist put it, "Behold! The Lamb of God Who takes away the sin of the world!" (John 1:29) The wine typifies the blood of Jesus. He told His disciples to drink all of it, because He was going to spill all of it. The blood of a newborn baby comes from the father of the child. Jesus blood came from His Father-God. That is why it was accepted by God, because God saw His own blood, and it was perfect, divine blood. Only that blood can wash away all of the sins of you and I. That is why is it called the blood of the

New Covenant. No animal blood would do, only God's Son own blood would do. When Jesus died on the Cross and said "It is finished" He was talking about that Old Covenant was finished and the Sacrifice for sins and sin (the sin nature) was finished. When He was buried, that Old Covenant was buried and the sins and the sin nature was buried. When He arose the third day, He brought in a new and living way, the New Covenant. With us as apart of Him, placed in Him by God our Father, we are apart of that New Covenant as is all believers, whether they are Jew or Gentile. Thank God, for the New Covenant that is totally based on Jesus Christ. Nothing in my hands I bring, simply to thy Cross I cling. Therefore, our salvation, our very life depends on Jesus Christ and the New Covenant that He brought about. I pray God will open the eyes of your understanding to the revelation of the New Covenant in the Person of Jesus Christ. It centers around and in Him. Amen and Amen.

Chapter 11
God Wants To Befriend Us

As we have seen throughout the Old Testament (Covenant) and the New Testament (Covenant) God has reached out to befriend individuals with individual Covenants and a Covenant with the nation of Israel. Starting with Noah, Abraham, Isaac and Jacob, he reached out to them. God doesn't just want us to be saved and on our way to Heaven. He really desires a Covenant Relationship, where He can enjoy friendship with us. It does not matter whether we are a Jew or Gentile, through the Lord Jesus Christ, He wants us to become a part of His family. Most believers believe if they just get baptized and participate in the Lord's Supper or Holy Communion when their local church administers it, that is good enough. But God wants so much more for us and offered it all through the sacrifice of His Son, Jesus Christ. In fact, the New Covenant is based on the sacrificial death of Jesus Christ and His resurrection from the dead. Jesus' death does away with the Old Covenant and His resurrection starts the New Covenant.

Actually, the New Covenant must be revealed to you by the Holy Spirit. (John 15:13-15) Hopefully, this book has opened your eyes to a New Covenant Relationship with God your Father and Jesus Christ, your elder Brother. The Holy Spirit will help and guide you into that Covenant Relationship. That has been my constant prayer—that you will have an understanding of the Covenants of the Old Testament (Covenant) and in contrast the New Covenant that is in Jesus Christ. That you will see that the New Covenant in Christ Jesus is far superior to that of the Old Testament (Covenant). That this New Covenant in Jesus Christ will change your life forever. That is my constant prayer in Jesus' Name. Amen!

God does not extend a Covenant Relationship to you just because you are saved and you are going to Heaven. You can get a glimpse of that in the Old Testament (Covenant). In the Old Testament (Covenant), God waited to see if Abel, Enoch, Noah, Abraham, Isaac, Jacob and Moses would follow Him after He revealed Himself to them. Then God befriended them and started sharing with them what was going to happen in their future. He extended His Covenant to them and by faith they had to walk it out. "But without faith it is impossible to please Him (God), for he who comes to God must believe that He is, and that He is a rewarder of those who diligently seek Him." (Hebrews 11:6) If you want God to befriend you, you are going to have to seek the Lord earnestly and walk by faith.

In the Old Testament (Covenant) most of the time, God required a sacrifice in order to enter into Covenant Relationship with Him. There were a few times in the Old Testament (Covenant) it was not mentioned. In the New Testament (Covenant) God sacrificed His Son, Jesus Christ, in order for us to enter into a Covenant Relationship with Him. That sacrifice, the sacrifice of Jesus, is the only acceptable sacrifice. In John chapter six, Jesus talked about eating His flesh and drinking His blood. This was hard for the Jewish leadership of Jesus' day to accept. (John 6:52-59) Even some of His disciples, not the original eleven, said this was a hard saying and some left Him that day. He explains it in John 6:63. "It is the Spirit who gives life; the flesh profits nothing. The words that I speak to you are spirit and they are life." Jesus' words were and are Spirit and Life to us. That is how we enter into Covenant with Him. Jesus Christ told individuals who wanted to follow Him, "And whoever does not bear his cross and come after Me cannot be my disciple…So, likewise, whoever of you does not forsake all that he has cannot be My disciple." (Luke 14:27, 33) The cross is a symbol of death that one might be called on to die for Jesus. It is not only a symbol of death to self, the world, the flesh, and the devil, but one may have to die period. He or she might have to make the ultimate sacrifice for Jesus. The church today has moved away from sharing that, because it is looked on as negative. But not so with God. "Precious in the sight of the Lord is the death of His saints." (Psalms 116:15) There are many saints in Africa, the Middle East, and Asia who have made that sacrifice. To enter into Covenant with the Lord, one must be prepared for this, in case it happens. You cannot be His disciple and enter into Covenant with Him unless you are ready to die for Him.

As we contrasted the Old Mosaic Covenant with the New Covenant in Jesus Christ, we saw that to enter into the New Covenant Relationship with Jesus and God the Father, we are going to have to accept completely the sacrifice of Jesus Christ as our sacrifice and the blood of Jesus Christ as the only way to wash away all our sins; past, present and future. This opens the door to a New Covenant Relationship with all the members of the Godhead; Father, Son, and Holy Spirit. Today, most churches around the world require new believers to be baptized (immersed) in water as a sign that they have completely accepted the sacrifice of Jesus Christ as their sacrifice for sins. New believers are also asked to participate in Holy Communion to show the Lord's death until Jesus comes back for His own. (Matthew 26:26-29; 1 Corinthians 11: 23-26) These two observances identify believers with Jesus Christ as their Lord and Savior. But they do not necessarily mean they are walking in Covenant Relationship with Jesus Christ, God's Son, with God our Father and the Holy Spirit.

Jesus' disciples walked with Him, followed Him and had daily communion with Him. But it was not until His last trip to Jerusalem that He called them His friends because they were walking in obedience to Jesus. This meant they were walking in Covenant Relationship with Him. It is in John 15:12-17 that Jesus calls them friends. "This is my commandment, that you love one another as I have loved you. Greater love has no one than this, than to lay down one's life for his friends. You are my friends, if you do whatever I command you. No longer do I call you servants, for a servant does not know what his master is doing; but I have called you friends, for all things that I have heard from My Father, I have made known to you. You did not choose Me, but I chose you and appointed you that you should go and bear fruit, and that your fruit should remain. That whatever you ask the Father in My name, He may give you. These things I command you, that you love one another." (John 15:12-17)

Notice in the Old Testament (Covenant) that God called Abraham, His friend. The Apostle James makes reference to this in James 2:23. "Abraham believed God, and it was accounted to him for righteousness. And he (Abraham) was called the friend of God." Note on several occasions, God let Abraham know what was going to happen in the future.

God told Abraham the future of Sodom and Gomorrah. God told Abraham, that Abraham and Sarah would indeed have a son the next year and would call his name Isaac. Finally, God told Abraham that his descendants would indeed inherit the land of Canaan.

Now, before Jesus was crucified, He shares with His disciples that He would be crucified and be raised the third day. He also forewarns them of the destruction of the Temple in Jerusalem and that the city would also suffer destruction. You may say what is the point? My point is, that if you have been called into Covenant Relationship with Jesus Christ, He will become your closest friend and He will tell you about things to come in your life and possibly those of your family and friends, who are near and dear to you. The destruction of the Temple and the altar at the Temple was another sign that the Old Covenant was passing away. Jesus said in Matthew 5:6, "Blessed are those who hunger and thirst for righteousness; For they shall be filled." But you have to desire and hunger for that Covenant Relationship with God. You must want it more than anything else.

Jesus Christ was very narrow minded about a relationship with Him and His Father. In John's Gospel in John 14:6, "Jesus said to him (Thomas), 'I am the way, the truth, and the life. No one comes to the Father except through me." In Matthew's Gospel, Jesus said in Matthew 7:13-14 "Enter by the narrow gate; for wide is the gate and broad is the way that leads to destruction, and there are many who go in by it. Because narrow is the gate and difficult is the way which leads to life, and there are few who find it." Jesus is that narrow gate and the only way, truth and life that will lead to the Father's House. You have to want Him more than anything else. Luke's Gospel is not any different. In Luke 14:26-27 and verse 33 Jesus says, "If anyone comes to Me and does not hate his father and mother, wife and children, brothers and sisters, yes, and his own life also, he cannot be my disciple. And whoever does not bear his cross and come after Me cannot be my disciple…So likewise, whoever of you does not forsake all that he has cannot be My disciple." Covenant Relationship to Jesus Christ and His Father requires an all-out commitment to Jesus Christ and His Father. All but one of Jesus' disciples had terrible deaths; they were all martyred. John, the beloved is the only one that did not have a terrible death. I believe it was because he was willing to die for Jesus from the very beginning. Why else would he march right into the High Priest's chamber and stand shoulder to shoulder with Jesus, while Jesus was on trial. No other disciple is found at the foot of the Cross of Jesus but John and Jesus commanded John to take His own mother in and care for her like she was his mother. And John did it. Therefore, the cost of following God in the New Testament (Covenant) is the same height as it is in the Old Testament (Covenant). As Jesus pointed out throughout the Gospels, walking in Covenant Relationship with Him might cost them everything and their very lives.

While Jesus was on earth, He used the supernatural to draw people to Himself. There was an occasion when Jesus healed Peter's mother-in-law. The fact that Jesus was at Peter's house and was supernaturally healing people caused a huge crowd to gather there. Listen to what it says in Mark 1:32,34. "Now at evening, when the sun was set, they brought to Him all who were sick and those who were demon-possessed…Then He healed many who were sick with various diseases, and cast out many demons and He did not allow the demons to speak, because they knew Him." It was during these times of the supernatural healings and deliverance when people were gathered to Jesus, He would preach and teach about the Kingdom of God. Notice next that even John the Baptist had doubts about Jesus being the Messiah and the Son of God. John the Baptist sent his disciples to Jesus and asked Him this question. "Are you the Coming One or do we look for another? Notice how Jesus answered their questions. "And that very hour He (Jesus) cured many people of their infirmities (diseases), afflictions, and evil spirits; and to many who were blind He gave sight. Then Jesus answered and said to them (John the Baptist's disciples), 'Go and tell John the things you have seen and heard; the blind see, the lame walk, the lepers are cleansed, the deaf hear, the dead are raised, and the poor have the gospel preached to them. And blessed is he who is not offended because of me.'" (Luke 7:19-23) Jesus again pointed to the supernatural power manifested through Him to others to declare that He was and is the Son of God. You might say that was Jesus; what about today? This is what Jesus told His disciples as He ascended to glory. "And

He (Jesus) said to them (His disciples), 'Go into all the world and preach the gospel to every creature. He who believes and is baptized will be saved; but he who does not believe will be condemned. And these signs will follow those who believe. In My name (the name of Jesus) they will cast out demons, they will speak with new tongues, they will take up serpents, and if they drink anything deadly it will be no means hurt them; they will lay hands on the sick, and they will recover." (Mark 16:15-18) Today, many denominations, independent churches and believers do not believe in the supernatural power of God and they don't practice it because they don't believe in the power of the Holy Spirit. These supernatural manifestations are a result of the Holy Spirit working in the churches and the lives of believers. This too, is a part of the New Covenant. God will bring you to a place where you are willing to let God do what He wants with you and through you, if you want the fullness of the New Covenant. The Supernatural power of God is a part of the New Covenant. Let Jesus have His way with you.

Walking hand in hand with the supernatural power of the Holy Spirit, is believing that the Holy Spirit is the third person of the Godhead and is for you today. Jesus told His disciples that He was going to send the Holy Spirit after He ascended to Heaven. "And you shall receive power when the Holy Spirit has come upon you; and you shall be witnesses to Me in Jerusalem, and in all Judea and Samaria, and to the end of the earth." (Acts 1:8) Many denominations, independent churches and believers say little or nothing about the Holy Spirit. Many of them are afraid of the Holy Spirit. Yet, Jesus told His disciples that they would be baptized or filled with the Holy Spirit and to not leave Jerusalem until this happened. On the day of Pentecost (Acts 2:1-4) the one hundred and twenty were baptized or filled with the Holy Spirit. Ten years later Cornelius' household and all those present were saved and filled with the Holy Spirit. (Acts 10) Cornelius, his relatives and all his friends were Gentiles, thus the Holy Spirit was sent to the Gentiles as well. If you want the supernatural power of the Holy Spirit working in your life, you must allow the Holy Spirit to fill and baptize you with His Presence and power. In the Old Testament (Covenant) only certain ones were full of the Holy Spirit and were used by the Holy Spirit. Under the New Testament (Covenant), God extends His Holy Spirit to all believers. Many today are afraid of tongues, because in the book of Acts on three occasions when the Holy Spirit fell on believers they were filled and spoke in tongues. (Acts 2:1-4; 10:44-48; 19:1-8) When the Holy Spirit comes into the life of a believer, manifestations and signs occur. The Holy Spirit wishes to fill all believers who are apart of the New Covenant. Let Him fill you today to overflowing and then the supernatural power of God will flow out of your life to others.

There is another step closer to God than friendship with God and His Son, Jesus Christ. It is when you come into revelation of Jesus Christ and you realize for the first time in your life that you are a son or daughter of God. God the Father through Jesus wants you to sit at His banqueting table and enjoy a meal with Him and His Father. Jesus said it this way in the book of Revelation. "Behold I stand at the door and knock. If anyone hears My voice and opens the door, I will come into him and dine with him, and he with Me." (Revelation 3:20) God desires a deeper Covenant Relationship with you. In far Eastern countries like Israel the door knob is on the inside of the house. There are no outside door knobs. No one can open the door and enter the house unless the individual living there opens the door. Jesus wants you to open the door of your house (your inmost being) and let Him in, to commune and fellowship with you. Open the door and let Him in and your life will be changed forever.

God wishes to befriend you and more. Many are still struggling under the Old Mosaic Covenant of Law and believe they must continue to do so. Many Messianic Jews have received Jesus as their Messiah, but have not given themselves over to the New Covenant and the blessed relationship they can have in Jesus Christ. They still think they have to fulfill the Law of Moses and do not realize that Jesus has already done that for them. Even some Gentiles have left their first love, Jesus Christ, and have become Jewish proselytes to the Law—all of it. They believe this will make them acceptable to God, but only Jesus can make them acceptable to God. Some are like Paul; they try to become under the Law to try and gain those who are living under the Law. But it did not work for Paul and it will not work for you. (Acts 21:17-26) In the long run due to the Holy Spirit it worked out for Paul and he did stand before all the Kings he was supposed to stand before. Yet his own brethren, the Jewish people, did not accept his witness. Later, Paul ended up writing the book of Hebrews years later showing the New Covenant is the Covenant we are to be under and will be under during the thousand-year reign of Jesus Christ and throughout all eternity. All who have put their faith in Jesus Christ and not the Law, will live under this New Covenant. God will write His Will on our hearts and we will have a Covenant Relationship with God our Father and our elder Brother, Jesus Christ. This will be under the power and sway of the Holy Spirit. Let God's Holy Spirit fill you and reveal this New Covenant to you. Please, let God befriend you today in this New Covenant of Jesus Christ. Amen and Amen!!!

Bibliography

All About Jesus.org>transfiguration.

Baker, Kenneth and Kohlenberger III, John (Editors), *The Zondervan NIV Bible Commentary, Volume I, The Old Testament*, Grand Rapids: Zondervan Publishing House, 1994.

Baker, Kenneth and Kohlenberger III, John (Editors), *The Zondervan NIV Bible Commentary, Volume II, The New Testament,* Grand Rapids: Zondervan Publishing House, 1994.

Barnabasaid.org>Praying for the Persecute Church, page 57.

Bible.org>Samaritans.

Biblical Calendar Proof.com> (Hebrew Calendar).

Bibleanswerstand.org.>Q.A. Enoch.

Bible Hub>timeline>Acts 71htm.

Biblicaltheology.com>act by J.W. Carter. The Power to Overcome Prejudice.

Blue Letter Bible>don_stewart_1319 Who were the Samaritans?

Carma.org>Isaiah—Malachi.

Davis, J.D., *Illustrated Davis Dictionary of the Bible,* Nashville: Royal Publishers, 1973.

Fausett, Andrew Robert; Brown, David; Jameison, Robert, *Jameison—Fausett—Brown Commentary of the Whole Bible,* Grand Rapids: Zondervan Publishing House 1871.

First Fruits of Zion: Wine, Messianic Jewish Center, Marsfield, Missouri by phone. 417-468-2741. Subject: *Wine in Old Testament Times and Now*, 2018.

Foxe, John, *Foxe's Book of Martyrs,* Alachi: Bridge Logos, 2001.

Got Questions/? a theophany.

Got Questions/? The birthright.

Got Questions/? The coat of many colors.

Got Questions/? Jesus Passover—atonement.

Got Questions/? What was the significance of weaning a child in the Bible (Genesis 21:8)?

Got Questions/? Hittite wives.

Got Questions/? The Times of the Gentiles.

Gower, Ralph, *The New Manners and Customs of the Bible Times,* Chicago: Moody Press, 2005.

Hagee, John (Editor), *Prophecy Study Bible,* Nashville: Thomas Nelson Publishers, 1997.

Henry, Matthew, *Matthew Henry Commentary, Genesis to Deuteronomy, Volume 1,* Old Tappan: Fleming H. Revel Company, 1706.

Henry, Mathew, *Matthew Henry Commentary, Acts to Revelation, Volume 6,* Old Tappan: Fleming H. Revel Company, 1706.

Henry, Matthew, *Matthew Henry Commentary, Joshua to Esther, Volume 2,* Old Tappan: Fleming H. Revel Company, 1706.

International Standard Bible Encyclopedia, Bible Study Tools.com>Abimelech.

Is it safe to drink blood?>Live Science>15899.

Kosor, Ronald, *Unveiling the New Covenant,* Camarilla: Xulon Press, 2005.

Larkin, Clarence, *The Book of Revelation,* Glenside: Reverend Clarence Larkin Estate, 1919.

Liberty Gospel Tracts>The Questions.

Morris, William (Editor), *The American Heritage Dictionary of the English Language,* Boston: Houghton Mifflin Company, 1981.

Myers, Allen C. (Revision Editor), *Eerdmans Bible Dictionary,* Grand Rapids: William B. Eerdmans Publishing Company, 1987.

Netfind.com/search—Isaac; Bible name meanings/ search here and browse.

Pink, Arthur W., *Gleanings in Genesis,* Ocean Shores: Watchmaker Publishing Company, 1951.

Pink, Arthur W., *The Divine Covenants,* Grand Rapids: Baker Book House, 1973.

Pink, Arthur W., *Gleanings in Exodus,* Chicago: Moody Press, 1981.

Reformed Health.net 7.>What does it mean?
Scofield (D.D)., C.I. (Editor), *The First Scofield Reference Bible,* Westwood: Barbour and Company, Incorporated, 1986.

Smith, Ralph, *The Covenantal Structure of the Bible,* Tokyo: Covenant Worldview Institute, info @berith.org., 2006.

Stewart. Frances, *The Amplified Bible,* Grand Rapids: Zondervan Publishing House, 1987.

Strong, James, *The Strong's Concordance: The Greek Dictionary of the New Testament,* Gordonsville: Dugan Publishers, 1890.

Swaggart, Jimmy (Editor), *The Expositor's Study Bible,* Baton Rouge: Jimmy Swaggart Ministries, 2010.

Taylor, Kenneth, *The Living Bible, Paraphrased,* Wheaton: Tyndale House Publishers, 1971.

Tenney, Merrill C. (Editor), *The Zondervan Pictorial Bible Dictionary,* Grand Rapids: Zondervan Publishing House, 1963
.
Thayer, Joseph Henry, *The New Thayer's Greek-English Lexicon of the New Testament,* Peabody: Hendrickson Publishers, 1981.

The Layman's Parallel Bible, Grand Rapids: Zondervan Publishing House, 1971.

Wikipedia.org/concubine Bilhah and Reuben.

Wilson, Marvin R., *Our Father Abraham,* Grand Rapids: William B. Eerdmans Publishing Company, 1989.

Wright, Fred H., *Manners and Customs of Bible Lands,* Chicago: Moody Press, 1953.

Zodhiates (Th.D.), Spiro (Editor), *The Hebrew-Greek Key Study Bible,* Chattanooga: AMG Publishers, 1984.

About The Author

Roy J. Myers is currently an ordained teaching elder at Westlake Fellowship in Montgomery, Texas. He received a Certificate of Bible from Berean Bible College in 1969. Later, Roy graduated from Louisiana Baptist University with a Master's Degree in Bible and Theology in 2012. Early in his life, Roy served as a missionary to Jamaica from 1970-1976 in which he taught children and preached most Sundays in a nondenominational church on the island. In his later years, he taught in several private Christian Schools from 1998-2008. Roy and his wife, Judy, have lived in Magnolia, Texas since 1996.

You can purchase Roy's book, *The Five Fold Ministry* now at amazon.com

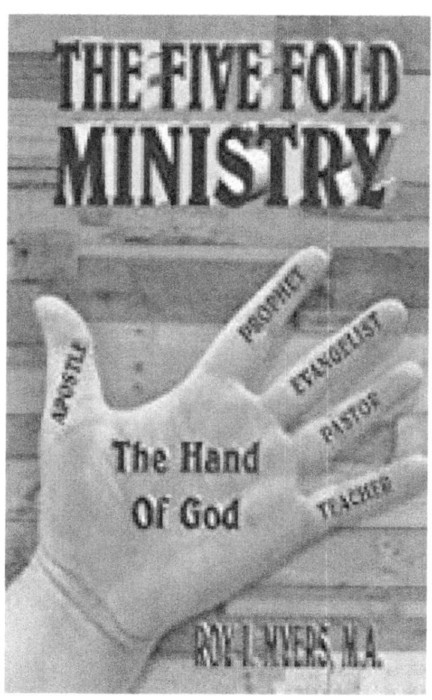

Made in the USA
Monee, IL
02 June 2022

97366022R00226